LES ANGLAIS

Philippe Daudy was born in Paris in 1925. Writer,
novelist and journalist, he travelled the world for
Agence France Presse from 1946–61 before working
in publishing, and later becoming a full time writer.
He is a founder member of the Franco-British Council and lives and works in London.

Isabelle Daudy, who translated and edited *Les Anglais*,
was born in Paris and educated in England at Mayfield
School and Brasenose College, Oxford. She is the
author of *People at Work in India*. She is the daughter
of Philippe Daudy and lives near Cambridge with her
English husband and their daughter.

Les Anglais

Portrait of a People

Philippe Daudy

Translated and Edited by Isabelle Daudy

HEADLINE

First published in Great Britain in 1991
by Barrie & Jenkins Ltd

First published in paperback in 1992
by HEADLINE BOOK PUBLISHING PLC

10 9 8 7 6 5 4 3 2 1

ISBN 0 7472 3842 1

Typeset in 10/11¾pt Times by
Falcon Typographic Art Ltd, Fife, Scotland

Printed and bound in Great Britain by
HarperCollins Manufacturing, Glasgow

HEADLINE BOOK PUBLISHING PLC
Headline House
79 Great Titchfield Street
London W1P 7FN

The trees are probably the most beautiful thing about England; obviously one must not ignore the fields and the policemen, but it is the trees mainly, their splendid bearing, ancient, free, venerable, huge . . . It is possible that the trees are what inspire the great English allegiance to the Conservative party. I believe too that it is they that encourage leanings, a sense of history, traditions, customs, barriers, golf, the House of Lords and so many other strange and ancient things.

Karel Capek, *Letters from England* (1925)

Dedicated to the memory of Christopher Soames
who loved France as I love England
and who believed, as I do,
that their common future lies in Europe.

Contents

Foreword

I was seven years old. We were living in Ethiopia, in the town of Diré-Daoua, where my father was working as a doctor for the Franco-Ethiopian Railways. The adventurer and man of letters, Henri de Monfried*, regularly visited us at home.

It was thanks to him that I first heard of England, though he spoke nothing but ill of it. A number of Her Gracious Majesty's ships had taken the liberty of inspecting his cargoes of smuggled goods on the Red Sea; by doing this they had, in his eyes, proved themselves to be the accomplices of his sworn enemy, the Negus†, and for this piece of treachery, he held them up to public obloquy.

Monfried was living on his estate in the province of Harrar, and had frequently urged us to take advantage of the old house he still owned at Obock in order to spend a few weeks by the Red Sea. My mother had finally accepted the invitation, and, accompanied by my two elder sisters, but without my father who could not leave his clinic, we went to Djibouti. From there we left in a dhow, also lent to us by Monfried, and made for the ship's port of registry on what was then known as the French Somali Coast.

---

* Henri de Monfried (1879–1974) spent much of his adult life in Ethiopia and travelling round North and East Africa. Pearl fisher, drug and arms smuggler, farmer and entrepreneur, he built a thermoelectric power station, and was thus instrumental in the electrification of Djibouti. Importing machinery from Hamburg and labour from Italy, he also set up an Ethiopian pasta-making factory. He wrote many autobiographical novels, the most famous of which is *Les Secrets de la Mer Rouge*.
† The supreme ruler of Ethiopia.

The wooden house, the only one to be seen on the beach, was set about a hundred metres from a hamlet of local fishermen living in their traditional *toucoul* huts*.

There had been a white man at Obock, the French colonial 'resident', Bernard. A few years earlier, he had been killed by some Dankali warriors, and since in the meantime Djibouti had become the colony's capital, he had never been replaced.

In this house, I was to live the most astonishing imaginative adventure of my childhood. But my fascination had nothing to do with Bernard's tragic death, nor yet with Abdi's stump – Abdi, the captain of Monfried's dhow, whom the writer was to immortalise in his tales of adventure under the name of *The Man with One Hand (L'Homme à la Main Coupée)*. Nor was I surprised by the torrid heat, which – thanks to the sea breeze – was less oppressive than the heat of Diré-Daoua; and I was neither thrilled by our solitude amid these reputedly ferocious Dankalis, nor astonished by the white and blue glory of the endless beach with its polychrome shells. In those days this was the only world I knew. Nothing in it seemed strange.

It was Dickens who gave me my first revelation of the exotic. Every evening after dinner, my mother used to read to us from a French translation of *Pickwick Papers*, and the familiarity of the language in no way diminished my astonishment at the unexpected heroes of these adventures: Monsieur Snodgrass, Monsieur Winkle, Samuel Weller or Madame Potts gave me the uncontrollable giggles, and seemed much more foreign than our black entourage, their woolly hair made blond with quick lime; Dulwich, Chelmsford and Gravesend – focus of the Pickwickian peregrinations – infinitely more surprising than Harrar, Djibouti and Obock. After Pickwick came Macbeth, still mediated by my mother's voice – Macbeth whose crimes were deliciously frightening, like those perpetrated by the gangsters who were always bested by Nick Carter in the illustrated periodicals which I bought each week for an Ethiopian piaster from Pantaléon, Diré-Daoua's Greek grocer-hairdresser. I owed these literary late nights to my two sisters, who were older than me by four and six years.

* Indigenous round mud huts with a thatched roof.

In 1941, almost ten years after our return to France, the elder sister, Alix – who had been well indoctrinated by my mother – made me read another translation, Samuel Butler's *Ainsi va toute chair**, followed by *Domaine Anglais*.

This prose anthology, translated by Valery Larbaud, was prefaced by the famous phrase, 'reading, that unpunished vice' – a phrase which, insatiable devourer of all printed matter that I was, I immediately adopted as my declaration of faith.

Other milestones in this literary vagabondage: the grey cover with green floral pattern that distinguished the books in the series *Feux Croisés*, and the white cover embossed with the prestigious initials of the *Nouvelle Revue Française*. The word literature seemed to me then to be embodied in the works of Aldous Huxley, Katherine Mansfield, Rosamond Lehmann, Margaret Kennedy and Richard Hughes. Later James Joyce, Virginia Woolf and D. H. Lawrence were to confirm for me that in the synonyms game, 'England' was equivalent to 'novels'. And since the only way I knew of refreshing myself from reading was by reading, I would abandon these masters for other friends, less reputable, no doubt, but just as faithful: H. G. Wells' *The Invisible Man* or Rudyard Kipling's Mowgli, detective stories by Agatha Christie, Dorothy Sayers or Edgar Wallace, and Sax Rohmer's terrible Doctor Fu Man Chu; not forgetting the great ancestor, Conan Doyle's Sherlock Holmes.

This literary trespass into an unknown country, in which – like a lucky thief – I stumbled across the best hidden booty, coloured my vision of Britain for many years to come. But although my reading gave the lie to the most common clichés about the country, I was inadvertently substituting others of my own. Certainly, I realised that the people of Britain were not composed entirely of retired colonels from the Indian Army or City employees in striped trousers and bowler hats. But I had a tendency to replace these in my mind with cohorts of travellers in tweeds and felt hats, carrying a luxurious train of leather suitcases and trunks covered in labels from the palaces of Europe. And when these pilgrims had returned from their voyages to pay homage to

* *The Way of All Flesh.*

Bavarian baroque or the Italian art of the Quattrocento, I saw them settling back into their wonderful country houses, buried amid the surrounding greenery, and being greeted by young wives with crystal blue eyes and sternly pleated skirts, whose hair – as straight as their chests were flat – was brushed back and held in place with a hairband. The German occupation of France was to fix these precious images in my mind, enclosing them – along with many others – in that pre-war album which I would leaf through in years to come with growing nostalgia and incredulity.

Had all this really existed? To this question, Marcel Ruff (whom the German invasion had, along with many others, brought to Aix en Provence) emphatically answered 'Yes'. Ruff was a wonderful Greek scholar. He used to read Theocritus to us in confidential tones, and within a term, had inspired me to become top of the class in Greek. A veteran of the First War, he was deaf and blind in one eye. These injuries had earned him the *Croix de la Légion d'honneur* – an honour which seemed of no particular significance to the boys of the lycée Mignet. Always ready for a laugh, they used to play cards in class under his hazy gaze, and gave voice to obscenities he could not hear.

The declaration of war in August 1939 had prevented him from returning to Eton, where he had taught French and Greek for about ten years. He occasionally referred to this 'Eton' as to another Arcadia. Then, at the end of the first term in the school year of 1940 to 1941, he revealed to us that he was Jewish. A new law – which had been introduced by the Vichy anti-Semites without any prompting from the Germans – prevented him, like all other Jews, from remaining in the teaching profession, and he was forced to leave the lycée.

Until this time, I had been a boarder. But, indignant at the way Ruff had been treated, and as a token of solidarity, I now obtained permission from my mother to go and live in his home. It was there that a new notion of England replaced for me the literary myth that I had created – an England which, in Churchill's words, promised 'blood, toil, tears and sweat', but also hope. The BBC, to which we listened together, and the lyricism – and occasionally comical grandiloquence – of those Frenchmen speaking to us French men and women at home, reminded us that there was just a narrow arm of sea between freedom and a captive France.

And soon our horizon was to be filled with the outline of Churchill's two fingers, splayed out in Victory. Fascinated by the power of the Americans and moved by the heroism of the Soviets, like many Frenchmen at the time of the Liberation, I did not immediately understand the significance of Britain's role in the war. I looked at it more in terms of the sacrifices involved than in terms of its military importance. It was only later that we found out about the realities of the Battle of Britain, the duel between Rommel and Montgomery in the Libyan desert, the Burmese epic, and the transformation of the United Kingdom into the gigantic arsenal which was to enable the Allies to reconquer the lost continent.

From 1946 I became a journalist with the news agency, *Agence France Presse* (AFP). It was still left to me to discover another side to British greatness – the art of gracefully shedding its greatness. While France was becoming enmeshed in the interminable Vietnam war, before being sucked into the Algerian conflict, Great Britain was quietly divesting itself of the largest empire the world has ever known.

But it was not until 1950 that I learned to speak English, first as a war correspondent in Korea, and then in Singapore, where I was running the AFP office covering Malaysia, Indonesia and Siam. And the Commonwealth was the first Britain institution that I tried to understand.

These long years of peripheral apprenticeship were not entirely useless. A number of points of reference had emerged from my reading, and thanks to them I felt at home during most of my subsequent travels: my peregrinations through London or Cornwall, Wales, Oxford or Edinburgh. These merely added a third dimension to my memories, the contours and exhalations of real life. I took up the habit of crossing the Channel. If there was no definite reason for doing so, I could always turn a visit to a museum or a garden into an excuse for the trip. In 1972, two friends – one English and the other French – asked me to help them organise regular encounters between representatives of the two countries. On the occasion of a state visit by Queen Elizabeth II to France, Prime Minister Edward Heath and President George Pompidou had decided to create a Franco-British council. I agreed to become its Secretary on the French side. I believed the task would take up a few hours of my time for a few weeks, or at the most a few months. This delusion now dates back some eighteen years, but did not last more than eight days.

Without exaggerating the importance of the ritual of seminars and symposia, there is usually something to be gained from any such meeting: an instant of enlightenment between the cheese and the port, half an hour's animated conversation stolen from the timetable of meetings and monotonous speeches. Ultimately, such moments are worth the trouble and the expense.

The fifty or so Franco-British meetings in which I have participated since 1974 – not to mention their preparation and follow-up – have enabled me not only to find out about men and women, fields and professions which I knew virtually nothing of, but also – and even more importantly – to make new friends. It is they who, for better or for worse, finally persuaded me to write this book.

Many people have asked me what kind of book this is. I do not have the false humility to call it an essay. Too many celebrated travellers have gone down that path, and I have not dared, like them, to limit myself entirely to making personal observations. Is it a piece of journalism? I am no longer a true journalist. I would like the title 'Reflections', if I could believe the reader would take the word in its literal meaning, asking no more of me than they would of a simple mirror.

Until the beginning of the century, the *dragoman* was one of the humblest and most useful French civil servants in the Ports of the Levant – the interpreter. He took pride in his knowledge of every language, and if, on occasion, he did not understand what he was meant to translate, he remained just as proud. Like the oracle at Delphi, his pronouncements were not always reliable; but his real function was to act as a guide to the guests whom the Consul entrusted to his care.

Dragoman: the word is of Greek origin. As a child I thought it was English. Why not stick to this useful mistake for the space of a paragraph: interpreter or intermediary, this dual role is a delicate one, but it requires more good will than erudition, and more experience than intelligence. As *dragoman* in the ports of Great Britain, I can accompany visitors of goodwill who wish to explore this mysterious island and get to know its natives.

Preface to the British Edition

Another dinner party, another explanation: the neighbour on my left is astonished, and discreetly attentive; the neighbour on my right shows a kindly curiosity. During the years in which – a Londoner by adoption – I was writing *Les Anglais*, the ritual did not vary a great deal. When introducing me, the hostess would inevitably trumpet my achievements, and did so with all the more enthusiasm if she had only just heard of me herself. Few dinners ended without the same question being addressed to me with pointed deference or a touch of aggression: 'Tell me frankly, do you like us on the whole, or not?' In my naïvety I had believed until then that the French were alone in wanting at all costs to be loved by the foreigners whom they despised. Yet, to my great surprise, I have more than once detected a trace of anxiety beneath the implacable English politeness. 'Frankly, you hate us don't you?'

The first British readers of *Les Anglais*, in its French edition, were relieved perhaps – or disappointed – to feel that I did not hate them. They gave me to understand that although the book might have its uses abroad, the English did not give a fig about the opinions of a Frenchman – unless they were either insulting or absurd.

My problem is that I do not love the English any more nor less than I love the French, the Irish or the Chinese. A couple of days before tackling this preface, I shared my perplexity with a fellow dinner guest*. He reassured me: 'Nothing is easier than to find

* I have to thank my table companion, James Spooner, for his contribution to this preface.

something disagreeable to say about a people. But it's true that – like Cyrano de Bergerac expounding on his nose – the best insults are those one flings at oneself. I'm Welsh, and I don't need more than one sentence to tell you all the ill that you can think of us: "A Welshman prays on his knees on Sunday and on everybody the rest of the week."' And since at this most British of dinner parties there was also a Scotsman, an Irishman and an Englishman, each of them felt obliged to attempt a definition of his own race. 'A Scotsman keeps the Sabbath strictly and anything else he can lay his hands on,' said the Scotsman. 'An Irishman has no principles but he will die for them,' said the Irishman. 'An Englishman is a self-made man who worships his maker,' said the Englishman. I leave each one of them the entire responsibility for his verdict, but I will at least have satisfied the lovers of insults.

I cannot conclude this preface without explaining to my readers that they are not my readers, for although my spoken English is comprehensible, my written French is untranslatable into English, and it is therefore my daughter, Isabelle, whom they are reading. French, like me, but Italian by her mother, English by marriage, and belonging to one of the first generations of women to have studied at Brasenose College, Oxford, she brought to her task as translator and editor an explosive mixture of filial love, intellectual respect for her father (the two do not necessarily go together), and academic rigour. This last quality and the innumerable additions, calls to order and corrections she imposed on me to make good the mistakes and omissions of the French edition, have confirmed me in the irritated respect that I have always felt for the only intellectuals I know of who think it is insulting to be called an intellectual at all: the British.

London, March 1991

Part I

The Virtues
of Pragmatism

1

An Englishman's House

'What is all the panic about? Why is everyone selling up? Is there some crisis I haven't heard about?' The Parisian, strolling through the streets of London is astonished by the array of 'For Sale' signs adorning the façades of so many homes.

Buying Time

There is no crisis, he discovers. Although high interest rates have punctured the euphoric consumer bubble of the late 1980s, houses continue to change hands. For the *house*, as every Englishman knows, is no more than a shell of bricks and mortar, quite different from the *home*, which is his castle. The home is an immaterial structure, a refuge from the aggressions of the outside world. It is constructed out of love, or at any rate, out of shared habits, and it has no price. An Englishman's house, on the other hand, is like any other consumer necessity. Like his wardrobe or his car, it answers to the need of the moment. It can grow with his family, improve or deteriorate according to his fortunes. For him, buying, selling, moving out, moving in, are merely staging posts in his career. His attitude is in marked contrast to that of the average Frenchman, for whom the most dreary of suburban bungalows is invested with all the permanence, the sacred aura of ownership, '*la propriété*'.

But if the majority of British home-owners feel less rooted to their property than their French counterparts do, there is good reason, for they really are less so. In Britain there has been no revolution to overturn the essentially medieval system of leases that persists today. Land, rather than buildings, has always been the source and symbol not only of wealth, but also of nobility and power. As early as 1086, inalienable land ownership was registered and enshrined in William the Conqueror's *Domesday Book*. Land was entrusted to lease-holders for farming, and long leases of seventy-five, ninety, a hundred and twenty years or more made it possible for the tenant to recover the cost of any building that was required. He retained the freedom of sub-letting, or of selling his lease to a third party, but at the end of the lease period, the entire property reverted to the owner of the land. To this day there are three men, the Duke of Westminster, Baron Howard de Walden and Earl Cadogan, who between them own most of the smartest and most exclusive districts of the West End of London.

In the eighteenth century, speculative builders (the equivalent of today's property developers) prompted major land-owners to carry out the first important property deals. The builder undertook the financing as well as the construction of substantial new developments. His need to reduce costs by rationalising building methods accounts for the regular layout of streets and squares – following a uniform architectural design – that is so characteristic of the British urban landscape. Among the best examples of this are the beautiful neo-classical façades of Edinburgh's New Town, the elegant curves of Bath's crescents and the straight lines of London's Eaton Square.

These urban residences reflected, on a reduced scale, the 'upstairs-downstairs' domestic organisation of the period's large country houses. Kitchens and staff were housed in the basement, reception rooms and masters' bedrooms occupied the main body of the house, and the servants lived in the attic. When architects lacked inspiration, or developers were aiming at more popular markets, admirable harmony often degenerated into boring uniformity, hypnotizing the eye with endless semi-detached or terraced houses repeating themselves identically along interminable streets.

The monotony of the streets in nineteenth-century working-class districts was compounded by the depressingly uniform deterioration of the houses. Jerry builders – or 'hats' as they were known in Liverpool – were responsible for the hasty erection of rows of back-to-back houses without foundations on ill-drained soil. These hovels, which had neither water nor any kind of sanitation apart from a few stinking collective latrines, were condemned by contemporary advocates of hygiene, and their construction was banned towards the middle of the nineteenth century. But many, although squalid, survived for a long time.

This differentiation between housing developments according to the wealth of their occupants tended to restrict the social mobility generated by the industrial revolution. On the other hand, the system of long leases did restore a certain flexibility to these over-rigid structures. A fine house on which the lease was running out might lose much of its market value, but its prestige was untarnished. It could be snapped up by an ambitious man of little wealth, for whom this short-term financial investment brought the high social dividends of a 'good address', which was almost as important as a 'good school' or a 'good accent'.

Today, with ever increasing land values – and despite the occasional slump in the housing market – estate agents can turn almost anything to profit. In London, where former hovels are cleverly renovated into 'luxury maisonettes', the boundary between a good address and a bad one is no longer so clear. But in spite of this trend, the speculative builder in England has to contend with the unrepentant individualism of rich and poor alike. The long lease continues to flourish and developers are given every freedom to withhold full ownership of the goods they sell. But they are quite unable to pile the English into the multi-storey apartment blocks which Parisians and Neapolitans, for instance, accepted as early as the eighteenth century, and which were uniformly imposed on the inhabitants of all Europe's big cities in the following century, and still are for the majority of them.

Neither the greed of developers nor the well-meaning efforts of social reformers trying to provide the poor with cheap council housing have managed to change this trait of the national character. No more than four per cent of the population live in high rise buildings, most of them concentrated in London, Glasgow and Liverpool, and no local authority today would consider building a new one.

And yet one of London's best-kept secrets is a block of flats. Not just any block: Albany has one of the smartest addresses in the city, between Regent Street and Piccadilly. It can be reached from a simple courtyard off Piccadilly itself, or from Vigo Street, which becomes increasingly narrow – discouraging importunate visitors – before opening out into Burlington Gardens, where two porter's lodges flank and at the same time disguise Albany's main entrance. Being rich and famous will not get you a set in Albany. Though it is no longer indispensable to be a bachelor, there are still two conditions that have to be met before an aspiring tenant can gain entry. First there has to be a vacancy. No one chooses to move out of Albany, but occasionally someone is considerate enough to die. As for the second condition, it is a more subtle one and precludes the tenancy of show-offs, parvenus and bores – or does it? Snobbery alone can settle this weighty question.

So, among the most privileged, there are some who like to distinguish themselves from the crowd by choosing the promiscuity of a block of flats. Indeed for some years there has been an increasing trend towards quality apartments; but four out of five British families continue to entrench themselves in the privacy of their individual houses.

Where Comfort was Born

Defying the cold and the rain, a coal fire glows in the hearth. This image always fills the Englishman abroad with deep nostalgia. No matter that the coal, more often than not, is today replaced by an electric bar heater giving out fake flames; the open fire retains its status as the beating heart of the British home. Even central heating has not successfuly dethroned it – and only serves to underline its symbolic importance.

Although the English tend to heat their homes more thoroughly than they used to, the axioms and taboos of a more heroic era still apply. True, the times are past when a visitor in a small provincial hotel had to get up at two in the morning because the heating had stopped working for want of a shilling in the meter. But the cold is still considered healthy, and warmth is thought of as enervating and a touch degenerate. In town, the desirability of a warm house is more or less accepted; in the country it is still considered normal to wander round corridors muffled up in several thick jumpers, red-nosed and breathing steam. Yet even in the depths of his agrarian retreat, the English die-hard is seeing his last frozen window pane melt in the insidious warmth of the radiator.

In the wake of her industrial conquests, Great Britain invented the notion of comfort. She allowed it at first to take on the elegant patina of time, then to rust like a disused piece of machinery, before rediscovering it, but this time in German, Japanese or American guise. The vast buttoned leather sofas; the irresistible welcome of granny's chintz armchairs; the old locks, shining like gold, with bolts that glide silently open; an ancient plate-warmer working as efficiently as on its first day of service; the *lazy Susan* enabling guests at the breakfast table to reach for the butter, jam or marmalade without having to interrupt the morning's peace with conversation; the triple gleam of brass, silver and polished mahogany; the suppleness of well-cured leather and the soft warmth of thick lining beneath the floral dress of a heavy pair of curtains: surely these things are more than mere creature comforts?

The conservatism of the rich and the parsimony of the poor have conspired to keep, protect and repair these family treasures. Despite their infatuation with video-recorders and computers, British consumers – unlike their European and American counterparts – are only just beginning to discover the intoxicating joys of modernisation at any cost. Though Victorian thrift has long been dead and buried in the cemeteries of the great industrial cities of the nineteenth century, in the family home it still exerts considerable influence. Flashy luxury is out of the question; not so, respectable bad taste with its doilies, its keys with tassels, its porcelain cups commemorating some royal jubilee and its machine-woven tapestries representing a pack of dogs, a Spanish dancer or a piper in front of a Scottish castle. To have a charming interior remains the first ambition and the first duty of a British household. For its sake a great many pleasures are foregone, the first of these being – without a qualm – the pleasures of the table.

Between the seventeenth and eighteenth centuries, the property owning middle classes and the aristocracy developed a notion of comfort that encompassed much more than simple relief from discomfort. It established a harmony between the new refinements of everyday life and the imposing décor was designed to impress on the common people a humbling reminder of the owners' power and of their aesthetic and therefore moral superiority. No less than accent and dress, this refined notion of comfort defined their superiority. It became the measure of an acceptable level of self-indulgence: below that line lay hardship and vulgarity; above it, dignity and self-esteem degenerated into sybaritism. It provided the ultimate proof that social superiority was not purely a matter of appearances, but reflected an innate delicacy of behaviour that would never hold any attractions for the crude populace. There is no real comfort without beauty, for beauty brings comfort to the eye. But whereas the classical notion of beauty, incomparably exemplified in Versailles, required the ordering of nature according to a principle, the English idea of comfort could encompass the disorder of practical necessity, or of a whim. With Louis XV, the French added elegance and ease to the splendours of the Louis XIV era, but the English went further: their achievement was to reconcile the order of art with the disorder of life.

A huge sofa to sink into, a table with light, easily moved chairs: it is good to sit and chat while embroidering or scribbling a few lines on a portable writing-box. In the admirable but austere colonnaded hall of the country house, a cosy corner has insinuated itself, nestling under the portraits of scandalised ancestors. Others are soon to follow, in libraries and pompous halls. The grand empty spaces of formal reception rooms fill up with chubby armchairs in floral chintz and small round tables laden with porcelain sweet-boxes, scattered next to partially read books and half-open work-boxes.

In France, it took the influence of Balzac – with his passion for antiques and modernism, fine cabinet-work and knick-knacks, luxury and simplicity, opulent masculinity and elegant femininity – before the salons of the Restoration were in their turn transformed under the leadership of du Marsay, the Duchesse de Langeais and their aristocratic following. Taking up the torch, the Parisian smart set of the Faubourg Saint-Germain remodelled themselves according to Balzac's imaginative portrayal of them, and introduced an astonished Louis-Philippe to décors that were novel, yet familiar, and that he imitated obediently. Today's interior decoration owes a great deal, no doubt, to this upheaval in which the familiar and the surprising are blended with an art that has created its own conventions. Is it too much to credit the English with having been in the vanguard in this field, as in so many others?

For the English comfort is not only a matter of material well-being. It is one more expression of their fundamental individualism which never expresses itself better than within the confines of the respectable and conventional. Originality consists not in breaking the rules of conformity, but in moulding them around one's own personality. The Royal Pavilion in Brighton – this 'folly' as some might describe it, this excellent joke, as I prefer to call it – is, first and foremost, a luxury bachelor flat, both comfortable and practical. But by decorating and furnishing it with fantastic *chinoiseries*, the Prince Regent was also providing himself with an escape into a world of enchantment.

Horace Walpole had more complex ambitions when he designed his Middlesex country house, Strawberry Hill. In rejecting the fashionable Palladian and Classical architecture of the time in favour of his own reinterpretation of the Decorated English Gothic style, he was primarily asserting his inalienable right to be different. But make no mistake: the theatrical character of his principal staircase, of the main sitting-room, of the Holbein room, and particularly of the gallery, with its ceiling elaborately ribbed with papier-mâché gothic vaults – none of these detracted from the material comforts which the hospitable bachelor demanded. On the contrary, having once made sure of his creature comforts, he could allow his imagination to soar. His fireplaces were carved after medieval tombs; Madame du Deffand*, who nurtured a hopeless passion for Walpole, provided him with an Aubusson tapestry for the decoration of his four-poster bed; the ebony table and

---

* Marie de Vichy-Chamrond, the Marquise du Deffand (1697–1780) hosted one of the main literary salons of the eighteenth century, frequented by artists, writers, wits, and some of the Philosophes and Encyclopedistes. After separating from her husband, Jean-Baptiste de La Lande, Marquis du Deffand, in 1722, she became the mistress of the regent, Philippe II, Duc d'Orleans. In her later years she fell passionately in love with Horace Walpole, who was twenty years younger than her. He accepted her passion with a good-natured indifference, and they maintained a firm and lasting friendship.

Elizabethan chairs in the Holbein room would inspire a new fashion for this furniture, which had previously been relegated to the attics; and who after Walpole – the arbiter of good taste – could doubt that it was possible to surround such furniture with French Louis XV armchairs? Later, he would not hesitate to borrow the plump contours of the Austrian and German Biedemeier style for his own small English buttoned sofas.

For surely the notion of comfort must reflect the pleasures of renewal as much as those of everyday life. Such, at any rate, must be the conviction of Terence Conran, who some twenty years ago created a style that will undoubtedly be remembered in art history books by the name of the worldwide chain of stores that he started, 'Habitat'. The Habitat style is like a splash of light in the shadows of a suburban semi. It has the carefree iconoclasm of cleanly scrubbed youth, pulling down old curtains, stripping away the flaking colours of long-gone generations and finding beneath them the grain of living wood. Habitat means simple shapes and industrialised production, accompanied however by a quality and prices that restrict the market; inspiration drawn from craft objects around the world – a partnership between yesterday's 'modern' and today's; invention and selection, eclecticism guided by strong individual taste. More than a style, it offers a mood that reflects the personality of its customers: artless, though well-groomed; rejecting fussiness, yet sociable; too busy or impatient for the daily grind of domesticity, yet attracted by spices, wholemeal bread and exotic dishes. The Habitat style is too simple and expensive for the poor, and a little too staid for the real bohemian, but it has nonetheless exploded the foreigner's image of a slightly old-fashioned and unadventurous England, replacing it with one of dynamism and success.

In the late eighteenth and early nineteenth centuries, an invisible array of complicated machinery began to make its presence felt under the visible trappings of luxury. Henry Shaw, in a kind of manual of interior decoration, describes what he considered to be an inexpensive and useful luxury – indeed, an indispensable item in the perfect country house: the bathroom. This small room, he explains, is reserved for showers and hot baths (cold baths being taken in the park, in an ornamental building on the banks of a stream), and should be placed in a part of the house where it can be fed with hot water by means of pipes connected to a boiler in the kitchen or the saddle room. In London, it is still possible to see traces of this historical development in the rows of little brick cubes overhanging the back gardens of elegant Georgian and Edwardian houses, from which emerge an assortment of pipes of varying length and bore. It is a safe bet that they still conceal those first bathrooms of the age of hygiene. A bedroom reduced by two-thirds of its area, a cut-off corridor, a landing with frosted-glass windows – any odd space was pressed into service for the sake of this new luxury. Today the '*en suite*' bathroom remains a most desirable asset in the eyes of an estate agent.

Though England gave the world the genteel initials 'W.C.', it was the French who first adopted the luxury of those *lieux à l'anglaise*, described by the architect Blondel in the eighteenth century. Since then the English have caught up: inevitably supplied by upper-class affectation with some euphemistic name – both esoteric and self-evident – the loo, bog or john has become the place which, after the drawing-room (or before it?) is the most agreeably furnished by the accomplished hostess. Every good W.C. comes with an array of books (preferably funny), a few engravings and some photographs (if possible amusing, or at any rate exaggeratedly stuffy) of the family – male and adult members only – and of the family dog.

Once again, it is thanks to early industrialisation and urbanisation that the English in the nineteenth century were so far ahead of the largely rural population of other European countries in matters of hygiene, and that they are trailing behind today. They were the first to acquire a modern system of sanitation, and were soon exporting their hardware throughout the world: their tin- or zinc-lined tubs, later to be superseded by enamelled sheet- or cast-iron baths, and their valve- or syphon-operated toilet bowls.

Despite this lead, the English were the last to be swept away by the fashion for fitted kitchens and gleaming new bathrooms, though today, with some twenty years' delay, they have finally acquired a taste for the modern. Naturally, they have left behind them a few sceptics: passionate lovers of industrial archaeology who continue to spit and polish the coppers and brasses once looked after by their grandparents' servants; and stern critics of contemporary vulgarity who, whilst dabbing at their mouths with monogrammed napkins, lull themselves into post-prandial torpor to the intestinal gurgles of the dining room's ancient pipes, furred with scale, rust and verdigris.

Let us leave aside the plumbing, and dwell a while on brushes, pumice stone and small stoppered bottles of crystal and porcelain, accompanied by silver, ivory and tortoise-shell. If there is such a thing as the romance of toiletries, its home is surely in England. From the transparent soap-cake to the shaving bowl, from badger-hair and linen to natural sea-sponges and pale wood: animal, vegetable or mineral, precious substances are allied to exquisitely plain ones in a fragrant metamorphosis. Strolling down Jermyn Street we catch the whiff of verbena or citron – that rare oil essence, of which one drop in a bath-tub is sufficient to dissipate an ocean of worries. For perfume we must go to Paris; for freshness only London will do.

Cosmetics know no frontiers, and television commercials are standardising tastes. Yet it will be many a long year before the world ceases to harbour a few obstinate individuals convinced that if they have not vigorously rubbed themselves down with English lavender water before slipping into their pyjamas, they will sleep less well.

A House of One's Own

With or without added luxuries, a privately-owned house would be an impossible dream for the average citizen, were it not for the saving grace of the detestable and inevitable mortgage. British building societies represent the oldest system in Europe for the acquisition of property. They were originally conceived as mutual credit societies with a working-class (or at any rate popular) base, and were not meant to survive beyond the achievement of their purpose – which was the provision of housing for each of their members. But it was not long before a few imaginative capitalists seized on them to attract and retain this growing form of popular savings. The success of the Halifax – which today remains one of Britain's largest building societies – arose in the last decades of the nineteenth century when a few earnestly religious great manufacturing families, such as the Aykroyds and the Crossleys, decided to put their spirit of enterprise as well as their sense of duty behind it. For many savers, then as now, the building society, with its solid, property-based collateral, seemed a far more profitable and, especially, more accessible option than the bank.

During the same period, a new kind of urban landscape was being created by a number of philanthropic businessmen, such as the founders of the Cadbury chocolate empire, and Sir Ebenezer Howard, who planned and built Britain's first garden cities. Without forming an architectural movement, they lent to British popular housing a particular quality that it was to keep wherever possible – that rather humble and touching individualism which delights in a breath of fresh air and a few flowers in a garden.

It is hardly surprising that the dynamics of this social and financial evolution should have given rise to a religion of house-ownership, of which Harold Bellman, president of the Building Societies Association, was to become the prophet, and his book, *The Silent Revolution*, the gospel. This gospel was welcomed with particular relief by the ruling classes, shaken by the violent advent of Bolshevism in Russia and the 1926 general strike. The young men who had been fighting for their country on the European battlefields of the First World War could so easily, on their return, have taken up the struggle for a roof over their heads. Fortunately the building societies were at hand to defuse this potential time-bomb by enabling them to acquire a house through their own work. As Bellman expressed it: 'By assisting men to the ownership of houses it gave countless thousands a stake in the country.' Mrs Thatcher's policy of council house sales was introduced with much the same aim in mind. It is ironic that for a number of years the Labour Party felt obliged to oppose a policy that accomplished one of the most effective transfers of wealth to the working classes in recent decades.

Today's problems of inner city deprivation and degradation have their roots in the massive expansion of six urban centres (London, Birmingham, Liverpool, Manchester, Leeds and Newcastle) that was taking place from the beginning of the century until the early

1950s. With the growth of the suburbs, city centres became increasingly depopulated, and even now, despite a general improvement in the standard of housing, they continue to deteriorate.

Since the war however, neither Labour nor Conservative governments have successfully tackled the housing question. In the last fifty years there has been little town planning worthy of the name. With a few rare exceptions, all the best British architects have been ostracised at home and forced to work abroad. Neither public nor private patrons have been encouraged to create something out of the ruins of the war; no artist has taken up where John Nash left off, constructing a new Regent's Park over London's bomb sites, or a modern version of Park Village East, or West, those exemplary prefigurations of the garden cities of the future.

Town and Country

The road curves gently down between mellow thatched roofs: for the past two centuries the village of Milton Abbas has been playing the shepherdess in a baroque pastoral with a Dorset accent. Lord Dorchester staged it, between 1773 and 1776, with Capability Brown – that greatest of British landscape gardeners – providing the design. But the real facts behind the set were less idyllic. To begin with Lord Dorchester commissioned the architect, William Chambers, to build him a house on the ruins of a former abbey. It then became an absolute necessity to get rid of the village that was spoiling his view. Not for nothing had Lancelot Brown been nicknamed Capability; better than the faith, he had the ability that moves mountains – or indeed entire villages. Since he had to knock everything down and rehouse the Dorchester tenant farmers elsewhere, why not apply to this task all the artistry that had already inspired him to recreate in England's fields the luminous Roman countryside of Claude Lorrain's paintings? The new village consisted of pretty cottages, grouped in pairs on either side of a wide road, each with its own small garden. These twin houses were separated from their neighbours by clumps of chestnut trees. A church and an almshouse completed the picture, giving the village its spiritual identity.

The fact that the architecture of these English tenant villages is often exquisite should be attributed, no doubt, to the vanity rather than the generosity of the great landowners who built them. The cottages were cramped, with low ceilings, and badly heated, offering little more than a shelter from inclement weather. But the gentleness of the landscape, coupled with the increasingly abundant produce of the fields and livestock, rendered life for the tenant less harsh than it was for the small independent farmer or the daily wage-labourer. His tenancy amounted to a work contract with reciprocal social duties. It reinforced the rights of the landowner, but it also defined his obligations. And although the integration within a community of the most humble with the most powerful smacked of feudalism, it had the virtues of creating a harmony that was not merely architectural, but also moral and metaphysical.

Not only in England, but also in Wales, in the poorest parts of the Scottish Highlands and in the most deprived villages of the northern isles and of Ulster, this harmony – which is one of the major attractions of the rural scene – has long survived the struggles between clans and factions. A few peasant revolts may have threatened it, but there has been no revolution to call into question the order established through the centuries by all sections of agrarian society. Even when industrialisation and urban expansion began to deplete the ranks of that society, radicalism continued to make little impact on the rural areas. Agricultural labourers were the last and the least numerous to join any kind of union or to go on strike. Naturally this indifference or passivity cannot be attributed entirely to the pleasures of the family cottage. But it can be admitted that the cottage has represented a microcosm of order and social harmony.

The last fifty years have given birth to many new cities. Some of the oldest have grown to such an extent as to be unrecognisable, and German bombs have permanently disfigured others, such as Coventry. But English villages are immutable and eternal. Even bearing in mind that since the eighteenth century at least, they have been almost entirely spared the destruction of war, and – with the exception of Northern Ireland – have rarely suffered the exactions of an army of occupation, the sheer number to have survived the vicissitudes of history intact is astonishing.

Villages are what inspire in us the love of England. And – as always in love – we idealise indiscriminately. We see only the impeccable lawns and forget the rain that makes them so green. We are blind to the pettiness, the poverty and the violence that sometimes underlie the beauty that overwhelms us. But how can we resist the comforting good cheer of these low-slung houses, with roofs tilted like hats to protect us from the weather, their doors and windows twisted with age but always freshly painted? The English themselves are the first to succumb to their charms, attributing to them all the virtues forsworn by the cities. Not all English villages are idyllic, nor are they equally well-preserved. Yet most of them have retained an individualism that goes beyond their regional characteristics, reflecting the individualism and docility which I believe to be the basic characteristics of English society.

The formula underlying English village architecture was originally that of the sixteen foot bay that separated the two branches of the tiny cottage's simple frame. Later more spacious models were equipped with beams and proper walls; the width of the bay was doubled or tripled, and a second floor was sometimes added. But the sixteen foot bay – just wide enough to house two oxen – continued to provide the basic unit of measurement. Beneath the cosy feline curves of its thatched roof, we can easily touch the cottage's low ceiling; like the ancestral hut warmed by animal heat, it surrounds us in a protective cocoon. In England, as in every country where stone is scarce, wattle-and-daub – that mixture of mud, chopped straw and wherever possible, cow dung – used to reign supreme. Whether covered in thatch or decked out in tiles or slate, it lent a genial portliness to walls that were whitewashed or painted year after year in pastel colours. In Devon, more than a century or two after they were built, you can still see cottages with overhanging roofs, their wattle-and-daub walls edged with stone to prevent them from disintegrating into the soil.

Apart from a ritual hop to Cambridge, foreign tourists rarely venture into East Anglia. They should do so, for the counties of Essex, Suffolk and Norfolk are particularly rich in those still landscapes where the houses blend into a timeless landscape. Here too the walls are made of an X-shaped supporting frame of beams infilled with wattle-and-daub. But whereas in Devon the wooden beams of the frame are almost always visible, in East Anglia they are usually drowned in heavy white rendering which is sometimes carved, or 'pargeted', into geometric patterns.

Except in places where it was produced, baked brick long remained too expensive a material for general use. In noble Tudor houses it was used instead of mud to infill the timber frame, but in peasant homes its use was restricted to the chimney which gradually replaced the simple hole in the roof through which smoke had formerly escaped. In the Highlands and Scottish isles, one can still see a few cottages whose rough stone walls have been so well put together that they have survived the centuries entirely without mortar. A few rare surviving examples testify to the use of this technique in Yorkshire and Cornwall. It was not until the seventeenth century that dressed stone, formerly the privilege of the powerful and rich, found its way into the village streets. Its triumph was that despite its splendour, it in no way altered their gentle familiarity.

Topography and situation have also been crucial in determining the layout of the English village. Many of the oldest settlements acquired their characteristic strung-out shape by threading themselves in double rows along the network of Roman roads, or taking over some later highway and transforming it into the high street. New generations of houses have gradually settled themselves behind their ancestors, giving these developments a more village-like aspect. Other villages took shape along the banks of a river, where possible a navigable one, or around easily cultivable land; and though their cottages were unmistakably English, their layout could have been that of any French or German settlement.

The village green, however, is a uniquely English product. Originally the green was a piece of common grazing land, and it is possible that the cottages and farms that developed around it were built to provide the livestock with protection at night from predators – most notably from wolves. With time, despoliation and an encroaching population, the village lost its outlying pastures. But the green has survived, as has the well or communal pump, and the pond – once a watering hole for livestock and a silt reservoir for wattle-and-daub – is now an ecological treasure-house.

Today the figure most notably absent from England's agrarian idyll is the farmer himself. He does exist, but being in a minority, his presence is not distinctive. Unlike his continental counterpart, he has the same education and the same tastes and wears the same clothes as his neighbour, the city commuter. He is a farm-labourer just as he might be a carpenter or garage-worker – undoubtedly a countryman, but not a peasant. Even when he lives on a genuine farm with stables and barns filled with agricultural equipment, his home is as comfortable – if not more so – as that of any city dweller of comparable economic standing. With a few rooms to spare, he can supplement his income by providing bed and breakfast. Whether employed by a great landowner or by a farming company, the tenant is likely to be better housed than the independent farmer, who is always short of cash. Conscious of his professional value (even in times of unemployment there is a shortage of qualified farm-workers), he is able to negotiate quality accommodation – which is his first requirement – from his employer.

The Englishman's Castle

Just as the village helps to perpetuate the image that the British have of themselves as country folk, so the primary function of the country house has become that of generating dreams: dreams of luxury for the English, of chivalry for the Welsh, of Bonny Prince Charlie for the Scottish, and of England for the rest of the world. Indeed, this function is so crucial that it mobilises everyone – from Government to local authorities, the National Trust and innumerable other charities and trusts, and of course the country house owners themselves, who have eagerly become farmers, industrialists or theme-park managers in an effort to perpetuate the myth. Far from breaking with tradition, such entrepreneurial efforts by a new generation of relatively impoverished gentlemen have helped to preserve it, enabling them to endow their ancestral homes with the prestige and preeminence that reflects their lineage.

As long ago as the Middle Ages, the importance of noble homes and fortified castles went far beyond their function as comfortable shelter or place of safety. Their size and splendour had to match the extent of the land that they dominated – first with their towers, and later with their colonnades and classical pediments. They were, after all, symbols of a power that was less precarious than royal favour, and more enduring than commercial or wartime prosperity. Yet without men to defend them in times of upheaval, land and riches were nothing more than a prize to be seized; and, without agents capable of exercising and imposing it, by force if necessary, power was nothing more than an illusion. For this reason one of the functions of the original country house was to house a following whose number and quality were worthy of their master's rank. Stewards, rent-collectors, tenants with special requests, all had to be welcomed, fed and – at a time when the endurance of the rider or of his mount determined the length of a journey – put up for the night.

The hall was the heart of the house and its outbuildings. Here the lord of the manor regularly held court, settled disputes, presided over meals and made merry with his retainers, or even his servants. For reasons of convenience the outbuildings – which at first had been as humble as the men and animals who lived and worked in them together – were gradually gathered round the hall, extended and ennobled, at least externally, finally giving the country house its full dimensions. In the seventeenth century, under the influence of Palladio, this somewhat disparate collection of rooms – including the hall, the noble and the servant quarters – began to be arranged symmetrically following the principles enunciated in the *Quattro libri di Architettura*.

A 'great chamber' and other, smaller chambers were increasingly built above the hall, which was situated if possible at the centre of the house on the ground floor. The master of the house no longer sat at the head of a communal table, but continued to take his meals in close proximity to his following, presiding from a separate table, in a dominant position befitting his rank. The hall was still accessible not only to servants, but also to tenants and visitors. Keeping an open table was as much a reflection of status as a duty.

But increasingly, the segregation heralded by the appearance of the great chamber began to make itself felt. The familiarity that had prevailed between the master and his retainers gave way to rigid hierarchy. Servants were now housed in a separate hall, or in the basement, and had to limit their appearances to a strict minimum.

Visitors and scroungers could no longer count on having their meals served in a main hall. Private apartments became increasingly elaborate. Corridors were turned into sumptuous picture galleries. Luxury abounded in cosy bedrooms (now accessible only to the most intimate visitors), and in welcoming libraries and gilded drawing rooms. Two divergent but complementary tendencies were bringing the master greater comfort in his private life, and greater ceremony in his public one.

In the second half of the eighteenth century, a new fashion for French windows opened country house drawing rooms to the pleasures of the gardens, which hitherto had been framed behind closed windows and admired like works of art. Now, these gardens were refashioned in an idealised version of the countryside, which the Romantics would extend to the entire world of nature. At the same time a new paternalism – whether severe or indulgent – ascribed idyllic pastoral virtues to those very tenants who were increasingly being relegated by this influx of new luxuries to their lowly role as producers. The beginning of the Victorian era would see the rehabilitation of those traditional festivities that had gathered servants round their master, in the manner of the feudal family. Yet beyond this high point, one could already detect the seeds of the country house's decline. Industrialisation and urbanisation were taking a heavy toll on the revenues of landowners, which soon became insufficient to sustain their patriarchal life-style. A few of the shrewdest learnt to survive by marrying their eldest son to some industrial heiress, or by accepting a directorship from a company in search of respectability. Many more survived by joining with other landowning families in marriage. Those who were unable to keep up with the enormous running expenses of their country seat allowed it to fall into ruin, or even knocked it down in order to free more land for cultivation. A few country houses were to survive for more than a century after this first economic shock, but gradually the names inscribed in their visitors' books ceased to reflect history in the making and began instead to evoke the history of ancestors long dead.

Chatsworth, home of the Dukes of Devonshire, and perhaps the grandest, if not the most beautiful of English country houses, was first opened to the public in the seventeenth century, almost immediately after it was built. Since then, even the wealthiest of country house owners – their fortunes strangled by exorbitant death duties and huge running costs – have been forced to follow the Devonshires' example. They either set up a trust, create their own management company, or start a leisure park (complete with restaurants, museums, or even a zoo) in the grounds of their home. They have replaced agriculture with tourism, and public opinion is behind them in their efforts to preserve a private heritage whose loss would undoubtedly be felt by the entire country.

2
Two Nations

'On either side of an invisible frontier, two nations eye each
other without favour: two nations "between whom there
is no intercourse and no sympathy; who are as ignorant
of each other's habits, thoughts, and feelings, as if they
were dwellers in different zones, or inhabitants of different
planets; who are formed by different breeding, are fed by
a different food, are ordered by different manners, and are
not governed by the same laws."

'You speak of . . .' said Egremont, hesitantly,

'*THE RICH AND THE POOR.*"'

These observations extracted from the political novel, *Sybil*,
remain almost as true today as they were when Queen Victoria's
future Prime Minister, Benjamin Disraeli, first wrote them in
1845.

The Gastronomic Gulf
The nation of fish and chips still eats with its back firmly turned
against the nation of lamb with mint sauce and venison with
redcurrant jelly. Breakfast alone unites the British people in
a common passion. For millions of households life would be
inconceivable without the morning ritual of opening the front
door and fumbling sleepily for the newspaper and daily pinta,
sometimes accompanied by fresh fruit juice and bacon and eggs.
Two incidents demonstrate the strength of feeling with which the
nation as a whole still views its favourite meal. When shops were
first inundated with imports of European long-life milk, there was

an uproar. This inferior product, with its low prices, threatened the very existence of the treasured doorstep delivery. And when the Junior Health Minister Edwina Currie dared to touch on the equally sacred subject of the British egg, she was overwhelmed by the public's reaction. Her tactless suggestion that egg production was widely infected with salmonella poisoning was enough to force her resignation in December 1988. For without eggs, what is left of the English breakfast?

Such occasional outbursts of public sentiment cannot hide the fact that this most traditional of meals has long since lost its integrity. The first ingredient to beat a retreat was the English cup of tea – beginning with morning tea, that early cup, accompanied by a light biscuit, with which one used to be woken by a housemaid or manservant in any decent household. Though this luxury is still offered in a few old-fashioned family guest-houses, more often than not the English cuppa has been dethroned, even at the breakfast table, by the cup of coffee – almost always instant, and always insipid. Even the faithful have forgotten the rules of their art. Gone are the days when the tea-pot was pre-heated with boiling water, the tea chosen and measured out with care – one teaspoonful per person and one for the pot. Today, the teabag is triumphant and tastes are ever less discriminating. Naturally there remain a fastidious rear-guard who will buy their tea only in specialised shops, where they carefully choose a classical or personal blend with an aroma that delights the palate of meditative souls. But their ranks thin daily.

Tea is not the only victim of this assault from modern trends. The real loser is the English breakfast itself. Heavy silver dishes laden with sausages, ham and bacon, kippers and mackerel, with tongue, venison, fried potatoes and eggs (poached, boiled, scrambled or fried), are as much a nostalgic anachronism as the country house and the club which were once their setting. Today, the frugal continental breakfast is rapidly gaining ground. The most robust defenders of the traditional breakfast (albeit in a simplified version) are manual workers – for whom this first meal remains essential – and travellers, who would feel cheated if the price of their room did not include a hearty English breakfast.

Lunch, on the other hand, is not considered an important

24

meal by manual workers. They are usually content to swallow a sandwich and a cup of coffee at work, or treat themselves to a visit to the nearest pub. But a lunch-time drink – though not a crime – is a slight infringement on the rules of sobriety which are associated with work, and even drunkards feel obliged to invent excuses for breaking them.

Industrial managers and city financiers alone surrender themselves without scruple to the rites of the business lunch, unanimously condemned as unhealthy and useless, but unanimously observed as a necessary evil by the international fraternity of businessmen. Though the last decade has seen a slight decline in the practice, it is far from dead. Like the hotel breakfast, it has the irresistible attraction of the free perk or of the benefit in kind wrung from the avarice of the employer and the degree of expense is a measure of the host's increasing prestige.

But the idea of a full weekday meal, with the family seated round the table for a gastronomic interlude between twelve and two, is virtually inconceivable to the average British household. Whereas in France, children and husband routinely come home from school and work to enjoy a good lunch and a bottle of wine, in England those few family members who are not out of the house at lunch-time might, at the very most, rummage in the fridge while boiling the kettle for their instant coffee. Between meals, companies producing sweets, chocolate bars and biscuits vie with each other to the tune of millions of pounds of advertising, selling energy to the labourer, tooth decay to the schoolchild, and superfluous kilos to the depressed housewife.

Ultimately, there is one huge social and geographical gulf dividing the north from the south, the provinces from London, and the working classes from the middle and upper classes. At least as much as his accent, it is the time at which he takes his meals that distinguishes the manual worker from his more privileged fellow citizen. For him, evening tea is the most important and the last meal of the day. For the white collar worker, it is no more than a quick break an hour before leaving the office. And for those who do not even need to work, it is an elegant afternoon pause, accompanied by the traditional cucumber sandwiches, crumpets, muffins and buns.

The less wealthy majority, in company with a few enlightened amateurs, spend a large part of their evening at the pub, leaving behind the children and often, the wife, who relaxes in front of the television watching soap-operas. Among the middle classes, the evening is usually lengthened, spent over dinner with family or friends, at parties (from the most elegant to the most dissipated), or perhaps at the theatre or the cinema. Private hospitality is usually simple, but the etiquette surrounding official functions is more elaborate than anywhere in the world. It has survived the centuries virtually untouched by revolution or political upheaval. At Royal dinners and Lord Mayors' banquets, at the Inns of Court or the smartest of clubs, everything – from the coffered ceilings to the wall tapestries, from the coats of arms to the polished mahogany tables, the table silver and pewter, the candelabra and the rare porcelain, the ancient rules of decorum religiously observed, the toasts, including the inevitable toast to the Queen – everything conspires to create an atmosphere of peaceful solemnity, gradually giving way to the animation which comes with the consumption of often excellent wines, culminating in the traditional vintage port at the end of the meal.

English cuisine, both popular and sophisticated, has received a bad press. Its worst enemies are the English themselves – not to mention the Welsh, the Irish and the Scots, none of whom do justice to their best local dishes, even when their patriotism requires it. They do not know what they are missing, for they have at their disposal a treasure-house of forgotten recipes; and their succulent meat and abundant fish, coupled with the freshness of their vegetables, gives them all the ingredients they need to rival the refinements of French gastronomy. But these refinements do not seduce so much as irritate them.

From the Production Line to the Dinner Table

Whereas in France every province and every village takes even greater pride in its local dishes than it does in its native customs, the British – who are so fastidious when it comes to housing – have uncomplainingly relinquished their strong and savoury ancestral cuisine and surrendered to the tyranny of processed foods. In the nineteenth century, the rapid industrialisation of

Britain's urban and industrial populations led to their isolation from the rural economy, including its fresh agricultural products and its culinary traditions. City dwellers were like naval crews on their travels, forced to subsist on dry biscuits and salt beef from the ship's storeroom, while at home the children lived on gruel. Naturally, the dry biscuit was an English invention. And Henry Ford would have admired the ingenuity with which the eighteenth century Navy cut its costs by introducing mass-production lines into its Deptford, Plymouth and Portsmouth bakehouses. Without biscuits there would have been no long-haul journeys, no adventure novels, no Huntley and Palmers, and none of those wonderful metal biscuit tins painted with garlands of flowers, portraits and landscape scenes. Without biscuits, the British processed foods industry might not have gained a fifty year lead over that of other countries and – who knows – a genuine British gastronomy might have survived.

As is often the case when capitalist dynamism is combined with humanitarian concerns, we find Quakers at the origins of industrial biscuit manufacture, as well as of the chocolate industry. In mechanising their output they were as concerned to improve the deplorable working conditions of their men as they were to increase their profits. First Jonathan Dogson Carr, then George Palmer, were to give the English biscuit a preeminence it has never lost. The industrialisation of the baking trade was to follow, though more gradually. The production and mass distribution of bread were soon to be merged, so that today, four major companies control more than ninety per cent of the entire bread market, in competition with a mere ten thousand independent producers. Even before that memorable night in 1762 when Lord Sandwich, wishing to avoid leaving the gaming table, ordered slices of bread and meat together, the English were already consuming this processed, bleached and homogenised product with a multitude of sauces. With the potato, it is still the staple part of the British diet.

But the universal consumer must be caught at birth. The traditional Scottish porridge – with its dual attributes of healthy and nourishing pulp for Baby, and cheap, filling main course for Father – first became popular in England, then in the United

States; and it was the former colony that subsequently gave birth to the protean breakfast cereal. Sweetened, caramelised, crunchy, puffed or flattened, these cereals were later reintroduced to their native land and imposed on British families with jangling advertising campaigns. In 1937 the terminal decline of the egg and bacon breakfast (by then served up in many households only at weekends) was finally confirmed when cereal preparations ceased to be categorised as food for children and invalids in the official statistics. In 1938 the annual consumption of cereals was estimated at 29 ounces per person; by 1972 it had increased to 113 ounces.

Thomas Lipton was a grocer of genius. He made a fortune by extending the principles which had enriched cereal producers to the entire retail food market. He standardised the manufacture of the smallest possible number of commonly consumed goods, and distributed them to the largest possible number of retail outlets. Beginning with a small shop, which he opened in 1871 with £100 savings, within twenty years he had created an industrial and commercial empire worth more than fifty million pounds, with 242 retail outlets in Great Britain, which comprised factories at home as well as numerous plantations abroad (including tea plantations in Ceylon), and a meat-packing factory in the United States. This hero of capitalism was an innocent incarnation of the ambivalence of progress. The imagination, the logic and the single-mindedness which informed his every step were to lead, inevitably, to our present consumer society. His greatest gift to the housewife was the time saved from those laborious tasks of food preservation – from salting, canning and bottling, not to mention the elimination of culinary disasters. Though he could not, like his successors today, ignore the seasons with the use of rapid transportation, he did succeed in eliminating the hazards of home production. Lipton sausages all have the same taste. His goods are satisfactory; one need fear no surprises. And who is to know whether another sausage might not be tastier, since – at this rate – the day may come when only his will be left?

Fortunately the rout of family butchers, bakers and grocers is not yet complete, but the trend has been set. The captive urban market ceases to complain as soon as it is presented with the irresistible argument of cost. From urban poverty are born passivity and conditioning. Henceforth fish and chips are what stimulate the salivary glands, and Britons eat some fifty thousand tonnes of fried fish a year. For the average worker they have become a powerful cultural symbol. Well trained electoral candidates, as everyone knows, kiss babies and old ladies. But they must also ensure that they are occasionally captured on television eating fish and chips, with an ecstatic expression on their face. Other cultural symbols are the English sausage (more often than not an unspeakable porridge of dehydrated meats, bread, starch and chemical preservatives), and the bracing pub meal – shepherd's pie, steak and kidney pie, fish pie, gammon, sandwiches of every dimension, tongue and pickles, and English cheeses (till recently absurdly neglected by the French) – not only the succulent Stilton, but also fat Cheddars and Cheshires, Shropshire Blue, Single and Double Gloucesters and many others.

Yet because of its early achievements, the British food industry has also produced a few successes that have not been diminished by time. Biscuit manufacture remains of an exceptional quality and variety (though even in this privileged domain the Germans are gaining ground). British sauces – Worcester sauce, brown sauce, mint sauce, innumerable pickles, chutneys, mustards and other seasonings – are unrivalled by foreign competition and continue to be exported throughout the world. But jams, including the illustrious Scottish marmalade, are under threat.

At this point I must mention the Eastern (essentially Indian but also Chinese) influence on British food habits and gastronomy. As in the rest of Europe, this influence first began to make itself felt in the Middle Ages with the opening of the silk and spice routes. For the British sailor, the curative and bracing qualities of oriental spices were, I imagine, soon appreciated as necessities rather than mere luxuries. The East India Company invested them with British nationality, and for a French palate of my generation, the taste of ginger conjures up England more than it does the Orient.

When independence was eventually won by those Indies which had so titillated the British palate with their curries and chutneys, a process of reverse colonisation was begun – at least in London and other major cities. The 'nation of shopkeepers' was overrun by the very shopkeepers they had formerly driven away from their counters. Anyone who has known the dead weekend streets of old, will daily bless the peaceful invasion of tireless Pakistanis and Indians, who – first imported into Africa by colonial commercialism, then sent to the devil by the obsessional chauvinism of newly liberated African nations – were finally reluctantly accepted by that unfamiliar homeland they had inherited from the late Empire. Today, the Londoner need not worry if on a Sunday, at midday or midnight, he suddenly feels hungry, or finds he needs a razor, some whisky, or a packet of aspirin: from Chelsea to Soho, from Hampstead to Fulham, the corner *Paki* shopkeeper, smiling, helped by his brother, his father or his nephew, will dig it out from a corner of his insomniac store, somewhere between the pears and the cheese. Always awake, always ready, the Asian newcomer has rapidly learnt how best to take advantage of British culinary laziness. Alongside the English, American or Italian chains of fast food with their graded sandwiches, their mass-produced pizzas, their hamburgers and their fried chickens, he displays his kebabs, his samosas and his take-away meatballs. As he increases his turnover, he expands the gastronomic curiosity of his clients. In the same way, Soho's Chinese supermarkets, filled with produce imported from Hong Kong and the People's Republic of China – fresh beansprouts, Chinese cabbage, dried mushrooms – conscientiously play their educational role.

With the exception of leaden imitations of Quiche Lorraine, French cooking has had little impact on the British menu. Its reputation, like that of anything French, is ambiguous. For the consumer of fish and chips – even though he may occasionally boast of a holiday meal he has enjoyed in a Normandy transport café – French cooking is pretentious, complicated, and drowned in too many sauces. If he mentions it, it is to compare it with the plain goodness of British food, and if he – in company with some ten million readers of the popular press – knows about the Queen's gastronomic habits, it is only to deplore the sad fact that her menus should still be written in French. Yet, when for the first time a French restaurant in London was awarded its third Michelin star, the achievement made headline news in all the newspapers.

A Campaign for Real Ale

Fortunately, Bordeaux wine – or claret, to call it by its proper name – like port and sherry, is an English invention. It is part of the legacy of Eleanor of Aquitaine and the Black Prince. Unlike perfume and *haute couture*, it is not tainted with French mannerisms and its origins can be forgiven. Though its importance cannot be compared to that of beer, the foreigner who peers through the glow of a claret-filled decanter in a good club is given his first glimpse of the English art of drinking. He is in well-bred company. He may be surprised to find his companions getting drunk – far more deliberately so than in France, where inebriation is a matter of accident and conviviality – but he will find that certain decencies are always respected. In clubs, officers' messes, universities or merchant bodies, the centuries have defined a line of bad conduct almost as rigorous as that which governs good behaviour. Yet good wine is genuinely appreciated, even if over-indulgence means that its distinctive qualities are sometimes blurred. Many consider themselves to be connoisseurs, some genuinely are. In 1979 a team of British experts soundly beat their French opponents in a blind wine-tasting competition.

Of course, champagne and burgundy also have their connoisseurs, and real wine-lovers are familiar with all the great vintages: Moselle, Tokay, the Vesuvian Lacrima Christi, or even – and why not – Californian Chardonnay. We are talking of an elite whose ranks are expanded every year by a number of less knowledgeable but no less enthusiastic amateurs. But it is the quality of his port that denotes a real gentleman. As every reader of detective stories knows, they really *do* exist, those retired colonels who – after waiting for the ladies to leave the dinner table – bring out a decanter of their best vintage port and pass it round, never handing it directly to their neighbour, but always pushing it along the table, in a clockwise direction. I know they exist, I have met them. Port culture is not as prevalent as it used to be, but it persists. We should all learn to savour this much admired and cherished ruby liquid, sparkling in its cut rock-crystal decanter. It has been lovingly aged in a barrel, then in a bottle, before being decanted for your benefit. And we must pity those unfortunate French – the greatest consumers in the world of a loathsome brew which bears the same name – abandoning them to their belief that they are drinking an *apéritif*. Still, in the matter of oenological credibility the English do not have much to boast about when they make their annual dash across the Channel to pick up the equally dubious red liquid they have baptised with the name of 'Beaujolais Nouveau'. The first day of its annual sale in Britain is celebrated with almost as much panache as the solemn opening of Parliament by the Queen at the Palace of Westminster.

In Britain the word 'wine' does not have the same connotations as it does in France. Speaking in Brussels at a European Commission meeting on family wine production, Lord Thomson of Monifieth – Chairman of the Centre for European Agricultural Studies – astonished his colleagues when he gave the figure (over a million, as I remember), for the number of producers to be found in Britain. Everything became clear when he explained the importance of home wine, brewed in many households from a variety of different fruits according to recipes transmitted from generation to generation. Today, England can produce better wine than these homemade brews. A few entrepreneurs decided that if Roman legionaries had been able to acclimatise their vines to the most northerly of their conquered lands, and if the monasteries after them had succeeded in sustaining their crops before they were destroyed by Henry VIII, then they too were capable of growing vines. What began in 1940 as no more than a scholarly horticulturalist's joke led in 1952 to the creation by Major-General Sir Guy Salisbury-Jones of the first commercial vineyard, at Hambledon in Hampshire. During the 1970s and 80s, the amount of land devoted to wine production in England increased from just over fifty acres (roughly what it was in the Middle Ages) to more than two thousand acres, and by 1989 almost three million bottles of English wine were being sold. The Ministry of Agriculture, Fisheries and Foods estimates that if the present rate of growth continues, England will have reached the ceiling allowed by the European Community for the production of ordinary quality wines by 1992. Today there are approximately 450 commercial vineyards, the majority of which are in Kent, Sussex and Hampshire. In Devon and South Wales, cultivators have also found suitable plots of land, and a few of the most daring have planted their vines as far north as Derbyshire and Yorkshire. In general they produce agreeable white wines, though somewhat thin and flat. Red wines are much less common. In a mood of indulgent good humour, they can be drunk without wincing. But we should be careful of scoffing at them. Grown with love, they improve from harvest to harvest. No doubt one of them will, one day, inspire a passion.

In the meantime, like everyone else, the British are drinking wine, and each year more of it – whether French, Italian, Spanish or, increasingly, German. Certainly the French are still highly rated for their great vintages, and their champagnes are better regarded than are other sparkling wines. But the less educated – and especially the less wealthy – consumer, prefers a Spanish Rioja or a Portuguese Vinho Verde. Most popular are the mixed, 'improved', sweetened and standardised German wines which are sold under a brand name rather than with reference to their origins or vintage. Their low price and uniform taste makes them attractive to the average consumer who compares them, favourably, with some appallingly rough red which he picked up by the litre in a holiday camp site on the Côte d'Azur, the Costa Brava, or in the Algarve.

Wine was finally established as a truly British drink the day, in 1983, the Government – ranking it with whisky, spirits, liqueurs and beer – decided to bring it under the umbrella of the weights and measures legislation by defining the official capacity of a standard glass of wine (7.5 cl), and of a large one (12.5 cl). But beer, even if it is losing ground, remains the national drink, and a great many more pints of ale are destined to disappear down thirsty Anglo-Saxon gullets before it is overtaken. For an Englishman, beer is a pass-word and a lullaby – a secret (yet another one) which a foreigner can never penetrate. Until the end of the seventeenth century, the ingredients of ale consisted only of malt, yeast and water. Hops were added later, not to mention that uncouth foreign interloper, carbon dioxide. From such chaste origins, true British ale has retained its modesty. For the continental drinker, beer must sparkle and froth and overflow its tankard as at a raucous Bavarian feast. In England, the clear liquid of a pint is unadorned except for a light foam that subsides gently on the lips. Slow and restful, it is a man's drink, consumed at home in the solitary tranquillity of dusk, or preferably savoured in the pub, between two lazy jokes, the flight of a dart towards its target, or the earnest analysis of a game of cricket or football. After a fourth or fifth pint, it becomes acceptable to laugh a little more loudly, become a touch too voluble, or begin to sing in chorus with the band of mates who have just shared the last round. But a true beer drinker is restrained, even in excess.

This picture bears only an arguable resemblance to reality, but it invites all those who recognise themselves in it to join forces in defending a threatened way of life. Around 1970, a group of Hertfordshire journalists, appalled by the decline of real ale before the brutal assault of continental-type beers, decided to put a stop to the trend. Under the combative banner of CAMRA (Campaign for Real Ale), they flooded the local and national press with statements and created a network of affiliated local bodies. At the end of a ten-year crusade, their combined offensive on public opinion, brewers and pub tenants finally earned them the rehabilitation of their forefathers' brew and its apparent victory over the obscene bubbles of German lager. But it was a Pyrrhic victory. Even the prestige of Guinness – that brand name which has become a household word – though still unaffected by the taint of financial scandal, was not sufficient to withstand the assault of foreign lager. In spite of accounting for a fifth of the entire beer market in Britain, the sales of Guinness were steadily declining, and – even worse – the decline could be attributed to the desertion of a new generation of young drinkers who were snubbing the inimitable liquorice-coloured stout. The rehabilitation of traditional ales, combined with the clever 'Guinless' advertising campaign, did much to help reestablish its sales. But the efforts and sacrifices of true believers have not been enough to contain the heresy. The number of defections in favour of those diabolical lagers is growing inexorably: over fifty per cent of British beer drinkers are renegades, and the number continues to increase . . .

Old England is growing young, and those who would drench her in the incense of the past can do nothing about it. Pubs are being modernised: along with video games and electronic fruit machines, they are quite happy to provide their customers with the lagers and wines they desire, just as readily as they accept their rainbow-coloured heads and Mohican haircuts. As for the great breweries and high-flying financiers who own them, the magic word is not ale but profit. What do they care about the merchandise so long as their pubs remain full? There are just over eighty thousand pubs in England and Wales, of which fewer than forty thousand are independent. Of the forty-five thousand or so that are owned by breweries, more than two-thirds are run by tenants enjoying a variable degree of autonomy, and about thirteen thousand are managed by directly appointed agents. Their origins are so ancient – often going back to the Elizabethan era – that in spite of a succession of more or less successful restorations and renovations, their architecture and décor still constitute one of Britain's greatest charms. Their Parisian copies on the other hand, though designed by one of the big English breweries, offer their French clientele no more than the most ridiculous counterfeit.

In the countries of the vine, where the heart of Roman Catholicism beats, the Church has never identified the wine of the sacrament and of the wedding of Cana with vice, and has long been indulgent in its condemnation of alcoholic abuse. In Protestant countries by contrast, preachers have vehemently pilloried all manner of distilled and fermented drinks, placing them next to fornication in the scale of iniquity. Pubs with regulated hours were, like brothels, a way of limiting sin. No doubt it was always possible for miscreants to find ways of refreshing themselves outside legal hours. At home, and even sometimes at the office, one could keep a few bottles in a cupboard and enjoy a drink, alone or with a friend. At eleven in the morning, and six in the evening – necessary rituals in the lives of these Protestant drinkers – the opportunity for sin was always there, as was the time for repentance during the long dry intervals in between.

In pubs, clubs, off-licences, grocers and supermarkets, the sale of alcohol used to be more strictly regulated in Britain than in the majority of other Western countries, with the notable exceptions of Sweden and Norway. Pub opening times were not only severely restricted, but also varied from one region to another – a classic subject of irritation for unwary tourists. For many years, religion, health and the protection of pub employees were all in turn deployed in favour of maintaining the status quo. No matter that in Scotland – where restricted opening times had already been abandoned – the people had not, as a result, sunk into the depths of debauchery, alcoholism, or social turmoil; popular opposition to the abolition of closing times remained strong to the very last. The time of restrictions is now past. Pubs can stay open all day long, and the British can tipple to their hearts' content. It is remarkable that they still have the stomach to drink so much tea.

The Gentleman and the Scarecrow

Of all the disguises for which the British have such a predilection, that of the gentleman is becoming rarer. The comfortable outfits by which one could, at a glance, pin down the sex, class, age and profession of the wearer, are increasingly being relegated to the attic to join cast-offs of a bygone era. To the despair of Savile Row tailors, men are ever more badly dressed, and – in this domain – their wives offer little competition. Long kept at a respectful distance by the multitude of barriers, traps and conventions that defend the privileged from intruders, the poorer classes (and manual labourers in particular) had chosen to accentuate the differences which separated them from their superiors. Since they already spoke a different language and ate different foods at different times of day, it was natural that they should dress differently as well. The peaked cap, which in the country could equally well be worn by an aristocrat as by a labourer, clearly distinguished the worker from the gentleman in the city. With women, it was the absence of a hat that gave away the modesty of their condition. As for the rest of a person's attire – whether it was overalls or a pin-striped suit, a donkey jacket or a tweed jacket – from head to foot, every item betrayed social rank.

Times have changed. American jeans have proletarianised the lower limbs of the upper classes. Successive onslaughts from the Italian, French and Chinese fashion industries have endowed the working classes with a middle-class look, and T shirts have announced a truce in the class struggle – at least in the streets.

The gradations from workers' blue to three-piece suit have become less distinct.

It is not so much class that distinguishes women from one another, as their own self-image. There are those who consider themselves to be guardians of tradition, neither willing to be corrupted by the passing fashions of the mass market, nor – if they have the means – by the daring inventions of *haute couture*, and least of all, by the provocations of liberated women. They believe in tweed and they love frills. Tweed is the standard-bearer of common-sense, of honest living, of marital fidelity and of the love of flowers. In frills we can find the charms of a cosy interior. The skirt – which looks as if it might have been borrowed from the legs of a chintz sofa – now drapes the hips of a woman who would not find herself out of place at one of the Queen's garden parties. How content she looks in the home that so resembles her. How comfortable she appears in the high street of her village, or at the hairdresser's where she is having curls put into that hair which she will dye blue when it has grown white. But the streets of London and of the other major British cities no longer belong to her.

In the cities, the visiting foreigner is astonished by the permanent carnival display of flashy rags, unpressed trousers and shapeless dresses which dump young and old, beautiful and ugly into the same lot, uniting them in a good-natured but resolute defiance of all the accepted canons of elegance. For the mutinous protagonists of this street show, good taste, like a scarecrow, is their best protection – the guarantee of their individuality. To dye their hair red and green with a hedgehog-spiky haircut, to stick some outsized old jacket over a moth-eaten mini-skirt that only just covers their knickers, to wear open-toed sandals under billowing long skirts and slightly grubby T shirts, to squeeze into jeans so tight that they hurt, or drain-pipe trousers that hug the ankle so closely as to look like wet suits: these are just so many ways of disowning their mothers, their sisters and their friends. It is their way of being different, at any price.

Julia, who has started her own publicity agency, is certain of one thing: 'We are not very good at behaving like good little wives in the manner of French and Italian women. Although we are living – at least as much as they are – in a society which is created and dominated by men, they have a family, whereas we only have a husband. Their children are all around them; ours are at boarding school. They attain power by emphasising their femininity; we assert ours by denying it. But sometimes we are more successful than we had hoped and men really do take us for their equals. That's when they stop looking at us altogether.'

During the past thirty years, two radically different fashions have attempted to enlighten the English male as to the personality of these women who want to be recognised for what they are, and not for what is expected of them by their men. The first was invented by Mary Quant and – with the opening of her Bazaar in the King's Road in 1957 – was responsible for the launch of the 'Chelsea Look', the mini-skirt and the myth of the carefree eroticism of ageless youth. Her commercial success underlined the cruel idea that all women are like well-adjusted teenagers, slim and desirable. Five hundred boutiques and a network of international companies soon transformed the dream sold by Mary Quant in Bazaar into a mass-produced fashion poster which, naturally, betrayed neither wrinkles nor excess kilos, nor any of the frustrations of life.

Laura Ashley, swimming against the tide, went searching in the past for her inspiration, and found England ripe for her nostalgic vision. Though Laura Ashley herself died in 1985, her empire continues to flourish. A customer who walks into one of her shops is as likely to be remembering an old family jam recipe, as she is to be thinking of the shy lover with whom she has made a date. She does not like her mother's frills, but she shares her love of domestic comfort. A jumble of small flowers against a slate background: a skirt, a bedspread or a dressing-gown, she hasn't yet decided. She is creating a doll's house for herself. She is an unostentatious young woman with a good deal of taste, and a little money. Laura Ashley's genius has been to give shape to her fantasies without resorting to dramatic effects. She has not attempted to turn her into a poppy or a panther, has not encircled her neck and ankles in a slave's collar; she has merely recreated for her Grandmother's old cottage where she used to play as a child.

Masculine elegance, though on the retreat, has not yet surrendered – and imitators beware! The subtle mistake betrays more cruelly than the obvious blunder. This pin-striped blue suit with a cut so elegant as to be barely noticeable is made of admirable cloth, but its surface – long and lovingly steam-ironed – has become slightly felted. This is its patina. The exquisitely fraying collar of a silk or poplin shirt which has been washed again and again by hand before being ironed to perfection, is as smart now as it was in the days when Brummel used to ask his manservant to break in his clothes, wearing them just long enough to tame the vulgarity of their newness.

A good pair of shoes with regularly polished soles is an ageless item, and has the patina of mahogany or ebony rubbed daily with a woollen cloth. If there still exists a rallying sign by which all well-dressed men recognise each other, it must surely be this horror of the new which so afflicted the prince of dandies.

Whether it is a question of the lawyer's wig or the robes of investiture of a peer of the realm, a pair of braces or a mackintosh, a hunting jacket, a smoking jacket or a morning coat, newness – when it is not ridiculous – is somewhat gross. The same is true of objects: your umbrella (which has never known the disgrace of being tucked into a sheath) was purchased at Briggs' naturally, and your pair of guns come from Purdey's. But they were bought thirty years ago, or else inherited from your father. And there is only one acceptable excuse for the desk-blotter in your study which has only just been delivered from Asprey's or Garrard's: it is a present from your wife. What a store of delightful vanities she is thus preparing for her grandson.

The sin of coordinating colours and textures too explicitly is also unpardonable. But knowing how to wear a pocket handkerchief with a tie that does not match, is a true art. Whether to retain or abandon the waistcoat, whether to relinquish trouser turn-ups, or to insist on them to your tailor, this secret garden of sartorial subtleties belongs to you alone. Only the *nouveaux riches* and the clumsiest of boys from a second-rate public school could make the mistake of trying to discover which way the wind of fashion is blowing. For to be well-dressed is, primarily, to be well brought up. And when you are well brought up, there are a number of things that go without saying. What also goes without saying is that this élite, whose reticence is so superior to the ridiculous ostentation of the parvenu, sometimes balks at the prices quoted by the tailor, and even more so before his insolent insistence on being paid.

Like the member of a club who has been thrown out for failing to pay his subscription, the Savile Row pariah – should he find in himself the strength to cross the gulf which separates him from Regent Street – can still maintain the illusion of smartness by resorting to a designer suit, humiliatingly signed by a French or Italian name such as Cardin or Ferragamo. And when, like Beau Brummel exiled to Calais by his debts, he is left with no alternative, it is with death in his heart that he ventures into Oxford Street (for the first and last time) to purchase an off-the-peg outfit made in Hong Kong or Taiwan. But he is not the only one to be retreating from the familiar London landmarks. Savile Row cutters too are looking to New York, Milan, Paris or Riadh for their customers – whose solvency only partially makes up for the sin of not being British.

They can still be found though, living in London's West End, a few survivors who can afford to pay their club dues and who frequent smart dinners and cocktail parties at court or in the city – or who ignore them with all the serenity of those who have nothing to prove. If they are still the best dressed men in the world, they do not make a fuss about it since it is only natural. Their hallmark is an imperturbable courtesy, which they share with their fair-skinned wives, wrapped in flowery chiffons such as only an English woman is capable of wearing without looking ridiculous.

From the Pyjama to the State Mantle

The composite image which today still constitutes good form was first evolved in Edwardian times. During the long years before his accession to the throne, the future King Edward VII learnt to cultivate the art of making the best of circumstances. While rejecting neither his own royal destiny, nor his solidarity with an aristocracy that still maintained many privileges, this lover of women and of amusing companions preferred the former to be pretty – without worrying too much about their social origins – and the latter to be rich and witty rather than well-born and boring. In 1901 he started wearing the *Homburg*, a felt hat from Prussia, and from one day to the next, it became the obligatory fashion. His kind of elegance was poles apart from that of a Lord Salisbury, who represented one of the last ramparts of a society whose twin pillars were prayer and success.

Neither stiff nor slovenly, the new fashion – unobtrusive enough to disclaim its own existence – was to trace in invisible ink the wavering but identifiable outline of the well-dressed man. Over the next few reigns, his hats and shirt collars took on a softer aspect. His spats disappeared, followed by his gloves. His waistcoat ceased to be obligatory. His cufflinks were brought out of their box only for special occasions, his tie-pin for the Ascot season, or for a wedding. Yet, give or take a few details, the silhouette of his descendants – though increasingly rare – is essentially the same today. And from the days when the British Empire nourished the first industrial revolution with its raw materials, we are left with long-fibre Egyptian cotton and Chinese silk, with Indian cashmere or Andean vicuña – while preserving Irish linen and Scottish wool and thread. Ivory from the Slave Coast, exotic leathers, tropical woods and essential oils – these and more were available, according to the whim of the client, to the skills of boot-makers and leather workers, to tobacco and cosmetics salesmen, purveyors of umbrellas and walking sticks and to all those ingenious inventors who clothe our everyday gestures as a tailor clothes our bodies.

One of the relics of this era is the pyjama, brought back from India around 1870. Its arrival was to transform the bedroom into an intimate living-room. At one stroke, it gave the masculine night-shirt a ridiculous, asexual and old-fashioned look, and restored a masterly bearing to the man who had previously been stripped by night of his day-time dignity and virility. His woman, by contrast, chose to accentuate the femininity of her night-time attire. Leaving aside the chaste white gown which had been the twin of her husband's, she began to wear satin and lace, transforming herself from daily banality into an object of desire. In his dressing-gown and embroidered slippers, accompanied by a mistress wearing *négligée* and high-heeled mules, this modern seducer was all set to leap headlong into a Noël Coward comedy. But it would be some time before the curtain fell on their last kiss, and the rest of the world was seduced by their kind of dreamy elegance.

As is only right, the last word was to be the woman's. Around 1920, from Paris to New York, or at crazy Hollywood parties, she appropriated her husband's pyjamas, without relinquishing her nightdress. True, worn by her, the pyjama took on a modified appearance: with a scooped-out back, and flared, elongated trousers, it was no longer used for sleeping in, but rather, for dancing.

By introducing pyjamas, the British had made night-time smart. In an inverse but symmetrical movement, evening dress became more casual and stiff shirt-fronts, white ties and tails were replaced with the most discreet of black-tie dinner jackets – which in France we have inevitably christened *Smoking*, since, as Proust once pointed out: 'we attribute to anything more or less British the name which it does not bear in England'.

Developed by public schools – in an orgy of fresh air and purifying Christianity – as the best possible protection against the temptations of the flesh and of the mind, sport gave rise to this new masculine dandyism. Freeing the body of all that constricted its movements, designed to warm it or cool it down at will, light and transportable, the sportsman's outfit was soon to become the uniform of the walker, the traveller, the countryman, and eventually, even that of the city-dweller in the privacy of his home.

It is a long time since breeches were of satin or leather, tapering below the knee to a pair of silk-clad calves. Now they are made of thick woollen cloth, revealing heavy wool socks in laced walking boots sturdy enough to make light of the rockiest paths. Just take a walk in the Lake District, or along some narrow Welsh track, and you are likely to meet – as you might have done more than a hundred years ago – one of those intrepid hikers whose pullover and trousers have changed as little as the small rucksack on his back. His face reddened by the bracing air, and without slackening his pace, he will greet you with equally old-fashioned politeness, before disappearing behind a hedgerow.

Jerseys, Guernseys, Ulsters, Shetlands and Tweed – it is not surprising that this outdoor fashion should have borrowed from its provinces, counties, islands and rivers, the names it has bestowed on its most loved garments and fabrics. A jacket, preferably a little threadbare, and a hat – or a peaked cap – both made out of tweed (but certainly not the same tweed), and, in a sophisticated discordance of colours, a check shirt, a woollen tie emerging from a hand-knitted jumper, a pair of well-worn trousers, and good waterproof walking shoes. A matching skirt and jacket over a frilly blouse, or a turtleneck jumper, a felt hat, a pair of woollen tights and sensible flat shoes. Husband and wife, walking in the hills together, or gardening in the morning mist, blend into the landscape they love.

But though masculine elegance, even in the cities, owes a great deal to sport and nature, it is nonetheless primarily the child of puritanism and prosperity, and heir to a tradition which it might soften and enrich, but which it on no account wishes to repudiate. It seasons the classic ingredients with that pinch of personal caprice without which even the best-dressed man would be no more than a shop-window dummy. But it never abandons the cardinal principle: self-control, that first commandment which dominates the whole of British education, and which also forms the basis of good style in clothes. A touch of negligence is but its supreme adornment. Slovenliness is never acceptable.

In deliberate and self-conscious contrast, the bearer of a uniform must abandon the pursuit of comfort. Bishop or soldier of the Grenadier Guards, master of a livery company, or Knight of the Garter, Eton schoolboy or Lord Mayor of the City of London – it is inconceivable for any of these to discard the pomp and ceremony associated with their origin and history. Capes, chains, swords, shoe-buckles and maces are relinquished only in times of violent upheaval. Two world wars have successfully robbed the armed forces of their panache; but should he be required to parade in full uniform, every soldier, sailor or pilot will, to this day, bring out his swords or medals, or at the very least the buttons which once held together the medal-strewn coat of his

43

ancestors. Every army, one might object, renders this nostalgic homage to its past splendours. But in Britain – and furthermore throughout the Commonwealth – thanks to the monarchy which has extended its brilliant cloak over the entire body politic, the humblest subject of Her Majesty the Queen can wake up one day wearing, as if by a miracle, the most ancient and the most splendid of ceremonial uniforms.

And since we are launched in the pursuit of these pompous relics, let us also admire the bowler hat, as well as the striped trousers worn by Dick, one of the foreign exchange dealers at Coutts's, the Queen's bankers. There are not many such trousers left in the City, but he is all the more attached to them since, aged twenty-six, he feels the need to look older. Besides, what was thirty years ago a professional necessity is today a charming anachronism, and therefore another way of being at the forefront of fashion. And let us weep for the top hat which Tom, former jobber at the Stock Exchange, used to sport. Alas, he no longer needs to wear it to distinguish himself from his erstwhile colleague, the broker. Since the reforming thunderbolt of the 1986 Big Bang opened up the City to the gales of competition, the once separate functions of jobber and broker have been amalgamated, and hats have all been blown away. When one is British, it takes nothing less than a revolution to make one change one's headgear.

The jumper, a gift from the Navy to the landlubber, as well as numerous other sartorial additions which the army – through the intermediary of Lord Raglan and Lord Cardigan (two of its most elegant and most inept leaders) – bequeathed to the civilian, are more up to date than ever; and the balaclava, a relic of the Crimean war, has since become the virtually obligatory uniform of any armed bank or supermarket robber.

To the list of achievements of Edward VII's reign must be added the sartorial liberation of the child. No longer forced to be the imperfect copy of an adult, he is free at least to move about without impediment. The sailor suits worn by Queen Mary's two sons (the future Edward VIII, later Duke of Windsor, and his younger brother who was to succeed him as George VI) allowed them to run around quite freely. And the fashion for these suits was soon to cross the Channel, lasting right up to the 1940s.

Indeed, among the European middle classes between the wars, everything connected with childhood – from prams and nannies (naturally christened '*nurses*' in French), to Eton collars and those raglan coats one used to buy in Paris at the Old England shop – everything had to be English.

Today the British youngster still offers an idealised image of childhood. But he too has exchanged the lace collars of Little Lord Fauntleroy and the rags of Oliver Twist, for the universal dungarees, the bright cottons and woollens in which today's child is clothed impartially the world over.

Only with the beginning of term does the small Briton recover his sartorial identity: a cap, well-pressed shorts or long trousers for the boys, a round felt or a summer straw hat and a pleated skirt for the girls; for either sex, a pullover with matching blazer in the school colours. Though many schools today have abandoned the much disliked uniform, parents, in their majority, still consider it to be the sign of a disciplined establishment in which traditional values prevail. The most ancient and famous of the public schools cultivate the peculiarities of their uniform with love, and though the boys and girls chafe at its restrictions, as adults, they look with nostalgia on their own brood, smartly decked out in well-pressed shorts and pleated skirts. The uniform is a symbol of the school and all it represents. The old school tie may never be worn again (except perhaps as a belt to fasten one's dressing-gown), but anyone who has been forced to wear it as a youngster will bear the mark through adulthood, and will immediately be recognised by his peers.

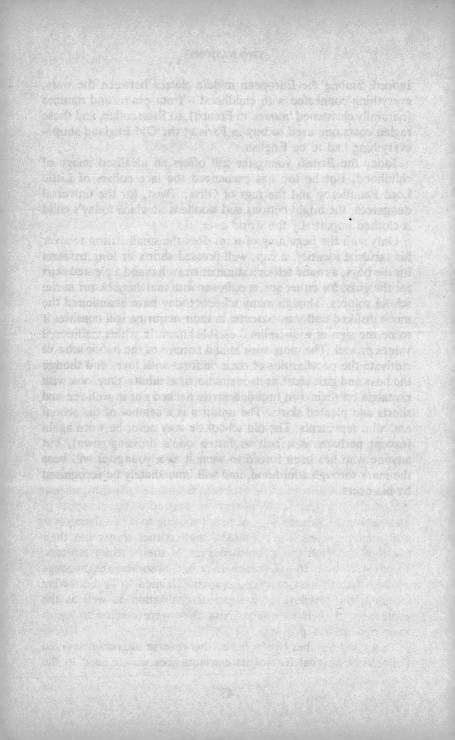

3
Life's Apprenticeship

For seven hundred years, the indisputable, inalienable privilege of being English was acquired by virtue of '*Jus soli*'. It was enough to have been born in England. Neither colour of skin nor social origins came into the calculation. From the first moment until the end of his days, the new citizen could rely on the promise made explicit by Lord Palmerston, torch-bearer of the *Pax Britannica* that was being extended, on land and on sea, from London to the antipodes – the promise that 'a British subject, in whatever land he may be, shall feel confident that the watchful eye and the strong arm of England will protect him against injustice and wrong'.

To Be or Not To Be British
Arriving after the end of the Second World War from every corner of the dislocated empire, from the Indian sub-continent, from Africa and from the Caribbean, fleeing religious or political persecution, driven out by poverty or enticed by the prospect of gain, a multicoloured influx of peoples came to settle themselves and their mosques, their temples, their corner shops and their ghettoes, beneath the astonished gaze of their former masters. From generation to generation they had absorbed the message of the white Protestant colonisers who claimed to be bestowing on them the privilege of a superior civilisation as well as the protection of their sovereign. Now they were coming to assert their right to this privilege.

To a good number of the hosts, this reverse migration seemed ominous. Irrational fear of its consequences was to lead to the

47

downfall of Enoch Powell, a politician of great intellectual gifts, moral rigour and personal charm. Having three times held ministerial office under the Conservatives, he could have aspired to the leadership of the party had it not been for his obsessive preoccupation with racial 'invasion'. What mysterious alchemy could transform this likeable academic into a Cassandra predicting 'rivers of blood' – the unavoidable consequence of harbouring coloured ethnic minorities in white, Anglo-Saxon Britain? Yet, as if to give the lie to his predictions about this fatal population explosion – and no doubt influenced by the example of her British sisters – a Jamaican woman who might previously have had four children, now limits herself to an average of two, and her Pakistani neighbour now has only four instead of six. In 1995 Britain's coloured population will only just have reached three million, and is not likely to go beyond 3,300,000 in the first years of the next millennium. These figures reflect a very significant assimilation, particularly evident in the weakening hold of religious and parental constraints. It proceeds neither from pressure by the white majority, nor from special educational methods, but from an internal mutation. It prefigures a genuinely multi-racial society in which attitudes tend to converge. To be anti-racist is the only possible attitude for a majority temperamentally hostile to the excesses of intolerance. But for all that, the racist virus has not been eradicated from people's underlying attitudes. Nor, as the Salman Rushdie affair has demonstrated, is racial integration a one-way process. Muslim fundamentalism is growing, in Britain as elsewhere, and with it the desire to assert a separate identity that is distinct from that of the host community.

Ayatollah Khomeini's death threat against Salman Rushdie for the allegedly blasphemous content of his book, *The Satanic Verses*, has also been the occasion of much anti-Muslim racist expression. But the incident merely highlights an underlying current. From Belgravia to the East End of London, just as in Marseilles or Geneva, Hamburg or Rotterdam, immigrants – the turbaned Sikhs and Parsi shopkeepers, North African labourers and waiters from Calabria, Turkish factory hands and refugees from Surinam – all provoke the same comments, endlessly repeated: 'Why don't they

go home? We have nothing against them but they're not like us.'
Other reproaches soon follow: 'They are violent. They are taking
our jobs.'

Since 1948, successive laws and regulations on nationality (culminating in the 1982 Nationality Act and various other restrictive
measures introduced during Margaret Thatcher's second period
of government) have had the avowed purpose of reconciling these
two contradictory attitudes. Their unavowed aim and their most
immediate consequence has been to dry up almost entirely the
flow of coloured immigrants. By 1985 the figure for permanent
admissions of applicants from the Indian subcontinent had already
shrunk to less than 20,000 – and more than half of this number
was made up of wives and children joining a breadwinner who
had already settled on British soil.

The new regulations with their inquisitorial requirements have
not been enough to allay public fears, though it would be unfair
to attribute these to plain racism. There is regret for a vision of
lost unity (even if it never existed), for no longer being able to
hear only English spoken at home, as one has done for centuries,
between comfortable silences. But rather than admit to this feeling
of unease, the host community inflicts pointless harassment on
their overseas guests, while keeping up the pretence of treating
them like fully fledged members of the community. Michael
Beloff, a respected jurist, maintains that the Nationality Act is
wrong precisely because it does not admit its true motives. His
attitude is officially shared by Labour, whose spokesman declared
in 1982 that as soon as his party was back in power, the Act would
be modified to take account of the multiracial nature of British
society today.

Should one trust the promises of a Labour party which, as
early as 1968, established a distinction between full citizenship of the United Kingdom and its colonies and the right
of abode, thus effectively confirming an earlier Conservative
measure which had taken away that right from citizens of the
Commonwealth? Yet the Labour Government had promised to
rescind that measure too. It neither did so, nor abolished any of
the laws introduced by the Conservatives in 1971; and in spite of
all Labour's protestations, Michael Beloff thinks it 'unlikely that

49

they will depart from precedent in relation to the 1982 British Nationality Act'.

So long as it was real, indisputable and undisputed for all subjects of the Crown, British citizenship did not officially exist. It was an invisible part of the fabric of England's Common Law and unwritten constitution. Every new law relating to nationality was therefore bound to introduce restrictions and exceptions to the notions of citizenship. Now that it has been clearly defined, this citizenship excludes, in one way or another, all persons who 'are not closely connected with the United Kingdom, the Channel Islands and the Isle of Man'. It is still possible to seek naturalisation after five years of continuous residence in Britain, but it is granted entirely at the discretion of the Home Secretary, without right of appeal – a right, paradoxically, enjoyed by the foreigner under threat of expulsion. For a foreigner married to a British citizen, it is possible to become naturalised more easily and rapidly, although the London Metropolitan Police has set up a team of investigators specialising in the detection of convenience marriages. The 1981 Nationality Act, concludes Michael Beloff, 'signals a diminution of national self-confidence, and an erosion of commitment to human rights'.

But these new regulations make little difference to the inescapable fact that, in all their multiracial diversity, the people now living under the shelter of the Union Jack can only be called the British. In spite of itself, Great Britain has demonstrated that it is easier to accommodate these foreign elements with their strange religions, than it is to resolve the ancient and bloody feuds – be they Irish, Basque or Corsican – of white, Christian Europe.

Religion and Religiosity

Both men were eligible for a post that had just been declared vacant. The first, David Sheppard, had been captain of the England and Sussex cricket teams. The second, George Carey, had long been an ardent supporter of Arsenal football club. In the event, it was George Carey who won the day, becoming the 103rd incumbent of the archiepiscopal see of Canterbury, head of the Church of England and Primate of the world Anglican community, which consists of some seventy million faithful.

As soon as Dr Runcie, then Archbishop, announced that he was going to retire at the end of January 1991 (nine months before his seventieth birthday), the bookmakers opened the betting. Although he showed no predilection for any particular sport, Dr Habgood, Archbishop of York, was considered to be a front-runner. Hard on his heels was the Right Reverend Sheppard (the former cricket player turned Bishop of Liverpool), whose work on behalf of the underprivileged – in close collaboration with the city's Roman Catholic Bishop, Mgr Derek Warlock – was cited as a shining example of ecumenicalism and efficiency. Despite their astonishment, the great majority of commentators welcomed the nomination by the Queen (on the advice of Mrs Thatcher) of Dr George Carey, Bishop of Bath and Wells, as the best possible choice.

Although it is not surrounded by the complicated rituals that distinguish the election of the Pope, the nomination of the Archbishop of Canterbury has to follow a procedure that has an element of mystery. A royal commission of ten lay and ecclesiastical members (the chairman of which is appointed by the Prime Minister) confers in secret and chooses two candidates who are put forward for selection by the head of the Government. In selecting Dr Carey, Mrs Thatcher was not required to give reasons for her decision, any more than her predecessors have been in the past.

Barely two per cent of the members of this curious Established Church – the only one in Europe since the fall of Franco's dictatorship in Spain – regularly attend its services. This indifference has long been the Anglican community's greatest problem – one that Dr Carey has now inherited, intact, despite his predecessor's best efforts. The similarities as well as the differences in the two men will enable us to judge the extent to which their actions are dictated by necessity, and how much they owe to personality.

'My father? . . . I can still hear him saying to my mother, "it is unhealthy that a boy should want to go to church so much."' This is Dr Robert Runcie, before his retirement, seated on a sofa in his Lambeth Palace study, talking about his childhood. 'And all that,' he adds, 'because I wanted to attend service on Sundays, and occasionally during the week as well . . .'

This surprising revelation was one of the first things that alerted me to the curious absence of religion in England's childhood folklore – which in all other respects is so rich and varied. Early childhood is a time of magic and dreams nourished by poetry, songs, sayings and books expressly written for it, not a time for prayers and metaphysical initiation. There are families and regions where most people still go to Sunday service, but religious attendance is frequently a social affair rather than an expression of deep conviction. Children who followed their parents to church – as to any other kind of family outing – often abandon the habit as soon as they are able. Others express spiritual aspirations which their religious practice has neither fulfilled so far, nor even attempted to elicit.

Dr Runcie, now Lord Runcie since his elevation, is the son of an electrical engineer. He describes his family and social background in Liverpool as 'Scots in general terms – Presbyterian. But non-practising . . . As a result, I wasn't brought up in any particular religious denomination'. The young Runcie adored his father, a keen sportsman with a healthy distrust of authority. 'His [my father's] great hero was Robbie Burns, the poet, who was also extremely suspicious of the clergy – and of the Presbyterian clergy in particular. I was thirteen when a friend, who was about to be confirmed in the Anglican Church, persuaded me to join him, and I began to follow what I suppose you might call catechism classes. The real reason for this neophyte's zeal is that we were both in love with the same girl, who was also attending these classes. But in the end, when we were confirmed by the bishop, I understood that the confirmation itself was more important than I had thought.'

With George Carey, we abandon the cosy middle-class nest. His father, no doubt, had not read Robbie Burns, and his religious convictions appear to have been simple but strong. In a rare reference to his private life, Dr Carey wrote of his father: 'He was a hospital porter, and had a very special colleague who was a black Roman Catholic. Both of them were outstanding witnesses in their work. One day his friend said to him: 'It grieves me we cannot meet as Christians round the Table of the Lord down here, but you know, one day we'll meet around the Lord in glory.'

The young Runcie's piety, on the other hand, was beginning to cause his father some concern. But, being a tolerant man, he allowed his son to do as he pleased. When progressive blindness forced the father to take early retirement, leaving his family in considerably reduced financial circumstances, 'the carefree and fun-loving boy that I was began to take life a little more seriously . . .' But Runcie's mother, he goes on to explain, 'was a sentimentalist. She used to read a great many detective novels and she loved going to the local cinema, where she used to chew dreamily on toffees. Her sentimentality led her to believe that the Church was a good thing, but she didn't go there much herself'. Naturally the entire family was in Church at Runcie's confirmation; but his two sisters and his older brother were no more religious than their parents. The eldest girl ended up as the wife of an Anglican Minister, while the second married an Irish Catholic, and the brother too married a Catholic from Switzerland.

A Casual Ecumenicalism

This casual ecumenicalism is not infrequent in British families that have known some social and geographical mobility. Ancient religious conflicts have left few traces, except in certain pockets of strict Presbyterianism in Scotland, or Catholicism in the North of England, particularly in Yorkshire. The time is long past when readings from the Book of Common Prayer and from the Bible, in its famous King James version, not only constituted the basis of religious life, but also nourished the English language and formed the style of generations of writers and poets. As early as 1851, a census of religious attitudes revealed that only half the population was practising, and that in the cities this proportion sometimes fell to a quarter.

The strength and durability of the Anglican Church has other roots. When asked about their religion, a large majority declare themselves to be Anglican without hesitation, even though they may not have attended a religious service for years. In their millions, they continue to get married and to bury their dead in the Anglican rite. In the space of a century the number of Anglican clergy has fallen by half, and today there are only just over ten thousand of them in England. The church, which has financial capital of more than a billion and a half pounds as well as a vast amount of property, can still afford to pay them and house them, train their successors and celebrate the services, without having to ask for too much financial assistance from a faithful flock which might balk at having to provide it.

Not dead so much as asleep and forgotten, not resisted so much as relegated, day-to-day religion is taught at school, like a lesson in spiritual citizenship. It is left to each individual in his own good time, to draw comfort from this religion, and to search within it for something to give his life greater meaning. Yet religiosity remains more firmly anchored in the national mores than this passivity would lead one to expect, and with it one finds a strong belief in God and in the divinity of Jesus Christ, in the existence of sin, paradise and hell, a belief in the usefulness of priests, and finally, the certainty that Great Britain is and must remain a Christian nation.

The majority of British people do not believe that religious practice is an obligation. Clearly, this considerably limits the role of churches in their lives. For them, church is a kind of institution, a respectable and useful one no doubt, but one whose role is primarily social. On the other hand, their particular notion of democracy easily accommodates the idea of an official religion, as well as the practice of obligatory prayers at school assembly, and even the fact that many of these schools, though mainly financed by the state, are denominational.

The Ecclesiastical Institution

Since its secession from Rome under Henry VIII, the head of the Anglican Church has been a layman – the monarch. Although a few voices have been raised in favour of the Church's liberation from the royal yoke, the majority of British people approve of the status quo. Yet that same majority also thinks that if the Prince of Wales were to become a Catholic, he should not be forced to relinquish the throne.

There are also twenty-six bishops, headed by the Archbishop of Canterbury, who by virtue of their office are given a seat in the House of Lords, where they are collectively known as the

Lords Spiritual. It is worth noting here that the new Archbishop of Canterbury, not content with leaving school at fifteen to become an office boy (as was natural for a young cockney of modest origins), and eventually a bishop, was elevated to the head of his church without yet having filled one of these seats in the Lords. But the situation has now been rectified: as Archbishop, he is a fully fledged member of the Upper House.

With the exception of a minority who are opposed to the entire principle of the House of Lords, it is rare to hear any objections to the participation of the Lords Spiritual in the affairs of the Kingdom (though admittedly, tradition limits their interventions to those areas which – theoretically at least – transcend all party divisions). And a Prime Minister has limited, though significant rights over the Church's choice of its bishops.

Like Roman Catholics, Anglicans have their Pope: not the Archbishop of Canterbury, nor any bishop elected by the Church's legislative assembly, the Synod. Their Pope is a collective body, the Westminster Parliament. It was Parliament and Parliament alone which, in 1974, confirmed that the doctrines of the Church of England were defined by the texts of the Book of Common Prayer. It is Parliament which legislates on the necessary procedures for the election of a bishop. And it is Parliament which, in the last resort, will settle controversies that have been troubling the Synod, such as the question of the ordination of women.

If for the moment no one is contemplating rebellion against this submission of the spiritual to the temporal, a number of the clergy would at least like to lighten the yoke; but the Anglican confession is secular at heart. It does not know exactly what it believes, nor very clearly what it is. It is simply alive and well, like each of its parishioners, and is not ready to die for anything but Queen and Country. God will surely recognise those who are truly His, and it is not man's business to do His job.

The 1559 Act of Supremacy, by which Queen Elizabeth I finally established Anglicanism as the national religion, is perhaps the purest example of those admirable ambiguities on which English society rests. Without denying tradition, without abandoning innovation, and especially, without prejudicing future compromises, it successfully removed the spectre of a Catholic restoration. Only fanatics, exalted souls and delicate consciences could object to such tolerance. Only enemies of the state could reject such a discipline. True, Catholics were deprived of the right to serve in the army as officers, and non-conformists were excluded from Parliament, but these restrictions were introduced only later and were finally all lifted in the nineteenth century. The initial tolerance of the Supremacy Act had been obscured but not obliterated.

Three tendencies have always coexisted in the bosom of the Church of England, sometimes convergent, sometimes neighbouring, sometimes separated by barriers of incomprehension or prejudice. The 'Evangelical' or Low Church tendency invokes the spirit of the Reformation and the thirty-nine Articles defining true doctrine in the face of Papist superstitions, and (especially nowadays) looks almost exclusively to the Bible for authority. The Anglo-Catholic tendency is attached to liturgy and ornament, and finds its inspiration in the unity of the Primitive Church. Its adherents celebrate mass, go to confession and pray for Pope John Paul II and the reunification of the 'catholic' church. From this tendency, the Oxford Movement emerged, a century and a half ago. It was founded by E. B. Pusey, John Keble, and the future Cardinal Newman – the only one of the three who was ultimately unable to reconcile his unitary aspirations with allegiance to the Anglican Church, and who eventually converted to Roman Catholicism. But in spite of their ecumenical aspirations, Anglo-Catholics seem closer to Catholic traditionalists than they are to the mainstream of Roman Catholicism. They deplore any kind of modernising trend and rise up against the moral laxity which refuses to condemn homosexual priests. They are vehemently opposed to the ordination of women and condemned the former Archbishop of Canterbury for his tolerance towards modernists, and for his desire to reconcile at any cost the opposing tendencies within Anglicanism.

At the opposite pole to the traditionalists, the most extreme spokesman for the liberal tendency is a theologian, the Reverend Don Cupitt, Dean of Emmanuel College, Cambridge, who publicly admits to disbelief in an after-life. He is ironic about 'walking corpses and empty tombs'. He believes that metaphysics has been superseded, and rejects the naïve vision of a supernatural God.

The choice of an Evangelical to take the place of Dr Runcie is clearly no coincidence. Mrs Thatcher, the daughter of a devout Baptist, is certainly closer to Low Church Anglicanism (by temperament as well as by education) than she is to the aristocratic Anglo-Catholic tendency, steeped as it is in pomp and liturgy, or to the liberal tendency (even in its moderate manifestations), with its show of indulgence towards homosexuality in the priesthood. Dr Carey is a genuine theologian and intellectual, and his evangelicalism is in no way sectarian. Although pastorally he relies heavily on the Bible, he is not unsympathetic to the Catholics, and no one doubts his ecumenical enthusiasm. Like the Pope, he is vehemently opposed to abortion and divorce, but he parts company with His Holiness on the question of the ordination of women, of which he approves. A man of the people by birth, a man whose commitments have steered towards the middle road, a man of broad culture and broad-minded attitudes – Dr Carey is the man with the best possible chance of checking the decline of the Anglican Church.

Precisely because they do not formally condemn any of the irreconcilable beliefs held by different sections of the Communion, Anglicans are not far from believing themselves to be, if not the best, then at least the most authentic of Christians. Even when they feel they have many affinities with Roman Catholics, they still reproach them with being weighed down by duties and dogmas verging on the absurd. And the many admirers of the Pope find his claim to infallibility and his intrusions into the private lives of his flock unacceptable. As for non-conformists, they have the right to believe what they will, but Quakers, Methodists and Presbyterians will never be quite 'one of us'.

Although the Anglican Church is national in its origins, it has sown its seed throughout the world, and succeeded in acclimatising itself without major difficulties to all kinds of different soils and environments. It has done this by setting up native Churches with close ties to their territories and traditions, though still maintaining the heritage of the Universal Church. Yet this moderate Church – wedded to common-sense – is beginning to lose its grip, and the most faithful of its members are also troubled. The election in September 1988 of the first woman Bishop, Barbara Harris, in the US state of Massachusetts, looked at the time as if it might prove to be the first crack dividing the Church in England from the rest of the Anglican Communion. During the 1988 annual gathering of the Synod, the then Archbishop of Canterbury declared that the Church of England would not recognise the episcopal consecration of women, nor even the ordination of women as priests. Events moved faster than he can have imagined. By November 1989, the Synod had taken the decision in principle to approve the ordination of women priests in England. Was this a sign that the main body of the Church was closing the gap with its more radical vanguard? Or on the contrary, was the Synod moving too fast for many of the Church's members, and could there be a backlash yet to come?

The position of the Anglican community is not much more comfortable within the frontiers of the United Kingdom than it is in the world as a whole. The Church, in the main, deplores its identification with the middle or ruling classes, and attempts a better definition of its spiritual identity. It tries to put a little more passion into its affirmations in favour of peace and the disinherited. It has rewritten the Book of Common Prayer in modern English, and at the end of the Falklands War, its Archbishop refused to celebrate the glory of victorious arms, but prayed for the victims of both camps instead. In doing this, it succeeded in alienating its warmest partisans, the 'Tory Party at prayer', for whom religion-and-conservatism are but another name for the pairing of Church and State.

While refusing to be appropriated in this way by any one party, the Church of England knows that if it ever ceased to be consubstantial with crown and parliament, it would lose its entire *raison d'être*. The attractions of Catholicism, with its certainties and its charismatic Pope, would become irresistible to some. The remainder would break up into innumerable rival sects or disappear into the agnostic crowds. The losers would be those curious parishioners who are born, marry and die under its protection, without ever giving it a thought, yet loving it – in their own way – like a mother.

Neither Traitors nor Damned

Like all her ancestors since the sixteenth century, Elizabeth II bears the title of 'Supreme Governor' of the Church of England. Yet the highest dignitary of her court, Earl Marshal and Hereditary Marshal, Chief Butler of England, Premier Duke and Earl, is a Catholic. Miles Francis Stapleton Fitzalan-Howard, KG GCVO CB CBE MC DL, Seventeenth Duke of Norfolk, Earl of Arundel, Baron Beaumont, Baron Maltravers, Earl of Surrey, Baron Fitzalan, Clun and Oswaldestre, Earl of Norfolk, Baron Howard of Glossop, is also President of the Catholic Union, as all his ancestors have been since it was founded a little under a century ago. For the first time, in 1984, four members of the Catholic Union attempted to oppose Fitzalan-Howard's reelection on the grounds that he had publicly approved of the use of contraception, in defiance of the Pope's oft-repeated teaching. In 1983, a report by the Roman Catholic Laity Commission had already presented the bishops with a long catalogue of complaints by Catholic women against the teaching and practice of the Church. While recognising that as a general rule abortion was to be condemned, they felt that in certain exceptional cases – such as that of a twelve-year-old girl who had been raped – it was 'the only action possible'. They strongly criticised the procedure of marriage annulments, and felt that the church should recognise that valid marriages sometimes broke down, and should allow the parties to remarry. They complained of the lack of understanding shown by their priests, and put this down to a traditional contempt for women. For English Catholics, such contradictions are routine. Since the sixteenth century, their life has been full of them. Yet after Anglicanism, Catholicism is the most important Christian denomination in Great Britain (perhaps, in fact, the most important in terms of church attendance), and it retains a vigour that the Latin countries – where it is the majority religion – might well envy.

The first and most essential of these contradictions confined Catholics to a sort of invisible ghetto whose doors were only gradually opened. In 1570, Pope Pius V declared Queen Elizabeth I a heretic, without rights to Crown or Kingdom. To obey her was a sin which carried with it the penalty of excommunication.

Thus the few great Catholic families which had remained loyal to their faith were now faced with a choice between treason and damnation. The majority refused to make the choice; remaining loyal to their sovereign, they did not weaken in their attachment to the Church, which in its turn did not reject them. For fear that they might turn to a foreign enemy (first the Spanish, then the French) to help them restore the authority of Rome, and in order to discourage them from conspiring together against her Majesty's government, they were forbidden from congregating for the celebration of the Catholic rite, and were disqualified from entry into public service. The Duke of Norfolk, born in 1915, can still remember a time during his early childhood in Yorkshire, when mass was announced with a single toll of the church bell because the laws restricting the public practice of Catholicism had not all been abrogated. It was not until 1924 that Catholic churches were allowed to let their bells ring out.

This embattled Catholicism, upheld by the wealth and pride of certain noble families, oscillated gracefully between asceticism and preciosity. Long after it had been restored to full freedom by the Catholic Emancipation Act of 1829, it continued to cultivate its own idiosyncrasies. Its children met on the school benches at Stonyhurst, under the stern eye of the Jesuits, or with the Benedictines of Ampleforth and Downside. It drew from its internal exile a romantic aura and a perfume of decadent melancholy of which we catch a final whiff in Evelyn Waugh's Catholic novel, *Brideshead Revisited*, set between the two world wars. Another convert to Catholicism, G. K. Chesterton (of Thomist persuasions and deadpan humour), used the humble remarks of his novels' hero, the amateur-detective priest, Father Brown, to set the metaphysical charity of the believer – which no human turpitude can discourage – against the inane optimism of the rationalist.

In placing Ireland under the direct control of the Westminster Parliament in 1801, William Pitt's only concern was to prevent Napoleon from using it as a base from which to attack Britain. But by taking this step, he also endowed the United Kingdom with five million Irish Catholics (equivalent to a quarter of its total population of Catholics) of which some 250,000 immigrants were to settle in England, mainly after the 1840 famine. It would have been anomalous, dangerous even, for them to remain outlawed from society, like potential traitors. In 1829 a new law restored to Catholics virtually all their religious and civic rights. But in a country that was preparing itself for the canonization of the middle classes, where poverty was considered a punishment from God and riches were greeted as a sign of His approval, the intrusion of these common hordes – though blessed by the State – was to rekindle the ancient hostility against Catholicism. Clearly, this was all that could be expected of papists: a rabble of foreigners, poverty-stricken, drunk, brutal, quarrelsome and superstitious – like a breed of English-speaking Latins.

Time was to temper these prejudices, without completely wiping them out. The first Catholic parliamentarians, the first judge, the first Viceroy of India: such intrusions no longer threatened the self-respect of the ruling classes. Today, whether in the House of Commons, the House of Lords or in the Queen's Privy Council, no one would question their right to accede to the highest positions – with the exception of the highest position of all, the Crown. The two world wars finally completed the integration – though not the assimilation – of Catholicism. On the occasion of the Papal visit to the British Isles in 1982, the Apostolic Pronuncio to the United Kingdom of Great Britain and Northern Ireland, Mgr Bruno Heim, was elevated to the rank of ambassador. The visit was a recognition that the Catholic question was no longer a burning issue. Yet the Pope has never lifted the Papal condemnation of the great Elizabeth, and in their loyalty to the second monarch of that name, English Catholics are still defying excommunication. Priests ordained by the Anglican Church are still not recognised by the Church of Rome. And when the sacrament of communion is performed within the Anglican rites, it is no more than a commemorative enactment of the Last Supper. The doctrines of the infallibility of the Pope and of the Immaculate Conception are treated as ethnographical curiosities by the more indulgent of Anglicans, and are considered by the more orthodox to be manifest idolatries, offensive to the Godhead. Although ecumenicalism is fashionable in Rome, as it is in Canterbury, everyone knows that the unification of the Christian churches is still a distant aspiration. When Anglicans, with their habitual realism, admit that the Pope could provide the focus for a world Christian body – even guiding it to a certain extent – they do not envisage him as the Vicar of Christ at the head of the Universal Church, but merely as the man most likely to save their coalition of faiths from the common peril of materialism. It is not at all clear that the Holy Father would accept the secularisation of his role that seems so natural to his Anglican interlocutor. The ecumenicalism of Catholics is a matter of doctrine and not of strategy.

These speculations are of little interest to the man in the street. If the different churches get on with each other, so much the better. If they fail, he will not lose much sleep over the matter. Theology is not his strong point. But though his sense of sin has been blunted, and though even death – sanitised, hospitalised, dispatched – may not arouse religious sentiments in him, a need for the supernatural survives, and all the more strongly if he is young and isolated. Sects are flourishing: Pentecostalists, Moonies, Jehovah's Witnesses, Seventh Day Adventists – the catalogue is never-ending. Black minority churches are on the increase, and in the difficult dialogue with the white majority, they are assuming political weight. Hindus and Sikhs have their temples, Muslims have their mosques, Buddhism is making converts outside the Asian population. Catholic monasteries are benefitting from an increasing number of vocations. Three-quarters of the population believes in parapsychology, sixty per cent in astrology, and half believes in ghosts and clairvoyance, as well as an endless stream of 'inexplicable phenomena'. Their common prayer could be: 'My God, even if you do not exist, give us a sign and we will believe in you.'

The Family, Society and the State
The family – natural pillar of the social order and object of concern for all the spiritual, moral and political authorities – is also suffering from an indefinable malady. It has never known the robust health, nor suffered from the excessive solicitude of its Latin counterpart. As early as the end of the fifteenth century, the Venetian, Andrea Trevisano, writing a report of his mission

to the court of Henry VII, complained indignantly 'that the want
of affection in the English is strongly manifested towards their
children; for after having kept them at home till they arrive at
the age of seven or nine at the utmost, they put them out, both
males and females, to hard service in the houses of other people,
binding them generally for another seven to nine years'*. Yet the
ideal of the family is endlessly extolled, as much by the Socialists,
who have offered it the protection of the Welfare State, as by
Margaret Thatcher, who placed her trust in its patriarchal virtues
to help her rid society of dependency on the State.

When asked about her profession, Mrs Thatcher used to call
herself a housewife. Her sentimentality on the subject cannot
conceal the fact that the British family, with its 2.07 children,
grows every day more fragile. Yet she insisted: 'The family must
continue to be the fundamental unit of society, and the most
important person in the family, who sets its standards more than
anyone else, is the mother,' adding, 'I think in many cases the
astonishing thing is not how lax society has become, but how
comparatively orthodox it is, and how it continues to believe in
and adopt the fundamental values – because there is something
there which people know that if you lose, the whole nature of
society would change, and change for the worse.'

In his book entitled *The Subversive Family*, the conservative
journalist Ferdinand Mount is equally fulsome in his praise of
the institution. The family, he explains, is subversive because it
has consistently resisted appeals to altruism and God knows what
other social imperative invoked by reformers, philosophers and
ideologues – be they called Jesus, Karl Marx or Hitler. Cemented
by love and marriage, the family is always – he believes – ready
to sacrifice the interests of the collectivity in favour of its own.
Though regimented by a society that tends to reduce everything to
the norm, and taken in charge by a bureaucracy that has assumed
the traditionally private functions of protection and education, the
indomitable, imperishable family continues to resist outside intervention, and in spite of every pressure, preserves its identity.

* Quoted by Alan Macfarlane in *The Origins of English Individualism*,
Basil Blackwell, Oxford.

In 1983, Mount was asked by Margaret Thatcher to establish a group for political debate that would help the Government in its deliberations. The group's remit was to encourage women to remain in the home; to break the rigid structures of state-funded old-age pensions by restoring to individuals the right to choose their own retirement saving schemes; to privatise a range of state services such as hospital catering; to develop the self-confidence and spirit of enterprise of the nation's children. While not allowing himself to question the fundamental principles of the State's duty to protect the weak, the ill and the underprivileged, he maintained nonetheless that by bringing these tasks under direct state control, huge resources had been wasted which would have been much better spent at the level of the basic social cell – the family. It was the family's duty to ensure its own protection and to display solidarity, as it had never failed to do in the past.

Institutions wear out and so do ideas. But the family, mean or generous, persists. In today's Great Britain though, the pendulum, which for the past half century had swung towards complete protection against illness, ignorance, poverty and natural disaster, has been returning towards the freedom of every man for himself. Prosperity no longer constitutes a right, merely a threatened privilege. State protection has proved to be insufficient. Dissatisfaction is growing. One injustice replaces another, and crime is on the increase. Though Mrs Thatcher balked before the implementation of the more extreme measures advocated by the partisans of economic laissez-faire, the society which she would have liked to build – after the model of a prosperous enterprise – would always, according to her detractors, have put productivity before justice.

One in sixteen people in Great Britain today is seventy-five years old or over. At the beginning of the century, the proportion was one in seventy-six. The number of old people left without surviving children – or even without any close relative at all – is growing every day. They want words of encouragement, but beyond that they need telephones, hot meals, and retirement homes. Worn out by poverty, demoralised by unemployment, embittered by fears and frustrations, and sometimes owing its very existence to an unwanted pregnancy, the new family is often no longer based on marriage. Whether it was created by love or by accident, it needs physical assistance rather than praise from the admirers of that ideal family whose address nobody knows.

And then there is that other British family, real enough but not necessarily on the council housing list, not necessarily struggling for survival amid debts and unemployment. It can sometimes be seen travelling in its new Japanese car towards a weekend cottage with monthly mortgage repayments paid without a thought. Yet this family is no more convinced of its great happiness by today's sirens of private enterprise, than it was by yesterday's sermons on the virtues of the Welfare State.

Good Children and Delinquents

In his book, *Exploring English Character*, the anthropologist Geoffrey Gorer writes: 'English is, as far as I can trace, the only European language which has a single word, nursery, for the place where both children and plants are reared.'

The Victorian era best exemplifies all that is darkest, as well as all that is richest and most powerful in British tradition. That latent or explicit antagonism between parents and children, and their shared belief in the natural perversity of the young, can be traced back long before the Victorian period, but they were never as clearly manifest. Reminiscing in the second half of the nineteenth century on his earliest years, Gladstone – pillar of a vigorous and self-confident society – writes with disturbing sincerity:

'I wish that in reviewing my childhood, I could regard it as presenting those features of innocence and beauty which I have often seen elsewhere . . . I do not think, trying to look at the past impartially, that I had a strong natural propensity then developed to what are termed the mortal sins. But truth obliges me to record this against myself: I have no recollection of being a loving or a winning child; or an earnest or diligent or knowledge-loving child . . .; the plank between me and all the sins was so very thin . . . I have no recollection of early love for the House of God and for divine service . . . Neither was I a popular boy . . .

If I was not a bad boy, I think that I was a boy with a great absence of goodness.'

What is the answer to so many imperfections and deficiences? In spite of the huge social, cultural and economic inequalities that divide the British people, there is one point on which they surely agree, and that is on the kind of education appropriate to so arduous a task. As with the pruning of trees, the role of education is to train the child to control itself and acquire good habits; to prevent it from reverting to its savage state, giving way to sloth and other suspect instincts. Though the belief in corporal punishment is decreasing, some two-thirds of the population remain as convinced now as they were thirty years – or even a century – ago of the imperative need to impose strict discipline on children.

'I always wanted to be a mother,' Mary Soames, Sir Winston Churchill's daughter, explains. 'In fact, I've had as many children as I used to have dolls, and those dolls were brought up very strictly by me. As for my children, I have tried to be as strict with them.' Naturally, this belief in authority does not always succeed in stifling the spontaneous demonstrations of affection that seem so natural across the Channel. From London to Newcastle, from Sussex to Lancashire, I have come across doting mothers and fathers who worship their children. What is certain is that – whether to castigate or to praise it – nowhere in the world has childhood been as closely observed and described as it has been in England.

Today the children of the poor no longer have to work in the mines and spinning mills as they did at the beginning of the industrial era, but they are still deprived of those cultural amulets which grace the lives of their more privileged contemporaries. In *East End Underworld: Chapters in the Life of Andrew Harding* – an autobiography recorded on tape between 1973 and 1979 – the near-centenarian Harding, recalling the East End slums where he was born, observed that by the age of eight or nine a child could survive without its family 'because it's got the instinct to survive . . . He'll thieve or beg . . .' Two themes emerge from this admirable autobiography: one is the way in which poverty eliminates childhood (one is forced very early to work, beg, steal, negotiate with society, like an adult), and the other is the survival of traditional values (one knows one's place, social hierarchy is part of the order of things, it is natural to respect some people and despise the rest).

In numerous households, childhood remains a precarious privilege even now. Though Conservative rhetoric extols the virtues of the family, Britain has no tradition of family policy, and even Mrs Thatcher's Government did not attempt to create one. This compares with France, where the family has much deeper cultural roots, and governments of every hue since the 1936 Front Populaire have elaborated a comprehensive set of policies encouraging family growth and extending material and practical help to working mothers. In Britain, child-care is provided on an entirely ad-hoc basis. In April 1990, John Major, then Chancellor of the Exchequer, allowed tax exemption on work-place nurseries. But despite the introduction of this measure, and the general growth in private child-care provision, the number of crèches per head of population in Britain is among the lowest in Europe. State nursery schools do not take children under the age of three, and have places for only about one per cent of under-fives. When both mother and father are working they often have to resort to improvised arrangements (with friends, neighbours, or semi-professional carers looking after too many children in inadequate accommodation), and – in extreme cases – even resign themselves to leaving their youngest child in the care of an older one, frequently aged less than ten years himself.

In April 1988, legislation finally abolished all discrimination between legitimate and illegitimate children. It was high time: in 1988, twenty-five per cent of births in the United Kingdom were illegitimate, compared to only twelve per cent in 1981, and if the present rate of growth is sustained illegitimacy will be the norm by the year 2010. The use of contraception is now standard, and the number of abortions is increasing despite a strong anti-abortion lobby and the recent reduction of the time limit for the majority of terminations from twenty-eight weeks to twenty-four. Clearly, couples who have children out of wedlock do so by choice. Many of these apparently precarious unions reveal themselves to be at least as stable as marriage, but a child's chances of finding himself prematurely deprived of father or mother are growing nonetheless. Between 1976 and 1986 there was a thirty-five per cent increase in the number of one-parent families in Britain, and today there are well over a million of them – that is approximately fourteen per cent of all families with dependent children.

The notorious 1899 Poor Law which – among other things – authorised the government to take a child away from his home if his family showed habits and a life-style rendering it incapable of taking care of him, no longer applies today. But it is only since an amendment to the Secure Accommodation Regulations in 1983, that the locking away of children in the care of local authorities ceased to be an entirely internal, administrative procedure, and was made subject to judicial control. Voluntary Childrens' homes have not even been subject to the same rules – though under a new Act, to be debated in Parliament in October 1991, this anomaly is due to be rectified.

And then there are all those ordinary children who go to school while their parents are working, who are shouted at by an exhausted mother when she returns from work, or ignored by a father on his way out to the pub. Short of joining one of those gangs whose activities are so disapproved of by adults, there is little for them to do. Deprived of early reading matter and of the more expensive toys, these young exiles share only one luxury with the well-to-do – television. Its advertisements have become their childhood fairy-tales.

The Eternal Nanny

For the middle and upper classes in England, childhood is a kind of protected state within the guardian state of adults, regulated according to the rules of a benevolent apartheid. Parents, when they can afford to do so, have an atavistic propensity to quarter their children in one of those reserves for the natives known as 'the nursery', preferably under the rule of Nanny, failing which a live-in home-help, or – at the very least – a young girl or boy *au pair* will do. Families who cannot afford these will delegate protective authority to a child-minder or the cleaning lady, and to baby-sitters in the evening.

A nanny is not only a faithful servant to the privileged. She is the guardian of the stern but shifting rules of table manners, she provides love when maternal warmth is lacking, a myth understood by all, regardless of class or fortune. Nannying is also a profession with a future. Employers have a different style and requirements, but with increasing numbers of affluent women pursuing a career like their husbands, demand is on the increase.

Winston Churchill's son-in-law, Christopher Soames (who died just a few years ago), spent his childhood in a real old-fashioned nursery, taking up an entire floor of the family house, and comprising, in addition to Nanny herself, Nanny's maid, and later the French governess. But his was the last generation to experience such a system. 'Even those who could afford to run a nursery such as the ones we knew have abandoned any idea of doing so,' he once explained to me. 'With my friends the N . . . s for example, their Nanny still has a maid, but the style is completely different. Everybody wears jeans now whether they are rich or poor.'

Old traditions are not entirely lost. I have met one of those pearls which the Norland Nursery Training College has been cultivating for the past 90 years to look after the education of well-to-do children. She was wearing a uniform – not, thank goodness, the unforgettable starched headdress over a blue veil, with white cuffs and a white pinafore – but a trim round hat with a pretty round-collared blouse and a small Spencer jacket over a pleated skirt. Still, one knew exactly whom one was dealing with. Susan G . . . (*professionalisme oblige*) has spent four years in a 'perfect' Argentinian family with five children, and two years with an English couple and their lovely twins (though the mother was a '*nouveau-riche* bitch'). Susan is twenty-seven years old. She is planning to stay in the profession until she is about thirty-two or thirty-three, unless she meets the man of her life or decides to retrain as a paediatric nurse, the one not excluding the other. Her biggest problem is that 'one gets too fond of the children'. Her golden rule: 'Never forget that they are not yours.' Her heartbreak: 'When the children become too fond of you.'

The twenty-one months of training at Norland cost £15,210. In spite of this high price, every year the college has a waiting list of five to six hundred candidates. The situation is about the same for the other great Nanny School, Prince Christian College, and in the remaining 150 private and state training establishments, there are approximately four candidates to every available place. The explanation: all these assistant-mothers are guaranteed a job somewhere in the world when they have completed their studies.

It is in the nursery that the child acquires that peculiarly British faculty of reconciling pragmatic respect for parental authority and tradition with the secret world of the imagination. In the nursery one can still catch a nostalgic glimpse of the days when children were selectively reared within its hothouse walls. The eldest son was carefully groomed for his role as heir and propagator of family values, while the others – those superfluous, untitled rejects – were left to their own devices, becoming penniless officers or merchants without capital. They fled from their families, sailed to the other end of the world where they planted the Union Jack, set up trading posts in the first sheltered inlet, compiled maps and inventories of unknown fauna, recreated for themselves all the luxuries they were denied at home, and finally returned to replenish ancestral coffers and royal caskets with their booty.

The Ritual Murder of One's Parents

Children's literature has contributed a great deal to the wanderlust of so many younger sons of good family. But its influence has been even greater on countless 'good' children, destined to become benevolent squires, ecclesiastics, or wives and mothers confined to their narrow duties. The first nursery rhyme, the first song, the first book: words far more than images represent the child's earliest escape from the constricting family circle.

In seventeenth century rural England, where a high level of literacy had already been achieved, books were available to a large population of children – though their purpose at this time was almost entirely didactic. With the increased prosperity that accompanied industrialisation in the nineteenth century, children's books underwent a metamorphosis. They were still ostensibly educational, but now aimed to give pleasure and distraction as well. Though written for a privileged minority, they were also read by pupils of the first state schools, whom they introduced to an extraordinary world of riches, power and overseas adventure. For the space of a novel, these children could believe in their capacity to leave the weak and join the strong. As for the children for whom this literature was primarily destined, they were left with whetted and unsatisfied appetites. Surely this vast world and its mysteries was theirs by right, since their fathers were already masters of it? Real adventure consisted precisely in escaping from the dominion of their fathers and mothers – the absentee landlords of the nursery – and discovering a world which was not subject to their law.

The secret of English children's literature lies in this journey within the heart of childhood. Its greatest authors are those for whom adulthood is just a mask behind which an eternal child is afraid, seeks reassurance, or flies away into a fantasy to which he alone holds the key. It is also perhaps the fruit – the most beautiful fruit – of the segregation of children in the traditional English family. As well as being a story about non-communication, *A Midsummer Night's Dream* is surely one of those cruel dreams into which only a child dares to penetrate without fear? Puck, asexual, prepubescent and cynical, could perhaps be seen as the symbolic ancestor, the first hero of that children's literature which was to flourish two centuries later.

In the world of the Comtesse de Ségur, doyenne of French children's literature, the occasional parent might be found wanting, but wisdom normally prevailed in the adult world. More recently, Tintin, the child journalist, took on the adult world and proved that he could do better. But the English child is invited by the child author (disguised as an adult) to forget, to pour scorn on, and even to annihilate his mummy and daddy, those adults who have relegated him to the nursery. Peter Pan, flying from window to window in Kensington Gardens, performs the ritual murder of his own parents, as well as of ours.

Grown-ups feature only minimally in this elaborate childhood world. But the rabbits of Beatrix Potter (yet another little girl hiding under a woman's dress), the games and the terrors of *Alice in Wonderland*, no longer engage children's sensibilities in the way

71

they did in the past, and even Shakespeare's magic is a little too forbidding for the majority of them. These siren songs are now distorted or made unintelligible by interference from other voices and other images – most notably from omnipresent television.

The number of children's books sold in Britain between 1960 and 1970 was more or less constant. Between 1970 and 1980 it fell by almost a third, a trend that was all the more worrying for the book trade since adults remain faithful to the habit of reading only if they acquired it at the tenderest age. Since then this decline has slowed down dramatically, and specialised publishers' attempts to revive sales have seen an increase in the children's books share of the overall market. More books are published in cheap paperback editions, and bookshops have expanded their childrens' books section from a few shelves to entire departments, assigning specialised buyers to the task of filling them. The major chain of bookshops, Waterstone's, has even opened two branches of Young Waterstone's, devoted entirely to children.

Parents continue to play a decisive role in purchasing a child's first books. *The Tale of Jemima Puddle-Duck* and the illustrated *Humpty Dumpty* (in which poor Humpty gets most cruelly dismembered) still find a place among those early purchases. Contemporary picture books, often beautifully illustrated, are also extremely popular with parents, who will frequently continue to buy books for their children even when they are cutting down on purchases for themselves. Yet many of the classics of childhood are sold in abbreviated adaptations. Some of the most popular modern books, such as the best-selling *Where's Wally* series – in which Wally, wearing a red and white striped bobble-hat, hides from his readers on every page – contain no text at all. How many children today can claim – as Mary Soames does – to have been brought up on John Bunyan's superb picaresque epic of faith, the *Pilgrim's Progress*? I doubt whether that fairy-tale Puritan novel has retained the importance in childhood culture that it had when it first appeared in the seventeenth century.

Between the ages of nine and ten, children begin to develop personal tastes independently of their parents. Like their parents, they are likely to read any book that has been shown on television, and classics such as C.S. Lewis's *Narnia* books can rapidly climb to the top of the best-seller list as a result of a successful TV adaptation. Contemporary authors, such as Jill Murphy with her *Worst Witch* books, have also benefited from being transferred to television. But most popular among young readers are cartoon strips and paperbacks with stories drawn from successful fiction films and programmes that first appeared on television; and that mass-product *par excellence* – the book of collected jokes and stories, whose scatological bad taste and frequently violent humour is as delightful to children as it is dismaying for parents.

Taking over from various leagues for the protection of decency, and inspired by the example of America, the Educational Publisher's Council has set up a working group in liaison with the Commission for Equal Opportunities which, like a progressive version of the Vatican, guides authors towards the straight and narrow path of purified literature. Its aim is to track down all forms of sexism, to expose masculine and feminine stereotypes, and to remove all expressions of racism or class prejudice, whether direct or implicit. Not content with going through babies' picture books with a tooth-comb, the group has extended its brief to poetry, history, and all works of fiction, whether ancient or modern. Their efforts are part of a wider trend. In August 1990, bowing before prolonged pressure over Enid Blyton's *Noddy* books – widely considered to be both racist and sexist – the publishers, MacDonald, finally announced that they were to withdraw the entire series, replacing it the following month with a new, sanitised edition: no more Golliwogs in Toytown, Gremlins instead; no more spankings, but plenty of punishment. Will these latter-day Puritans now ask for *Robinson Crusoe* to be banned for racism, or will they rewrite the fairy tales of Grimm and Perrault in order to cut out all sexist and classist implications? The prickly moralists who pore so anxiously over the torrent of contradictions, violence, repression and subterranean sexuality of which English children's literature is composed, have taken on a labour of Hercules. Nor can they afford to confine their efforts to output of a less enlightened age.

In his immensely popular children's stories, the writer Roald Dahl maintains the continuity of a quintessentially English tradition in which innocent cruelty dallies gaily with the absurd.

Parental clichés burst under the sharp point of his pen, and children wallow in the wicked joys of his unedifying stories and *Revolting Rhymes*, recognising in Dahl the last in England's long line of child authors in adult guise. And surely Roald Dahl himself, whose infantile sadism is clothed in the refined art of the accomplished writer, must have recognised a kindred spirit in the naïve and cruel output of the twelve-year-old Lewis Carroll:

> 'Sister, do not raise my wrath.
> I'd make you into mutton broth
> As easily as kill a moth!'
>
> The sister raised her beaming eye
> And looked on him indignantly
> And sternly answered, 'Only try!'
>
> Off to the cook he quickly ran.
> 'Dear Cook, please lend a frying-pan
> To me as quickly as you can.'
>
> 'And wherefore should I lend it you?'
> 'The reason, Cook, is plain to view.
> I wish to make an Irish stew.'
>
> 'What meat is in the stew to go?'
> 'My sister'll be the contents!'
> 'Oh!'
> 'You'll lend the pan to me, Cook?'
> 'No!'
> *Moral:* Never Stew your sister.

4

The School of Inequality

Certain English landscapes are so English that one wonders whether an imp has stepped into God's shoes and hung up on the horizon a water-colour of the English school, lifting it from the wall of a local squire's house: meadows, trees, lanes flanked by hedgerows, overhung by clouds and bathed in a vaporous, dewy light.

Sheltered in the folds of the plump green Mendips, there are villages which are a thousand years old or more. Chewton Mendip, with its school and its church and fifteenth-century tower, is perhaps the most pleasing among them. The colourful cottage gardens and red cheeks of the children testify to the wholesome qualities of its rainy climate.

Sport and Caning

It is at Chewton that I first sat on an English school bench a few years ago. With the quiet confidence of one stating a self-evident truth, the school's headmaster, John Shakesby, smilingly explained the primacy of sport and games to me. This primacy has been inculcated in generations of schoolboys for more than 150 years, and it remained for him the basic principle of any truly English education. Indeed, it was to his proficiency in sport that he owed his present appointment – in preference to three other candidates, who in other respects were as well qualified as himself.

Nonetheless school sport – which has given birth to the majority of modern sports, not only in Great Britain, but all over the world – is beginning to lose ground. Competitive games have for some time been under attack from the 'loony left', who object to the rivalries they create between children, exposing the weak to a sense of failure. But the majority of schoolteachers continue to believe that without the keen edge of competition to give children a sense of solidarity with their school team, other kinds of sporting activities – the only sort the reformers would like to preserve – would also gradually be abandoned. For a boy to be described as 'very good at sport' (in France one might say 'a likeable dunce') is still, in the mouth of a British schoolteacher, the greatest of compliments. Its hidden meanings are: 'He is well-adjusted, he is popular, he is trustworthy.'

Until very recently, and to the astonishment of most foreigners, the question of corporal punishment remained a very live issue among both parents and educationalists. Until 1986, caning and belting were still common in a large number of schools, and even today the debate is not closed. The partisans of corporal punishment make great claims for it: it is the best deterrent because physical fear is universal and nothing strengthens the character more than overcoming fear. It is a punishment reserved for grave offences, which does not have any of the psychologically damaging effects of alternatives such as temporary expulsion from the school, with all its deleterious consequences for the family. It cleanses the child of his fault and – unlike punishment such as depriving him of a special outing or requiring him to do extra homework – it does not hang over him for days. It is a natural outlet for natural feelings, and therefore quite harmless. A few strokes, a few red stripes on the buttocks, and everything is forgotten, by master and by child alike. After all, caning has been practised in Britain for centuries – to no ill effect. Like fox hunting and kippers for breakfast, it is a truly British institution.

Opponents of corporal punishment are equally forceful in cataloguing its baleful influences: it is responsible for the inhibitions and masochism which characterise the English; it does not strengthen the child's character so much as encourage homosexuality. At best it is an inadmissable abuse of power which degrades the abuser as much as it does his victim.

Praise and opprobrium are equally excessive. Experienced teachers know that caning is neither a panacea nor a poison. Maybe its use is merely pointless. It certainly does nothing to contain the violent outbursts of a difficult school population; it might even provoke them. In any case, abolitionist parents have now won the day. First from Scotland, then from England, they fought in the European Court of Human Rights in Strasbourg and obtained the right to object to the caning of their children at school. In August 1987, corporal punishment was finally abolished altogether in state schools. In 1988, the Chairman of the Conservative back-bench Education Committee, James Pawsey, proposed that the balance be restored by giving parents who were in favour of corporal punishment the right to demand it for their children. But in spite of such rearguard action, it is likely that the last vestiges of this tradition will crumble away like so many others before it. The evolution of British society is reflected in its educational system: authority is no longer fashionable.

From Education to Consumerism

One of the first things that the foreigner – especially if he comes from France or Germany – notices about the English educational system is that it is considered almost self-evident among educators that there is no such thing as a universally good teaching method to suit all children. The teacher's first duty is to assess the personality of each of his pupils and to adapt his teaching accordingly.

In practice, two distinct philosophies of education have divided the nation since the war. One is traditionalist, placing emphasis on academic achievement above everything else, and accepting – perhaps even applauding – the creation of an élite, raised in exclusive grammar schools or expensive private schools whose origins go back to forgotten times. The other, inspired by the Labour movement, gives comprehensive schools (open to all children between the ages of eleven and eighteen) the task of breaking the cultural mould that isolates different social classes, and redistributing among all children the assets monopolised by a handful of predetermined winners. But while the privileged fork out uncomplainingly for an education which they consider to be the best in the world, state education, which is the only accessible education for ninety-five per cent of the population, provokes a cacophony of more or less justified criticism, even amongst its partisans.

Under banner headlines, the conservative tabloid press continually publishes horror stories about ignorant teachers in shabby clothing who are unable to make themselves respected by the hooligans who fill their classes, and who go on strike without a thought for their pupils. Meanwhile, *The Guardian* and other organs of the soft left worry over the depressed condition of a teaching body that is underpaid, misunderstood and harassed by uncontrollable students and overbearing parents. But studies of any thoroughness and countless inspectors' reports show that hostility and violence are the least of the teachers' problems. The great majority of pupils are docile, or numbed into a hopeless torpor. In the end, it is the substance of what is taught that has had to be called into question. However attached they may be to the principle of school autonomy, teachers have had to admit that although the system they inherited was appropriate in the days when schools catered for the sons of doctors, lawyers, artisans and gentlemen farmers, it may no longer deliver the kind of education that would allow Great Britain to regain its position as a world industrial leader.

In 1880, ninety-seven per cent of the population in Britain was literate. Thanks to the efforts of religious foundations, the education of the masses proceeded rapidly. The creation of scholarships allowed the children of a small number of poor families to gain access to grammar schools. In 1944, under the coalition government, and on the initiative of the Conservative Minister of Education, R.A. Butler, a new Education Act extended and rationalized a system that had been operative for a century. It raised the school-leaving age to fifteen, while reorganising schools into primary and secondary sectors and making it possible for all children to complete their secondary education if they wished. At the time, the statute was hailed as an immense step forward. From a distance it is easier to measure its shortcomings. Undoubtedly it favoured the perpetuation of a hierarchical culture which stifled social mobility and preserved the pre-eminence of an aristocracy, whether of social origin or of wealth. Even when they were fighting that aristocracy in the political arena, the middle classes, as they prospered, tended to imitate its tastes, attitudes and prejudices – most of all in the domain of education.

In 1976, the Labour Party abolished the long-standing eleven-plus examination which until then had sifted the supposedly brighter children – destined for the academic grammar schools – from the others, relegated to the secondary moderns. As a result of this measure, during the next three years (before the election of Mrs Thatcher's first government), most of the country's old style schools were either closed down, or amalgamated and turned into egalitarian comprehensives. But this did not so much abolish as move the frontier separating the education of the élite from that of the masses. The same divisions that once separated comprehensives from grammar schools and the better independent establishments were soon to manifest themselves within the comprehensive school system. Depending on their location, the social origins of the majority of parents, and the results obtained in examinations, particular schools acquired a more or less favourable reputation.

Real power was in the hands of the local authorities, whose composition (with certain nuances and qualifications), reflected national political divisions. They acted independently, and found unanimity only when defending their prerogatives. Engaged, under the watchful eye of the minister, in interminable negotiations over salaries and working conditions with the six teachers' unions, they temporised, and were easily scared by educational innovations. The more active among them, on the other hand, found themselves accused of a sectarianism which demoralised more than it encouraged the teaching corps. In practice, good schools continued to improve, while bad ones got worse, and the indifference of children, coupled with the dissatisfaction of parents continued to grow.

During the first two parliamentary terms after their 1979 electoral victory, the Conservatives, encouraged by the disaffection among a majority of the electorate, initiated the return to a system which took account of natural inequalities between individuals, and began by restoring the eleven-plus examination – thus saving some 150 remaining grammar schools from eventual extinction. For Labour, as one might have expected, the solution to these problems lay in the opposite direction – towards greater democratisation of the system. In addition to advocating the abolition of private schools* which, in their present form, they believed

79

to be responsible for the division of British society in two, they called for a general improvement in the standard of education, from nursery school to university level. As for the failure of the comprehensive schools, they denied it. According to them, the shortcomings of the system could be attributed primarily to successive Conservative governments' penny-pinching education policies.

In fact (with the notable exception of Japan), Western democracies have all been more or less unsuccessful in their attempts to replace the élitist educational system they inherited from the nineteenth century with a truly egalitarian one – and undoubtedly inadequate funding has been a large part of the story. In their obsession with the externals of equality, they largely abandoned traditional teaching methods – which relied on the exercise of memory and the acquisition of basic skills and information – and placed a grossly excessive emphasis on the stimulation of creativity in children, at the expense of knowledge. In this way, they even managed to destroy their primary education (which had been the sole concession made by the paternalism of their forebearers to all people without restriction), while doing little to modify the substance of what was taught in secondary schools, where the virtues of the old humanist tradition (with its concentration on the liberal arts) continued to be proclaimed despite its élitist antecedents. But the task of imparting this old-fashioned education to a much broader constituency proved to be incommensurate with the abilities of teachers and pupils alike. The prestige and calibre of a much expanded teaching corps gradually declined as the funds made available to education failed to increase in proportion to the size of the undertaking. At the same time, it became increasingly clear that this kind of education was inappropriate to the less academic majority of pupils, and throughout Europe, various kinds of obstacles (such as the imposition of high doses of mathematics in France and the perpetuation of élitist examinations in England) had the effect of disheartening all but an intellectual

---

* Today, the abolition of the independent education sector has been dropped from Labour Party policy, and has been replaced by the promise to 'review' the nature of private schools' charitable status.

minority. There is a mass of people who have been abandoned by a system that tends to reject not only the less bright, but also the less well-off, as well as recent immigrants, drop-outs and eccentrics, and there is no doubt that society could discover or elicit all kinds of qualities essential to its own development amongst them.

Whatever their ulterior motives may have been, the British Conservative governments of the last ten years have had the merit of breaking with a tradition that implicitly abandoned the task of educating the underprivileged to the Labour Party. But for all that, they have not been tempted, like their adversaries, to believe that it is necessary or possible to establish a unified educational system ensuring the same opportunities to all children, regardless of their social origins or individual aptitudes.

To Mrs Thatcher – who liked to call a spade a spade – it was obvious that some students are gifted while others are dunces, that some work diligently while others are idle. It would be wrong, she believed, to inflict on the former the lack of intellect or laziness of the latter. Similarly, there are good schools (more often than not in the private sector) and bad ones (usually in the public sector); and it is only by getting rid of the bad ones that one can hope to improve the others. Finally, it was clear to her that those who are best placed to judge the quality of the education provided are not politicians, and even less teachers (who are too closely implicated in the process), but parents – who are the customers.

Totally confident in the justice of her convictions, Mrs Thatcher (who had herself been in charge of the Department of Education and Science under Edward Heath), handed over to three successive Secretaries of State (out of a total of five), the responsibility of entirely restructuring the school system according to her criteria. The first of these was Sir Keith Joseph, an intellectual who was behind many of her most daring ideas on the economics of the market-place, and had been one of the architects of her accession to the leadership of the Conservative Party. He seemed the ideal man to promote and impose a radical reform of the state school system.

A powerful free-trade lobby in the Conservative Party accused the local education authorities of having created what amounted to an educational monopoly which was not subject to the healthy discipline of competition, and which imposed on its dissatisfied customers – the parents – a product that was considerably inferior to that offered by the private sector. The solution, it was suggested, was a school voucher system, in which schools would not be funded directly by the state, but would be forced to compete for the custom of parents – empowered by the voucher in their pocket. In this way good schools would flourish while bad ones would not survive.

In the event, Keith Joseph proved to be too close to the academic community, which considered him to be one of their own – too subtle perhaps, and not enough of a politician to fall in with the rhetoric of the extreme wing of his party. He was vehemently opposed to the idea of a National Curriculum, and though in favour of making the educational system more responsive to the needs of industry, remained unwilling to embrace an entirely market-led approach. He was at heart a humanist of the old school, and Mrs Thatcher saw herself obliged to part company with him, while thanking him for his loyal services by elevating him to the peerage.

It fell to his successor, Kenneth Baker (better known for his ties with the former Prime Minister Edward Heath, than for his Thatcherite convictions), to carry out the most radical reform of the British educational system since Butler's Education Act of 1944. According to Michael Marland, Honorary Professor of Education at Warwick University, and Headmaster of the North Westminster Community School (a highly regarded London comprehensive), the most important aspect of Baker's 1988 Education Reform Act* consists in the complete redistribution of powers between the State, the local authorities, teachers and parents.

In theory, the administration of education before the reform was placed in the hands of the local authorities 'under the control and direction of "The Minister"'. In practice, since the powers of the Minister were nowhere defined, he never exercised either

* Separate legislation broadly on the same lines was also introduced in Scotland in 1988.

direction or control over the educational system. Perhaps because in 1944 there had been an unspoken consensus on what the young ought to know, the content of the curriculum was left entirely to the discretion of local authorities and schools. Yet over the last twenty years it had also become obvious that public opinion was beginning to tire of the vagaries of the system. Free to determine their own curricula, yet corsetted by the administrative rules imposed on them by local authorities, schools seemed incapable of providing a sound basic education for the benefit of the greatest number.

In August 1990, adding his voice to that of numerous other academics, Sir Claus Moser, President of the British Association for the Advancement of Science and Warden of Wadham College, Oxford, declared that Britain was in danger of becoming one of the worst educated countries of all the advanced nations. Speaking to the members of his association in Swansea, he stated that 'hundreds of thousands of children have educational experiences not worthy of a civilized nation'.

A study published in 1988 showed that only thirty-five per cent of young people between the ages of sixteen and eighteen were pursuing full-time studies – a percentage that was lower than that in any other developed country, and compared appallingly with the figures of seventy-nine per cent in the United States, seventy-seven per cent in Japan, seventy-six per cent in Sweden, and sixty-six per cent in France. And in 1990, the publication of two Government-funded enquiries gave further substance to people's anxieties. The first included a Britain-wide survey of children aged eleven to sixteen, and revealed that one in three believed the sun rotated around the earth. A report on the survey concluded that young people are wary of scientific change, and half do not understand the basic principles of physics, chemistry and biology. The second enquiry, carried out among a representative group of more than a thousand sixteen- to twenty-year-olds in England and Wales, showed that a quarter of them had difficulties in reading, and when tested on their ability to understand the content of a text, showed themselves to be not only uninformed, but more worryingly still, remarkably uninterested in the questions asked of them.

Without burdening himself with an undue respect for logic, Kenneth Baker established a system that combined centralisation (the establishment of a National Curriculum and standardised national exams) and decentralisation (the devolution to schools and parents of powers hitherto entrusted to the local authorities and the Department of Education and Science). The now defunct Inner London Education Authority was outraged, and the largest teachers' union was also highly critical of the changes. Commentators highlighted those aspects of the legislation that took powers to the centre, and one writer calculated that the Act has given the Secretary of State 349 specific new powers. The very phrase 'National Curriculum' encouraged many to think that all curriculum planning was to be done in the Department of Education and Science. In practice, the Secretary of State is required to take advice from two bodies appointed by him under the Act – the National Curriculum Council (NCC) and the school Examination and Assessment Council (SEAC). According to Michael Marland, 'The redistribution of power has actually made the governing body the centre of responsibility . . .', transforming it 'from a watchdog to an executive'.

The National Curriculum is not a complete curriculum, nor is it intended to be. It does not govern how a school organizes its day, nor the full range of courses or subjects a secondary school timetables. In fact, not only does it not control how the school should deliver those aspects of the curriculum that are established nationally, but one section of the Act expressly forbids the Secretary of State to lay down such controls. It requires the National Curriculum Council to establish the content of the 'core' and 'foundation' subjects listed in the Act, but, says Michael Marland, 'there is still immense freedom for content, delivery, source pattern and style. Secondary schools should find the exercise makes it possible to produce coherence, so that the curriculum will stop being just a list of separate individual "subjects". It will be an immense undertaking, and will fundamentally alter ways of planning in schools.'

The most bitter criticisms of the new National Curriculum do not come from the Left, as one might have expected, but from the small group of Conservatives who believe that the Baker reform has not gone far enough, and has left far too much power in the hands of the teaching profession. According to them, the committees that are in charge of drawing up the Curriculum are dominated by teachers. Their deliberations are made in secret, and there is no reason to suppose that they are any more convinced today than they ever were of the superiority of solid vocational training over a broadly based humanist education of the kind they have always dispensed. The inclusion of a few technical and practical disciplines is just a smokescreen. Far from endorsing the specific talents of individual school students, national exams tend to reduce them to their lowest common denominator.

Since April 1990, schools have been funded according to the number of students on their register, enabling those that are popular with parents to attract both more students and more funds, while the rest – it is hoped – will either be forced to improve, or have to close down. 'There is no doubt,' says Michael Marland, 'that the increased local accountability, the much greater power of governors, the immensely greater power of parents through and on governors, and the national assessment will make a greater regard for the "client" and her or his family necessary for all, and sharper and more sensitive even for those already committed to that stance.'

For Mrs Judith Scott, Vice-Chairman of her local Parents' committee, and herself a parent on the Board of Governors for Burntwood Comprehensive (an all-girls school in Wandsworth, where she has two daughters), 'Parent power is a nonsense. It's no good giving people power unless you also give them the wherewithal to carry out the responsibilities. All the Government is doing is shifting the responsibility on to unpaid governors.'

Though it is true that the ambitions of the reforms have not been matched by a commensurate increase in spending on education, the Act places another weapon in the hands of the client by giving schools the possibility of opting out of local educational authority control, and turning themselves into grant-maintained schools directly funded by the Department of Education and Science. The creation of City Technology Colleges, intended to be financed largely by local businesses, was planned as yet another way of breaking the monopoly of the LEAs, while at the same time promoting the development of vocational training. However, this policy is collapsing as the funding has not been forthcoming.

It fell to Mrs Thatcher's third main reforming Secretary of State for Education and Science, John Macgregor, to defend the Act against its numerous detractors, as well as to refine and amend it. By way of a welcome, four thousand head teachers wrote to him to complain about the underfunding of school education and the terrible deterioration in the fabric of school buildings themselves. But this was not enough to make him lose countenance. As meticulous and lacklustre as his predecessor was dynamic, John Macgregor patiently explained that, for better or for worse, the reform was not a myth but an irreversible reality. He did not try to claim that the National Curriculum or any of the other changes in the system could provide a miracle cure; it would take some time before their beneficial effects would be felt.

Sure enough, at the end of 1990, fewer than fifty schools had taken advantage of their new freedom to shake off the tutelage of the local education authorities. Perhaps this freedom will one day lead to a dramatic redrawing of the British school map, but to date this has not happened. It is possible that the City Technology Colleges have a brilliant future ahead of them, but at present there are not enough of them to make much difference to the system as a whole.

How does this compare with the situation in France? For a century and a half or more, French state education has been the standard bearer of quality, compared to a mediocre private sector with second class teachers. The quarrel between Republican education and religious education had nothing to do with their respective academic qualities but turned on the principles of universal and impartial secularism versus those of 'religious obscurantism'. On the other hand, the success of primary schools and the lycée system in France was entirely attributable to the intellectual calibre of the education it dispensed, and was quite unconnected with the superiority or otherwise of secularism over an ideology of religion-based education.

Today, the great and admirable primary schools of the Third Republic have fallen under the influence of unions and psychologists, and are just a shadow of their former selves. The lycée has more in common with some sort of Madame Tussauds of learning than it does with any living institution, and Catholic private schools are, in their majority, gaining new prestige – not because the French have suddenly become converted to the Catholicism of their fathers, but because they provide – at a price – a better education. Like every other Western nation, France is feeling its way uncertainly towards an educational system adapted to the social revolution it has undergone.

There are good schools in Britain – and not all of them are public schools. Numerous comprehensives have much to be proud of. The education dispensed in Northern Ireland is of exceptional quality – largely because it is still based on traditional teaching methods emphasising the importance of knowledge acquisition. Scotland, where the school system differs substantially from that in England and Wales (and where traditional teaching methods have also been maintained), can to a large extent serve as a model for the reformers. In particular, 'Community Schools' – immersed as they are in their local communities and maintaining close links with local industries and professional bodies – could well foreshadow the schools of the future. But perhaps these Community Schools – with their heavy reliance on ideas of self-discipline among the children – must abandon their most militant characteristics before their experience can be transposed to the educational system in Britain as a whole.

Ultimately, it is from the Baker reforms themselves that we must hope to see the much needed and decisive mutation in Britain's education. While accepting that a core of knowledge and skill must be imparted to every young person, it has created more flexible structures that could perhaps – with adequate funding – lead to the development of a diversified system of education, catering to the needs of a far broader spectrum of the nation's youth than is at present the case.

For the moment, the hope remains a faint if not impossible one. The education budget is not large enough to meet the tasks which Mrs Thatcher's governments set themselves. Far from leading the secondary school student to new perspectives, the present examination system closes the doors of the universities in the face of the great majority of school leavers, abandoning them without any kind of professional qualification to a world where unskilled labour is increasingly obsolete. A scattering of short training programmes is supposed to make up for this deficiency, but they are of benefit to only a small number of young people. They are both too specialized and of an insufficiently high level to train the kind of versatile, skilled labour-force increasingly required by industries that are themselves having to change constantly in order to survive.

Diversification does not imply a hierarchy from the most to the least gifted; on the contrary, it provides the key to a multitude of doors. It has always been the strong point of the English pedagogic tradition that it has understood and appreciated the individuality of every student, and it is ironic that this tradition has flourished within a system that has justly been accused of neglecting the non-academic majority of its pupils. Is there any reason why this flexible English approach should not be extended to the choice of the best kind of school for a particular kind of student?

Public alias Private Schools

On May 29, 1990, Queen Elizabeth II was invited to Eton to celebrate the 550th anniversary of the famous school founded by Henry VI. One thousand two hundred and seventy Etonians, wearing their traditional uniform, heard the sovereign telling them once more what they were already quite convinced of: that Eton is unique, and that its reputation is second to none.

A year earlier, almost to the day, John Rae, former headmaster of Westminster School, was recommending that Eton, Harrow, Winchester and Westminster be turned into state schools because of the 'malign spell' which their insolent élitism placed on the rest of the educational system. But during the past ten years the percentage of students in public schools has increased from 5.8 to seven per cent. Theoretically, independent schools can ignore the National Curriculum, but in practice they have to take account of it, as well as the particular requirements of the major universities which will take in a large proportion of their students.

Lord Soames, Ambassador in Paris during the period of

estrangement between Britain and Gaullist France, and later Governor in charge of preparing Rhodesia for a perilous independence, attributed his great adaptability to the education he had received at Eton. 'I think that Eton in particular dispenses a certain *savoir-faire* in the world which no other school, in my opinion, not even one of the other "sacred nine"* can teach . . . Not so much *savoir-faire* as *savoir-vivre* – a unique grace in the relations one has with other people. I think it is Eton's secret. I don't know how it's done, but it is done . . . In the past it was Eton's function to prepare young gentlemen for the job of governing the colonies, and to teach them how to feel at ease with anyone.'

While condemning public schools on principle, the old Etonian and left-wing philanthropist, Ben Whitaker, has quite good memories of his old school. It was a place where one's individuality was respected. Like all his contemporaries, he had a room of his own and got involved in many extracurricular activities. 'Eton,' he admits, 'is much less conformist than the other public schools. It instilled extraordinary self-confidence into one – a self-confidence to last a lifetime.' But the boys prided themselves on being anti-intellectual. It was good form to despise or ignore the industrial world. As for women, one merely expressed a vague antipathy for them. 'Perhaps,' he suggests, 'it was the reaction of sons against mothers who had separated themselves from their children without a qualm.'

The great pride of these schools – called 'public' at the time of their creation in the Middle Ages to differentiate them from family education dispensed by a private tutor in the home – is their ancient origin. *King's School*, in Canterbury, first opened its doors around the year 598. The spirit which still animates them, and which – thanks to them – has spread throughout the

---

* The nine most ancient and most prestigious public schools in the United Kingdom. *Winchester College*, the eldest of the sacred nine, was founded in 1382, *Eton College* in 1440, *St Paul's School* (a day school) in 1509, *Shrewsbury School* in 1552, *Westminster School* in 1560, *Merchant Taylors School* (also a day school) in 1561, *Rugby School* in 1567, *Harrow School* in 1571, and *Charterhouse* in 1611.

English school system, originates in the thinking of a number of nineteenth-century educators, most notably Thomas Arnold, headmaster of *Rugby* who summarised good education in three precepts: fostering religious and moral principles in children, training them to behave as gentlemen, and finally, developing their intellect.

While being a repository of tradition, public schools also encouraged that constant social osmosis which has always been the strength of the British class system. Although difficult of access, they never refused entry to the children of success. On the contrary, they were the sovereign instrument of their integration. They helped a small but continuous stream of children to lose the accent that revealed their embarrassing family origins, substituting it for a good accent, the essential passport of a gentleman.

In 1923, when Stanley Baldwin was asked by King George V to form a government, his first thought was that he should make it 'a government of which Harrow would not be ashamed' – a wish that he fulfilled, since six of his cabinet ministers were indeed old Harrovians. For the past twenty years or more, in the successive versions of his *The Anatomy of Britain* and finally in *The Changing Anatomy of Britain*, published in 1982, Anthony Sampson has been devoting himself to the task of unmasking the old boys who occupy the top places in the economic, political, administrative and judicial spheres of British life. His revelations are impressive, but with time have become less convincing – not only because the three last Conservative Prime Ministers, Edward Heath, Margaret Thatcher and John Major are products of state education, but also because public schools themselves have been undergoing a revolution which is not yet complete. So thoroughly have they been castigated by sociologists, politicians and writers that they have been obliged to reform. Aristocracy is taking a back seat to meritocracy. No doubt privilege still makes discreet appearances, but the time is past when it was enough to be the son of an old boy, automatically enrolled from birth, to be granted a place at his father's school, rather as one might receive an inheritance. Enrolment is now merely a preliminary and carries with it no guarantees.

Today, as a result of these changes, only five per cent of the students at Westminster are children of former pupils, and in the majority of public schools the proportion does not exceed a quarter. Only at Eton does it rise to half, and to a third at the major Catholic public schools: the Jesuits at Stonyhurst, and the Benedictines at Ampleforth and Downside. This democratisation has its limits. Whereas in comprehensive schools only one in five pupils are from the upper-middle class or above, this proportion increases to four out of five in the public schools. Nonetheless, academic excellence is the criterion by which public schools now wish to be judged. Indeed, though they provide only seven per cent of secondary school education, they continue to account for just under half the student population at Oxford and Cambridge.

The religion of sport has not explicitly been called into question by public schools, but it features less prominently in their canon of values. Their syllabuses have also changed dramatically. Just after the First World War, more than seventy per cent of public school teachers were in the humanities. Even today, there are very few headmasters who come from a scientific background. But at Winchester, the place once occupied by Latin has now been taken by mathematics. And with a kind of reverse snobbery, this grand old school congratulated itself in 1982, when for the first time it sent more of its pupils to the redbrick universities than to Oxford or Cambridge.

During the past forty years (as indeed, throughout most of their history), the most audacious educational innovations have been introduced in the public schools before being taken up by the state sector. The notion of discipline, in particular, has radically changed over the last ten years. Until the fateful year of 1968 – less heated in Britain than in France, but punctuated by the same kind of protests – the country's future élite was certainly not pampered at school. Corporal punishment itself was bad enough, but worse than that, brutality was erected into a principle, and conformity stubbornly enforced. All were impartially subjected to ridicule for physical weakness, independence of thought or the appearance of sensitivity.

Such was the training of those lost generations of empire builders so necessary to the nation – but it was achieved at the cost of festering humiliations, scars and infirmities that were all the more painful for being invisible and inadmissible. Fagging, the right of older boys to beat the young ones, the generous administration of the cane for all infringements of the elaborate rules governing this world cut off from the world, the daily obligation to attend religious service, the emphasis on sport to the detriment of all intellectual or artistic expression (judged to be feminine and therefore contemptible), enforced military training in the cadet corps – the catalogue is repellent.

But this litany of obligations and prejudices gives a distorted picture of day to day life. The glorification of sport was also the guarantee of a healthy way of life. Camaraderie and a sense of honour and of responsibility were not necessarily the expression of latent homosexuality or of class prejudice. The academic excellence of the masters offered gifted pupils an excellent opportunity for development. An architecture laden with the symbols of centuries past, the accumulation of traditions whose emotive power easily made up for the constraints, colours, style, a web of loyalties, a tradition of rules transgressed: all these were to embed themselves forever in the memories of those who had experienced them.

It was precisely these 'Victorian' values (so prized by Mrs Thatcher) that the British youth of the late 1960s were rejecting. They refused to sing hymns in chapel, to play rugby in the cold, to carry out their supervisory duties as prefects – demonstrations of discontent were on the increase. Though the protests never became very widespread, the shock was sufficient to encourage headmasters (already anxious about rapidly rising labour costs and the need to charge correspondingly high fees) to begin reforming their schools.

Even in schools where corporal punishment was not abolished, it was much less frequently used. Fagging began to disappear (though Eton did not finally abolish it until 1980). Again at Eton, although Daily Service was retained, older pupils were given the choice of attending an 'alternative assembly'. Nonetheless, frequent contacts between children and their parents during the school year were discouraged. Today certain schools allow their pupils to return home every weekend from Friday afternoon to

Sunday evening, and the majority authorise two or three family weekends at term. It is also no longer compulsory nowadays to join the cadet corps. Many schools have relinquished the uniform, at least for the older pupils, or have limited the hours and occasions when it must be worn. And it is now possible for a boy to prefer athletics or tennis, or even drama or music to team games. The most significant of these varied reforms has been the admission of girls to about a hundred of the country's public schools, including Charterhouse, Marlborough, Rugby, Uppingham and Westminster. The majority accept them only in the sixth form, though a few take girls of all ages. In either case, headmasters agree that the move has been a success.

But despite so many changes, there remains a corpus of traditions – a style, a tone proper to each public school – which survives all innovation. The Eton schoolboy, in his Victorian gentleman's dress with high starched collar and tails, is fully conscious of his pedigree, and revels in the slang (incomprehensible to any outsider – let alone a Frenchman) that distinguishes him from any other kind of schoolboy. And what can we make of the Eton Wall Game – that extraordinary pastime involving a wall, a ball, a tree, a garden gate and a few rules with the most mysterious of objectives?

Measured out with care, the injection into the public school system of a few foreigners and a number of bright children of modest background with state-assisted scholarships, does not seem to have broken this mould of exclusive conformity. And where are the iconoclasts who would wish to do so? It is true that when Neil Kinnock was Shadow Education Secretary, before becoming Leader of the Labour Party, he suggested that Eton should be closed and its buildings used to house Vietnamese refugees. But is he likely to carry out this project as Prime Minister, and would his majority follow him if he did?

Selection without Shame

It is regrettable but quite natural that, with their great beauty, Oxford and Cambridge, those two coquettes who for the past seven hundred years have been vying for the courtship of the nation's youth, should have seen their identities merge under a name more suited to a brand of canned soup – the hybrid, neatly packaged name of 'Oxbridge'.

That beauty is evenly shared between them, and is immediately apparent to the newcomer, but its secret will be revealed only gradually to the casual visitor. And it will be fully perceived only by those who, year after year, have worked and lazed in splendid colleges, read or dreamed in wood-panelled libraries, eaten the same execrable food in halls of noble proportions, and seen the light change across quadrangles and courts. It is primarily this beauty which bestows such an exclusive privilege on members of the two universities. One day, perhaps, all students in Britain will benefit from a comparably good education with equally qualified teachers, but the students of Oxford and Cambridge will always possess an extraordinary advantage – the benefit of that particular harmony and beauty which is shared by the two universities, yet which makes them so visibly different from each other.

Buried in an industrial agglomeration, a diamond in a bucket of coal, a refuge offered by the past to the future, at first sight the University of Oxford appears to be on the defensive. But one only has to see the cyclists, with their ruffled hair and scarves blowing in the wind like battle standards, for that impression to disappear. Oxford remains a bastion of impenitent youth.

The city of Cambridge barely extends beyond the limits of the university. It lies like a cat in a basket, its back curled against the comfortable curve of the river, enjoying the sun and shade as they play between the branches of the trees and through the stained-glass windows of the chapels, occasionally stretching indolently on the lawn or following the slow trajectory of a cricket ball.

The alliance of the monumental with the discreet constitutes Oxford's greatest charm. You can walk past the gate of New College ten times without noticing it, despite the handsome Renaissance statues which dominate it. Once inside the college, carry on until you reach the garden. Nestling within a curved fragment of medieval city wall, its garland of flowers welcomes you all the year round. It gives colour to the coldest and greyest of November mornings, and the most timid spring is transformed into precocious summer by its magic. From New College a few paces takes you into the great, rectangular Queen's College quadrangle with its chapel and hall designed by Christopher Wren. The architect of St Paul's, who had a genius for simplicity, was no simple genius. His art in marrying classical buildings with Oxford's Gothic profusion has a scholarly verve in which one can detect echoes of Italy.

In Cambridge Wren's genius was to express itself, if not more perfectly (the Sheldonian Theatre in Oxford is one of his most accomplished works), at any rate more freely. The chapel of Emmanuel College with its arcade is a triumph of *trompe-l'oeil* and *chiaroscuro* which does full justice to those Neapolitan architects who were such masters at offering the eye an open perspective within a closed space. James Gibbs does not have Wren's grandeur, but could we today conceive of Oxford, or of the Bodleian library without the adjacent cupola of the Radcliffe Camera?

Nowhere is the past created anew every day as successfully as it is in Oxford and Cambridge. Architecture is only one of the elements of this spell; sounds contribute to it even more suggestively – the 101 strokes sounded each evening at five past nine precisely by 'Great Tom', the six-and-a-half ton bell which, as Max Beerbohm wrote, is indeed 'the solemn and plangent token of Oxford's perpetuity', tirelessly repeating 'All's as it was, all's as it will be'. From the top of Magdalen Tower, a seventeenth-century eucharist hymn is clearly heard, at six o'clock, in the silence of the spring morning. Since its composition in the seventeenth century, it has been sung by the College's choristers every year at the same time, on the first of May. Or more prosaically, there is the trumpet which calls members of Queen's College to dinner every evening.

On this Christmas Eve, the choristers of King's (six boys and four men) are lined up in the stalls of the College chapel, wearing cassock and surplice. The service is attended as it is every year by the Provost, by College fellows wearing gowns and fur-lined hoods, and by a few guests from Cambridge and elsewhere. As we file out of the chapel, I see them again, my small choristers in their pin-striped trousers, tail-coats and black top hats. They are a tiny élite, selected from all over the country for these prestigious choral scholarships, and they are looked after entirely by King's, which houses, feeds, dresses and educates them, and in addition teaches them music.

The traditional annual service at King's, consisting of the nine lessons of Advent interspersed with popular Christmas carols, goes back only to 1918. Its introduction by the then dean, Eric Milner-White, was intended to revive the languishing Anglican liturgy. Since then colleges and parishes throughout England have adopted it, and the BBC has turned it into a national institution, transmitting the service every year since its inception in 1928, with the single exception of 1929. Even during the Second World War – at a time when the chapel's stained-glass windows had been removed because of the danger of German bombs, and the very name of the college was not mentioned on the radio for security reasons – the British people were still able to listen to their favourite service and believe that, in spite of everything, life continued 'as before'.

Never mind the age of a tradition, what gives it pedigree and assures its durability is success. Life in England, surely, is founded on respect for precedent; English wisdom consists in constantly referring to it, rather than venturing unnecessarily into the dangerous realm of innovation. Yet it would be a gross distortion to picture the flower of Britain's youth abandoning itself complacently to the charms of an outdated pantomime. The script is theirs and they are masters of the art of improvising. It is their inalienable privilege to exploit or challenge established customs, to subvert or ignore them, and to invent new ones which suit them better. Here, as in the public schools, there are rules which govern the art of transgressing, but the code is unwritten. It is the tribal nature of Oxbridge which, today more than ever, really distinguishes it from all other universities in Great Britain, or indeed in the world. Like all tribal communities, it worships its ancestors and has its own laws, rites and taboos, as well as its own places of refuge and channels of communication (for Michael McCrum, master of Corpus Christi, Cambridge, the college 'staircase' is a crucial factor in the creation of friendships).

Each college has its own character – one is rich, another poor, each has a particular smell and dimension. Although most colleges are no longer able to provide accommodation for everyone, they still require first year students to live in – just long enough for them to be impregnated with the spirit of their particular institution. In subsequent years those same students usually move into a flat or house where they share domestic expenses with four or five friends, but the umbilical tie with the college is not severed. They continue to receive most of their mail in college; they rely on the college porter to receive or give out messages; they relax in the college bar, join the college History or Philatelic Society; and, in Oxford, they turn to their former scout (the cleaner in charge of their former 'staircase') to provide them with a second-hand gown for examinations.

With every new generation of students, a college's style and individuality renews itself. Nonetheless, the stiff selection of all newcomers ensures some continuity, and for that reason the interview is a key element in the selection process. It reveals a candidate's personality and general culture, and shows whether he possesses curiosity and a sense of humour. This method of selection is defended by a former student from Magdalen College, Oxford (now an Ambassador known for his caustic humour) on the grounds that it makes it possible to spot qualities – such as a sturdy character or truly free imagination – which are not revealed in examination results. The important thing, he adds, is not to miss the most gifted twenty-five per cent. As for the remaining seventy-five per cent, does it matter exactly how they are selected? They will disappear noiselessly into the anonymity of an honourable career.

The cornerstone of the college is the tutor at Oxford and the supervisor at Cambridge. Oxbridge has never known the kind of solemn and autocratic methods of teaching which are still prevalent in France despite the 1968 student revolt. Unlike his French counterpart, the student at Oxford or Cambridge can choose the lectures that interest him, and can enter into an active dialogue with his supervisor with whom he regularly discusses his work. The quality or insufficiency of these discussions can spark new enthusiasms or drown incipient interests. Some students claim that the supervisor is a myth, a ghost or a stuffed dummy. Others merely hope that he will not snore too loudly during their next meeting. Though the tutorial system is not exclusive to Oxford and Cambridge, no other British university seems to have taken it so much to heart. It is a concrete symbol of that extraordinary mixture of rigour and informality which is the very air one breathes in Oxbridge.

Yet in this climate of enlightened amateurism, the Cambridge Medical Research Council molecular biology laboratory has – on its own – won more Nobel prizes than any other European country. Thirty years after their historical discovery of the molecular structure of deoxyribonucleic acid (DNA), the transmitter of inherited characteristics, the American James Watson and the Englishman Francis Crick are both working separately in the United States. But in 1953, Cambridge was surely the only place where a twenty-five-year-old zoologist, fresh from his doctorate, and a thirty-six-year-old physicist who was bored with his discipline, would have been given the opportunity to work together on a project in biochemistry – a discipline neither of them knew anything about – simply because they were excited by an idea.

There is undoubtedly a Trinity College snobbery. Two Kings, Edward VII and George VI, and a future King, the present Prince of Wales, all pursued undistinguished student careers at the famous Cambridge College. But Trinity also trained one of the greatest scientific geniuses of all time, Isaac Newton, as well as Prime Ministers (Balfour, Nehru), poets (Byron and Tennyson) and philosophers (Francis Bacon, Wittgenstein, Bertrand Russell). Like all contemporary luxuries, this sophisticated and expensive education is available to students from any kind of background. But the background it provides is of the most exclusive. It is understandable that moralists should become indignant about a system which so successfully co-opts an élite and excludes the majority.

The Drive against the Universities
In February 1983, for the first time since the beginning of the century, a Royal Charter granted the status of university to a private establishment. This was all the more remarkable since, in general, higher education was undergoing a painful phase of

retrenchment. Founded by the eminent Conservative intellectual, Lord Beloff, University College, Buckingham, sells a thorough preparation for the world of business. About half the students are foreigners, and all are wealthy. For some, the college – which offered the outstanding advantage of not asking for a single penny of subsidy from the State – seemed to represent the advance guard of the revolution undertaken by Mrs Thatcher's third Government with the aim of providing British society with the agents of modernisation. For others it was a Trojan horse, dedicated to the destruction of the Welfare State's educational system. Whatever the case, it symbolised the advent of that new class which places profit above knowledge, its own skills above any title or honour, and for whom Mrs Thatcher was both the herald and the heroine.

Until the beginning of the nineteenth century when London, Durham and Belfast universities were created, there were only two universities in the whole of England (Oxford and Cambridge, founded in the twelfth and thirteenth centuries respectively), and four universities in Scotland – St Andrews, Glasgow, Aberdeen and Edinburgh, founded in the fifteenth and sixteenth centuries. Between 1850 and 1950, fifteen new 'redbrick' universities were created to service the egalitarian society which was being forged by the Welfare State. In 1963, for the first time, an official document (The Robbins Report) unequivocally formulated the objective of offering some kind of higher education to 'all those who are qualified by ability and attainment to pursue it, and who wish to do so'. The next ten years were to see the creation of eighteen new universities – almost as many as had been founded in Great Britain during the preceding three centuries.

In spite (or maybe because) of their popular character – and with certain notable exceptions – the countless technical colleges and crowded polytechnics are considered by many to be mere excrescences in the British higher educational system. Polytechnics were created by the Labour Party in the 1960s with the aim of providing advanced technical education and training, and so filling a gap left by universities which had always been reluctant to cooperate with industry. As Anthony Crosland (then Secretary of State for Education) made clear when he launched the idea of polytechnics in 1965, they were also meant to transform the cultural attitudes of the young. 'Let us move away from our snobbish, caste-ridden obsessions with university status,' he urged.

Today there are thirty polytechnics in England and Wales, many of which are equal in size to universities. Their courses are often excellent, providing a vocational education with heavy emphasis on science and technology and strong links with industry. Indeed, it is polytechnics and not universities that have led growth in higher education over the past decade. Between 1979–80 and 1987–88 the number of full-time polytechnic students rose by thirty-seven per cent, while admissions to universities went up by only six per cent. Polytechnics now have the largest share of the country's 580,000 students, and produce about a third of all graduates. Optimists, such as John Stoddart, chairman of the Committee of Directors of Polytechnics until September 1991, feel confident about the role of these institutions in the higher educational system, and reject the idea of rechristening them as universities with the aim of boosting their status. 'Some universities in Britain do things we don't, such as running medical or veterinary schools,' he explains, 'and good luck to them. We *are* universities in the European sense, but the issue of our formal name is not of the first importance.' Despite a chronic and increasing shortage of funds, he sees polytechnics in the future as growing in status and public recognition.

Nonetheless, the problem of status remains a very real one. A pamphlet published in March 1990 by the Association of Polytechnic Teachers complained that many people thought polytechnic business was retaken GCSEs rather than degrees, while 'even MPs' seemed unaware of their research activities. As in the primary and secondary school sectors, the enthusiasm of politicians and educationalists was destined to come up against social obstacles they had not anticipated. Even nowadays – though their job prospects have improved considerably in comparison with ten years ago – polytechnic graduates often emerge from their studies into a social limbo. Children of the middle classes shamefacedly avoid mention of the source of their degree, while the sons and daughters of factory hands and of lower-middle-class white-collar workers receive an education which enables them to measure the distance they have travelled from their fathers, and peer over the abyss which separates them from the truly privileged.

As I was able to observe most clearly in the hard hit industrial towns of the North, the reaction of such young people is often to idealize their working-class roots, while themselves becoming more radical. Like their parents, they look to the Labour Party for an answer to their frustration. But their choice is more sentimental than political, and only the left wing of the Party speaks in the language they expect to hear. A few of them join the Communist Party, but they rarely become die-hard Marxists or Trotskyites. Their quasi-mystical condemnation of injustice is more reminiscent of a seventeenth-century non-conformist sermon than it is of a lecture on dialectical materialism.

As for industrialists themselves, they long neglected the polytechnics entirely – not for fear of political contagion, as one might have expected, but because of their traditional contempt for any kind of technical education. Today, their attitudes are beginning to change, and they recognize the merits of certain degrees from the more prestigious establishments. Though the roads from the polytechnics do not automatically lead to the gate of success, they are no longer inevitably dead ends.

The Conservative ideology of meritocracy has dominated the educational debate of the eighties, just as the ideology of the social contract had coloured the fifties and sixties. A persistent loyalty to the ideal of academic freedom, however, makes it impossible to make any simple predictions about the future of higher education. The only thing that is almost certain is that decentralisation (the virtues of which accord so closely with the British spirit) will be defended tooth and nail by resolutely individualistic universities.

The years of growth, often disorderly but rich in invention and hope, have given way to the era of cut-backs and criticism. Nonetheless, the great medieval universities, their nineteenth-century heirs and the best of their junior partners strive to maintain their standards despite continuing pressure on resources. And while Oxford and Cambridge are still confident of attracting the finest specimens of the nation's youth, Durham, Bristol, York,

Southampton, Exeter, St Andrews, Edinburgh and a few others carefully select those who are most likely to benefit from their care, in the hope of challenging the supremacy of their elder sisters.

In his inaugural address as Chancellor of Bristol University in May 1989, Sir Jeremy Morse emphasized the importance of challenging the dominance of Oxford and Cambridge in the university world, and of London in government. 'I can't think of anywhere better to challenge both dominances than this city of Bristol, and this University,' he said.

The selection of students destined for university is more confused and more brutal in Britain than it is in other European countries, but the vast majority of those who are given a university place will come out with a degree at the end of three or four years. Although the pecking order among universities encourages healthy competition, it also lends undue glamour to certain degrees and diplomas, while others of equal merit are neglected. Yet how can one cure the disease without killing the patient? Thirty years ago the question was how to increase the number of students; today, with falling electoral rolls, the problem is one of contraction. An analysis of the Japanese miracle, and the proximity of 1992, led Mrs Thatcher's third Government to a re-examination of the social and economic goals of education. Universities were encouraged to finance themselves and to strike up deals with industry, thus placing themselves in a position to prepare the young of ambition for a system of universal competition such as Thatcherite Conservatives dreamt of. As for the students – the future agents of the market economy – they were encouraged to take out loans to pay for an increasing proportion of their own education, thus not only lightening the burden on the tax-payer, but also preparing themselves to face a world where higher education is no longer the privilege of wealthy dilettantes, but has become the ultimate weapon for economic development.

Degrees of Failure
I clearly remember a journey I took in 1980 to the East London suburb of Barking. Alone in my tube carriage, I was looking out of

the window at the dismal urban landscape with its waste ground, its abandoned factories and its interminable streets of identical terraced houses with pocket-handkerchief gardens, which could not make them any brighter on this early March morning. Three stops before my destination, a wan adolescent carrying a vast radio stepped inside. He had that muddy complexion which comes of a diet based on sandwiches, sweets and a variety of inexpensive fizzy drinks. He was wearing blue jeans and was decked out in a pin-striped jacket two sizes too large for him. His bleached hair was shaped into a glutinous crest at the top of his skull. Politely he tried to find out which of several cassettes of pop music I preferred, then hesitantly enquired who I was. Seating himself next to me, he asked, 'What are you doing here? I've got a good idea, come with me and I'll show you the good spots of East Ham.'

I couldn't make it? Shame. I was French. I didn't have any friends? As if to prove his good intentions, he told me his name – Jerry. I asked him what he did in life. He said he was finishing school in July, but he had not been going since Easter. What was the point? His girlfriend's parents were loaded. Her mother ran the cloakroom in some fancy Mayfair club and got masses of tips. Stepping out of the carriage, he held the automatic door open with his foot and turned towards me, his eyes half shut and a faint smile on his lips: 'No joke, you can't live without friends. Come on . . .' It was not until he had left that I became aware of the smell which was still floating in the carriage. It was the smell of glue – glue which my young East Ham punk had been sniffing. This poor youngster's drug had introduced him to a paradise of woolly benevolence and sweetness which he had tried to share with me.

For Jerry and many like him, then as now, school is not an open road leading to exams and university, nor to any other kind of professional training. It is more like an interminable moving walkway which for years they have been treading in the wrong direction. What strikes me however, not only about Jerry but about others I have met since, is a certain mental and emotional vacancy which – according to one's mood – can be taken for indifference, sluggishness, resignation or pessimism, but which is occasionally overtaken by a sudden craze for some singer or a new fashion in clothes, for the anti-nuclear campaign, a football club or Princess Diana, or the possibility of getting work as a car washer . . .

It is sometimes difficult to remember those other adolescents, so vigorous and sometimes so charming, whom we saw only yesterday (or was it some centuries ago?) running in the park or playing cricket on the green in their uniform of yesteryear. They have matured and developed behind the high walls of their medieval universities; or on some modern campus, they have acquired a speciality, some sound professional training; they live on a different planet from that of the school leavers. Their future is inscribed in an elegant trajectory. The future of the school leaver is so uncertain that he is included in the official statistics under that name, which defines him like that of 'student' or 'plumber'. In 1988 there were some 650,000 school leavers, of whom about two-thirds were from working-class backgrounds, and nearly half were unemployed. They constitute a new class, but despite its youth, this class is already frozen in its past and its lack of qualifications.

This army of unqualified youngsters has a poor reputation: they are supposed to be lazy, undisciplined and immoral and to indulge in violence and excesses such as alcohol and drugs. They are accused of all kinds of crime, from pickpocketing to mugging, robbery and car theft. Public opinion demands more policing and harsher punishments to cope with this nebulous threat from potential delinquents, whether real or imaginary. Yet when they manage to get beyond the barrier of monosyllables which separates them from language, my young interviewees are docile, and reveal themselves to be surprisingly yielding when confronted with the rules and taboos which they are so often accused of transgressing. They are fatalistic about unemployment (which for the young is not the castrating failure it is for the old, but is merely one of the routes to maturity), and indifferent about politics; they passively accept the most traditional of social codes. But they powder this insipid mixture with spices and colours which distinguish them from the youth of other countries. They have invented a softer kind of nihilism, one that is more cheerful, and perhaps more radical, and that they celebrate on singles, LPs and cassettes at the four corners of the world.

On the map of pop culture, Rome is to be found at Nashville, and Liverpool is the new Athens. Elvis Presley is a demi-God. The Beatles have been canonized by the new religion, while Pink Floyd and the Rolling Stones are apostles of the church which emanates from it. As is only right for such prestigious figures, their priests, their faithful and their imitators are still numerous. Every day their hagiography is enriched. There has not been a year when some British singer or musician has not succeeded in rising to the top ten of the American hit parade.

The hippy dreams of the sixties first gave way to the anarchic nihilism of the Punk revolution dominated by angry slogans from bands such as The Stranglers, The Clash, The Jam, and the angriest of them all, The Sex Pistols, whose album *Anarchy in the UK* set the tone for the whole punk movement. Then the eighties brought a smoother kind of hero, the fashion-conscious stars of bands like Eurythmics, Culture Club and Duran Duran. Boy George, in his peacock feathers and heavy black tresses, is perhaps yet another surprising avatar of the eccentric dandy, that figure who has always played such an important role in British history. No doubt the Punks and their rivals, the New Teds, the Mods, the Skinheads, the Neoromantics, the Soul-People, the Rude Boys, the Futurists or the Rockabillies owe more to Beau Brummel's shimmering waistcoats than they do to any working-class or revolutionary ideology.

Attracting attention is to them an end in itself. It is a mild provocation to parents and police, a talisman against the moroseness of the times, a rallying standard. In most cases, Punk & Co do not go any further. In spite of their war paint and the occasional escapade, in the main they conform. Their music – even the cries of revolt of West Indian reggae, or the more outrageous railings of marijuana smokers or cocaine sniffers – is not a challenge to society so much as it is a highly profitable consumer product, exported throughout the world, much to the satisfaction of the chancellor of the exchequer.

In 1990, Liverpool's prestige has faded somewhat, and Manchester, 'Madchester' – with its fashionable night clubs, The Hacienda,

Thunderdome and Conspiracy, and its star groups, New Order, Happy Mondays and The Smiths – is now the centre of attraction. But the United Kingdom has kept its lead in the pop universe. The production of pop video-clips and the insatiable hunger for new programmes created by American cable television are at the root of the fantastic success of British music in the United States. At the beginning of the eighties it already earned the mother country over 150 million dollars a year – more than four times the annual profits of the entire American record industry. Consequently, millions of young people, from Seattle·to Miami, continue to be influenced not only by the music but also by the lyrics and by the entire life-style of British youth today.

Brutal and Malevolent Louts

'We have always known that there were two Britains, one extraordinarily pleasant, inhabited by mild, tolerant, kindly people, the other utterly disgusting, inhabited by brutal and malevolent louts,' fulminates Auberon Waugh, son of Evelyn, and vitriolic columnist on the right-wing *Spectator*. On this occasion, his anger is provoked by events during the European cup final in Brussels on the 29th of May 1985, when English football fans ran riot, leading to the death of thirty-eight spectators – almost all of them Italian. For some time now, skinheads – who previously seemed more at home in the streets, or in one of the pubs in their territory – have been joining the hooligans on the football grounds. Because they wear the swastika or one of the SS symbols, and are sometimes members of the National Front, the popular press has not hesitated to print banner headlines on the growth of neo-Nazism in Britain.

The racism of skinheads is real enough, but it stems mainly from the desire to create an easily identifiable 'enemy'. In the absence of any blacks or Asians conveniently at hand, they will fall back on punks or New Mods. As for their tattoos and Nazi insignia, they wear them only as a way of frightening people. Many of them have never even heard of Hitler, and do not have the slightest notion of what National Socialism was. Since 1974, Peter Marsh and a group of researchers from Oxford Polytechnic have been studying the 'rules of disorder' surrounding the football pitch. For Marsh 'football is largely a ritualised display with the illusion of violence rather than actual violence'. It is true that the vandalism, the violence, even the murderous stampede in Brussels have the character of an accident, like driving too fast down a steep hill and miscalculating the last curve. If the road is empty, the driver will kill himself alone. But he may provoke the death of forty passengers in a passing tourist coach.

'When magistrates and the police refer to fans as animals and savages,' continues Peter Marsh, 'and when teachers are unwittingly engaged in the process of systematic humiliation and depersonalisation of pupils, order is threatened.' In strengthening security at football stadia, the police are either acting in ignorance of the internal hierarchy which operates among gangs of the young, or they are denying that it has any authority. In either case, they are disrupting the internal constraints which held the most aggressive elements in check, while simultaneously setting themselves up as targets for that aggression.

Violent crime is on the increase, and most worryingly, so is armed robbery. In London, more than half of those arrested by the police are under the age of twenty-one. The alienation of the young is paralleled by that of the adult population, who feel insecure and refuse to accept psychological explanations which they consider to be simply excuses. They are deaf to the argument that, historically, the criminal population has always been young. They do not want to hear of understanding, but only of repression. In Great Britain, as in every other industrial society, unemployment and the urban ghetto are the backdrop of juvenile delinquency. Since 1980, the problem of solvent abuse (most commonly glue) has been overtaken by an alarming growth in the consumption of hard drugs. Between 1980 and 1989, the number of registered addicts rose by more than six times – from 2,240 to 14,780 – and it is estimated that the real total figure is about five times greater still, and has grown proportionately over the same period. Perhaps even more worrying is the growth of alcoholism among the young. Seventy to ninety per cent of teenagers sent to Borstal offend again before they are eighteen.

Under his shaven skull, this skinhead still has the chubby cheeks of a child. For the past four months he has been waiting in jail for his case to come before the courts. 'I would never go out with a girl who sleeps around,' he tells me categorically. 'When we're in a gang, if one of us is attacked he's not alone. We wouldn't let him down . . . I get on with my family . . . I live at home . . . I had a fight with three blacks in a kebab house. There were two others waiting for me outside and they started shouting at me. My house is just down the road. So I went home to get an axe and some hammers. When I got back they were still there. They landed me this one. (He shows me a large bruise on his right cheek.) One of the guys had his stomach slit open. You could see his guts and we thought he was going to die. (He doesn't say that it was his blow of the axe that caused the damage.) So that's why I'm in for GBH (Grievous Bodily Harm). Here I've got a black mate . . . the screws, they're OK. They're doing their job.'

The young black later confirms his friendship with the skinhead, whom he considers to be a bit mad. 'They beat up guys and they don't even know why . . . but he's not a bad sort. Me, I'm in here for theft.'

He steals because it is more profitable than working. If he gets caught, that's his own stupid fault – he should have been more careful. He will stop when he is twenty-one and start up his own business.

Whether honest or delinquent, these young people seem to look at the world around them, at the rich and the law-abiding poor, with the same amused indulgence. From where do they draw these reserves of cheerful nonchalance which they carry with them through poverty, failure and crime? Perhaps they are fatalistic, rather than conformist, but they are nonetheless as imbued with the rules and customs of standard morality as if they respected it.

5

Leisure and the Consumer Industry

A Gentler Life-Style

Life is perhaps less comfortable in England than it is in France, but it is gentler; less comfortable because at every level of society the French today cannot do without small daily luxuries that the English either do not know or do not indulge in; gentler because a traditional friendliness, a combination of indifference and good will, softens the edges of everyday life; gentler also because contentment and resignation are more common than insistence and aggression.

Tensions exist in Britain as they do elsewhere; more than elsewhere perhaps, behind a reserved façade – family tensions as well as financial, political, social and racial ones. From the world of the penniless job-seeker to that of the goldfingered super-broker in the City, violence bares its teeth, but generally retreats before a moderate response. Some people complain that such moderation is pointless since it does not help to solve the problems of drug abuse, AIDS, physical insecurity, the conflict in Northern Ireland or any of the other ills of contemporary society. But thanks to this moderation, the everyday gestures of everyday life are performed without conflict. Somebody is reading his newspaper, somebody else potters around the house; the shopping gets done; holidays are saved for and booked long in advance; and if in the meantime, television and the pub do not provide sufficient distraction, there is Bingo or the bookmaker, a football match or a game of golf, or there is always the possibility of just going for a walk in the countryside. Time slips by unnoticed, and it is lovely simply to get home at the end of the day, to sit in a favourite armchair and finish reading that article which had to be abandoned in the morning for work.

Who will be the first to get up this morning? Will it be Pamela, who has to prepare breakfast for Judy and Vanessa, her older daughters, and for Walter, her thirteen-year-old son, before leaving the house to open the gift shop where she works part-time? Will it be John, her husband, who works as an accountant in a furniture factory in North London, an hour away by tube? Or will it be the children, who have to take the bus to school? In fact it is Walter, who for the past month has been getting up at six in the morning to do his newspaper delivery round.

It is against the law to employ children under the age of fourteen, even part-time. But Walter is tall for his age, and besides, enforcing this law would require prosecuting half the country's newsagents, not to mention depriving several thousand young Walters of an innocent source of pocket money, and – worst of all – depriving the British citizen of his inalienable right to receive the morning newspaper at home. This method of delivery (which extends to the Sunday newspapers with their copious illustrated supplements), perhaps explains why the British still have an insatiable appetite for newsprint despite being gorged with television. Only the Japanese read more newspapers than the British, although British consumption of newspapers per head has been steadily declining since the fifties. As well as delivering the news, the daily paper serves as a political identity card, a filter for pasteurised pornographic fantasies, a sporting Bible, a second-hand market-place and a job centre. Every advertising agency knows that the most persuasive of television campaigns is fully effective only if it is backed up by parallel advertisements in the appropriate newspaper.

At first sight the British housewife – the real one, the one who works only at home – looks like the twin of her continental sister. Yet she spends less time cooking than does her French counterpart, for whom the stove – on which lovingly prepared dishes simmer for hours – is the centre of the universe. Even Italian and German housewives take longer to prepare family meals than she does. She is also more careful with her money; she tends to have things repaired rather than replace them, and she still believes that a vacuum cleaner should live as long as she does. She is also more independent of her man, and even of her children. Though she leaves political militancy to a minority of activists, she is quite secure in her opinions. She is particularly conscious of her social responsibilities, and firmly believes that her personal efforts can make a difference. She may volunteer to drive the sick to hospital, help someone to obtain legal aid, fight for the consumer, and champion the rights of dogs, flowers, tramps, homosexuals – or even deprived children, though she may have little time to fuss over her own at home. She was the pioneer and remains the patron of all good causes, without waiting for an unimaginative state apparatus to step in. Whether she is defending peace, natural child-birth, or single-parent families, she will always look to her fellow women for support in preference to the politicians, whom she distrusts. She is self-reliant and dislikes any institution over which she does not have direct control.

A People on the Move

John and Pamela are 'commuters', a word the British have borrowed from the Americans. The commuter is not defined by sex, face, or profession, but by mobility. Clustered around Great Britain's six sprawling urban centres, there lives a population on the move.

The railway was invented by the British. But though they are condemned to long hours on public transport, these migratory city dwellers have retained a strong – and usually platonic – faith in the bracing virtues of walking and cycling. Unlike the peoples of the Mediterranean, they make little use of mopeds or scooters. The big motorcycle – once the pride of British industry – is now Japanese, in Britain as elsewhere. The car is as much an object of passion for the British as it is for the French or the Italians, but the vocabulary of love is different. The French are perhaps even more chauvinist about their cars than they are about their cooking. They sulkily ignore even the most glamorous of the foreign beauties, preferring the discreet banality of a car that says nothing about their income. The Italians dream of lightning acceleration and of an engine that is as powerful as the car is small. If he is thrifty and

111

has a practical turn of mind, the British driver will certainly choose a German, French or Japanese model in preference to one made in the United Kingdom. But for the automobile romantic, nothing can compare with that limited edition convertible produced by some family-run factory in the heart of the English countryside, or that fifty-year-old model which gleams as brightly today as if it had come straight off the production line.

For me, all the romance of the railways in Britain is expressed by those two juxtaposed London stations: Saint Pancras, with its superb cast iron vault spanning seventy-three metres and overlooked by the Midland Hotel – a Gothic palace built by Sir George Gilbert Scott in 1865; and Kings Cross, one of the first great examples of modern architecture, built by Lewis Cubitt in 1852. Train spotters and miniature railway collectors cultivate this romance with passion. They fight for the preservation and restoration of small abandoned stations, or stretches of uneconomic narrow-gauge track with their old fashioned trains chugging through cosy or magnificent landscapes. They lovingly polish the heavy brass fittings of old locomotives and organise excursions through nostalgic puffs of white and black smoke, a world of steam and coal in half-mourning for the demise of a great industrial power.

This pious celebration of the railway's golden age is of small comfort to the exasperated traveller daily exposed to the chronic delays of dirty and outdated trains. Neglected tracks, overmanning, a productivity rate that is among the lowest in Europe, union resistance to any kind of innovation: according to Conservative doctrinaires, all the ills that afflict British Rail can be attributed to the familiar indifference of nationalised industries to the needs of the public. But history is more complicated than their simple vision allows. It was the Victorians, those model free-marketeers, who first sacrificed profitability and passenger comfort by indulging their bureaucratic passion for rules and regulations. On the other hand, by nationalising the railways after the Second World War, the Socialists made a paradoxically handsome present to the capitalist shareholders who were indemnified for their stake in a near-bankrupt enterprise.

Since then successive governments of the Left and the Right

have completely failed to formulate a coherent transport policy. Over the past ten years or more, while Switzerland, Germany and France improved their infrastructure with heavy subsidies to the national transport system, Margaret Thatcher set about systematically cutting state funding to British Rail and urging all the public transport enterprises to become more competitive and financially self-sufficient. But at the end of her tenure as Prime Minister, her policies had not transformed them into the vigorous and efficient services she envisaged. The Channel Tunnel agreement, including the proposal for a high speed train linking London and the continent, constituted one of the few notable initiatives in favour of the transport consumer in almost a century. Meanwhile the deficiencies of the system continue to cost the country dearly in lost time and frayed nerves, and recently two major accidents dramatically focused public attention on the questions surrounding the role and management of public transport: the Kings Cross underground fire in November 1987, which killed thirty-one people; and in December 1988, the Clapham Junction train crash, in which thirty-five people died.

Though the modernisation of the railway system in Britain has been a failure, its integration with the Greater London transport network is remarkably successful. Since its construction in 1863, the London tube has had the same size of track as the railways, and the two systems have always provided parallel and complementary services in the suburbs. By contrast, the Parisian population at the turn of the century was hemmed into the city boundaries by competition between the *métropolitain* and the great railway companies. The Parisian commuter had to wait until the 1960s before the Réseau Express Régional (commonly known as the RER) was built to provide a link between the suburbs and the city tube.

But time is beginning to take its toll on Europe's oldest underground system. Dirt, overcrowding and delays are now the passengers' daily lot. The lyrical interlacing of Hector Guimard's arches does not light up the subterranean corridors, as in Paris; no marble cathedrals welcome the passengers, Moscow-style. The rounded carriages slip, snake-like, into snug-fitting burrows. And when the clock strikes five, with shadows lengthening slowly over

London's green parks, the Londoner sheds his city skin and buries himself in his tube, riding through suburbs and industrial wastelands while dreaming of an English cottage garden.

Londoners mostly do their shopping by bus. These bright red buses are as beautiful as toys. You can see them everywhere, and travel in them anywhere. They even have the good grace to dress themselves in green for trips out of London when the shopping is done. But the foreign visitor should beware the bus queue: one step out of line and the native – normally so courteous – may enrich his vocabulary with one or two choice words which should be repeated only with care.

If there is a vehicle the entire world would do well to envy the British, it is the taxi, the real and only one, designed by Carbody – black, square, high-slung, with a baggage compartment next to the driver, and roomy enough to accommodate an Englishman and his top hat on the way to Ascot or to the Lord Mayor's banquet. Even if you are not wearing a top hat, you can enjoy the incomparable pleasure of stretching your legs while admiring the view out of the cab's large windows; there is plenty of space for all your parcels, and the driver calls you 'guv' – or 'love', if it is a woman – in the cockney accent which is London's song.

Over the years the taxi has prudently adopted a few modifications – diesel engine, automatic gears, electronic meter, central door locking; such have been its discreet concessions to modernisation. Refusing rather self-consciously to yield before the laws of aerodynamics, it has allowed itself to flirt with colour. Though the majority are still black, a significant number now sport fresh new coats of royal blue, burgundy, scarlet or bronze. And when the Carbody monopoly was finally broken by a competitor, Metrocab, the interlopers were very careful not to draw attention to themselves. The two rivals could be mistaken for twins.

The only characteristic that the British driver shares with his counterpart around the world, is that he believes himself to be the best. He makes a point of distrusting all foreigners behind the wheel, but he is particularly frightened of the French. He is more indulgent towards the Italians, whose alarming driving feats do not scandalise so much as astonish him. For their part, the Italians and the French accuse the British driver of having slow reflexes. It is true that in general, he does not treat pedestrians like objectionable vermin. He is usually as patient sitting in a traffic jam as he is standing in one of those queues that punctuate his everyday life; and British roads are among the safest in the world. Yet Britain was one of the last Western countries to introduce the compulsory wearing of safety belts, the fear of infringing individual liberties being for many years stronger than the fear of death.

For the British, the car is primarily a vehicle of escapism. But escapism, in the modern world, is a luxury. It is no coincidence that the British car industry created the Rolls Royce – that celestial chariot, as immortal as the Gods. One of the Sunday Times's regular classified pages is entirely devoted to listing new and second-hand Rolls Royces for sale, together with their equally exclusive Bentley cousins. Britain was one of the last countries to start making cars for the mass market, and found itself correspondingly ill-equipped to compete with foreign producers. Today, more than half the vehicles registered in Great Britain are built abroad.

Until a recent upturn, even the British luxury car had been losing its prestige and clientèle. But of all inventions, beauty is the most difficult to imitate – though it precludes neither commercial dynamism nor increased productivity. After a period of apparently terminal decline, Jaguar was nationalised, and sold back to the private sector once it had regained its strength. Unfortunately, this miraculous recovery did not prove sufficient to save Jaguar as an independent company, and in 1989 it was taken over by the multinational, Ford. Though the mystique of British-made luxury cars survives, its *cachet* is increasingly being appropriated and cannibalised by the giants of the car world, and the days of a truly British automobile industry are probably numbered – as indeed are those of all the national car firms in Europe. Cooperation, pacts and mergers spell the future of car manufacturing, and the time will soon come when some four or five multinationals dominate the entire world market.

Model Consumers

Apart from his regular trips to work, the British citizen – like any Westerner – rarely goes out of the house except to go shopping;

and during the past thirty years his purchasing power has been growing regularly. This progression has partially concealed from him the ever-greater distance between his standard of living and that of other developed countries. It has also blinded him to the regular increase in the number of the poor. Between 1979 and 1987 the number of people living on or below the supplementary benefit level increased from twelve to nineteen per cent of the population.

Yet again, the modest aspirations of this unimaginative consumer can be attributed to his acceptance of a social hierarchy which circumscribes the scope of his ambitions and lays down his behaviour. Whether he votes Conservative or Labour, he is neither a thorough-going capitalist, nor entirely a socialist; he considers birth and education to be so clearly superior to wealth (and so subtly preferable to merit) that he will applaud a duchess – since naturally she can do no wrong – for doing her shopping at Marks & Spencer, just like him, and for abandoning Bond Street to Arab sheiks and to Americans. For the same reason, he will feel that he is not entitled to cross the threshold of those shops which make their living as much by discouraing some as by encouraging others.

He is suspicious of provocative chic, except in the case of the young, who are allowed to be outrageous on the cheap. Luxury must be reasonable to make him fall – maybe because only then does it remind him of the Royal family. Even if he cannot afford to do his shopping at Harrods, he will go there occasionally to feast his eyes on its display of unostentatious prosperity; in this national monument (the most frequently visited in the whole of the United Kingdom), in this middle-class temple, lovers of discreet luxury can be agreeably tempted.

Back on earth, the average consumer prefers to shop in chain stores, whose familiar names immediately allow him to place their merchandise: at the bottom of the scale there is Woolworths; half way up lies Marks & Spencer, where quality and price are so well matched that it attracts customers from every sphere; W.H. Smith & Son serves as a glorified newsagent, stationers and record store all in one; Dixon and Curry provide audio-visual equipment; Sainsbury's and Tesco are kings of the food trade. In every town and every district, these commercial poles of attraction can be found. The majority take credit cards without demur – as they would need to in a country where there are more than twelve million Access cards and well above fifteen million Visa cards, making Britain the European champion of plastic credit and stamping the British as model consumers.

Even in areas such as stationery, printing and photocopying and beauty products, chain stores like Ryman and The Body Shop are increasingly taking over from the traditional independent retailer. They deck themselves out in easily identifiable colours, and are all immensely successful. Branded products of reliable quality and price are more attractive to the consumer than originality and variety.

By contrast, the giant French and American-style supermarket situated on the city's outskirts is a relative newcomer to the British scene. It was not until 1976 that the first of them was built at Brent Cross, in Hendon, and it was another ten years before the giant Metro Centre at Gateshead (still the largest at two million square feet) was opened. Since then three more Regional Shopping Centres have been completed (two of them in 1990), three are under construction, and a further eighteen are planned. High interest rates and the corresponding slow-down in retailing probably means that not all will actually be built in the near future – but these mercantile palaces continue to exert irresistible fascination. The dilapidation of the urban ghetto and the mediocrity of popular housing have endowed them with a magnetism quite separate from their commercial function. They are not just consumer paradises; the attractions of the superfluous would not be enought to keep the punter interested – what they provide in addition to material goods, is an escape into a fantasy world of splendour such as he could previously find only in great media spectacles, or in the reflected glory of the monarchy.

Beside the retailing giants, a web of small food shops, general stores and Asian newsagents have spread over every corner of every city, welcoming all comers at any time of the day. These rescuers of the forgetful and the disorganised are always there, whenever and wherever they are needed.

117

The average consumer is no less demanding for being un-adventurous. He expects efficient service with no frills, and wants to know exactly what he is being sold. When this tacit contract is broken, meek lambs turn into avenging wolves. The appearance of the magazine *Which?* some thirty years ago was to give these militant consumers a remarkable weapon with which to fight abuses of every kind. Initially, the magazine was run by a small group of idealists determined to clean up the marketplace. They worked from an abandoned garage, and wondered how they would manage to clear their £187 debts. By 1990, *Which?* had more than nine hundred thousand subscribers, and the Association for Consumer Research (descendant of the Consumers Association which created the magazine), had a turnover of more than forty-one million pounds, and an annual surplus (not a profit since the Association is a registered charity) of about ten million pounds. A few purists are offended by the commercial success of these consumer crusades. But the Association justifies its methods by the results, and public opinion backs it entirely.

Here once again, we can see the professional rigour of the amateur; it is perhaps the most spontaneous expression of that robust British individualism that relies neither on the State, nor on institutions and religions, nor even on God, but on personal effort alone. Only by self-help can the individual save himself and his community.

Hi-de-Hi!

Of all the numerous publications brought out by the Consumers Association, *Which Holiday?* is one of the most successful. For along with washing powders, video-recorders, cars and chocolate bars, holidays have become the ultimate consumer good.

No sooner have Christmas decorations and the New Year Alka-Seltzer been put away, than daily newspapers, colour supplements and television screens are invaded with images of blue skies, silvery sands, golden sunshine, cascades of happy laughter, the Pyramids with their camels, India with its Taj Mahal, Venetian gondolas . . . Holiday brochures flop through every letter box. The first day of the Harrods January sales is celebrated by Londoners with as much fervour as the Queen's official birthday, but the customers are no longer just interested in sheets and crockery. While hunting for bargains in the world's most famous shop, they may also drop into the Harrods travel agency where they will be offered a choice of holiday camps, lake-side hotels, mountain chalets and bungalows surrounded by palm trees. The major travel agencies compete with each other fiercely, offering incentives of every sort – free trips for firstcomers, discounts for latecomers, discounts for off-season travellers, special family rates, special youth rates, special old age rates. In the cold of January, Great Britain takes out an option on summer. The only losers are the small-scale tour operators who face increasing problems trying to match the prices of their giant competitors. Many are taken over by the larger companies, some fold altogether.

Until relatively recently, only the upper classes took their holidays on the other side of the Channel, while the majority of beaches at home (with the exception of a few smart resorts) were reserved for the working population. Blackpool, Scarborough, Bridlington in the North, and Eastbourne, Ramsgate, and Southend-on-Sea in the South, are factory towns just like Liverpool, Sheffield or Birmingham, but what they mass-produce is leisure. Theirs are the endless sea-fronts lined with cabins, striped tents and pedal-boats, and conscientiously festooned with multicoloured lights; the miniature Eiffel towers, the ferris wheels, the Sea View, Park and Marina hotels, the gaming halls and pornographic cine clubs, the bed and breakfasts and boarding houses; the Indian, Italian and Chinese restaurants, the fish and chips establishments, the wax museums, the clusters of souvenir shops, and – in the evenings – the sheds surmounted by fluorescent strip lights next to broken down hoardings. A little further on, there is emptiness – or so it seems at night. In the grey light of the morning rain, a garage emerges, a kitchen furniture factory, and a bit of wasteland just in front of the neighbouring town with its interminable sea-front, its cabins, striped tents and pedal-boats . . .

From 1936, the mandatory provision of paid holidays was to bring some festive colour to the greyness of chilly English resorts. And Billy Butlin, creator of the jolly holiday camps which bear his name, was to invent a rigid timetable for them. The war itself was a mere blip in the smooth growth curve of the Butlin's camp.

Skegness, Clacton-on-Sea, Filey: for thousands upon thousands of faithful Butliners, these names were synonymous with good health and schoolboy high spirits. Every Butlin's camp was divided into two 'houses' which were expected to compete with each other in a series of games and sporting contests, with prizes at the end. The Butlin's anthem began with the words: 'Now we're at Butlin's, Dear old Butlin's'; and the Butlin's day began every morning at seven forty-five with a song broadcast across the entire camp over powerful loud-speakers:

> Roll out of bed in the morning,
> With a great big smile and a good, good morning.

At the end of the day another song rang out: 'Good night campers!' Between the two, every hour of the day was organised into 'events' which were announced and exhaustively commented on by Radio Butlin. The 'Butlin Buddies' (also known as the 'Red Coats') wandered around the camp showing off muscles and good cheer, and gathered at meal times to greet each other with the famous 'Hi-de-Hi', to which the 'Happy Campers' invariably replied with a hearty 'Ho-de-Ho'. Once the holidays were over, the weekly *Butlin Times*, and the *Butlin's Physical Recreation and Social Club* both strove 'to stimulate and encourage the Butlin spirit amongst all members and to keep in touch with old campers'.

Butlin Camps have been the butt of endless jokes, and the television series *Hi-de-Hi* continues to exploit the inexhaustible comic vein they offer. But the '*Gentils Organisateurs*' and the '*Gentils Membres*' of the up-market *Club Meditérrannée* should pay homage to the 'Happy Campers' who were the first to clear the ground for the Elysian fields of collective leisure.

Even Yorkshire miners and Birmingham mechanics were finally seduced by the Mediterranean sun. In 1986, Butlin's began a general reconstruction and modernisation of its sites in order to tempt them back to the fold. But this marked the death of the old Butlin's camps, and their rebirth in another guise. Butlin's had been one of the last heirs of that religious and paternalistic capitalism which presided over the creation of the first workers' garden-cities. It was now abandoning optimism at any cost in favour of luxury at any price.

Voulez-Vous Jouer Avec Moi?

Apart from a short Easter break and the year-round escapades of the very rich and the retired, most holidays are bought in winter and consumed in summer. Dreams would not be quite enough to sustain one through the rest of the year, were it not for the astonishing variety of sports and games without which British society would collapse like a pack of cards.

'In *memoriam* English cricket which finally passed away at The Oval, 14th August, 1984, will be sadly missed. RSVP.' This obituary notice was published in *The Times* after the England team suffered an ignominious defeat at the hands of the West Indians. The very same words had been published in *The Times* almost exactly a century before, in 1882, to mourn an equally devastating defeat of the national team by the Australians. The remains of English cricket, the original obituary pursued, were to be incinerated and sent to Australia. No sooner said than done: cricket balls were solemnly burnt and their ashes placed inside an urn. Such are the origins of that most important of cricket tournaments, The Ashes, in which the English are still frequently defeated. No matter: defeat on the Commonwealth pitches spells victory for the Empire's erstwhile pupils, and – thanks to cricket – Britain can continue to observe her greatness. But English gentlemen now have better reason to mourn. They are witnessing the slow death of amateurism and fair play, once synonymous with cricket. As with so many other games, the financial motive is taking over. Matches are increasingly commercialised, and professional cricketers continue to play in South Africa against all political odds and in spite of violent protest – not for the sake of the game, but for the enormous sums of money involved.

A pub is not quite a pub if it does not offer its customers a board and a set of darts. While the rules have not changed, darts have been transformed by the advent of television – a rival turned ally, only the better to triumph over the spirit of the game. From being neglected in pubs for the sake of television, the game was to find its way on to the television screens; now well-known professionals are pitted against each other in public matches played for very high stakes. This transformation by television of a good-natured game into a professional competition of national proportions is even more spectacular in the case of snooker. Entire evenings are devoted to it on the small screen, and its heroes are showered with riches. Their love affairs, their whims, their tantrums and their spectacular successes have all become headline news in the popular press.

The time is long past when the pre-eminence of British tennis players seemed to be almost a law of nature. But though champions may be made at Roland-Garros or at Flushing Meadow, connoisseurs believe that only at Wimbledon can kings and queens be consecrated. But Wimbledon is not just the Mecca of tennis. To the south of the courts lies the Wimbledon croquet lawn; and surely no one would dare to suggest that the English have ever lost their supremacy in this game? Britain boasts more than a hundred croquet clubs, which organise some eighty annual tournaments, and every year about one hundred thousand croquet sets are sold. Scoffers are mere philistines – croquet is no mere light-weight entertainment for school girls; it offers opportunities for refinements of malice unsurpassed by any other game.

The royal regatta at Henley and the Oxford and Cambridge boat race both figure prominently in that calendar of events in which England celebrates itself according to a liturgy that is incomprehensible to all but the English. From the simple pleasure of punting down the Cam, to the rigours of tussling with a strong swell in a sailing boat off Cowes, the most anodyne and the most audacious of nautical pastimes are there to remind the English that water is their element. The Scots, who are equally proficient sailors, also possess rivers and lochs filled with trout and wild salmon. Fishermen from all over the world pay dearly for the privilege of raiding their stores – but nobody knows when the rivers will run dry.

On land, the British do not have the same passion for democratic massacre as the French, for whom the indiscriminate shooting of any kind of game is the annual confirmation that the Revolution did indeed strip the aristocracy of its cynegetic privileges. In Britain, shooting is an art with its own ethics and social conventions. Well-worn, comfortable clothes, healthy dogs and an immaculate gun are essential preliminaries for the aspiring shot. But he will be fully co-opted only if he manifests the requisite manners – prudence, courtesy and modesty. Grouse shooting requires a great deal of calm, an accurate eye and complete silence – which is no doubt why it is particularly favoured by British sportsmen, enemies of bluster and noise.

Deer stalking exists in Britain just as it does in France or in Germany, but for the British there is nothing to match the fox hunt. Over the past few years however, some enthusiasts have discovered an alternative quarry – the hunter himself. No sooner has the season begun, than packs of animal lovers gather together to plot the disruption of the day's sport. Sometimes the hunters win the day, the fox gets killed and his brush is added to their trophies. Occasionally victory for the pack saves the life of the fox. Some of the hunting fraternity go so far as to claim that their own lives are threatened by the fanaticism of the hunt-saboteurs, but their alarm is no doubt excessive. True, the saboteurs have succeeded in persuading the Labour party to include a ban on hunting in their manifesto. But French socialists had also sworn to put an end to the practice, only to go hastily back on their word when faced with popular protest. Aristocratic lovers of the hunt can rest easy then for, as in France, they have in effect opened their ranks to all social classes, from farmers and artisans to young city dwellers, and these newcomers would certainly add their voices to the battle cries against reform. Practitioners of the oldest sport in the world can also take comfort from seeing their opponents so excited by the scent of their blood. It little matters what the prey is, so long as the sport is good.

Boxing, athletics, horse-riding (the list could go on indefinitely) – at some point all these sports had to conform to a set of rules, and to find a style of their own. It was the British, well-known masters of fair play, who were to endow them with these rules. Today, falconers, pigeon-fanciers and similar exclusive fraternities constitute a world-wide commonwealth over which the British enjoy as little authority as they do over the other, but a great deal more prestige.

The art of breeding and racing greyhounds has been transplanted to the United States, but it remains an essentially Anglo-Irish affair. With his tiger-striped coat, crowned by a splash of white at the end of the tail, Ballyregan Bob was one of the most beautiful greyhounds of all time. When he did the impossible and ran, ears pricked, to his thirty-second consecutive victory, London and Dublin, forgetting their political differences, applauded in unison. Twenty years ago, greyhound racing attracted three times as many spectators as it does now, yet it remains one of Britain's most popular sports. Despite the closure of a number of venues in London because of the high value of land in the capital, there remains a total of eighty-eight tracks in Britain. Approximately four and a half million tickets are sold every year, providing the bulk of thirteen and a half million pounds of annual revenue for the tracks, while punters spend a further four hundred million pounds on bets.

'Do away with the trappings, and it would descend to the ordinary level.' Lord Abergavenny said so himself, at Royal Ascot one fine Sunday, and he surely should know since he was there as the Queen's representative. For the horse-lover, an invitation to the Royal enclosure during Ascot week is a unique opportunity to meet the flower of the equestrian world, from the monarch downwards. But for those who crave social recognition, it represents primarily the crowning of their success. Even more flattering perhaps, in that it is addressed to a tight circle of friends over the heads of social climbers, is a July invitation from the Duke of Richmond (direct descendant of King Charles II and his French mistress, Louise de Kéroualle), to the private dining room of the race course at Goodwood, which he owns. In any case, no outsider would know how to wear his straw boater with quite the smart casualness of the Goodwood *habitué*. Kingdom of the horse, capital of the jockey, home of the trainer, Newmarket lives only for its breeding stables and race courses. But for the past two hundred years, the most famous race in the world – the Derby – has been held at Epsom.

This society of initiates with all its money, its outdated etiquette and its elaborate social distinctions, has no more fervent supporter than the public at large, to whom its secrets will always be a closed book. But what do the members of the public care? The tickets they get from the bookmaker offer them a peep into paradise, and on a lucky day an obliging thoroughbred might open the gates for them. On the race course you can still find a few of those legendary bookmakers, dressed in checked jacket and beige bowler hat, who transmit messages to each other using their arms like semaphores over the heads of their clients. They have lost neither their cockney accent, nor their loquacity. But although bookmaking has not been turned into a state monopoly as it has in France, it has become concentrated in the hands of a small number of conglomerates specialising in leisure, bingo halls, hotels and tourism.

Luck too is a mass consumer good which the English, along with the Chinese, enjoy more feverishly than any other nation. Since the days when Phileas Fogg made his famous bet, it takes less time to travel round the world, but the number of punters has not decreased. The distance of a hare's leap, the stamina of a mare, the probability of an extra-terrestrial landing, the name of the next Miss World – so long as a hypothesis permits a minimum of two possible solutions, there is no bet that the bookmaker will consider too absurd to take on. Nonetheless, the wheel of fortune is less colourful than it used to be. While race courses and old fashioned bingo halls find it increasingly difficult to draw the public, casinos have become ever more popular since their legalisation in 1968. For some ten years after 1975 they were stuffed with petro-dollars, and they continue to attract big gamblers despite the fall in petrol revenue. Less wealthy punters get their kicks from the football pools or from the massive bingo competitions organised by the tabloid press. Meanwhile, the Government earns tens of millions of pounds in tax revenue from gaming machines in pubs and arcades.

Speaking in a surprising bass voice tinged with an English accent, the clown, Grock, used to address his public every evening at the circus with the same invitation: *'Voulez-vous jouer avec moi?'* To get the English to play, an invitation is hardly necessary. Or perhaps one should say that the English would not think it possible to refuse such an invitation. It is as if they were conscious of being protected from the violence inside them by the ritual enactment of combat in play; as if self-control and that famous 'fair play' (that is, the magical transmutation of defeat into another kind of victory) were alone sufficient to contain the excesses of an explosive temperament. Games impose a common discipline on all participants, whose egoism is restrained by the rules which they have freely agreed upon. The penalty inflicted on cheats is heavier than the humiliation of defeat. And so the indestructible individualism of the English is curbed, and their desire for power is harnessed to the good of the collectivity. But this playful apprenticeship to the laws of society also has its price. By taming violence and channelling the emotions, games inhibit darker impulses which would upset the harmonious development of socialisation – sensuality, sexual desire, and a certain kind of creative laziness that some might call day-dreaming and others would denounce as culpable self-indulgence.

The Latin, who has spent his childhood buried in his mother's skirts or exploring his sexuality with sisters and friends, preserves and nourishes within the depth of his soul a curiosity that games cannot satisfy. For him the attractions of intimacy are more compelling than the distractions of an active social life.

By contrast, the historical propensity of the English to separate themselves from their children, the development of the public school and the emergence of puritanism, crowned by Victorian prudery, have combined to create the ideal environment for a childhood robbed of sexuality and perfectly preserved in adulthood, where it remains intact till death. Play remains the adult child's refuge against the confusions of life. The particular violence which has developed around football matches, in England more than in any other country, is perhaps a determined, if unconscious, attempt to expose through provocation the conventions of play, and thus to restore to it the functions of initiation and ordeal. Perhaps the young hooligan who plays a kind of Russian roulette with the police is looking beyond fair play – in which he never really believed – for the genuine rules of the game of life.

6
Taboos

However intimately a foreigner may have come to know the country to which choice or necessity has brought him, there are two areas that almost always remain inaccessible to him: snobbery and sexuality.

The mystery of snobbery is more impenetrable and better defended than any personal or state secret. Every nation, every class, every caste, every clique delights in and tortures itself with its own brand of snobbery. The English alone are at once the active agents, the consenting victims and the guardians of a snobbery that is both universal and yet so particular that any attempt at defining it is in itself an admission of crass ignorance. It is prudent therefore not to venture into such treacherous terrain, with all its inaccessible delights, nor to expose oneself to profound humiliation or countless small reprisals; better to confine one's adventures to the exploration of that other mysterious province – sexuality. And forgetting, for a moment, the complexities of Scottish puritanism or Irish Catholicism, let us merely attempt to follow in the more or less visible tracks of the English libido and its avowed or repressed desires.

Like snobbery itself – the irrefutable expression of an inscrutable hierarchy – sexuality has its source in the deepest and most vital recesses of one's being. Although it is intimately tied up with the survival of the individual and of the species, with the defence of family and territory, with the organisation, protection and development of personal and collective interests, it remains the most cerebral of activities. To speak of sexuality is to speak of the imagination. It is impossible to gain any intuition about the

127

sexuality of another before one has understood and accepted one's own. But from generation to generation, this indispensable understanding has been replaced by the creation of stereotypes. Faced with a different ethnic or social group, people throughout the world have tended to avoid making the effort of comprehension required by tolerance, and – armed with a stereotyped version of their own sexuality – have resorted to denigration and ridicule.

The peoples of the West have all inherited from the same Christian cultural patrimony. Yet each of our nations, viewing itself through a series of prisms and deforming mirrors, has built up a sexual iconography of itself that is distinct from that of any of its neighbours, whose most intimate behaviour is generally looked on with severity. Shared or divergent memories, chaste and obscene postures, subconscious fantasies and the rules imposed by religion and society have all played their part. In their description of the sexual map of Europe, natives and anthropologists contradict each other vehemently, or occasionally agree – as can sometimes happen between a policeman and the suspect he is interrogating.

Latins – the French, the Italians, the Spanish and other southerners of similar mould – are the first to recognise themselves in the picture painted of them by Anglo-Saxons, Scandinavians, Slavs or Germans: a warm-blooded cohort of young males, watched over at a respectful distance by castrating mothers, encouraged or held back by the advice of patriarchs and the homilies of priests, and tirelessly pursuing ripe young maidens who are waiting to metamorphose – for their benefit – into submissive wives, before finally turning into castrating mothers with warm-blooded sons and ripe young daughters . . .

Comfortably settled in his seducer's persona, the Latin is only too happy to charge his potential Germanic rivals with ponderous clumsiness, while accusing the Slavs of madness, and assigning to those islanders across the Channel the roles of effete young man or timorous lover. English history and literature abound in characters who have nothing of the fastidiousness or frigidity that continentals attribute to the Anglo-Saxon archetype. A succession of Royal mistresses and Royal bastards, the coded confessions in Samuel Pepys' diaries, Moll Flanders and her escapades: the image of seventeenth and eighteenth-century England that these convey is no less racy than that of France, conveyed by accounts of the high-jinks of the young Louis XIV, or the saucy tales of La Fontaine. And in France the eighteenth century has left us no one to compare with Henry Fielding's hero, the incomparable Tom Jones – the jovial ladykiller whose triumph over treachery and wickedness can be attributed to a quality more remarkable even than his innocence – his charm.

But the collective myth – or *cliché*-making factory – does not stop churning with so little reason. Those serious, cultured Frenchmen who are quietly convinced of the superiority of French cooking and literature over any other, would probably not dream of bragging about their sexual feats. Yet they remain convinced that if English women are for the most part frigid, it is not their fault, but that of their men, who do not know how to go about awakening their desire. Climate and puritanism must bear some of the blame for this state of affairs, but the heart of the problem is that English men have the misfortune not to be French. Let us be fair: some of my compatriots are ready to admit that a young Englishman, straight out of a good public school, is not automatically tempted by the delights and dangers of homosexuality. But they will be very disappointed if they do not see him turn scarlet and dumb before the delightful young woman they have just introduced to him, and whom they know so well how to charm.

The Francophile Englishman is not taken in by simplistic descriptions. He appreciates the psychological subtleties of French cinema, and is a discerning critic of *nouvelle cuisine* and the *nouveau roman*. Like Theodore Zeldin, he carefully avoids spotting those caricature Frenchmen – with their berets and baguettes – who crowd the streets of Paris in Hollywood studios, and can occasionally be seen in Paris itself. He knows the French, and can tell you how laconic and cool they can be – masters of the stiff upper lip. He has travelled much, and everywhere has come across romantic young couples, faithful husbands and discreet lovers.

But the old hacks of the popular press and writers of cheap detective stories, television serials and mass-market films are only too well aware that such images of the French would not go down with their public. Theirs is the small, greasy Frenchman who hardly ever washes and slobbers at the sight of a woman; who cheats at

129

cards, is arrogant with the weak, obsequious with the powerful, cruel to animals, and cowardly before an enemy.

Can we ever get out of this vicious circle of *clichés* and counter-*clichés*? It is all the more unlikely since one of the few things that all nations have in common when it comes to sexuality is lies and self-delusion. Every sexual confession masks a tide of shameful emotion; every explicit image robs desire of its potency. In this trial without end which sets conscience against sexuality, middle-age is the final false witness. Time takes the edge off the conflict and teaches the litigants to live with each other, settling into their different moulds: marriage, adultery, divorce.

In our consumer society, differences of class and education, no less than specific national characteristics, are gradually fading. Yet however open a foreigner may be to the peculiarities of another culture, something of it will always escape him, and he will never cease questioning and being astonished. But the thing that most surprises the English when they are placed under scrutiny in this way, is the very astonishment that their behaviour provokes. Silence for instance, the silence so loved by my English friends – their own silence, which they compare to the cacophony of foreign languages. They cherish it as an expression of calm in the face of futile agitation. It is their antidote to excesses of emotion. Whereas the French consider *le shake hand* to be an English custom, the British hold out their hand in a parsimonious gesture that maintains distances more than it expresses cordiality. This reticence is perfectly encapsulated in the famous 'How do you do?' to which the polite reply is 'How do you do?', leaving the parties unencumbered with information about their respective health and families. It is true that in certain circles kisses are liberally exchanged, cheek brushing cheek. But these sexless greetings are no more than tokens by which members of a coterie recognise each other, the prelude to chit-chat at a cocktail or dinner party.

Silence
This reassuring silence, made up of shared culture and certainties, is not always as comfortable as the English would like to believe. At times it feels more like the muteness of a prisoner who has forgotten how to speak after long years of incarceration. 'Children

must be seen and not heard', that old maxim of a good English nursery education, is only too well observed – especially by boys. Chit-chat is a feminine occupation, it seems. Of course, every street gang has its passwords, every public school its slang, and every profession its own dialect. Men talk about common preoccupations – sport, their taxes, how they are doing at work. But what of a boy and a girl; what of a woman and a man? Apparently they have nothing to say to each other. Or rather – one thing only, and that is not really a subject for conversation. The silence of the shy and the innocent, followed by a naked assault. The silence of gratified love, of conjugal understanding, or even – in the best of cases – the peaceful silence of complicity: between the two sexes, everything begins and ends with silence.

People throughout the world have problems with sex. The English have a problem with language. For more than a century the English were taught that they should never discuss money or food, and were left in complete ignorance about sex. But their ignorance, as much as their reticence, was a matter for pride. Today's more liberal mores could have been expected to do away with such taboos, but they have merely replaced the silence of prudery with the silence of inarticulateness.

For boys as much as for girls, the loss of virginity remains an embarrassing mystery relegated to some dark corner of consciousness, or exorcised by a joke. The earlier one has lost it, the easier it is to forget the experience, or to think of it as merely the last in a series of childhood transitions. People generally agree that earlier generations made far too much fuss about the subject. It is true that in those days there was syphilis, and the pill had not yet been invented – but AIDS did not exist then either. As in other Western nations, few people in Great Britain today are shocked by the idea of young lovers living together before marriage. Yet this easy cohabitation has done little to promote a more intelligible dialogue between the sexes. It has merely robbed their early encounters of that element of furtiveness and adventure which at least had the virtue of opening a few windows into the unknown. Young couples are now freely accepted in the homes of an older generation which no longer reacts with incomprehension. They are spared the rigours of an isolated

131

relationship, and, like cherished infants, feel no need to break their satisfied silence.

Failing a common language to unite the sexes, the rhetoric of love assumes greater significance, and that rhetoric has hardly changed: Love still has a capital letter, as does Fidelity – especially among girls, who continue to disapprove of those among them who have emancipated themselves from it. Though marriage is less common than it was, the monogamous ideal is as firmly anchored as ever in the nation's morals. Separation and divorce are unthinkable, even if they happen every day. And even if it only lasts six months, Love is eternal, the couple indissoluble and faithlessness unforgivable.

In Great Britain, as elsewhere, anthropologists, pollsters and agony aunts vie with each other for the privilege of making statistics out of sex and aphorisms out of sentiment. Their discoveries are unsurprising. A majority (though still a modest one) of British women agree that it is no longer imperative to be a virgin before marriage. Yet contrary to common belief, more than three-quarters of them will not lose their virginity till the age of eighteen to twenty-four, and more than ten per cent of women over twenty-five have still not experienced full sexual intercourse. Between the ages of eighteen and forty-five, about half of those living with a man have sex with him about twice a week – which amounts to a ten per cent increase in frequency since the seventies. Some thirteen per cent of women have sex five times a week or more, though among married women the proportion is even lower – a mere five per cent in 1970. The middle classes seem to be more enthusiastic about sex than the working classes, and among the young, men and women display an equal appetite. However, marriage or prolonged cohabitation dampens female ardour sooner than it satisfies masculine needs.

Smut and Morality

The British press is as prolix on the subject of sex and its confusions as the public is silent about it. Newspapers luxuriate in intimate details, analysis, and unexpected or spicy revelations. Looking through the headlines, it would seem that two different moral codes cohabit in Great Britain – one reflected and cultivated by the popular press, and one that the so-called quality press tries to inculcate from its superior position.

In general, popular newspapers deplore easy divorce and condemn pornography, which they automatically connect with violence. The broadsheets proclaim a pluralistic morality resting on the sacrosanct principles of democracy and individual liberty. Each paper adopts its own minority causes, according to whim and political outlook. Worried parents, independent adolescents, prostitutes, campaigners for the clean-up of television – all these and many more are defended in turn.

The Times and the *Daily Telegraph* defend the mother who wants to prevent doctors from prescribing the pill to under-age girls without the approval of their parents, and bemoan the predicament of ordinary women who no longer dare to walk alone in streets which have been taken over by prostitutes. The *Guardian* is indignant about the fate of divorcees unable to remarry in church, and homosexuals prevented from adopting homeless children.

A closer look at the written press reveals that the difference between the two moralities is less marked than it seems. The success of the *Sun* (most popular of the tabloids) rests on a formula that reconciles smut with morality in an orgy of juicy indignation. The more lustful that country vicar, the more disgusting the perversion of paedophiles who collect pornographic photographs of children, the bloodier the rape, murder and mutilation described on the front page, the more appalling the details of that sado-masochistic film – the more implacable is the indictment of the *Sun* in the name of outraged virtue. Every day twenty million British citizens contemplate some eight million pairs of breasts spread out on the page before their still sleepy eyes. No doubt the regular and lucrative *Sun* bingo competitions also contribute to its popularity. But it is probable that fewer female chests would be bared if the average reader did not find in them some compensation for the silence that surrounds the mysteries of desire. The editors of the *Sun* know their job. They spare no effort to reassure their readers that bare breasts and moral rectitude make good companions. Homosexuals and drug addicts are not the only ones to be turned into the scapegoats of this demonstration. Militant trade-unionists, the women's peace movement, universities, foreigners – all potential trouble-makers are scrutinised with uncompromising vigilance. True, the *Sun* has been forced to tone down its sensational profile a little, perhaps as a result of libel cases such as that instituted by Elton John, which cost the paper a million pounds in damages. But the basic recipe remains the same.

The quality press is not much more coherent in its liberalism than are the popular papers in their right-thinking obscenity. A clinical detachment enables journalists and readers alike to disassociate themselves from the subject matter, however outrageous. Besides, the fine Anglo-Saxon tradition of philanthropy must be maintained. Fetishists and exhibitionists will always find a benefactress, an adviser and well-wishers (all with an irreproachable sexual history) to fight for their full integration into society. Nothing escapes the sanitised compassion of these champions of sexual minorities.

Television viewers regularly update their repertoire of possible romantic and sexual predicaments by watching soap operas. Until the beginning of the eighties, these always had 'positive' heroes, through whom social developments were reflected and sanctioned, while any kind of unseasonable audacity was avoided. It was possible to make love or to give birth outside marriage without being branded as infamous. But tolerable licence did not go further than this. Even the goings-on of American magnates in *Dallas* or *Dynasty* – as popular in Britain as anywhere else – remained firmly outside the traditional code of sexual behaviour. Two soap operas – Channel Four's *Brookside*, and more especially *Eastenders* (produced at considerable expense by BBC1 since 1985) were to revolutionise the *genre*. For the first time physical poverty as well as emotional destitution, sexual and romantic confusion, were openly displayed. The success of *Eastenders* was immediate.

Since then a curious phenomenon has emerged: the huge popularity of the Australian soap, *Neighbours* – a middle-class paradise in which conventional morality is firmly rehabilitated. Lying somewhere between the fantastic dreams of splendour, inordinate wealth and great wickedness of *Dallas*, and the social realism of *Eastenders*, *Neighbours* is a sort of Western of everyday life, offering the escapism of the exotic (permanent sunshine and Aussie accents), with the reassuring quality of the familiar and trivial.

But despite the countervailing trend that the success of *Neighbours* demonstrates, there is no going back on the soap opera revolution. The popularity of *Eastenders* continues unabated, and even the long-running *Coronation Street* has been forced to modernise its dreary image and incorporate themes of sex and violence. The collective psychotherapy which the new-style soap offers to its public does not yet amount to dialogue, but it brings into full light a reality the public knows and has been reluctant to accept.

The heavy-handed jokes of popular television comedians are a purely English product. Every foreigner has heard about the famous English sense of humour. English farce and low comedy are less well-known, but they do exist – coarse, iconoclastic and often scatological. The great and the good are pitilessly taunted; priests and politicians are branded with all the vices that a heavy beer drinker might dream up between two pints, or between two burps. But it is women who provide the greatest store of jokes – women, and the men who undress them with a look. This barrack-room humour is made up of adolescent frustrations translated into a virile buffoonery that unrelentingly ridicules all shameful temptations. It is no coincidence that the play, *No Sex Please, We're British*, has been one of the greatest successes in contemporary English theatre (second only to Agatha Christie's eternal *Mousetrap*), running uninterruptedly for seventeen years, from 1970 to 1987.

The conflation of sex with violence is another stratagem used by the English in their constant battle to expel sexuality from their lives. The campaigns that are periodically launched to stem the tide of contemporary aggression almost always denounce pornography, prostitution and the laxity of modern morals in the same breath. To confuse the debate even further, literature, cinema, and especially television are also accused of generating the violence they describe; and their frequent portrayal of sex (seen as the mainspring of the criminal's mentality) is often cited as one of the principal contributors to that violence.

In 1983, a number of MPs, throwing themselves headlong into the *melée*, simultaneously attacked the pornography of some films and the violence of the so-called 'video nasties'. Under the impetus of a campaign launched by Mrs Mary Whitehouse's pressure group, the National Viewers and Listeners Association, the controversy was whipped up into an election issue, and most newspapers joined in the collective outcry against the unbridled portrayal of violence, which threatened to traumatise defenceless young viewers permanently. The furore culminated in the passing of the Video Recordings Act, in 1984, which stipulated that videos – like cinema films – must be submitted for censorship and classification by the British Board of Film Classification.

Yet no one was forced to watch such films. No parent, guardian or teacher was obliged to show them to the children in their charge. Violence, though a real enough social scourge, has no need of fictional inspiration to flourish. Surely children – at their imaginative worst – are able to inflict far greater tortures on themselves and on their peers? The exaggerated violence of the video nasties took the edge off their horror by making them less realistic, and their impact was further blunted by the possibility of endlessly repeating them on the television screen. Perhaps their very artificiality transformed them into the best possible antidote to the real violence of the world. And without the freedom to wander into the dark as well as the light zones of the imagination, are not the English in danger of denying themselves one of the first stages in the education of the soul?

Treachery and Lust

In 1980 the Catholic magazine, the *Tablet*, carried out an opinion poll on the relative importance of the ten commandments. The British were alone among Europeans in putting the injunction against fornication and adultery in second place, after the commandment, 'Thou shalt not kill'. For everyone else, adultery came at the bottom of the list. In a MORI poll conducted some nine years later, only fifty-two per cent of respondents thought that 'having sexual relations with someone who is married to someone else' was 'morally wrong'.

Could it be that the Thatcher years have really seen such a dramatic rejection of the Victorian value of fidelity? Or is this another manifestation of the Victorians' notorious hypocrisy in matters sexual? Significantly, at forty-nine per cent, the proportion of MORI poll respondents who thought that pornography in the cinema is immoral, was almost as great. Summing up the results of their researches on 'Moral Britain'*, the journalist Eric Jacobs, and Robert Worcester, the chairman of MORI, write: 'People, we found, are far more likely to be outraged by seeing something violent or sexually explicit on their television screens than they are by sexual behaviour that offends conventional religious belief. Many more people . . . deplore full frontal male nudity than do divorce. If there is still something puritanical left in British attitudes,' they conclude 'it is about what is seen in public rather than whatever people may want to get up to in their personal lives'.

Nothing is more symptomatic of this state of mind than the sex scandals that beset British political life. Naturally, people everywhere enjoy bawdy gossip about their politicians, but Britain is probably the last European democracy to take it seriously. 'He who cheats on his wife will betray his country' – such could be the slogan of those who set themselves up as defenders of the nation's morals. The 'affairs' which keep cropping up from one year to the next say less about the corruption of those who govern than they do about the immaturity of those who are governed.

The Profumo affair in 1963 remains one of the classic examples of its kind, and continues to raise interest and controversy today. The scandal centred around Christine Keeler, a glamorous young model, who was found to be sharing her favours with John Profumo – then Secretary of State for Defence – and with a member of the Soviet military mission.

A security enquiry soon revealed that no state secrets had been endangered and that the titillating coincidence between the bedroom antics of the politician and the Soviet diplomat were of no consequence. But the relentlessness of the press, which continued to hound Profumo long after suspicions of treachery were shown to be unfounded, led him to commit the only unpardonable sin – that of solemnly declaring to the House of Commons that he had never had sexual relations with Christine

* From the book, *We British. Britain under the MORIscope*, Weidenfeld and Nicolson, 1990.

Keeler. His career was ruined. Slipping meekly into the role assigned to him by public expectation, he resigned from public life to devote himself to charitable works. In 1975 he received a CBE, a sign that he had finally paid the penalty and deserved forgiveness. Having enjoyed the peep-show at his expense, the public now gave itself the ultimate luxury of magnanimously acknowledging the fact that he had discharged his debt to society.

Nearly thirty years after the Profumo affair, mundane sexual activity continues to provide entertainment and scandal. In March 1989, the *News of the World* lifted the curtains on the first act of an *opera buffa* featuring Pamela Bordes (a much publicised House of Commons research assistant), Andrew Neil (Thatcherite editor of the *Sunday Times*), and Peregrine Worsthorne (then editor of the *Sunday Telegraph* and a traditionalist Tory). Once the scene had been set with initial revelations about Miss Bordes' extra-curricular activities, Peregrine Worsthorne stepped in to accuse his colleague of undermining the dignity of the *Sunday Times* by appearing in public with Miss Bordes. Leaping to the defence of his own outraged reputation, Neil successfully sued Worsthorne for libel, and – in the crowning act – demonstrated that Worsthorne himself was no stranger to hanky panky, of the public-school variety. Andrew Neil was awarded £1,000 damages by the courts, and the episode was covered in great detail by all the newspapers.

It is now also nearly thirty years since homosexual practices between consenting male adults were legalised. When the death of Lord Wolfenden of Westcott was announced in January 1985, numerous obituaries rendered well-deserved tribute to the historical initiative of this liberal reformer whose 1957 report had eventually led to the updating of the law on homosexuality. Yet even today, the legal position of the British homosexual is full of inconsistencies. Lesbians are not included in the updated law, since female homosexual practices were never illegal in the first place. Consequently, while the age of consent for heterosexual couples is sixteen, female homosexuals can legally make love at any age, and male homosexuals have to wait until they are twenty-one. Furthermore, the notion of 'public indecency' is interpreted far more strictly where homosexuals are concerned, and gay couples have occasionally been arrested for the crime of kissing in public. These gaps, compromises and occasional severities in the law are an exact reflection of the contradictory and uncertain feelings of the average British citizen when faced with homoerotic love.

The misogynist élite of the public schools continues to flourish as it always has done – though perhaps a little more openly today than in the past. Some are quite forthright about their preference; other discreetly admit to their difference. They have inherited the art of reconciling freedom with convention. But for the great majority of homosexuals – civil servants, politicians, family men – there is no way out of the limbo of their original sin. They are neither plainly rejected nor truly accepted by the population at large, while from within the gay community itself, they are under increasing pressure to 'come out' and face the Damoclean sword of condemnation that might fall on them at any time.

In 1982 Michael Rauch, a male prostitute, disclosed his brief liaison a few years earlier with Michael Trestrail, officer of the security personnel to the Queen. Rauch, who had already tried to blackmail Trestrail several times without success, finally decided to make capital out of the story by selling it to the *Sun* for £20,000. The next day, Trestrail resigned from his job. His professional competence and integrity, as well as his devotion to the Queen (who was known to hold him in real friendship) were never in doubt. Yet newspapers across the board expressed particular indignation that a homosexual should have been allowed to slip through the net of positive vetting. Hardly anyone questioned the assumption that it was impossible for someone of unorthodox proclivities to be entrusted with such a responsible position.

In the light of such pervasive public attitudes, one can legitimately ask what the law on homosexuality is worth. In what way do the private activities of a citizen expose him to danger so long as he stays within the law? And if he is exposed, surely the law should enable him to stand up to threats? By refusing to bow to pressure from Michael Rauch, Trestrail answered both these questions, and fully justified the confidence placed in him at the time of his appointment. Yet the diplomatic service continues to exclude known homosexuals from foreign postings, and the army still expels them from its ranks as if they were unfit for service.

Meanwhile, the militant left builds up an arsenal of weapons against institutional fortresses. Islington Council provides a grant in support of Irish lesbians fighting against discrimination in London, and Hackney Council offers to help local gay couples in their fight for the right to adopt children. 'Heterosexism is pernicious', proclaims a left-wing activist, while a female student at Wadham College, Oxford, inveighs against 'heterosexual propaganda' in one of the student satirical magazines. The passive intolerance of the masses is pitted against the active fanaticism of minorities whose activities ultimately strengthen the very prejudices they set out to combat. The results of their valiant efforts have not been long in coming: in 1988, Margaret Thatcher's Government introduced the now notorious Clause 28 into their Local Government Act to prevent local authorities from 'intentionally' promoting homosexuality in 'published material', or from promoting 'teaching in any maintained school of the acceptability of homosexuality as a pretended family relationship'.

There is less dialogue between the two sides today than ever before. Sex is still a battleground, and the fear of Aids is unlikely to help the antagonists settle their quarrel. But short of exorcising the ancient demon of desire, it must surely be possible to apply the subtleties of language and thought to understanding its mysteries. A little semantic prudence might soften the edges of the argument. With such an ancient and abundant language at their disposal, the English have every opportunity to avoid the reductive spell of certain words. Why not talk of flirtation, desire, pleasure and shame – or even sexuality – rather than always resorting to the brutal and mechanistic catchword 'sex' in its numerous manifestations (having sex, sex-life, sex-scandals, sex-play, sex'n'violence)? Why deprive oneself of the word 'gay' and not restore to it the traditional role of expressing *joie de vivre*, instead of dwelling on the difference (which is actually quite immaterial – except in terms of fecundity) between homo and heterosexuality. For

140

whatever the tune, whatever the particular promptings of body and soul, sexuality is always and everywhere condemned to the same dance of attraction, seduction, love, pleasure, frustration and guilt.

7

Here Come the Artists

The French claim to love art and venerate artists, but they are afraid of being thought ridiculous, and in order to avoid appearing out of touch, they buy nothing and criticise everything. The English have no particular admiration or respect for artists. They are happy to applaud them from their comfortable seats in the stalls, but they have no desire to meet them behind the scenes or visit their workshops, and even less do they want to invite them to their homes. On the other hands they know and appreciate their work, for which they are prepared to pay without demur. Had it not been for the Second World War, the word 'culture' might still be one of those high-flown words which pepper the speeches of foreign Heads of State, but which should never cross the lips of a self-respecting Englishman.

The Best for the Most

During the war, privations, bombardments and the threat of invasion made it imperative to find some way of sustaining the nation's morale. The Crown Film Unit was created to depict the hardships and triumphs of the population at war and of its armed forces, thus reviving an industry which had been squeezed by competition from Hollywood. ENSA, the Entertainment National Service Association, was established to mobilise actors and other variety artists in an effort to distract the military. As for the civilian population, it had to be convinced that to fight under the Union Jack was to fight in defence of a homogeneous nation with uniform values, not merely a mosaic of social classes dominated by an aristocracy of title, wealth and accent. The Council for the Encouragement of

Music and the Arts (CEMA) was meant to introduce the masses (till then confined to their pubs and working men's clubs) to the pleasures of high art previously reserved for the happy few.

'The best for the most' – this article of faith gave rise to a controversy which still rages: should one be making the traditional culture of the privileged accessible to the masses, or should one be ennobling and exalting popular culture? In 1946 – golden age of the Welfare State – the Arts Council of Great Britain took over where CEMA had left off, and today it continues to distribute modest annual subsidies to more than one thousand artistic bodies of every kind.

Over the past ten years, this well-worn debate has been spiced by an additional argument about the role of market forces in regulating the arts. Mrs Thatcher's reputation as a philistine has hardly been improved by her insistence that art should be profitable as well as uplifting. During her premiership, public funding for the arts in Britain sank lower than in any other Western country. Artistic companies, unaccustomed to private fund raising, were forced to learn quickly, and business sponsorship increased dramatically during the last years of the decade. But this was not enough to close the gap created by cuts in government funding. In 1989, the new director of the Victoria and Albert, Elizabeth Estève-Coll, spent well over £150,000 on an advertising campaign to promote the museum, but a year later, she was sacking eight distinguished scholars from their posts as senior curators. In November 1990, the Royal Shakespeare Company was forced to close at the Barbican Theatre for four and a half months, in order to save money. The Royal Opera House is three million pounds in debt, and the English National Ballet narrowly avoided bankruptcy at the beginning of 1990.

Yet the Arts Council is criticised every year because it subsidises the extravagant and élitist spectacles at the Royal Opera House, Covent Garden (much less extravagant than those at *La Scala* in Milan or at the *Opéra de Paris*) and is not generous enough towards companies of deserving young actors in Manchester or Birmingham. But the majority of the art-loving public defends the established arts and is suspicious of troublemakers who want to impose incomprehensible aesthetic innovations.

In the post-war days of full employment and Keynesian euphoria, the notion of popular sovereignty was easily elevated to mythical status by Marxist intellectuals, who arrogated to themselves the right to represent the 'people'. Enemies of bourgeois art, they attempted to undermine it from within by gaining control of such organisations as the Institute of Contemporary Arts and the British Film Institute. But in the absence of a strong communist party, voices were soon raised against the imposition on the working class of an ideology no less alien for being allegedly proletarian in spirit.

Today, although British theatre often borrows its décor from dingy suburban streets (as in Arnold Wesker's plays), it remains comfortably ensconced in the Victorian stucco world of the West End. And when, from time to time, a small theatre company stages some *avant-garde* show in the back room of a pub, it usually does so less out of empathy with the people than in the hope of capturing the imagination of the producer who will introduce the show to a smarter audience.

It is a curious fact that the British – supposedly the least demonstrative of nations – have the best theatre in the world. A unique acting tradition, and the work of playwrights such as Harold Pinter, Tom Stoppard, Alan Ayckbourn, and Caryl Churchill have jointly contributed to its exceptional importance today. All of these writers have, in their own way, laid bare a few of those secret miseries that modesty or social hypocrisy normally conceal. With Pinter, sexual obsession, family hatred, violence and madness are exposed in a voice that is so distinctive, yet so familiar, that its echoes in the real world are immediately identified as 'Pinteresque'. Master of the moral dilemma, Stoppard delves into the darkest recesses of the conscience, and forces awkward questions into the glare of open scrutiny. All the hypocrisy, brutality and the hidden wounds of a middle class that refuses to see itself for what it is are mercilessly satirised by Alan Ayckbourn, while the most firmly anchored public prejudices are shaken by Caryl Churchill's blunt feminist radicalism. Could it be that the stage offers the British a mask behind which they can explore unacceptable passions? The famous impassiveness of the Englishman is a meagre disguise for desire, violence and hatred, or even for shyness and inhibition. But on stage, the alibi of fiction allows him to give way to the cries of joy, pain, love or triumph that decency normally forbids.

In the last decades, perhaps more than ever before, the British have looked to theatrical fiction, with its lighting tricks and *trompe-l'oeil* scenery, as a means of expressing their deepest feelings and true thoughts. After the Second World War, it seemed imperative to lift the curtain on poverty, destitution, loneliness and alienation, and playwrights became deeply involved in ideological controversies. Later, as the self-confidence of the Welfare State was eroded, British theatre became correspondingly less political and more intimate, abandoning ideological dichotomies and social critique in favour of multifaceted exploration. Particularly under the influence of experimental theatre and theatre workshops, the personality and feelings of the actors, as well as of the audience, were implicated in the narrative action of the play, and professional concentration on the art and craft of acting and the aesthetics of action, movement and lighting, replaced a more simple concern with the delivery of a political message.

John Osborne's *Look Back in Anger* is undoubtedly the most important play of the immediate post-war era. Written in 1956, it is the indictment by youth of all the 'virtues' of middle-age, and of prosperity by indigence; it celebrates anger in the place of passive resignation to modern life and its hypocritical certainties. Although the play's content is iconoclastic, its form and style are traditional. By prudently observing the conventions of theatre writing, Osborne wanted to make sure that his rage would be accessible to the most hidebound and obtuse of his audience.

It may seem paradoxical to cite *Nicholas Nickleby* as one of the most important productions of the eighties. But although it is based on the Dickens novel, apparently so firmly rooted in its Victorian context, the play occupies a unique place in recent theatrical history. Apart from being an adaptation of extraordinary imagination and verve, it perfectly illustrates the eighties trend away from straightforward social critique towards a purer form of theatrical exploration.

Like his predecessor Osborne, David Edgar – author of the stage *Nicholas Nickleby* and an ardent admirer of *Look Back in Anger* –

is a man of the left, passionately hostile to Thatcherism and committed to political writing. But when, in 1979, he was asked by the celebrated producer, Trevor Nunn (then Joint Artistic Director of the Royal Shakespeare Company), to adapt Dickens' novel, he became as absorbed in the technicalities of conveying action and emotion on stage, as he was in the narrative and meaning of the play. Working closely with the Royal Shakespeare Company, he shaped the script out of repeated live readings of the story, to which actors and artists all contributed. Writing later about the production, he said that the play had been created and interpreted by 'a group of late twentieth century actors, who sympathised profoundly with what Dickens wrote and his aspirations for society and the human beings within it, but who were telling his story six generations later, and who knew 150 years' worth of things about men and women and their affairs that Charles Dickens did not know'.

His treatment of this Victorian chronicle transforms it into a contemporary parable in which the central character is the composite incarnation of all the play's other characters, as well as of the actors and the audience, all of whom contribute to the narrative's evolution. The action moves forward continuously, sometimes intense, sometimes nonchalant, multifaceted, projecting good and evil, pain and tenderness in a play of light, movement and emotion which is reflected from the stage to the auditorium and back. It is a work one might be tempted to call 'global' if the word had a meaning, but which is at any rate living and constantly evolving.

Despite the originality of the production, *Nicholas Nickleby* remains a very accessible play, a thrilling story wonderfully told. For all its brilliance, British theatre fights shy of the kind of *avant-garde* experimentation on which French producers have based their reputations. It is surely no coincidence that the Englishman, Peter Brook, should choose to stage his unorthodox productions in Paris. In London, and in Britain's innumerable provincial theatres, playwrights and producers prefer to work within the conventions, using them to their own ends – and with what skill and virtuosity they do so!

The National Theatre, on the South Bank of the Thames, and the Royal Shakespeare Company, in Stratford–upon–Avon and in the City's Barbican, are not merely academies of traditional dramatic art. Artistic and commercial pragmatism has freed them from the respectable cultural ghetto in which they traditionally belong, and producers in search of commercial success now look to them for their next Broadway show. It is also in London that they look for best-selling musicals to fill the American stage, and if they are lucky enough to land a contract with the young and inexhaustible Andrew Lloyd Webber, they know they cannot go wrong. From the Royal Shakespeare Company's musical adaptation of Victor Hugo's *Les Misérables*, to Lloyd Webber's *Phantom of the Opera* and *Aspects of Love*, Britain's contribution to the coffers of world theatre has been far from negligible.

Aging cinemas hastily restored with cheap materials, unimaginative programmes (Hollywood block-busters, science fiction, violence, heavy-handed sexual titillation), and a declining industry: compared with the wealth of invention in the theatre, it is hard to explain the shameful poverty of cinema in Britain. It was not always so. In 1932, Alexander Korda founded London Film Productions, which was to generate such masterpieces as *The Private Life of Henry VIII* in which Charles Laughton masterfully inaugurated his film career, before giving an unforgettable performance as Captain Bligh in *Mutiny on the Bounty*. *The Third Man*, produced shortly after the war, immediately confirmed Korda as one of the best film directors of the period, rivalling the Hollywood greats. In 1949 alone, the release of several films – including *Passport to Pimlico* and better still, *Kind Hearts and Coronets* – established a comic style as English as the the neorealism of Vittorio de Sica in *Bicycle Thief* was Italian, and as universally appealing. A whole generation of films produced by the Ealing Studios in the decade after the Second World War came to be known as the 'Ealing Comedies', and have survived as real classics of the *genre*. Thanks to television, *The Lavender Hill Mob*, for example, continues to convey a sparkling portrayal of good-natured wickedness to viewers of every age.

The grumpy populism of the generation of 'angry young men' was translated to the screen with films such as *Saturday Night and Sunday Morning* in 1960, *A Taste of Honey* in 1961, and *The Loneliness of the Long Distance Runner* in 1962. However, these flourishes of the imagination, which had seemed so promising, faded almost as suddenly as they had appeared.

The extreme concentration of cinemas and distribution in the hands of two or three conglomerates such as Rank and EMI is one of the main reasons for the comparatively rapid decline of the film industry in Britain. At the first signs of public disenchantment, rather than spending money on renovating out of date and uncomfortable cinema halls, they chose to transform them into bingo halls, rent them out to garages or sell them to developers for office blocks. During the past thirty years the number of available cinema seats has decreased by a staggering ninety-five per cent. Today fewer films are being made than ever before, and several top directors, such as Alan Parker and Ridley Scott, have moved to Hollywood. Goldcrest has collapsed, George Harrison and Denis O'Brien's Handmade Films is in severe crisis, and the film arm of Thorn EMI has produced no significant films since its takeover by Cannon. The production of a film in Britain today is a genuine *tour de force*, and its commercial success is possible only if it can be sold abroad. Producers always have an eye on the American market. They are suspicious of subjects they judge to be inaccessible to American audiences. A few low budget horror films (still a national speciality), some depressingly bad comedies for internal consumption, and from time to time, like a flower in the desert, the work of a headstrong young film-maker – these are all that is left of a once great industry. The talent is there, but the means are not.

Successive governments have done little to help revive the flagging industry. In 1986, responding to widespread criticisms about the low level of funding available to British film producers, Mrs Thatcher – true to her unshakeable faith in the market-place – replaced the National Film Finance Corporation (which had been funded entirely by the public purse), with a Government subsidised private sector company, British Screen Finance. Abolishing the so-called EADY levy on the sale of cinema tickets (from which public funds for the cinema industry had previously been raised), she pledged a fixed annual Government subsidy for British Screen Finance, which – for its part – was expected to raise further funds from the private sector. But though these changes have replaced the vagaries of the old system with the security of a regular Government grant, at a mere two million pounds a year, the sum represents a paltry contribution to national film production. In June 1990, Mrs Thatcher announced the creation of a European Film Making Fund to encourage the industry further in the run-up to 1992, but the Government's contribution to this new fund amounts to no more than five million pounds over three years.

Today however, it looks as though video and television, which for many years were among the principal grave-diggers of the British film industry, could become its ultimate saviours. In particular, Channel Four's policy of direct investment in quality productions has made it possible for a number of films to be made that might never otherwise have seen the light of day.

Paradoxically, this has also been a period of employment and prosperity for cinema professionals. Major Hollywood companies have increasingly seen the advantage of using British film studios, with their low production costs, to make films such as *Batman* or *Indiana Jones*, from which they can reap colossal profits (seventy million US dollars in the first weekend). Nonetheless, the hostility of unions, resentful of competition from foreign actors, has put a brake on the growth of co-productions despite greater willingness by the City to finance projects where the risks are shared.

From time to time, an important British film does emerge in spite of this bleak financial picture. The noble thrust of David Puttnam's *Chariots of Fire*, the epic imagery of Richard Attenborough's *Gandhi*, the intimacy of *Room with a View*, the heterodoxy of *Letter to Brezhnev* and *My Beautiful Launderette*, the strange charm of *Shirley Valentine*, the wacky humour in *A Fish Called Wanda* – these and a handful of others throw the occasional spark on the dying embers of British cinema, though they cannot revive the fire.

A Passionate Tradition of Musical Amateurs

In the realm of music, yet again, quality without ostentation reconciles national pride with a horror of affectation and Latin display. The English are in love with music and musicians, yet they take pride in their philistine reputation. Scratch the polished surface of this feigned indifference, and there is music everywhere:

the music of choirs and brass bands; music at school, at church, in friendly societies; music improvised on synthesisers and electric guitars, before being mixed and recorded in some back room in Liverpool or Hackney. And then, just across the English border, enthusiasts shed all inhibition and revel in their musical traditions – Irish ballads and Scottish bagpipes and the music of Welsh miners' choirs.

It is the music of amateurs, but these amateurs have all the rigour of professionals, to which they add the enthusiasm of true believers. The Bach Choir of London is known throughout the world, yet – with the exception of its director – it is composed entirely of amateurs. The reputation of King's College Chapel choir in Cambridge is equally enviable. In Britain people do not talk about music, they make it.

Most British music lovers have never had the privilege of going to Glyndebourne and hearing their favourite aria sung by an unknown young performer whose name will be on everyone's lips the next day. But the majority of these absentee music lovers would consider themselves somehow the poorer if the festival at Glyndebourne did not open every year in May and close in September.

In addition to being a rural paradise for wealthy opera lovers (or alternatively a shrine for snobs in search of social and cultural acceptance), Glyndebourne is a precious nursery of talent – to the benefit of a musical community whose frontiers extend far beyond those of the United Kingdom. At Glyndebourne, singers, musicians, producers, designers, electricians, costumiers and carpenters all live together (sometimes for several weeks at a time), in a context of shared creativity unknown elsewhere. It is the only private opera company in Britain to survive entirely without public subsidy. Each one of its productions is an artistic event of which music lovers across the world can catch the echo on record and on video cassettes.

For those who dislike the exclusivity of Glyndebourne, there is the Aldeburgh festival, founded in 1948 by Benjamin Britten and Eric Crozier. To the tourist it offers the additional advantage of being held in Suffolk, on the shores of the North Sea – a region he would otherwise never visit, believing, like other foreigners, that England begins at Dover and ends in London. Although it is primarily given over to the works of Benjamin Britten, the festival aims to reflect the spirit of curiosity and eclecticism of its founder. At Aldeburgh, mufflers and tweed jackets are more in place than black tie and long dresses. Yet in this casual and very English atmosphere, the international patriotism of music thrives.

From the point of view of musical interpretation, the most notable event of the last decade has been The City of Birmingham Symphony Orchestra's rise to international fame, with Simon Rattle as conductor. Under the directorship of the Czech conductor, Libor Pesek (appointed in 1987), the Royal Liverpool Philharmonic Orchestra, which celebrated its 150th anniversary in 1990, is now also gaining an international reputation. But in spite of the benefits which a great institution can bring to its city, the Liverpool orchestra – like so many other artistic institutions – is severely under-funded, receiving a mere twenty-three thousand pounds a year from the City Council. In accordance with Mrs Thatcher's cherished principle, this amount is supplemented by a notable increase in funding by private enterprise.

The major orchestras, opera companies and musical theatres are at times a touch too respectful of established reputations, a touch too suspicious of innovative new works. BBC Radio Three is perhaps a little pompous at times, but it redresses the balance to some extent, broadcasting more new work than virtually any other radio station in the world. Thanks to Radio Three, music is available to everyone, and remains – for those who make it as much as for those who listen to it – an affair of the heart and not a dictate of fashion.

London has become an international musical capital, supporting no less than four resident orchestras – not counting the BBC Symphony Orchestra, which brings the total to five. Every summer from July to September, London's famous Promenade concerts offer a feast of music at the lowest prices. Night after night, great works by great composers of every age are played by the greatest orchestras and led by the greatest conductors. The Proms, as they are more commonly known, were founded in 1895 by the twenty-six-year-old conductor, Henry Wood, who continued to direct them until his death in 1944. Today the international reputation of a musician is not fully established until he has taken part in at least one of these concerts. And let those who believe in the tired *cliché* about English reticence and *sang-froid* visit the Albert Hall on the last night of the Proms. The vast auditorium is filled to capacity. The so-called *promenade* gallery and arena have been stripped of their seats to accommodate impecunious music lovers or those who simply prefer the charged atmosphere they find there. And when the last note has sounded in the most religious silence, they will be able to yell out their enthusiasm, in a unison of uninhibited thanks to the artists.

In spite of so many virtues, the Proms are not without their critics. The most exacting music lovers complain that Henry Wood's innovative example is no longer being followed, and that too little time is devoted to contemporary music, and – curiously – to living British composers. Yet it must be admitted that despite such an open and enthusiastic public, British music is curiously elusive. It is not possible to talk of an English school – nor of a Scottish, Welsh or Irish school – with nearly as much assurance as one can describe a German, Italian or French school. Even Russian, Hungarian, Polish and Czech music are more firmly rooted in national traditions. Yet there is no shortage of great British composers, nor even of very distinctive folk music, much of which has inspired foreign composers. Yet in this domain, insularity has not fulfilled its promise of stubborn originality.

In the wake of the 1066 Norman landings, the English musical landscape was invaded by bands of *trouvères* (the northern equivalent of the Provençal troubadours), singing in their own language – French. French was also the language of the first formal music in England. It was the music of the court and its nobility, an ornament of power, a form of expression quite foreign to English society which had no courtly traditions of its own. The Normans soon became anglicised, and French gradually disappeared from common usage. Yet aristocratic culture long preserved its French flavour. As late as the second half of the seventeenth century, Charles II was sending the talented young musician, Pelham Humfrey, to perfect his art in the court of Louis XIV. The great Henry Purcell himself was influenced by the music of Jean-Baptiste Lully, and the Italianate echoes in his own music are entirely mediated through his knowledge of contemporary French composition.

Though dance does not have a language, it does have a style, and that style was also to remain French for a long period. Masked balls '*dans la manière Italienne*' were very fashionable under the Tudors at the beginning of the sixteenth century, but in 1521, Robert Copland published a manual of dance 'according to French usage', which – in a delightfully provoking association – he appended to a French grammar book. In 1706, Raoul Feuillet's *Des ballets anciens et modernes*, which had been published in Paris five years earlier, was translated into English by John Weaver, a dancer and choreographer at the Drury Lane theatre. The Branle and the Minuet are French dances; the Sarabande and the Chaconne (both Afro-American dances imported by the Spanish from their empire), as well as the Allemande were thought fit to dance only when Frenchified. And until the beginning of this century there was not a dance master worthy of the name who was not – or did not claim to be – French.

After ignoring it for many years, the British have finally done justice to the splendours of Elizabethan music. Dowland, Purcell and Byrd enjoy the reputation they deserve, and Handel – English by adoption, as Lully was French – is the object of a particular cult. Delius and Elgar, so unjustly neglected in France, are well appreciated at home. Among twentieth-century composers, Walton, Tippett and Vaughan Williams have an audience. Benjamin Britten is heard and known worldwide. Yet the works of contemporary composers such as the South African Priaux Rainer, who died in Britain – her country of adoption – in 1986, George Benjamin, and Hugh Wood, are very rarely played. Though the BBC regularly commissions new works to be played at the Proms, the public generally receive these with more good will than genuine enthusiasm. The English certainly do not disown their musicians, but neither do they believe in a national school of music.

The Loneliness of the Painter's Studio

It is easy to imagine the courtesy tinged with embarrassment with which William Rothenstein, an English portrait artist of solid reputation, must have greeted the twenty-five-year-old Jacob

Epstein who came to him for advice in 1905. Rothenstein was too much of an artist not to recognise the talent – not to say genius – of the drawings he was being shown. But what would his colleagues make of them, or his aristocratic clientèle? He advised the young artist to go to Paris, where he would receive a warmer welcome than in London. The future Sir William (he was later to be knighted and made director of the Royal College of Art) was right. At the beginning of the twentieth century, London was still a desert for any young artist wanting to break new ground. But though Paris was a haven for British painters and sculptors, it also represented their exile.

In 1911 Walter Sickert, whom Virginia Woolf described as 'a novelist in paint', founded the Camden Town Group in collaboration with his colleagues Spencer Gore, Harold Gilman and Malcolm Drummond. But although their avowed purpose was to show the poverty behind the beautiful Edwardian façades of Greater London, their gaze remained firmly fixed abroad. During a visit to Paris, Sickert – already a friend of Whistler's – became acquainted with Degas. Later he was to spend two periods of six and seven years in Dieppe, and he regularly made visits to Venice in winter. It was not until 1926, at the age of sixty-six, that he finally came back to live in England. Spencer Gore was influenced by his friend Lucien Pissarro (son of Camille Pissarro), whose *pointilliste* technique he adopted. He admired Gauguin and was fascinated by Cézanne's paintings. Harold Gilman adopted a lighter palette as a result of a trip to Paris with his friend Charles Ginner, another painter from the Camden group. And Ginner was captivated by the paintings of Van Gogh.

Roger Fry was a painter, historian and art critic, with ties to the Camden Town group as well as the Bloomsbury artists. In 1910 and 1912 he organised two major exhibitions of post-impressionist art, and theorised about 'significant form', in contrast to subject matter, which he considered to be of minimal importance. Influenced by his ideas, Duncan Grant and Clive Bell tried their hand at producing the first non-figurative paintings in England. Mark Gertler, a member of the Bloomsbury group and the son of Jewish immigrants, looked primarily to his own people for inspiration. Yet he owed the structural solidity of his canvasses to the influence of

Picasso and Cézanne. Matthew Smith was already thirty when he discovered Paris in 1904. From that date he hardly ever left it again, except for the occasional plunge into Mediterranean light. Augustus John often made visits to the French capital. His sister Gwen lived there. Their art developed in very different directions, but both continued to be invigorated by that Paris air without which English artists obstinately refused to believe they could breathe.

In 1934 Paul Nash organised an exhibition in London entitled Unit One, with the aim of demonstrating the existence of an English school of modern art. The attempt was not successful. Some people explained the failure by claiming that the artists Nash had tried to bring together were too different from one another to constitute a school. Yet the *Ecole de Paris* is hardly a model of homogeneity. But it did exist, subdivided into different currents and antagonistic groups, and embracing artists from Spain, Russia, Italy, Romania and even France.

It is curious that not one of those English artists who lived and worked at the same time as Picasso, Chagall, Giacometti, Brancusi and Matisse, should ever be mentioned in connection with the Paris school. Paul Nash was right: English modern art does exist. It is clearly identifiable, powerful and complex. Yet it was not until 1987, when the Royal Academy of Arts organised a magnificent retrospective exhibition of British art in the twentieth century, that the English showed any sign of recognising this. In the same year, the Scottish National Gallery of Modern Art also rendered justice to its own painters by putting on a parallel exhibition entitled 'The Vigorous Imagination: New Scottish Art'. It was the Americans who finally identified the talent of today's young British artists and gave them recognition in the form of a major exhibition, lasting from November 1988 to January 1989, at the Center for Contemporary Arts in Cincinnati.

In the light of these three important shows artists such as Francis Bacon, Lucien Freud and Henry Moore no longer loom like isolated giants in a drab, provincial landscape, but are shown to be surrounded by an astonishing family of artists. The youngest generation, seen in Cincinnati, are confidently abandoning abstraction and returning to figurative art. Painters such as Ian McKeever, Thérèse Oulton and Christopher Le Brun are developing a new, romantic conception of landscape, while Eileen Cooper, Steven Campbell and Andrzej Jackowski, spiritual descendants of Stanley Spencer, are using myths to feed their own subjective vision. With Graham Cowley, Peter Howson and Ken Currie, social realism is overtaken by an earthy and painful, but overwhelmingly powerful expressionism.

Could this mean an end to the isolation which British artists have so long had to suffer? British painters themselves have always been the first to minimise their artistic heritage and vocation. The Pre-Raphaelite fraternity were so pessimistic about their patrimony that they felt obliged to turn to the Italian Quattrocento for a past which they believed their own country could not provide.

The abolition of the monasteries by Henry VIII was to lead to the secularisation of art in England. On the Continent, the master-pieces of baroque art reflected and were enriched by wars and reconciliations, alliances and defections, Lutheran morality, Calvinist austerity and loyalty to Rome. The Counter-Reformation, which led to the resurgence of medieval iconography – with its golds, its *trompe-l'oeil* skies and expressive statuary – throughout most of Europe, did not have the same impact in England, where there was also a stubborn refusal to exalt absolute power. The worship of God did not require idolatrous painted images. Art was irrelevant to prayer, nor was its purpose to proclaim the glory of a divinely appointed King. Painters were at the service of nobles who wanted to embellish their personal residences and increase their prestige. Their own portraits, those of their families, of their dogs, or of the view from one of the windows of their country house – these were subjects suitable for pictures. Also popular were the great historical paintings which noblemen brought back from Flanders or Italy on their return from the 'Grand Tour'. In the Netherlands they gathered many of those small paintings which only the Dutch – whose love of interiors was as deep as their own – could produce to such perfection. But their favourite paintings were by Claude le Lorrain, and the Frenchman, Nicholas Poussin, both of whom had the good sense to paint reasonably sized canvasses from which their English clients were able to draw ideas for the design of their parks and gardens.

Gheeraerts, Holbein, Van Dyke, Peter Lely, Kneller: all these foreigners had successful careers in England because they were portrait painters. The Swiss artist, Fuseli, with his literary subjects; and the Venetian, Canaletto, with his views of the Thames, were also extremely successful, but they were rare exceptions. The English artist, George Romney, dreamed of becoming a history painter; his clients wanted only portraits. Reynolds, first president of the Royal Academy, went as far as to claim that historical paintings was the only kind that really mattered, and that every other *genre* was inferior to it. Yet he was to build his reputation on portrait painting, although he tried to ennoble the *genre* by idealising his subjects and inserting allegorical personifications at their side. Constable, who painted sublime and quintessentially English landscapes, was not very popular in his lifetime. The portrait painter, Thomas Lawrence, who was revered throughout his career and died, paint brush in hand, like an army general on the field of battle, sank into oblivion immediately afterwards. There were others to take his place. Gainsborough was unable to sell his landscapes. Turner, to whom official recognition was so important, had the good fortune to be taken under the wing of the third Earl of Egremont who offered him the refuge of Petworth House. Without his encouragement, who knows whether Turner's genius would ever have achieved the incandescence of his final paintings.

At the height of the Victorian era it became acceptable to paint great historical and allegorical themes, but this was for social and political rather than artistic reasons. Leighton, Watts, and fellow members of the Aesthetic Movement acclaimed Britain's Imperial and mercantile glory in their paintings, and they were richly rewarded for their efforts. Leighton's first great success was the painting entitled *Cimabue's Madonna*, which was purchased by Queen Victoria herself. Subsequently she was to pay him the extraordinary honour of making him the first and only hereditary baron of English art. Today, the painter Maclisse would be better remembered for his exquisite manners than for his work had he not painted the *Death of Nelson* and the *Meeting of Wellington and Blücher at Waterloo* on the neo-Gothic walls of the Houses of Parliament at Westminster.

Similar examples of official promotion and recognition were

not sufficient permanently to improve the standing of the artist in British society. Stubbs is one of the most noble and mysterious of English painters – so penetrating an observer and so learned an anatomist that he seems to uncover the souls of animals beneath their ribs. Yet to his clients, he was merely another portrait painter, specialising in horses. Hogarth was perhaps the only painter to be thought of as specifically English, and as important because he was English, with an English conception of life. But the idea of an artist of national stature seemed pretentious, and it was Hogarth as draughtsman and caricaturist – not as painter – who was celebrated. Only now is his genius as a painter beginning to be recognised. The isolation of William Blake is typical: he thought of himself as a prophet, bringing the word of God to the people through his poetry and engravings. Yet the public at large were never interested in his art.

Thus the solitude of the British artist persists, while even art lovers, surrounded by their collections, persistently deny the importance of art.

Montaigne and Shakespeare

The most important public building to have been started in Britain this century has been a library. It was begun in 1962, amid general indifference, and most people do not even know which Government commissioned it. The new building will for the first time gather the entire collection of the British Library under one roof (at present it is held in nine separate depots, of which the most famous is the British Museum, with its superb reading room). Only the French Bibliothèque Nationale or the Library of Congress in Washington can rival the treasures, accumulated since the Middle Ages, which it will shelter. Yet unlike their French counterparts in similar situations, British politicians seem remarkably unconcerned to know who will be in power on the day of its inauguration. Libraries, public and private, are numerous throughout the United Kingdom. They are well organised, well equipped, and do their job quietly and extremely well – too well perhaps, as they take custom away from the bookshops. Writers have had to fight a long campaign before obtaining the Public Lending Right. Their royalty is still tiny, but the principle has been established, and they hope that the payment will be increased with time. Membership of the London Library, in St James's Square, is a hedonistic privilege. Those who have never had the opportunity to wander quietly around its five shelf-filled floors, choosing a book at leisure (or ten, or fifteen) to take home with them, have been deprived of one of the world's purest pleasures.

Talking about literature is not exactly shocking – unlike sex, food and money – but it is a little ridiculous, except perhaps for an academic. One should not attach undue significance to this pose, but it does reflect a traditional English wariness of anything overtly intellectual. The Scottish, and in particular the Irish, are much more continental in their attitudes and unblushingly render homage to the Literary Muse. The English are self-conscious – except when saluting Shakespeare, whose genius is so purely national that he can be admired out of patriotism, as one might admire Nelson's Column or the green velvet of a hundred-year-old lawn.

The French, as heirs of the Enlightenment, are apt to choose their masters from among their intellectuals. The biblical traditions of the British render them more susceptible to the teachings of a prophet. This difference was particularly underlined by the great success of certain works published in England in the 1940s. Arthur Koestler's *Darkness at Noon*, brought out in 1940, warned of the frailty of intelligence when faced with the deadly logic of ideology. In 1945, George Orwell published *Animal Farm*, followed three years later by *1984*, in which he explored the horrors of a life dominated by ideology.

In England, as in France, a generation of novelists and playwrights found their inspiration in working-class subjects, but unlike Aragon or Sartre for example, they did not build up theories about the working man's transcendent virtue, nor did they prepare him for revolt. Their writings seem to exude apathy rather than despair, and the heroes of these gloomy chronicles are not offered salvation except in the form of individual effort or an imaginative retreat into the fringes of society. The mood of the fifties in England is encapsulated in two novels of the period: *Saturday Night and Sunday Morning* by Alan Sillitoe, and *Room at the Top* by John Braine, both of which were made into rather good films. They portray the dreary greyness of the proletarian condition and offer the working man a single escape route – social ascent through hard work or by marriage.

These parallel literary developments merely accentuate a long-standing difference between the attitudes of the two nations. The 'stupidity' of the English is compared to the mental agility of the French. The English are more than happy to give credit to the French for intellectual feats which they consider to be useless at best, and possibly even dangerous. The French are naïvely delighted to have their superiority in this domain confirmed by the hereditary enemy. But in the end, the English have become prisoners of their own conceit, and have come to believe – quite sincerely – that the French are all men of culture. They also believe that the French – Cartesians long before the birth of Descartes – are prisoners of their logic, which cuts them off from reality, feeds their pride, serves as an alibi for their cowardice and masks their fanaticism. As for themselves, the English are pragmatic and have a monopoly on realism, as well as all those other reassuring qualities which derive from it – common-sense, tolerance, courage, dignity, and of course, modesty. In this cultural confrontation, the two nations have one thing in common – they both have the best literature in the world.

In spite of this rivalry, there are many similarities between English and French writers. They hold values in common, and have borrowed much from each other. Yet revealingly, each culture has kept hidden from the other what it does not know about itself. There is a France which the English do not see, refuse to see, or pretend not to see: it is the France of uncertainty, ambiguity and incommunicability, a France that is tender, joyous and melancholic, a France where things and habits exist just because they have always existed and not because they are better, a France where history is lived and not merely talked about, the France of Montaigne and not that of Descartes.

What the French do not understand is that England is not just a country which proclaims its own narrow-mindedness with too much insistence to be really believed. Masked by this impressive confession, which is merely another form of national pride, there is an England which harbours violence and internal conflicts, fermenting hatred, explosive laughter, frustrated appetites, devasting emotion, burning love and consuming guilt; this is Shakespeare's England, not that of P.G. Wodehouse.

Shakespeare read Montaigne, or at least he read the version of Montaigne's *Essais* translated by his contemporary and perhaps also his friend, John Florio, in 1603. Although Florio's translation is full of mistakes, it is faithful to the Frenchman's spirit, and is written in splendid prose which inspired Shakespeare when he was writing *The Tempest*, as well as Hamlet's famous monologue, and no doubt numerous other passages in his work. From Charles Cotton to the Hazlitts, father and son, the translations of Montaigne have continued to multiply. Their imperfections do not mask the essential fact that those who are in love with Montaigne, on both sides of the Channel, belong to the same family. Must we say that these Frenchmen who believe in tolerance, in the uncertain lessons of experience, in gentle humour, and who know how to make fun of themselves, have somehow made off with merchandise which was 'made in England'? Or that the English have acquired these attributes, of which they are so justly proud, from the French? Why not give credit both to Montaigne and to Shakespeare for their equal love of knowledge, for their refusal to accept ready-made ideas, and for their common exploration of man and nature?

Hobbes against Descartes

The French know nothing about the English Revolution except that Charles I was beheaded – and even that they have learned only thanks to Alexandre Dumas. They generally deplore the fact, forgetting to draw any parallels with the decapitation of Louis XVI, 140 years later, during their own revolution, the only real one, the only one that interests them. They pay ritual homage to Milton, as they might salute Dante in Italy – without ever having read either. But they have no idea that he was in any way connected with the Puritan revolution, and though they think he is admirable, they are contemptuous of the English philosophy which was to emerge from these troubled times. Yet it is in the English Revolution, not the French, that one should look for the first social mutations and the ferment of ideas from which modern Europe and American democracy were to emerge.

Thomas Hobbes' *Leviathan* is a masterpiece of contradictions.

It coolly reconciles political liberalism with the legitimacy of absolute power (though not the divine right of Kings). But these are viable contradictions, rooted in the art of the possible. The empiricism of Francis Bacon (yet another admirer of Montaigne) leads directly to Hobbes' rationalist pragmatism. Thomas Hobbes was an opponent of Descartes, but a friend of Gassendi and of Father Mersenne.* Fleeing civil disorder and Puritan domination in England, he came to Paris where he taught mathematics to the Prince of Wales. After this self-imposed exile, he was determined to return to England permanently, and being as much of a pragmatist in his actions as in his writing, he took the oath of allegiance under Cromwell, and after the Restoration, placed himself under the protection of the monarch – thus avoiding a sentence by parliament for atheism. Hobbes' writings were perhaps more influential and representative of the century than were those of his celebrated young contemporary, John Locke, who was so admired by Voltaire. Nonetheless it is thanks to Locke (also admired by Montesquieu and the *Encyclopédistes*), and later thanks to the Scotsman David Hume with his *Treatise of Human Nature*, that a bridge was created between the thought of the English, who had just given birth to their Revolution, and the French, who were still pregnant with theirs. It was and remains a fragile tie. For the French, philosophy – starting with Leibnitz – is a German speciality. With some reluctance they acknowledge the genius of Newton (and, in his day, of Darwin), but they do so by uprooting it from its native soil, as if it had emerged

---

* Abbé Pierre Gassendi (1592–1695), French philosopher and mathematician. He revolted against scholasticism, and became an early critic of Descartes' new philosophy. He was a friend of Galileo and Kepler, and his *Institutio Astronomica* gives a clear picture of science in his day.

Le Père Marin Mersenne (1588–1648), French mathematician, philosopher and theologian, strongly opposed to mystical doctrines (alchemy, astrology, and related arcane arts), and an ardent supporter of science, defending Descartes' philosophy and Galileo's theories. One of his most significant contributions to the period was the link that he provided between philosophers and scientists. It was said at the time that 'to inform Mersenne of a discovery, meant to publish it throughout the whole of Europe'.

by a happy accident for which English culture was in no way responsible.

If the public face of the English Revolution remains little known by the French, the very existence of its private face has remained undiscovered by them. Behind the obvious struggles of the puritan Roundheads and the royalist Cavaliers, Protestantism was fragmenting into endless sects, and the nature of society itself was being brought into question. Millenarians, Calvinists, Presbyterians, Baptists, Quakers, Ranters, Seekers and many others fought or joined forces in the name of True Religion. The Levellers – moderates ahead of their time – advocated a social and parliamentary republic which they were brutally refused. The Diggers wanted nothing less than to change the world. Their agrarian communism was more than an ideology; it was a way of life. The revolution, they said, had been a struggle against the King and wealthy landowners on behalf of the poor, and now that the poor had won they should reap the benefit – common land was there for common cultivation. In 1649, twenty landless labourers, under the leadership of Gerrard Winstanley and William Everard, took possession of the village common at St George's Hill in Surrey, and began to work the land together. Within less than a year they had been expropriated and their millenarian republic broken up. Yet Winstanley's communist vision, described in writings of startling clarity, remains as powerful today as it ever was; his lyricism is the natural expression of his certainty. If the French read Winstanley they would begin to see another side to the English personality, one which is as implacable in its thirst for justice, as the first is pragmatic in the pursuit of its own interests.

But the return of Charles II to the throne was no mere coincidence. It initiated a historical compromise between the power of the King and the growing political will of a flourishing society. It was not until James II's exile and the joint accession of William of Orange, and Mary, that this tacit pact was finally ratified. But in the meantime, the English court was never as cheerful and lively – nor, it must be said, as French – as it was under Charles II.

Count Anthony Hamilton was born in Ireland in 1645 or 46. He was the son of a Scottish nobleman, and grandson of the Duke of Hamilton, who also possessed the French title of duc de Chatelherault. His mother, Marie Butler, daughter of the first Duke of Ormonde, Lord Lieutenant of Ireland and one of Charles II's closest advisers, was of equally good stock. Writing in the lightest French prose, the 'Scotsman from Ireland', Hamilton, offers us a delightful chronicle of life and its amorous adventures in the English court. His account captures the mood of the times better than any other, and gives a perceptive description of the King whose personality coloured that mood – a King who 'showed great abilities in urgent affaires, but was incapable of application to any that were not so: his heart was often the dupe, but oftener the slave, of his engagements'*.

Hamilton's small book bears the unexpected title of *Mémoires de la vie du comte de Gramont*, and contains an amusing portrait of the man who married his sister. But his brother-in-law, Gramont, is merely a pretext. The chronicle's real hero is Hamilton himself, and his youth is the subject. But these recollections are more than just a collection of anecdotes. In 1772, sixty-three years after Hamilton's death, Horace Walpole published at Strawberry Hill a second edition of his compatriot's frivolous masterpiece. He dedicated it to the marquise du Deffand, offering it as 'a monument of admiration and respect. To you, whose graces, wit and taste revive in this century the century of Louis XIV and the charms of the author of these memoirs'. For aristocrats who already possess everything, the only aristocracy that really counts is that of the mind, and there are no frontiers except those between the sharp-witted and the dull.

'The King's restoration,' wrote Hamilton, 'having drawn a great number of foreigners from all countries to the court, the French were rather in disgrace; for instead of any persons of distinction having appeared among the first who came over, they had only seen some insignificant puppies, each striving to outdo the other in folly and extravagance, despising everything which was not like themselves, and thinking they introduced the *bel air*, by treating the English as strangers in their own country.

---

* From the *Mémoires de la vie du comte de Gramont*, in an undated translation by Horace Walpole. Walpole, whose admiration for Hamilton is discussed below, not only translated the memoirs, but was also instrumental in the publication of a second French edition of them.

'The Chevalier de Gramont, on the contrary, was familiar with everybody; he gave in to their customs, ate of everything, and easily habituated himself to their manner of living, which he looked upon as neither vulgar nor barbarous, and as he showed a natural complaisance, instead of the impertinent affectation of the others, all the nation was charmed with a man, who agreeably indemnified them for what they had suffered from the folly of the former.'*

Like his compatriot Gramont, Saint-Evremont was estranged from the French court and was forced to cross the Channel in a hurry. He soon became another favourite of 'all the nation', which later also welcomed Voltaire and Montesquieu with open arms. The French Revolution, and even the Napoleonic wars never severed the ties that bound people of distinction on either side of the Channel. Meanwhile the majority of the English – those who did not form part of the élite 'all England' of enlightened spirits – continued to frown on the cynical futility of French culture, and on their own aristocracy, which they judged to be of the same stamp. The revocation of the Edict of Nantes and the subsequent influx of Huguenots finally convinced them that an unholy alliance between papist obscurantism and royal absolutism was chasing from its frontiers all that was left of decency in France.

Henceforth, French ignorance of English radical thought and (after a brief flirtation) of English philosophy, was matched by English disregard of certain crucial aspects of French culture and temperament. Confident in their dislike of all things Latin and popish, the English ignored a whole side of France that was patriarchal and Catholic, but of Gallican rather than Roman persuasion, respectful of order and morality, and quite as scandalised by the licentiousness of the court as the sternest Roundhead. More significantly, they entirely ignored another, less visible, strain of Catholicism, though it had so much in common with English Protestantism. From Port Royal to the seminary of Saint Sulpice, French priests and parishioners were living their Jansenist faith with austere fervour, defying the authority of the pope and setting their democratic ideal against the reality of royal arbitrariness. Yet

* ibid.

the English have rarely even suspected that beneath the banner of a France that was confident, revolutionary, ideological and secular, there existed this other Christian nation, divided by conflicting religious attitudes. Though literary influences from both sides of the Channel were, and continued to be, numerous and powerful, they were felt only in restricted circles, and the cultural image each country formed of the other was unchanged by them.

Even among the literary élite, these influences were patchy and fashions did not necessarily reflect what was best in the literature of the two nations. Ronsard and the Pléiade poets stimulated considerable interest in the sonnet form among English poets of the sixteenth century, but the reputation of John Donne and the metaphysical prose and poetry of the seventeenth century did not cross the Channel. France, for its part, soon turned its back on the preciosity and baroque of the first years of Louis XIV, just as the King himself had left his flamboyant mistress Madame de Montespan for the dreary Madame de Maintenon; just as Mansart wiped out the Italianisms of Le Vau at Versailles; just as Corneille and Saint Amant were succeeded by Racine and Boileau.

In England the Augustans (so-called because they believed that the Romans had reached a pinnacle of literary achievement during the age of the emperor Augustus) paid tribute to what they considered to be the pre-eminence of contemporary French literature. John Dryden hailed Boileau and Father Rapin, author of the *Réflexions sur la poétique d'Aristote* (and now almost forgotten), as 'the greatest of the century'. Yet the work of Dryden and Alexander Pope remained virtually unknown in France. Half a century later, Voltaire was to discover some merit in Shakespeare, as well as publishing a work entitled *Eléments de la Philosophie de Newton*. The now forgotten Cyclopedia by Ephraim Chambers inspired the great *Encyclopédie* of Diderot and d'Alembert.

This exchange of compliments was not to last. As at Fontenoy, it was merely the preface to a battle in which French classicism was routed by a decisive English assault. And as in other wars, an obscure deserter was at the origin of the defeat: his name was Pierre Le Tourneur. Not content with translating the complete works of Shakespeare in twenty-four volumes, he dared to claim in a sacrilegious preface that the English bard was the greatest of all tragedians. This was too much for Voltaire. True, he had been the Englishman's champion, but between that and dethroning Racine there was an abyss. He rebuked Le Tourneur in no uncertain terms: French tragedy alone was worthy of the name.

But it was too late: the fashion for English was already rooted. Sentiment had won the day over reason. Laurence Sterne's *The Life and Opinions of Tristram Shandy* and *A Sentimental Journey through France and Italy* spawned a rich posterity of shapeless and intimist French novels such as Diderot's *Jacques le Fataliste et son maître* and *Oberman* by Etienne Pivert de Senancour, which were in their turn admired by the poet Matthew Arnold. The Celtic bard, Ossian, through the good offices of Macpherson, carried his French readers into a world of Irish mythology. Le Tourneur followed up his work on Shakespeare with numerous other translations: *Night Thoughts on Life, Death and Immortality* by Edward Young, *Miscellanies* by Richard Savage, Thomas Gray's *Elegy in a Country Churchyard*, and in particular, Samuel Richardson's *Clarissa*. With the exception of Gray's admirable elegy, all these works were in remarkably poor taste, and all prodigiously successful. Wealthy sentimentalists all over France could now retire to the bottom of their '*jardin anglais*', settle down in front of a fake Roman ruin designed by an English architect, and devour, with copious tears in their eyes, some pathetic story written with heart-rending realism by an Englishman.

From 1700 to 1740, a total of sixteen English novels were translated into French. Between 1740 and 1805 there were a further 630 translations or adaptations of English works – the majority of which were published before 1789. England was all the rage. But the infatuation of the French (supposedly the most discerning public in the world) was inversely proportional to the quality of the authors they discovered. Henry Fielding's joyous truculence and Tobias Smollett's directness – though they had so many affinities with Alain René Lesage – never earned them the same popularity as was enjoyed by the mawkish and sententious Richardson, or by the grandiloquent Young.

Henceforth it seemed as if the cultural poles had been inverted. While France was swamped in sentimentality, the English lost interest in their cross-Channel neighbour. 'French' novels were thought to be synonymous with cynicism, licentiousness and abstraction. If the English learned, generally from hearsay, of the existence of some short work by the *abbé* Prévost, by Crébillon *fils*, by Duclos or by Choderlos de Laclos, they merely condemned their too predictable immorality. Yet in spite of the Napoleonic wars and the continental blockade, the Gothic novels of Mrs Ann Radcliffe and Matthew Gregory Lewis continued to be translated and brought into France, where their influence was considerable and long lasting. Was it a Gothic novel that prompted the young Balzac to choose, among many others, the pseudonym of Lord R'Hoone? Prosper Mérimée, an amateur of the bizarre, kept up a correspondance with Mary Shelley, widow of the poet and author of *Frankenstein*, which was published in 1818. Later the surrealists – also lovers of the fantastic – were in their turn to discover *Le Château d'Otrante*, a translation of the first novel in the *genre* by Horace Walpole, that great creator of fashions.

The Unity of Language

After 1815, wealthy and educated Europeans were once more able to enjoy that freedom of the continent which their parents had known before the French Revolution. The Papal police, the suppression of national movements, civil wars, struggles for emancipation – none of these really hindered the movement of affluent travellers who exchanged ideas as they might have exchanged louis d'or, gold sovereigns or thalers.

In the nineteenth century, French and English literati became more cosmopolitan and less obsessed with each other. Germans and Italians were the next to join the international literary community, soon to be followed by Russians, and later by the Scandinavians. In spite of Benjamin Franklin (the only American known in France), and of Fenimore Cooper's Red Indians, the Americans were not admitted into the charmed circle until Charles Baudelaire translated Edgar Allan Poe into French – and even then it was only as second class members. True, American authors such as Nathaniel Hawthorne, Henry Wadsworth Longfellow, Mark Twain and Walt Whitman were frequently read in Britain. But it was still widely felt that true literature was European while American writing was merely a crude copy of the real thing. Even the impact of Henry James' genius at the end of the century was muted. His writing was too European for the Americans, and too American for the Europeans. It was not until after his death that he was properly recognised by the French. In France, Walter Scott, Byron and Dickens enjoyed considerable reputation or success, but the English were not equally enamoured of Victor Hugo or Honoré de Balzac. Translations of Alexandre Dumas, Eugène Sue, George Sand and Paul Féval were published in popular editions, but Stendhal was not read by the English until the twentieth century, and even then very little. On the other hand, the few French who had ever heard of Jane Austen thought she wrote only for teenage girls. As for George Eliot – whose writings they never sampled – she was considered by the French to be a mere plagiarist of the only real George, their own, George Sand.

There are numerous reasons for this gradual distancing. With the growth of imperial ambitions, the rivalry between France and England took on greater proportions. The French did not want to give up their second empire to the British, as they had the first. And since the new imperial frontiers were still not clearly drawn, each new demarcation traced by the colonial pioneers gave rise to further disagreements and confrontations.

But beyond these historical interpretations, there is a simpler explanation for the misunderstandings between French and English – it is a question of language. The Victorian era, which was so confident in all other respects, was afraid of words. Prudery and cant – so hated by Stendhal, despite his anglophilia – were now triumphant in London. In Paris on the other hand, the imagery and vocabulary used by contemporary authors were increasingly plain and unvarnished. Because of this, many French books of the period were untranslatable, or rather unpublishable in Great Britain, while the circumlocutions and equivocations of English writers rendered them equally incomprehensible to the French. In spite of his popularity, Dickens was to suffer from this lack of understanding; his French readers accused him of having a mawkish vision of people and their motivations, whereas the British, with their famous 'hypocrisy', were able to interpret much more clearly the telling silences and the coded language in which he expressed the cruelty of life.

A number of popular writers succeeded in breaking down this barrier of incomprehension, reaching a wider public than the élite of French anglophiles and British francophiles. Zola and Jules Verne had a large English readership, and later, Rudyard Kipling's *Jungle Book* became immensely popular in France. Sherlock Holmes was as famous in France as in the rest of the world, while Edgar Wallace, Agatha Christie and Dorothy Sayers finally established the detective story as an Anglo-Saxon *genre*.

Thanks to the awe in which the French hold their intelligentsia, a renewed fashion for British writers developed in France after the First World War. Respected intellectuals such as Valery Larbaud and Gabriel Marcel introduced the public to authors they particularly loved – Samuel Butler or Aldous Huxley, Samuel Taylor Coleridge (translated by Larbaud only in 1901), Richard Hughes or Joseph Conrad. Publishers soon caught on and began to commission many more translations. D. H. Lawrence's *Lady Chatterley's Lover*, which had been banned in England, was immediately popular in France where no one was shocked by the sexual images, though they were a little by the religious overtones. For French readers – already familiar with Malraux's *La Condition Humaine*, which had come out two years earlier – T. E. Lawrence's *Seven Pillars of Wisdom* elevated adventure to a mythical status. The British saw the book in a more down to earth light, hailing it as a classic memoir of the war, or condemning it for the romanticised exaggerations of the author's role in that war. Virginia Woolf, Katherine Mansfield, Rosamond Lehmann, Ivy Compton-Burnett, Margaret Kennedy, Mary Webb, Daphne du Maurier, and recently Barbara Pym, have all been translated into French and are avidly read by a public that is delighted and astonished by such feminine fecundity.

In this praiseworthy educational enterprise, British poetry remained something of a poor relation. Yeats, Auden and Spender were completely unknown in France, and few people realised that T. S. Eliot (the only contemporary English poet that anyone had ever heard of) was American by birth, like his friend Ezra Pound, and had taken English nationality only at the age of thirty-nine. And when W. H. Auden was finally translated into French, the phrase 'a good lay' in his poem *In Praise of Limestone*, was

171

rendered by '*un bon poème*'. English literature was exacting revenge for a century of being patronised by the French for the coyness of its expression.

Between the two world wars, the British literary establishment became increasingly inward-looking, cutting itself off from the philistine public. Patrons and their *protégés* retired to their *salons* or to the last country houses surviving from the Edwardian era; academics remained secluded in their colleges, while critics and poets sheltered in their literary magazines. Only a few writers, such as E. M. Forster and Somerset Maugham, were able to reach a broader educated audience, who in their turn influenced the public at large.

This same narrow intelligentsia liked to think of itself as cosmopolitan and compared the *Atheneum* of John Middleton Murray to André Gide's *Nouvelle Revue Française*, or recalled Valery Larbaud's memorable lecture on Joyce in Adrienne Monnier's famous bookshop. Here, Gide and the majority of contributors to the *Nouvelle Revue* frequently gathered, and it was in this shop too that Beckett enjoyed meeting Joyce. Russian literature and surrealism, Marinetti's futurism or the poetry of Rilke were the daily bread of this élite. The next generation of intellectuals (including Evelyn Waugh, Anthony Powell and Graham Greene) maintained its prestige and influence beyond the Second World War, sometimes even extending it thanks to cinema and television. Nonetheless, the literary world they had known was fast disappearing. The privilege of reading and being read had once united writers and their public like members of an extended family. Now the media was increasingly taking over, appropriating the image of the author and his work, accumulating the ingredients of the nation's culture, and serving them all up to the public like a mass consumer good.

Today, neither France nor England have produced any literary giants to step into the shoes of an Orwell, an Evelyn Waugh or a Graham Greene, a Sartre or a Paul Morand*. No contemporary French or English writer can claim to have such a genuinely

* Paul Morand (1888–1976), diplomat and writer, widely considered to be one of the great figures of twentieth-century French literature.

international reputation as, for instance, Gabriel García Márquez or Milan Kundera. The exception of Salman Rushdie merely confirms the rule since his fame has little to do with literature. Despite the alleged blasphemy which took *The Satanic Verses* to the top of the best-seller list, the novel has neither the lyrical power nor the rigour of *Midnight's Children*, which remains Rushdie's best book.

In France, a number of literary prizes – including the prestigious Goncourt – and later, the emergence of a unique and truly popular television programme about literature, *Apostrophe* (sadly discontinued in September 1990), have combined to sustain some kind of mass public interest in new writing. In Great Britain, prizes such as the Booker or the Whitbread began to gain real popularity only from the early eighties. Today the winner of the Booker has a first print run of some thirty or forty thousand copies. To protect the prize from commercial pressures and cliques, the jury is replaced every year. But despite some distinguished choices, the Booker and other prizes are no less bitterly criticised for polarising opinion and discouraging readers from tackling reputedly difficult books. Whatever the virtues or vices of these awards, there is no doubt that the reading public in Britain has changed. Educated book-lovers who formerly would have died of shame to be caught reading a popular novel, now show no signs of indigestion when devouring British and American best-sellers. These are sold in hundreds of thousands, to the detriment of authors who would never before have found themselves keeping such bad company.

Some six thousand novels are published every year in Britain, most of them in the autumn – as in France, but with even lower print runs. The most successful authors can expect a paperback edition of their work a year or two after hardback publication. But with the exception of a few professional cookery book writers who become tax exiles, the vast majority of authors cannot even begin to think of living by the pen.

Publishers in Britain are in thrall to the triumphant success of their language, which they share with the United States, not to mention Australia, New Zealand, South Africa, and Canada. The expanded market available to books in English works to the advantage of a number of well-known authors whose writing is appreciated on both sides of the Atlantic. The Canadian novelist, Robertson Davies, expresses what is most subtle and fertile in this cross-cultural fertilisation. The American school of novel writing continues to exercise considerable influence on the British, in spite of the purists who deplore the invasion of English by American-isms, just as their French counterparts rail against the growth of *franglais*. But the importance of the American market has another consequence that is less beneficial. Literary agents and publishers lie in wait to grab any work they can publish simultaneously in Britain and the United States. Books are being conceived and made to measure for this hybrid market, and manuscripts are increasingly turned down because they are unpublishable across the Atlantic.

The rest of the Commonwealth does not place such a heavy burden on British literary production, but the global currency of English does encourage writers from all over the world to contribute to its riches. V. S. Naipaul – an Indian Brahmin born in the Caribbean – and the Australian, Patrick White (who died in 1990), have acquired well deserved international reputations. One of the youngest of these, the Japanese-born Kazuo Ishiguro, was awarded the 1989 Booker Prize for his third novel, *The Remains of the Day*. His work masterfully demonstrates that, without denying their origins, these outsiders can discover a voice for themselves in the most secret depth of English culture.

The pages of *The Times Literary Supplement* and now the *London Review of Books* are the main forum for discussion among Britain's literary élite. Protected from the *hoi polloi*, liberal and cultivated critics continue to write in beautiful English – if sometimes a little pedantic – about the merits of works whose language their compatriots do not understand and which they have no intention of reading. Marguerite Duras and Michel Tournier are the only two contemporary French writers who have any kind of broader following, though it is nothing like that of García Márquez, Milan Kundera or Vargas Llosa.

In France, the courteous obstinacy of Michel Mohrt (Larbaud's discreet successor at the Gallimard publishing house), the eclectic refinements of Christian Bourgois in his 10/18 collection, and the

isolated whims of a few brave publishers give the resolute anglo-
phile a fairly full picture of contemporary English language literature. Graham Greene, Angus Wilson, William Golding, Anthony
Burgess – no bookshop neglects these established names. Julian
Barnes, whose novel *Flaubert's Parrot* won the *Prix Médicis*,
also has a faithful following. But what cannot fail to surprise
the French observer is the proliferation of English women who
turn to the pen. Following in the footsteps of their remarkable
elders, Iris Murdoch breathes life into what one might call the
Anglo-Russian psychological tradition, and Doris Lessing, far from
sticking exclusively to the realm of science fiction as so many of
her French readers believe, explores the feminine world which
feminism cannot quite encompass. That feminine world – and not
its ideological representation – is also at the heart of the work
of Margaret Drabble and Fay Weldon. Mary Wesley epitomises
a well-mannered upper-class view of morality, to which she adds
a personal dose of wryness and cynicism. Could it be that these
female novelists are turning to the written word as a defence
against the silence with which men are forever meeting their
questions? Beryl Bainbridge, Muriel Spark, Alice Thomas Ellis,
the late Angela Carter, and Jeanette Winterson have all been
writing during the last decade, and they neither condemn nor
question, but merely bear witness to their place in society today.

Piers Paul Read, Peter Ackroyd, Martin Amis, and their Scottish
colleagues, James Kelman, Allan Massie and Alasdair Gray are
all genuine writers. The late Bruce Chatwin restored a certain
lost quality to travel writing. But the last figure of undeniable
greatness in either French or English literature was a figure who
belonged to them both – the Irishman Samuel Beckett, who died
in Paris in 1990.

This celebrated interpreter of the inexpressible wrote the first
half of his work in English, translating it into French himself, and
the second half in French, which he later translated into English.
Like Graham Greene, Anthony Burgess and many other British
writers and artists, Beckett lived in France. While working as
an English *lecteur* at the *Ecole Normale Supérieur* in 1928, he
met James Joyce in Paris and struck up a friendship. He wrote
on Proust, and was one of the founders in France of what is

known as the '*Théatre de l'absurde*'. In the Anglo-Saxon world, his theatrical posterity runs from Harold Pinter and Tom Stoppard to Athol Fugard. He reduced characters to the status of shadows, action to unformulated regrets and dialogue to half abandoned sketches. Yet his passion for language was unconditional. 'Words have been my only love,' he said in an interview in France shortly before he died, 'some of them.' Only some of them, true enough, but words from both his languages: English, the language of his birth, which he inherited; French, the language of his daily life, which he acquired.

Part II

A People by
Divine Right

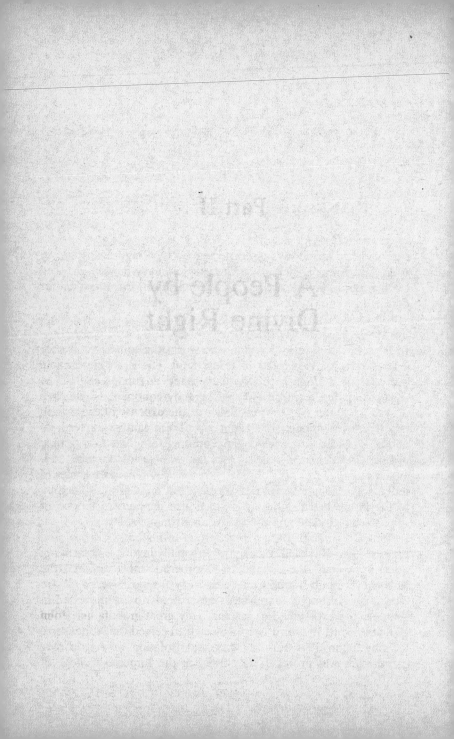

1

Production and Exploitation

Continentals are always disconcerted by the English attitude to work. They appear neither to view it as a heavy burden imposed by fate, nor to embrace it as a sacred obligation. Effort is a matter of personal choice, and payment simply a quid pro quo.

The Most Glorious Industry

In French, '*un paysan*' is a man who works the soil. He may own a few acres, or vast tracts of fertile land. His is an honourable profession. In English the word 'peasant' is condescending, or – when applied to those dirty and greedy continentals who live off the Common Agricultural Policy at the expense of the British tax-payer and mindlessly slaughter innocent lambs – a term of abuse. But a British farmer is quite another thing. He may or may not be a gentleman, but he always knows how to recognise one. Whether daily labourer or landowner, whether tenant or farmer of independent means, employee or manager, he is proud to belong to the most ancient industry – which also happens to be one of the most up to date and productive in Britain.

John Strutt, sixth Baron Rayleigh, is in his early thirties, and the first Lord Rayleigh to become personally involved in farming, injecting a new tone of modern meritocratic efficiency into the substantial family farming business. 'My forebears were all too busy distinguishing themselves in other fields to be interested in farming,' he explains. 'For instance, my great-grandfather, John William Strutt, the third Lord Rayleigh, received the Nobel prize for physics in 1904 for his successful isolation of Argon. My grandfather was professor of physics at the Imperial College of

179

Science, and my uncle, from whom I inherited the title, worked in the Stock Exchange. Traditionally, the running of the estates has always been handed over to the younger branch of the family.'

Throughout most of the nineteenth century the family land was mostly rented out to tenants who looked after it themselves. But by the 1870s agricultural recession was driving numerous tenants away, prompting the physicist, John William Strutt, to look at alternative ways of earning the income he needed for his scientific research. In 1876, he asked his youngest brother, Edward, to take over the family's Essex estates and farm them himself on behalf of the family. Today Strutt & Parker (Farms) Ltd farms some fifteen thousand acres of land, of which three thousand acres are rented. The company's ninety shareholders as well as the board of directors are almost all family members, and the company chairman, David Nutting, is the present Lord Rayleigh's third cousin. Lord Rayleigh himself is a non-executive director of Strutt & Parker (Farms) Ltd, as well as being sole director of Lord Rayleigh's Farms Inc., which farms some eight thousand acres (mostly rented by the company from him). In addition he is chairman of the immensely successful Lord Rayleigh's Dairies Ltd, which processes, packages and distributes about one per cent of the country's entire milk production. The two businesses with the Lord Rayleigh prefix are principally owned by him, and the other five shareholders are also all family members or family trusts.

Although the various companies are run independently of each other, they frequently confer on policy and some of them share offices. Lord Rayleigh's Farms Inc. and Strutt & Parker (Farms) Ltd own a joint sheep venture, and have about one thousand milking cows each, providing between five and ten per cent of the milk processed by Lord Rayleigh's Dairies Ltd. In addition, Strutt & Parker farms and Lord Rayleigh's Dairies recently joined forces to purchase a yoghurt-making business called Bridge Farm Dairies Ltd. The four companies have a joint turnover of some seventy-five million pounds, of which approximately sixty-five million is accounted for by the dairy and yoghurt making business.

The present Lord Rayleigh calls himself a strong family man, and is deeply attached to the countryside where he spent his childhood. Having been in the army for four years, and fought in the Falklands war, he decided to devote himself to the business full time, and in 1984 enrolled himself in a three year business and rural estate management course at the Royal Agricultural College in Cirencester. 'I never felt the army would be challenging in the long term,' he explains, 'but having been born and brought up around here, I wanted to make a contribution to the area.'

Such sentiments of loyalty and pride in the family, its land and its traditions should not blind one to the tough businessman's motivation underlying Lord Rayleigh's courteous and amiable manner. 'Family and business are two different things,' he insists. 'The primary function of the companies is a commercial one, and sometimes in business you have to be a bit hard. I don't think this should impair family feeling, but unfortunately it can happen. Ideally, I would like the companies to be less dominated by the family than they are. In fact, this is probably the most radical difference between myself and my predecessors.'

Rayleigh also believes in a clear and defined hierarchy in which every person knows his exact job specification and is treated 'fairly and firmly'. No one should rely on getting a job, just because his father or grandfather had it. Yet in spite of such attitudes, there remain a number of local families some of whose members have worked for the Strutt estates over several generations, and Rayleigh does not deny that 'everyone appreciates the stability this encourages'. Ultimately the practice of farming, however progressively run, has to be about stability, and the perspective is a long-term one. 'Inevitably, when you have been in farming as long as our family has, you are not interested in short-term gain. The long-term fertility of the land is of primary importance. Unless the business is profitable we cannot achieve anything, but assuming that everything is going well we want to be as generous as possible to our staff, and to the environment as well.'

Nat Sherwood farms in Essex. Sherwood & Sons Farms consist of six separate establishments which Nat owns and manages. His land is not far from the Strutt and Parker estate, which he excludes from his description of the area: 'Most houses around here are normal farm houses, there aren't many large estates. I have got some arable land and some expensive bloodstock. Wheat cultivation is my bread and butter; peas and oil seed provide the jam. Out of three thousand acres I own, I cultivate 1,400. It is very hard to tell you what the price for land is nowadays because it's no longer quality which is the main factor, but the property that goes with it.'

Two tweed caps, three or four shapeless hats hanging on the wall, a procelain art nouveau umbrella stand full of walking sticks with brass knobs; a collection of wellington boots of every shape and size; an engraving of a paddle steamer framed in varnished wood – Nat Sherwood's hall has a kindly and welcoming air. A faint smell of hay and cinnamon pervades the house like a childhood memory. The sofas are covered in floral chintz. Against the wall, there is a handsome Welsh dresser of polished oak complete with pewter mugs and plates. The scene is almost too good to be true – too close to every Frenchman's dream of England to be quite believable. Tea is served, with crumpets and cucumber sandwiches. It is true after all: this English farm really exists.

'My father was a seed merchant,' explains Sherwood. 'But he died when I was fifteen, and I wasn't able to go into the family business. I inherited the farm from my grandfather. I studied agriculture in Cambridge between 1945 and 1947. After that I had to support myself. Since the beginning of the nineteenth century, when they made money, most English people have bought land – which gave them a position in the county. It was considered rather common to be in industry, and the same for trade . . .'

Sherwood's business is a successful one. In addition to farming, he runs a commercial shoot and is now a partner in a stud farm. Yet in order to maintain the profitability of his own farm, he has been forced to stop replacing agricultural workers as they retire, and over the past ten years he has shed as many as four out of eight labourers.

The situation on Sherwood's farm is part of a national trend, and the majority of farmers' children, like his own, have chosen other careers. There remain a few young people who know no other world. There is still a future for them, but technology has made it imperative that they should receive increasingly specialised training.

In the less prosperous and fertile areas of Britain, farmers – like any peasant in Italy or the South of France – have to rely heavily on subsidies from the EEC simply to survive. Paul Staley is a hill farmer in the Pennines. He was brought up on his father's farm, and went to agricultural college for three years before doing an exchange programme for a year and a half in Minnesota, finally returning to run his father's establishment.

The farm consists of two thousand acres of hill land (which is larger than the average for the area), and has seven hundred sheep and thirty cows. Like all the farmers around him, Staley grows no arable crops. 'Throughout the eighties,' he explains, 'farmers were encouraged to breed sheep and get out of arable and dairy farming – for a short period the hill farmer enjoyed a boom as he was the only person producing sheep at the time, and other farmers had to buy their breeding ewe lambs from him. But now everyone is breeding and there is over-production. In 1988 one of my breeding lambs would sell for fifty-five pounds per head. Two years later the price had gone down to thirty-nine pounds. Most of the farmers here make just enough money to survive. But if things don't improve some of them will simply go out of business – a few have already. Everyone knows everyone else, and we help one another out, which makes sense, since we're all doing the same thing at the same time.'

Half the farms in the area are tenant farms. Nearly all of them are family-run, and since farmers cannot afford to employ extra labour, it is quite common for their wives to help out. Paul runs his farm with the help of his three sheep dogs, while his wife combines a part-time job with looking after the baby son who, Paul hopes, will one day take over from him.

As well as the Hill Livestock Compensatory Allowance which he gets jointly from the European Commission and the British government for farming in a 'less-favoured area', Staley also receives a per capita subsidy for his livestock. In Cumbria, as in Cornwall, the Highlands of Scotland and other areas where agriculture is a hard and unprofitable business, the majority of farmers could not survive without subsidies of this kind – even though the value of the subsidy to the farmer is eroded by the over-production which it encourages, bringing down the price that his goods can command. Yet without small farmers and their sheep, the countryside would also die, and the land would deteriorate, gradually reverting to scrub. But since the Second World War, government policies have encouraged the development of intensive farming in large institutions and holdings. It is now estimated that some twelve per cent of holdings in the largest group account for 55.8 per cent of activity, while small farmers (forty-four per cent) account for only 2.6 per cent. Subsidies have also indirectly encouraged the production of winter cereals, leaving ploughed land exposed to the first severe rains between September and November. The effect of this intensification has been to impoverish the soil, leaving between five to ten per cent of arable land in England in serious danger of soil erosion. According to the Soil Survey and Land Research Centre, about seventy-five per cent of this erosion could be stopped almost immediately if appropriate policies were adopted.

Today British farming is at a cross-roads. Present subsidy arrangements continue to encourage farmers to keep more animals than they have the capacity for, and to glut the market with unwanted goods. The government runs a number of environmental protection pilot schemes, offering payments to farmers for putting land out of production. In 1988 for example, the Farm Woodland Scheme was introduced to encourage the planting of new wood-lands on land currently in productive agricultural use, in order to 'help in the diminution of agricultural surpluses, to enhance the landscape, and to create new wildlife habitats'. The political agenda now also includes the encouragement of so-called 'extensification', involving crop rotation and a lower use of fertiliser on arable land, and less intensive cattle and sheep rearing elsewhere. But the sums involved so far are paltry, and do not make up for the contrary incentives still given by the Common Agricultural Policy (despite a significant reduction in farming subsidies). Whether in France or Britain, Italy or Spain, instead of subsidising livestock and produce, the CAP should support small farmers directly, enabling them to survive as guardians of our countryside, without overgrazing their land, or diverting resources and energy into the creation of mountains of produce which are expensive to store, and even more expensive to distribute.

Independent farmers, whether they own vast tracts of land or rent a few acres, tend to vote Conservative. But the waged agricultural labourer, though he remains primarily a farmer with a farmer's outlook, has a slightly different perspective on life. Ray Johnson has long been an activist member of the Labour Party. He was born in the city, in Leeds, but has worked on the land, in the Vale of York, all his life, and on the same farm for nearly forty years. 'I joined the National Union of Agricultural and Allied Workers in the forties,' he tells me. 'Everyone around me was Labour. Labour meant blue collar, Conservative meant rich. This constituency has always been Conservative. The farms around here are prosperous. They combine cereal cultivation with sheep and cattle rearing. My union was never able to get over the problem of our being so dispersed. It's very difficult to organise agricultural labourers. They work too closely with their masters.'

Johnson also believes that tenants pay excessively high rents to landowners, and have to fight for an improvement in their conditions. But there is no solidarity between them and agricultural labourers, who feel themselves inferior to tenants.

English farmers are a peaceable and easy-going breed. Unlike their French counterparts, they would never dream of barricading the roads or spreading liquid manure or tomatoes outside the Ministry's doors. Yet the British do not love their farmers any more than the French appreciate theirs. Housewives suspect them of having sold out to foreigners (specifically, to the European Commission in Brussels) in order to be able to charge more for their produce. Conservationists, bird-lovers, fox-lovers and butterfly-lovers, as well as friends of the cornflower, the poppy and the hedgerow, all accuse them of upsetting the balance of nature for the sake of a productivity which is as dangerous as it is pointless. But farmers argue that the ancient nightmare in which Britain was isolated by war from the rest of the world and unable to feed herself (having to import more than seventy per cent of her food from her colonies and dependencies) has been exorcised only thanks to an efficient, modern agriculture which can now provide for two-thirds of the nation's needs.

Between 1975 and 1985, overall agricultural productivity increased by sixty-nine per cent, while for wheat it increased by ninety-eight per cent, and during two successive years, in 1983 and 1984, the harvest exceeded national needs. At the same time employment in the industry has been falling dramatically. In 1946, there were nearly a million farm workers alone in Britain, but by 1989, a total of just 573,000 people were engaged in agriculture, exploiting some forty-five million acres of land, equivalent to seventy-seven per cent of the total area of the United Kingdom. According to Sir Simon Gourlay, President of the National Farmer's Union, during the decade to 1990, the farming industry lost some sixty thousand jobs, and twenty thousand full time businesses. Today just 2.2 per cent of the working population are engaged in agriculture – a lower proportion than in any other major industrialised country. During this period, the country was self-sufficient in wheat, barley, eggs and poultry. In was also producing eighty-three per cent of its beef and veal, sixty-nine per cent of its pork, ninety per cent of its potatoes and seventy-one per cent of its cheese.

These remarkable figures have not been achieved without cost. Factory farming has increased dramatically, spurred on by demand for cheaper food, and made possible, not only be mechanisation, but also by biotechnology and genetic scientific developments. Intensive farming in the poultry industry has widely been held responsible for recent outbreaks of salmonella poisoning (in the first nine months of 1988 there were twenty-six outbreaks involving 450 people), while the suspected cause of the newly identified condition, Bovine Spongiform Encephalopathy (better known as BSE, or mad cow disease), is infected mass-produced feed made of recycled farm animal and poultry remains.

After forty years of uninterrupted prosperity, farmers are now suffering from an unprecedented identity crisis. There are hundreds of bankruptcies and liquidations every year. The future offers a bleak perspective, with revenues amputated by the progressive withdrawal of subsidies from Europe. But British agriculture is vigorous enough to overcome this trial. Two out of every three farmers today have a secondary source of income. Organic farming, though expensive, is increasingly popular. Cultivators who had previously dismissed it as the inoffensive obsession of a few fad-ridden city-dwellers are now beginning to think that it might represent the agriculture of the future, and in 1987, the government stepped in to regulate the trend by establishing the United Kingdom Register of Organic Food Standards. Unlike other sectors of British industry, some of which have gone into terminal decline, agriculture has survived every crisis and has always emerged healthier. Its strength is not a mere product of chance, and its history deserves more attention than has been granted by admirers of the industrial revolution.

Britain's individuality owes less, perhaps, to its insularity than it does to an early transition from ancient forms of subsistence agriculture to the vigorous market agriculture that we know today. According to some historians, English society was highly mobile from as early as the thirteenth century, and did not resemble the peasant economies of other European nations, in which the extended, patriarchal family was both the unit of production and of consumption. The possibility of buying and selling land turned the English family into a precarious economic association operating for the greater benefit of the individuals within it. There were numerous labourers working for cash on other people's land. Rather than working at home on the family plot, children were frequently put out as servants in other people's households, while at home, labour was hired when necessary. Though predominately rural in the Middle Ages, it was essentially an economically 'rational', market-oriented and acquisitive society. The subsequent growth of industrialisation did not therefore destroy the mythical patriarchal family, which had never existed in England, but was the logical outcome of this historical pursuit of riches by the individual.*

Us and Them

'You looked into an immense hollow of smoke and blurred buildings and factory chimneys. There seemed to be no end of it. In the vague middle, dominating everything, was an enormous round white tower, which I afterwards learnt was a new gasometer.' It was with a sense of fascination and horror that, in 1934, J. B. Priestley stumbled across this 'temple of some horrible new religion', in the Black Country, near Birmingham, where the dismal landscape

---

* The ancient origins of a specifically English market agriculture, and of its consequences, are discussed in *The Origins of English Individualism*, Basil Blackwell, Oxford, by Alan MacFarlane, lecturer in anthropology and Fellow of King's College, Cambridge.

of industrial Britain spread before his eyes 'like a smouldering carpet'*.

In Rusty Lane, West Bromwich, Priestley visited a sheet metal depot. 'The whole neighbourhood is mean and squalid,' he wrote, 'but this particular street seemed the worst of all. It would not matter very much – though it would matter – if only metal were kept there; but it happens that people live there, children are born there and grow up there.'†

Has anything changed during the past fifty years? The Victorian cottages which Priestley found so hideous, seem full of charm in comparison with the cement barracks built just after the Second World War, whose flaking façades fill me with gloom. In Coventry, Priestley had admired the Daimler works: 'hundreds and hundreds of mechanics were at work making and testing parts'. In the British Leyland factory at Longbridge, where Metros and Maestros are produced, automated assembly lines apply complex mechanical procedures to cars which are supposed to persuade British consumers to abandon their Japanese rivals.

After years of enduring taunts about the great age of their country's industrial machinery, the British set to rectifying the situation. By 1984 Britain had more industrial robots – a third of them produced in the United Kingdom – than any other country in the world, with the exception of France and Japan. And even since then, the number of British firms using robots has more than doubled. Heron-like, elegant pointed machines, they jab, pierce and rivet, without taking the time for a fag, which – in 1934 – the Daimler workers were allowed to do for half an hour twice a day.

Factory workers are a dying breed, but a few of them survive. Strangers to the world of retired colonels, City financiers, gentlemen farmers and country vicars, they remain as typically English as the best of them. 'For us, working class people . . .' – this 'Us' immediately opposes the speaker to 'Them' the rich, 'Them' who do not speak like us, 'Them' who do not dress like us, 'Them' who do not eat like us. The factory worker is attached to his

* From *English Journey*, by J. B. Priestley, first published in 1934.
† ibid.

house, his road, his job (when he hasn't lost it), his pub and his club, but his territory is hemmed in by a domain that is not his own. The only thing he has in common with 'Them' is this frontier that both unites and separates them. This differentiation was inscribed in national custom by the industrial revolution, and has been almost universally accepted as if it were a natural law. Historically, it had the advantage of defusing the violence and disorder that egalitarian demands might have provoked. Though at opposite poles of society, the landed aristocracy and the common people – the tenants, the agricultural labourers and the servants – were tied by daily mutual dependence, and could nurture the sense of their importance one to the other.

The middle classes were tormented by the uncertainty that comes of social mobility. Between the lowliness of their origins and the height of their ambitions, success or failure dictated whether they felt closer to the masses who knew how to keep their place, or to that élite which might one day condescend to accept them. The middle classes were the source of Britain's dynamic energy. They were soon to forget their proletarian origins and increasingly to share real power with the great landed nobility – though without always adopting the aristocracy's pomp, or their traditional paternalism. Through the impetus given by the middle classes, a new kind of worker arrived to swell the cities' populations, finding employment in the thriving production and service industries. The least well-paid shop attendant might try to save money on meat, candles, clothes for himself and shoes for his children, but he would keep two house servants in order to avoid the degradation of manual labour, and thus confirm his social superiority. By creating jobs, he was further developing the social mutation in which he was himself participating.

In the 1850s Britain had about 1,300,000 servants, making up the largest single occupational group after agricultural workers. Ninety per cent of these servants were women. Like agricultural labourers, they were more likely to identify with their employers than to resent them. During the First World War, the growth of employment prospects in offices and industry began to deplete their numbers, and by 1945 only 0.5 per cent of British families could still afford the luxury of a servant. Similar trends could be seen throughout Europe in the nineteenth century, but on the continent wars, popular insurrections or the excessive rigidity of absolute monarchies had led to a corresponding loss of respect. In Britain the tranquillity of the *Pax Britannica* allowed a good-natured understanding to evolve between master and servant, both of whom shared a respect for the established order.

In the 1860s, the rapid growth in the number of craft workshops and highly specialised small factories near the labour-intensive centres of coal, metallurgic and textile production, and the general development of commerce were all contributing to an increase in the number of skilled labourers, and so to the dawn of a new era. This new aristocracy of labourers, unlike the indistinct masses of the proletariat, took pride in their work. They had acquired dignity through their skills, and were to impose recognition of that dignity on the rest of society by creating the world's first trade unions.

Trade Unionism and Decadence

British trade unionism was élitist in its origins, but it eventually opened its doors to the unskilled labour force. From then on, the movement became irresistible. From defending the professional interests of individual members, it gradually took on the task of promoting the interests of the entire working class, and from there it aspired to conquer political power. But despite a broader base, British trade unions could not entirely shake off their origins: when first organising themselves in the face of increasingly powerful and unyielding employers, the working-class élite had given priority to upholding professional hierarchies and defending their status, education and salaries. With these aims in view, they had readily adopted the principles of a strategy which went from direct negotiation with the employer to collective bargaining, arbitration and finally, strike action.

Mutual aid and instruction, both individual and collective, were the next priorities trade unions set themselves in order to confront the educational superiority of the ruling classes. In their adoption of the values associated with those whom the revolutionary left dubbed as their 'exploiters', British trade unions have often been accused of reformism. But although they rejected the extreme outcome which Marxist theory assigned to the class struggle, these reformists were as active as the communists in their efforts to politicise the trade union movement. And whereas the intellectual leaders of Marxist-Leninism thought of the Bolshevik Party as being the engine of the Revolution, and merely used the unions as a conveyor belt to lead them towards their goal, the British unions were themselves the driving force behind reform. Indeed, in founding a political party that was truly their own, they went further than any revolutionaries in the world.

The Labour Representation Committee (LRC) was created in 1901 to stand up to an anti-trade unionist offensive by employers. Five years later it was turned into the 'Labour Party', which was to act as a parliamentary pressure group on the Liberals (who were more dependent on the popular vote than the Tories) to adopt legislation favourable to the trade unions. But the momentum was unstoppable. The trade union movement, while remaining open to the democratic socialism of the Fabian Society* (without however turning its back on Marxism to the extent that has been claimed) was to consolidate its hold on the burgeoning party. In the struggles between left and right that the Labour Party has experienced since its inception, the trade unions – with the money and their block votes – can still tip the balance to one side or another.

In addition to standard dues, the trade unions soon added a political levy to their annual subscription rates. This union contribution to the Labour Party remains at the heart of a controversy which has been going on for years both inside and outside the unions and the Party. Like secondary picketing and the now illegal closed shop† – it has long been considered one of the outward signs of working-class solidarity. But many have objected that although individual union members have always had the option of withholding the sum, not everyone is aware that part of their annual dues are in fact diverted to the Labour Party. An opting-in system, they argue, would be much fairer (as well as more indicative of real solidarity) than the present one.

* The Fabian Society was founded in 1883–1884, and participated in the creation of the LRC. It is still affiliated to the Labour Party.
† The closed shop was a contractual agreement imposed on employers by the unions, making union membership a condition of employment.

During her eleven years in power, Mrs Thatcher set about systematically undermining this traditional working-class solidarity in the name of the freedom to work. In the 1984 Trade Unions Act, she required unions to ballot their members at regular intervals about the political levy (in the event, every union voted to retain the fund), and in the 1988 Employment Act, she finally removed all remaining statutory justification for the closed shop, relegating it to the status of a nostalgic union memory. With the remarkable intuition that characterised her, Mrs Thatcher had sensed that in order to break down trade unionism, it was necessary to attack its most sacred dogmas. To the surprise of everyone – including her own supporters – the denunciation of trade union excesses proved too popular for the offensive to be curtailed in mid-stream. Every good melodrama has its villain and here was an excellent one. And since trade unionism was godfather to the Welfare State – from which public opinion had expected too much for too long not to be disappointed – it was natural to blame the unions for its shortcomings. From there it was also tempting to blame them, indiscriminately, for all the country's economic mistakes, past and present. They were responsible for pressurising governments into bureaucratic meddling in business affairs. They blinded the workforce and led them down a path of self-destruction through excessive strike action. In short, the decline of British industry could be laid at their door.

These convenient over-simplifications bore only a distant resemblance to reality. The unions were authoritarian, moderate and resistant to change. They were even more violently attacked by the hard left for their class collaboration than they were by the right. As for management, it was not as blameless as its defenders had claimed, and trade union responsibility for its misfortunes was less clear than most people wished to believe.

Certainly industry had known a period of former glory. Britain's extraordinary economic expansion at the end of the eighteenth century (in which manufacturing industry had played a notable part) had gained new momentum after Napoleon's defeat. Considerable fortunes were amassed in mining, metallurgy and textiles. Never had British industry been more flourishing; but in Germany, rural France and distant Japan, industry also began to develop vigorously from the end of the last century, and in America it progressed by leaps and bounds. By the beginning of the twentieth century, industry nearly everywhere was catching up with the British model, frozen in its sovereign pride.

By then, Britain's real economic strength lay in different directions. In the area of food, drink and tobacco, several dynasties were founded which still survive today, and some of them retain an enviable position in world markets. But it was in the service industries – especially in the financial sector – that the British showed real genius. Great Britain's prosperity is based less on the creation of wealth than on its exploitation. It is not the unions so much as the money makers who have sacrificed the future of British industry to their appetite for immediate profitability. As for the industrialists themselves, their problem was not lack of strength – as they repeatedly demonstrated in major confrontations in which the unions were forced to capitulate. They seemed afflicted instead by a surprising lethargy which prevented them from making the most of the advantage gained to invest, modernise, increase their productivity or go in search of new markets. The supremacy of the pound sterling and that admirable tool of commerce forged during the course of centuries, the system of imperial preference (which survived for a brief period after decolonisation), allowed them a brief respite before they found themselves very suddenly supplanted in every market, starting with their own.

At a time when the Marshall Plan and the Treaty of Rome – whatever their drawbacks – were heralding a new era for Europe, the British were firmly set in their ways. Assuming they had gained the upper hand, trade unionists set to wresting from management all the concessions so far denied to them. Drunk with success, they multiplied demands for wage increases, restrictive practices and protective measures as if they had discovered an inexhaustible treasure, thus finally justifying the popular resentment which Margaret Thatcher was to exploit so skilfully. For their part, employers – who today proclaim their outrage at such profligacy – offered only token resistance to the unions. Thinking they could ignore the little European Community of the six, they simply raised their prices and relied on the rest of the world to buy their unique products, as they had always done.

The British have always enjoyed the fruits of their industry while treating it with a condescension tinged with repugnance. It is not trade unionists who ruined Britain's enterprises, nor the early entrepreneurs; but their children. Having cleansed themselves of the soot from their fathers' factories in a bath of Latin and Greek, they went straight from their public schools to their country residences, or to the colonies, far from their factories and their workers' cottages. They left their workshops to the engineers, and took refuge in company of their own kind, in the discreet luxury of their clubs and their boardrooms.

Ancients and Moderns

Public opinion, like army generals, is often one war behind, and the trade unionism which provokes its enmity is already on the road to extinction. The real battle is taking place within the unions and is not so much a confrontation between Left and Right, as between the ancients and the moderns. Resistance to the Conservative offensive relies less on an uncertain counter-attack by the unions, than on a redeployment of their troops.

On the 17th of January 1985, the National Portrait Gallery unveiled a new painting in the presence of the former Labour Prime Minister, Harold Wilson, now Lord Wilson. It was a large portrait of three well-known trade unionists: Joe Gormley, who became Lord Gormley on his retirement from the presidency of the National Union of Mineworkers; Tom Jackson, former leader of the Union of Post Office Workers, now an antiques dealer; and Sidney Weighell, former General Secretary of the National Union of Railwaymen. This triumvirate had been judged by the National Portrait Gallery – which had commissioned the portrait – to be particularly representative because they had presided over the three toughest strikes of the sixties. Yet all three of these men were considered right-wingers in the trade union movement. It was not, in fact, a lack of fighting spirit that set the Right against the Left; but whereas Gormley, Jackson and Weighell had fought to defend the professional interests of their membership, the militant left were pursuing the wider aim of establishing a working-class society. Ironically, Tom Jackson was unable to make it to the picture's inauguration because of a railway strike, while Lord

Gormley was forced to take one of the gallery's side entrances in order to avoid a group of miners waiting to take issue with him over his opposition to the strike being conducted for the past year by his successor, the left-wing Arthur Scargill.

Gormley and Scargill could not have been more different from each other in temperament, opinions and methods. The former was chubby, conciliatory, and accepted the political order. The latter was forceful, doctrinaire, intolerant, and believed in forcing political change through industrial action. Yet each in turn enjoyed the unstinting confidence of the majority of miners because both of them had worked in the pits, and – though their styles were completely different – both were formidable negotiators. But after the debacle of the 1984 to 1985 strike, Scargill lost considerable support among his membership; his impressive oratory could not compensate for his failure to deliver the goods, and his uncompromising left-wing stance was becoming unfashionable in the miners' union, as elsewhere. His popularity took another dive when it emerged, in July 1990, that between £1,000,000 and £1,800,000 donated by Russian miners to the NUM had been diverted to the coffers of the impenetrable communist-backed International Miners Organisation – of which Scargill is the president. But in spite of this rather unpleasant episode, Scargill remains – for a dwindling constituency – the unblemished hero of the radical left.

Another complicating factor in the balance of power within the unions was the role of the Communist Party, which had successfully infiltrated sections of the union movement, sometimes openly and sometimes clandestinely. But despite conflicting tendencies within the movement, the different factions frequently compromised with each other and did not hesitate to put up a united front before any external danger. Union leaders all pursued the same objective. As Ronald Utiger, managing director of Tube Investments, put it to me in 1981, 'They would prefer to have a larger slice of a small cake, rather than enlarging the cake.' Even when the Labour Party was in power, union leaders were unable to start an open-ended dialogue with the Government about the economy without being accused of compromise or capitulation, and talks could immediately be put into jeopardy by savage strike action. The Advisory Conciliation and Arbitration Service was created by the Labour Party in 1974 and given official status a year later, but most people thought ACAS merely institutionalised the very conflicts it was meant to defuse.

Until Mrs Thatcher's election to power in 1979, successive governments – both Labour and Conservative – had merely tightened the knot they were delicately trying to unravel. Mrs Thatcher's approach was to cut straight through it. During her first term of office she introduced several measures: postal ballots, financed out of the public purse, to discourage fraud during the election of union leaders; compulsory secret ballots of the workforce to consult them on any strike decision; restrictive rules on strike picketing; restrictions on the closed shop; compulsory periodic polls to check whether union members still wished to contribute to the political levy.

The effect of these measures began to make itself felt shortly after Mrs Thatcher's first re-election. Union leaders prophesied a mass revolt by workers determined to undermine the new legislation, but three massive defeats brutally and definitively gave the lie to their forecasts. The first of these defeats was inflicted on the powerful National Graphical Association by Eddie Shah, then the obscure proprietor of a local free newspaper; the second, in 1985, forced the miners to go back to work, unsatisfied, after a year of industrial action; the third, when Rupert Murdoch transferred The Times group of newspapers to Wapping, finally broke the hold of newspaper and printing unions over Fleet Street.

During previous periods in power the Labour Party had tried in vain to curtail the strength of the unions, in a sort of ritual murder of its parent. Now in spite of vocal protests at the role of the courts and the police in enforcing the new despicable legislation, Labour soon let it be known that it would not be putting the abolition of the Thatcher union reforms in any future manifesto. The party's second defeat in 1983 had forced the unions to become more pragmatic and less political, and the new Labour leader, Neil Kinnock, was successfully distancing himself from the coterie of union leaders. Their names were removed from the lists of party platform speakers in the 1987 election, while the regular seventies-style meetings between the

TUC and the Labour Party Liaison Committee were all but formally ended. During the 1990 Labour conference, the unions' own voting strength was mobilised to bring in a number of structural changes to the Party, the net effect of which was to curtail union power in the constituencies, as well as reducing the union block vote from ninety to seventy per cent. In the meantime Tony Blair, the Party's employment spokesman, was able to steer Labour's new policy on employment and trade union law through conference despite rearguard action by the left-led unions. While proposing a new Industrial court 'which will have a conciliation role in addition to its normal duties', as well as a number of measures designed to soften the impact of some of Mrs Thatcher's union legislation, the new policy effectively endorses many of her most radical measures. *Looking to the Future*, a 1990 Labour Party publication, boldly states, 'We fully support and advocate a hundred per cent trade union membership at the work-place,' but the real point of the assertion is contained in the preceding phrase, 'whilst recognising the freedom not to join a trade union'. The closed shop is not about to be resurrected by the Labour Party. Industrial action, it also states, 'requires the support of a properly conducted ballot', and while the reader is assured that 'Labour will restore the right to take sympathy action', including secondary picketing, it is later specified that this will be permitted 'only where the second employer is directly assisting the first employer to frustrate the dispute'.

Curiously, it was in Tory ranks that Mrs Thatcher's legislation sometimes occasioned a certain disquiet, for Conservative wisdom is suspicious of needless legislation and prefers self-regulation and mutually binding agreements to the impositions of the law. Furthermore Britain had seen enough savage strikes in its history to know that, law-abiding though its people may be, no legal bolt can ever be strong enough to resist forever the onslaught of legitimate demands.

In 1985, the year of the miners' defeat, the Amalgamated Union of Engineering Workers signed a new kind of agreement with Nissan, giving it – in preference to two rival unions – exclusive rights of representation over the entire workforce in the Japanese car manufacturer's British subsidiary. In return for this exclusivity, the AUEW agreed to reduce to two the numerous professional categories which compartmentalised the car industry, and never to resort to strike action while some form of negotiation, mediation or arbitration was in progress. The Electrical, Engineering, Telecommunication and Plumbing Union (EETPU) had already signed a 'no-strike agreement' with another Japanese company, Toshiba, in which conciliation and arbitration procedures were to replace strike action entirely. A few years later when Rupert Murdoch opened his new premises at Wapping, it was once again the opportunist electricians who took an unprecedented step by agreeing to take over the jobs of NGA members, thus enabling the newspaper magnate to sack his Fleet Street staff *en masse* without losing a single day of production on any of the papers in his News International group. In July 1988, the Trade Union Congress suspended the EETPU while considering their possible exclusion from the TUC for having betrayed the printing workers. Anticipating their decision, the electricians voted, five to one, in favour of retiring voluntarily from the Congress. Two months later during its annual conference, the Labour Party, anxious not to be dragged into a witch hunt by its left wing, refused to exclude the rebel union from its ranks.

In April 1987, Kenneth Clarke – then Secretary of State for Employment in the second Thatcher Government – claimed, entirely without irony, that the union movement should be grateful to the Conservatives for having saved it from decline. The new laws enacted to protect individual freedom within the unions, in his view, had restored power where it belonged – to the workers – and forced union bosses to abandon unworkable policies which only they still supported. It was, in fact, difficult to contest this argument. The real reason for the unions' decline had little to do with the new legislation, and everything to do with unemployment and the decline of labour-intensive heavy industries, and the rise of service and largely automated precision industries. At the June 1987 elections, less than half the union membership voted for the Labour Party, thus effectively ratifying the very policies against which their self-declared champions were attempting to mobilise them.

The growth in part-time jobs, with their shifting workforce, was also unfavourable to trade union recruitment. Women were turning in large numbers towards a kind of work which was compatible with their domestic duties, and they put little faith in a trade-unionism which was dominated by men and where they were only grudgingly given positions of subordinate responsibility.

Women, racial minorities, temporary and part-time workers, and employees of multiple chains or restaurants are not interested in traditional forms of union solidarity. What they require is advice about health and social security; they need education, legal assistance and good quality childcare provision. It is by offering them this kind of help, as well as cheap holidays and preferential house and car insurance rates, that the unions can hope to attract them within their ranks. Because of their dispersion and the precarious nature of their work, their recruitment is difficult and costly and their loyalty uncertain. But without them the union movement cannot hope to regenerate.

At the end of the last century there were 1,200 trade unions in Britain. By the end of 1988 there were only 354 left, and by the year 2000 the figure will probably be as low as two hundred. In order to avoid ridiculously low membership figures, they will have to regroup into broader categories of representation and be more willing to sign the kind of agreement in which only one union represents the entire workforce within a company – a strategy which is at present denounced by the die-hards. They will also have to forge closer ties with unions in other European countries, and to define a precise strategy to deal with multinationals. Like the new businessman, the trade unionists of the future will have to adapt and change, or perish.

The Wrong Accent with the Right Attitude

In May 1987, the City University Business School turned to a novel kind of guru for a lesson on the rules of good management. His name was Alan Sugar – neither a Cambridge economist nor an expert from the City, but a self-made man whose personal fortune is worth more than three hundred million pounds. Amstrad, the company which he created for the production of low-cost computers and a range of other electronic products, has become the largest personal computer manufacturer in the United Kingdom.

The glamorous multi-millionaire Richard Branson is in his thirties. He left his public school, Stowe, when he was fifteen, and became an entrepreneur 'to survive'. His company – named Virgin 'because I was as ignorant about business as a virgin is about life' – now has one of the largest world networks of record shops. In addition, Branson personally controls a large number of other companies, including the airline company, Virgin Atlantic. He suffered a small disappointment when the launch of his company on the stock-market coincided with the 1987 share crash. In a princely gesture a year later, he decided to buy back, together with his employees, all the shares at the price of their issue, for the sum of 238 million pounds.

Terence Conran, the creator of Habitat, gave up art school at the age of eighteen, without a diploma, because he was 'wasting his time'. Sir James Goldsmith, one of the twenty richest men in the world, left Eton at the age of seventeen after having placed a £1,000 running bet on a horse, and the late press baron, Robert Maxwell, never set foot in a university. Universities, on the other hand, have taken to providing courses explicitly aimed at promoting the creation of new enterprises.

Over the years I have been meeting an increasing number of these employees and company directors who have the wrong accent with the right attitude. They come from obscure state schools, and if they have any kind of diploma – which is not always the case – they could have obtained it with relative ease at some provincial university, or from Oxbridge, after a hard struggle to prise open its doors. A few are heading some of the biggest concerns in the country. Others have gone bankrupt. A few have constructed a second fortune from the ruins of the first. The majority accept a less spectacular fate, working hard for a salary which in all objectivity they believe to be inadequate, but which they are determined to improve.

In 1979 – before the new Conservative team had fully worked out its monetarist and ultra-liberal theories – Ian Henderson, Director General of the Swansea Viscose Group Ltd, was already an adherent of Thatcherism without knowing it. 'I belonged to a working-class background,' he explained to me, intimating that this was one of the keys to his success. He regretted that there were not more company directors from working-class origins, like himself; they would have an easier relationship with the unions. But the unions 'stood in the way of progress and new machinery quite often'. He was as critical of them as he was of managers who 'expect to be beaten by the unions'. His political convictions were in harmony with his vigorous faith in the capacity for survival of the fittest: 'If the Left get in, we've had it. The manufacturing base will go completely because the unions will rise and managers will acquiesce.'

It is more common than one might imagine to hear other Ian Hendersons say that they have all the weapons they need for victory. True to her electoral promises, Mrs Thatcher rewarded these heroes of front-line capitalism in kind for the material and moral benefits they brought her. Her policies rested primarily on them. Without them Thatcherism would have been a mere dream, and Mrs Thatcher herself would have been swept away by history.

Making the Wealthy Wealthier

In the race for power and money, these uninhibited and ambitious men who have shaken off their social handicaps, have been joined, and often overtaken, by a gaggle of foreigners and Commonwealth immigrants whose direct style upsets the hushed elegance of traditional boardrooms.

The international magnate Rupert Murdoch, owner of the *Sun* (Britain's biggest selling tabloid newspaper) and of *The Times*, was an Australian before acquiring American nationality. Michael Edwardes, the saviour of British Leyland, the troubleshooter successively called in to save the situation at International Computers Ltd (ICL), Dunlop, and the Chloride group, is South African. Ian MacGregor, formerly in charge of British Coal – the man responsible for the miners' defeat – is of Scottish origin, but is an American citizen, as is Richard Giordano, President of the British Oxygen Company (BOC) group. And the opening up of the City to foreign firms in 1986 led to a mass invasion of Americans and Japanese that was barely slowed down by the 1987 stock-market crash. Whatever their origins, these new-style managers prefer risk to security and change to tradition.

Yet besides a handful of stars with exceptionally fat salaries, industrial managers in Britain are paid half of what their American, German or Swiss counterparts receive, and a good deal less than the French and the Italians. It was therefore without qualms, that Nigel Lawson – then Chancellor of the Exchequer – introduced his March 1988 budget, cutting the maximum tax rate from sixty per cent to forty per cent, and thus incurring the wrath of the Labour Party for shamelessly throwing money at the wealthy. Quite unworried by the hullabaloo, he merely called attention to three triumphant electoral victories, a balanced budget, a generally improved standard of living, and a regular fall in the unemployment rate. He might also have pointed out that unless managerial salaries in industry become competitive with the City's, there is every reason to believe that the most gifted graduates will continue to ignore it in favour of finance – with the exception of those who emigrate to America, where industrialists know that talent is expensive, but profitable.

In spite of this handicap, between 1980 and 1987 Britain's annual growth in productivity was in the region of five per cent – a rate similar to that of newly industrialised countries such as South Korea and Hong Kong, and superior to that of Singapore or Taiwan. Forty years after a defeated West Germany, and some twenty years after the other countries signatory to the Treaty of Rome, Britain too at last appeared to be overcoming its post-war blues. The recession of the early eighties had led to a 'shake-out' of manufacturing industry (particularly large industries), hitting the north of the country, as well as Scotland and Wales, with greater severity than the south and east, but bringing about a significant regeneration of a number of inefficient businesses. A paradigm case is that of British Steel, which was transformed from one of the least to one of the most efficient steel industries in the world.

Next to the well-established companies, a new breed of entrepreneurs was also falling into step – the creators of small businesses. According to Mrs Thatcher, it was these small new concerns – in Britain as in every other developed country – that would gradually reduce the rate of unemployment. What is certain is that during the

1980s, the stock of businesses, most of which are small, increased by as much as twenty-nine per cent. In 1989 new businesses were being set up at a net rate of 1,700 a week, compared with just over 300 in 1980. And it is also clear that a number of these did very well.

When in 1976, Anita Roddick stepped into her local branch of Barclays Bank, wearing jeans and pushing a pram, to request a £4,000 loan for a cosmetics boutique, she was politely shown the door. The second time round, she came wearing smarter clothes, accompanied by her husband – and was successful. With the money she opened a small shop in Brighton, which she called The Body Shop. The herbal products which she offered were sold loose, and it was up to her customers to fill pretty containers of every size with the creams, crystals or essences of their choice and to put their own labels on them. Encouraged by her immediate commercial success, she applied for another £4,000 loan to open a subsidiary in Chichester, only to be turned down once again. It was a family friend, Ian McGlinn, who finally gave her the necessary sum in return for a half stake in her business. Today there are some 150 Body Shops in Great Britain, and well over four hundred of them abroad, though the majority are franchised. In April 1985, when the Body Shop was floated on the stock market, Ian McGlinn sold for more than £400,000 a part of the shares which he had bought for £4,000, while still retaining a £2,000,000 pound equity in the business of his friends, the Roddicks.

One could multiply the number of examples demonstrating that in Britain, as elsewhere, small businesses provide one of the mainsprings of economic expansion. Throughout much of the seventies and eighties, Britain heavily increased its involvement in industrial research and innovation. At the very time when more traditional manufacturing industries were suffering from the worst consequences of Mrs Thatcher's first recession, the growth potential in the electronics, technology and related sectors seemed enormous. In 1983, the State's monopoly on patents developed with the help of public funds was abolished in order to encourage researchers to exploit their inventions commercially. In 1984, the British Computer Society was given a Royal Charter, again with a view to encouraging the development of new technologies. Yet a

Midland Bank report, brought out in March 1987, showed that it was precisely in the areas of manufacturing demanding the highest intensity of research that Britain was losing the most ground. The budgetary constraints required by Thatcherite orthodoxy were dangerously depleting funds for university research (a fact which Mrs Thatcher strongly denied). In answer to the complaints of university dons, she offered her usual panacea – an invitation to find money in the private sector; and in order to improve their chances of getting it, she suggested charitably, it was necessary for them to have a clear notion of the potential economic application of their work. But neither research nor business was ready for a marriage of convenience in which both parties were afraid of being the dupe of the other. Meanwhile American universities and businesses were creaming off the ablest British researchers, as well as the best scientists from the laboratories and universities of the Commonwealth. Today, about a thousand British scientists and engineers a year are granted permanent residence in the US.

The bleakness of this picture should not be unduly exaggerated. In order to promote cooperation between the universities and industry, and in order to ensure the fruitful cross-fertilisation of applied research with the latest industrial techniques, there has been a great expansion in the number of science parks located in or around universities. One of the first to be established (in 1972), and still the largest, is the Cambridge Science Park, where some eighty companies occupy most of a 130 acre site, with room for further companies. By January 1989, there were thirty-eight such science parks in the country, with a further twenty under construction or planned. Furthermore, a new law granting financial autonomy to university faculties, polytechnics and other establishments of higher education, enabled them to market the fruits of their research directly.

In Scotland during the eighties, the entire industrial belt surrounding Edinburgh and Glasgow successfully exploited the conjunction of its underused industrial potential and the scientific talents nurtured by the Scottish universities. The zone, which had been one of the hardest hit by the crisis affecting all the traditional industries of the north, is now known as Silicon Glen – by analogy with Silicon Valley in California. It was electronics that brought it back to life. Between 1979 and 1989 Scottish electronics output more than quadrupled, creating about 11,400 jobs in the region. By mid 1988 some 230 plants were employing about 45,200 people (equivalent to thirteen per cent of Scotland's manufacturing workforce), and creating eighteen per cent of the nation's output and investment. This represents one of the biggest concentrations of the electronics industry in Western Europe. It is true that in 1988, more than forty per cent of those working in the Scottish electronics industry were actually employed by American owned plants, and it is possible that by limiting the activities of their subsidiaries to the exploitation of products conceived and designed at home, American, Canadian and even Japanese multinationals – which are so dominant in the area – could eventually compromise this technological revival and dry up Scottish creativity. On the other hand, the high volume of export orders that this generates has protected the Scottish electronics industry from the worst effects of the early nineties recession, and in the long term increasing demand and the growth of related service activities probably minimise the danger.

In the university and laboratories of Cambridge, scientific creativity has been blossoming, giving rise to highly lucrative projects. Between 1979 and 1987, the number of firms established in and around the city rose from forty to more than four hundred, and the most interesting thing about this boom is that it was entirely spontaneous. Two major factors were at the root of the development. The first was ancient: it lay in the university's unique scientific personnel and equipment. The second, on the contrary, was very recent: it was the discovery by high-flying researchers that they had an aptitude for designing and organising the technical implementation of their discoveries, as well as – in some cases – marketing them successfully, and in either case, making a profit from their skills. The third axis of this high technology revolution has been the six lane M4 motorway, which links London and Heathrow (the most important airport in Europe), with Bath (whose university is actively cooperating with regional industries), Bristol and South Wales. The present recession has not spared these innovative industries. Yet in early 1991, the lettings on the Cambridge Science Park were still buoyant, and whatever the fate of individual companies, the new spirit of cooperation between enterprising academics and entrepreneurial business remains a legacy for the future.

The owners and managers of these up-to-the-minute firms are, for the most part, under forty. They are energetic, sporting types and not in the least stuffy. But although they are quite as inventive as their Silicon Valley counterparts, they have remained faithful to that peculiarly British style that is moulded from centuries of tradition. As if to distance themselves, not only from traditional industry, with its factories and offices, but also from the trappings of modernism, they have taken their headquarters and their laboratories into splendid country houses, of which they are the new lords.

The Logica company was started in 1969 by four friends to produce computer programs and peripherals. It was floated on the stock market in 1983, and by 1991 had expanded into a holding company with five subsidiaries and a total staff of 3,700 worldwide. The headquarters of Logica Aerospace and Defence, one of the subsidiaries, are based in the former stately home of Cobham Park, in Surrey. Before being taken over by Logica, the house had been entirely neglected – abandoned to the frogs and disfigured by fluorescent tube lighting on its eighteenth-century ceilings. Five hundred thousand pounds were spent on removing the pipes which covered the walls, and an expert from the National Trust restored the gold leaf on the ceiling mouldings. Hallam Court, formerly used as horse stables, and in Edwardian times, to stable motorcars; Milton Hall, an eighteenth-century country house near Cambridge; the annex of a convent at Windsor – all are historic buildings which have been rescued by these architects of post-industrial society. But for all the nostalgia, the primary aim of such companies is still to place themselves and Great Britain at the forefront of world development.

In the fields of electronics, biotechnology and comunications the British have indeed taken great strides into the future, and in the late eighties, high technology industries showed levels of output, productivity and exports well above the average for manufacturing. Between 1985 and 1990, the computer sector was greatly expanded. Britain is now one of the top three markets in Western Europe for data-processing equipment, and many of the leading overseas manufacturers in the sector (such as IBM, Compaq and Seiko) have established plants in the country. Since 1984 there has also been a rapid expansion in the market for cellular telephones, with the British at the forefront of technology in this field. Sales of telegraph and telephone apparatus and equipment by British firms more than doubled between 1979 and 1989. An important part of the industry produces transmission equipment and cables for telecommunications and information networks. Well over half the world's undersea communications cables have been made and laid by a British company, STC Submarines Systems, and Britain also has the world lead in the transmission of computerised data along telephone lines for reproduction on television screens.

Though this renewal of the industrial fabric has been most striking in Scotland and the south of England, the north has also participated in the innovative boom, and next to abandoned old factories, a new generation of highly specialised workshops are sub-contracted to produce goods for the industrial giants.

With the old rules of the game disregarded, there was an unprecedented growth in consumption – the driving force behind production – during the boom of the eighties, outpacing that of all other European Community countries over the past decade. Poverty was no barrier to acquisition; one merely got into debt in order to live better today, in the expectation of becoming wealthier tomorrow. During the five years to 1989, spending increased by a staggering 28.3 per cent in real terms. For the retail trade, the gulf separating the depressed north from the prosperous south barely seemed to exist. The biggest commercial shopping centre ever offered to the public was opened in 1986 in Gateshead near Newcastle – a city which had the highest unemployment rate in the whole of the United Kingdom. Over the last ten years more than half of British households came to own a car, and nearly a quarter of these possess a second one. Families without a refrigerator have become a rarity, and more than one in three own a freezer as well.

Financial deregulation has been the principal motor behind this extraordinary spree. While Mrs Thatcher was assiduously advocating the Victorian values of self-reliance, hard work and good housekeeping, her Governments made possible a huge expansion in private sector borrowing, which fuelled an economic boom, and sustained the public's confidence in the Thatcherite miracle. After the severe depression of the early eighties, the economy did indeed pick up significantly, and with the new possibilities for credit, the British – encouraged by Mrs Thatcher's policy – were able to indulge the dream of owning their own homes on an unprecedented scale. Between 1971 and 1988, the number of owner-occupied homes increased by about fifteen per cent, and today two-thirds of Britain's housing is owner-occupied, compared to 50.7 per cent in France and only thirty-nine per cent in Germany. With the growing value of houses leading the growth in the rest of the economy and boosting the confidence of the consumer, home-owners thought they were sitting on the proverbial golden egg, and borrowed even more heavily on the security of their property to finance the purchase of all the other consumer durables of their fancy. A true revolution in British attitudes to spending was taking place.

The euphoria of the eighties has today been curbed. With rising unemployment and inflation now in double figures, many economists are gloomy about the economy's future. Productivity growth has slowed after the surge of the mid 1980s. House prices have dropped significantly for the first time since the mid 1970s (in some places by as much as twenty-five to thirty per cent), and the construction and related industries have naturally suffered badly. Between a hundred and two hundred estate agents' branches have closed, with the loss of up to ten thousand jobs. Sustained high interest rates, introduced to curb the consumer boom, have hit industry across the board, but particularly the small businesses which flourished under Mrs Thatcher in the south and east. In 1990, 24,442 businesses failed in England and Wales – a figure which easily beats the previous record of 21,682, established in 1984. According to Philip Mellor, marketing manager in the business information company, Dun & Bradstreet, 'the 1990s have not started well for new businesses . . . It is very disturbing that the level of business failures is now nearly twice as high as it was ten years ago. All the signs are that for the foreseeable future the situation will get worse rather than improve . . . The more new businesses, sadly, the greater the rate of failure'.

The electronics sector, with a high preponderance of small companies, has inevitably suffered badly from high interest rates, while the Stock Market – which is nervous of high-risk industries at the best of times – has been particularly wary of investing in electronics during the current recession. In 1990 the sector as a whole underperformed the market by about ten per cent, with capital equipment companies such as laser manufacturers tending to perform less well than software businesses as industry postponed expenditure on capital goods. Despite the general gloom, certain companies (particularly international innovative ones able to attract overseas investors) have succeeded in maintaining growth. Amstrad, for instance, recovered strongly from the problems of 1989, and in 1990, outperformed the market by sixty-one per cent.

At the beginning of 1991, while some pundits are already talking of 'the worst recession since the war', not everyone is as gloomy. The forecasting company, Cambridge Econometrics, predicts that the current downturn will be 'much less serious' than the early eighties recession, largely because manufacturers, profit margins and industrial efficiency are higher than in 1980 and employment levels are lower. Though the number of small businesses going into liquidation is unprecedented, large industry may well be able to weather the current recession more successfully than the last. In the meantime, British consumers have taken stock of the situation and have curbed their acquisitive urge – curbed it, but not stifled it entirely. According to a report published by the Economist Intelligence Unit in October 1990, provisional indications were that real consumer spending growth (adjusted for inflation) had slowed down from 4.1 per cent in 1989 to something under two per cent in 1990. And in 1991, the report forecasts, it would recover again to 2.8 per cent. Neither the pockets of poverty, however scandalous, nor continuing – and now growing – unemployment, however unanimously condemned, nor even inflation, has been sufficient to kill the new credit mentality. Deaf to the exhortations of economists who urge him to accept a lower salary in order to avoid pricing himself out of the market, the average consumer keeps one hand on his credit card, the other on his pension plan, and – his eye glued to the television screen – lets his mind wander covetously over an array of goods each as irresistible as the next.

2

Financiers First and Foremost

With the abolition in 1986 of all the barriers that used to defend the Stock Market from foreign competition, the ancient City of London has given Great Britain – and with it the whole of Europe – the opportunity of maintaining its primacy in the stock exchange markets of the world (a primacy it has enjoyed without challenge in a number of other financial markets). The strategy has not been without risk, and failure could still relegate the City to the status of a glorious memory.

The Square Mile

The merchant oligarchy of the City is resplendent in its ostentatious finery. But this is no permanent fancy-dress party. It is the outward expression of those franchises, large and small (many of them going back to the middle ages) which the law has not expressly abolished. Through its municipal council, the City of London Corporation, including all its ancient corporations, its Court of Aldermen, its Court of Common Council, and its officials – Town Clerk, Chamberlain, Comptroller and City Solicitor, Remembrancer, Secondary, Under-Sheriff, High Bailiff of Southwark, Protonotary, Medical Officer of Health, City Surveyor – the City proclaims an identity over which the centuries have no influence. It holds on to its schools, its retirement homes and its open green spaces – notably the six thousand acres of forest which it owns at Epping. It is entirely responsible for the upkeep of the square mile (or to be precise, the square mile and thirty-seven acres) which contains it. It is also responsible for the repairs and, if need be, the reconstruction of the four Thames bridges (Blackfriars, London,

211

Tower and Southwark) which it owns, and would never dream of asking the State or the local authorities for an assistance which would only impair its authority.

The City has its own police force, entirely independent of the London Metropolitan Police and with exclusive authority over its own territory. That territory includes not only the Bank of England, but also the headquarters of more than five hundred banks (the world's greatest concentration), the Stock Exchange, the commodity markets and Lloyd's, the most prestigious insurance market in the world. Every weekday morning its narrow streets are invaded by the City's 350,000 employees, and every evening the square mile is emptied of people, and its treasures are left in the sole charge of the City's personal guardians of the peace. At the weekend it is almost deserted.

City of London Police regulations state that their policemen have to be at least five foot eleven tall, and their policewomen, five foot six, and, until recently, their horses had to be dapple-grey. But this is no operetta army. The City Police was one of the first forces in the world to use electronic equipment for the prevention and detection of crime, and its financial fraud division is the best in the United Kingdom.

The Old Bailey is situated in the City, on the site of the former Newgate Prison, whose sordid and distressing image is firmly implanted in the memory of every reader of Dickens. It is a Crown court, the principal criminal court of the Realm, and the City therefore exercises no authority over it. Nonetheless, it is the Lord Mayor of the City who inaugurates its quarterly sessions, as well as the ten or so sessions in which a High Court judge presides over a civil action. Because of its location, the civil court – which elsewhere would be known as the County Court – is here called the Mayor's and City of London Court. Its jurisdiction covers a zone which was once vital for commerce in the City, and which extends from the banks of the Thames at Chertsey in Surrey to the sea. The Lord Mayor's home, Mansion House, is the only private residence in the whole of England to comprise a court of law – one of the City's two Magistrate Courts, the other being situated in the Guildhall. The Lord Mayor is, *ex officio*, the City's chief magistrate, and actually presides over the court unless prevented from doing so by some more pressing engagement.

The City jealously protects its judicial prerogatives, official and unofficial. At the beginning of every November, crowds gather in the square mile to watch the Lord Mayor's Show in which the Mayor – taking part in an ancient and solemn procession – reaffirms his position as the heir of those merchants who, for the past thousand years or more, have kept supreme control over the City and the world of money. He owes his legitimacy to election by his peers – the Liverymen in Common Hall Assembled – but he sits like a sovereign on his throne, stiff in his ample robe, his chain of office and his golden carriage. It is to him in fact that foreign Heads of State on an official visit pay their respects, not to any democratically elected representative of London.

Yet the Lord Mayor is little more than a living parable. He reigns more than he rules. Anyone who wishes to wear this ephemeral crown at the end of an honourable career, and who is prepared to spend a small fortune during his year in office, has a chance of being elected. The year 1984 even saw the election of a woman to this ancient honour. But despite the associated pomp and prestige, the Mayor is nothing but the City's public relations officer, selling merchandise produced by the City.

By common consent of the experts, this merchandise is still worth its weight in gold. And the price of that gold is fixed every day for the entire world, between 10.30 a.m. and 3.30 p.m., by five experts (who would raise their eyebrows at such a description) gathered in a small sitting room with five telephones, on the first floor of the N.M. Rothschild and Sons Ltd Bank. Yet until late 1981, the smell of fish from the nearby Billingsgate market, and the sight of crowds of customers and porters in their white overalls, served as a reminder that high finance – at its most abstract and esoteric – nonetheless boils down to a transaction, a purchase or a sale. After at least seven hundred years of activity in the heart of the City, Billingsgate was finally forced to move to hygienic modern premises on the Isle of Dogs. Smithfield meat market has also moved, but continues to set the daily national meat prices.

A fragment of Roman wall, the Guildhall, Mansion House, the majestic dome of Saint Paul's and the Georgian homes of a master mariner, a tea merchant or some Huguenot weaver driven out of France by the Edict of Nantes: these and other vestiges survive to testify to the City's ancient credentials. But fire and war have taken a heavy toll, and what remains is essentially Victorian architecture, itself mutilated by the German V2s during the Second World War. On these remains has been grafted the most ponderous modern architecture imaginable. Only the National Westminster Bank skyscraper and the new Lloyd's headquarters stand out from the general banality, epitomised by the vast concrete monstrosity of the Barbican. Completed in 1982, with the aim of restoring life to the City each evening after it has shed its daytime population, the Barbican's giant windswept corridors simply add to the gloom of the surrounding solitude. But as a saving grace, the world's best acting troupe – the Royal Shakespeare Company – has dug out a home for itself in the heart of this shapeless ant-hill, creating a theatre like a conch of shadow and light.

The Club of Clubs
In 1914, at the height of British imperial power, when pound sterling and not the dollar was still the world's major reserve currency, the City contained only twenty-nine foreign banks. In 1978 there were 395, and by 1984 as many as 460 – twice the number of foreign banks in Wall Street. Only ten of the hundred most important banks in the world are not directly represented in the City, and even they all have a foot in it thanks to some form or other of participation. With its nine discount houses*, the London discount market is still without rival today. Primary commodity markets (spot or futures), the London Metal Exchange and a market in furs establish a bridge between financial transactions that involve no more than an exchange of paper and the trade in physical goods that once formed the foundation of the City's wealth.

---

* Specialised institutions acting as financial intermediaries between the Bank of England and the rest of the banking sector, promoting an orderly flow of short-term funds between the authorities and the banks and lending to the Government by guaranteeing to tender for the whole of the weekly offer of Treasury Bills.

The Baltic Exchange, a freight and shipping exchange, was created in the seventeenth century in two coffee houses – the Jerusalem, and the Virginia and Maryland, renamed the Virginia and Baltic in 1744. It has outlived the glorious days of the British merchant fleet, most of which was swept away by competition from container ships built in South-East Asia, Greek cargo vessels flying Panamanian flags, or Norwegian tankers with Liberian colours, and it still remains the world's foremost international shipping exchange. Two-thirds of naval freight and half of the world's ship sales are negotiated on the Baltic Exchange. A market for cereals and oilseeds has also been developing, and in 1985 the Baltic International Freight Futures Exchange (BIFFEX) was opened. In addition, Britain's agricultural futures markets are now operated entirely from the Baltic Exchange.

The City cannot forget that before becoming a marketplace or financial centre, it was itself a port. Its power has always come from the sea, and it was natural that it should give birth to the idea of insurance against maritime risk. No sooner had Lloyd's of London stripped its headquarters of scaffolding in 1986, than the futuristic new building by Richard Rogers (one of the architects of the Pompidou Centre in Paris) was nicknamed the 'space shuttle'. Its users, less imaginatively, compared it to an airport waiting lounge, to a multi-storey car park or a supermarket. But the ancient bell of the *Lutine* frigate, captured by the English from the French at Toulon in 1793, will continue to be sounded in the new building's main hall, as it has been sounded for the past two centuries in Lloyd's successive headquarters, to warn of any piece of news liable to affect the market – traditionally, one stroke of the bell for an overdue vessel, two for its safe arrival back at port. Today its use is largely ceremonial – one stroke at the annual Lloyd's remembrance service, two for a visit by a member of the Royal Family. In January 1991 the bell was poised to ring for the outbreak of the Gulf War, but in the event hostilities began at night and Lloyd's remained silent.

In the eighties, the historical reputation for probity and the consequent aristocratic serenity of Lloyd's were shaken by violent storms. A series of scandals were to cost the underwriters of the prestigious insurance market more than 150 million pounds.

The most notorious of these involved the broker, Kenneth Grob (known as 'the grobfather'), who was accused of dishonest conduct by a Lloyd's inquiry in 1984, and was subsequently expelled – one of forty-seven brokers and underwriters to be thrown out of the organisation during the early eighties. In 1987 he was arrested on charges of theft, but two years later was found 'not guilty' in one of the most complicated criminal trials of the decade. By September 1990 however, the Department of Trade and Industry had brought out a report which effectively convicted Grob and three of his colleagues (known as the 'Gang of Four') of 'false accounting' and 'plunder' in what is probably the biggest Lloyd's scandal since the war. In reply to the report, Grob simply said: 'After all, can you make wealth and still occupy the high moral ground?'

In 1982, the conclusions of an enquiry prompted Lloyd's themselves to reform their internal organisation and self-regulatory mechanisms, tightening the rules governing the relationship between brokers and underwriters, and so forestalling – for the time being at least – the danger of Parliament's imposing outside regulation on them. For even among Conservative Members of Parliament – normally jealous guardians of the autonomy of Lloyd's – several voices were being raised in favour of placing it under the authority of the body already responsible for the regulation of the stock market, the Securities and Investments Board (SIB). The Labour opposition promised to give this body official status independent of the City, and to extend its powers of control and sanction to include the Lloyd's insurers. It is not the first time in their history that people have taken issue with Lloyd's unique organisation, but government interventions to modify it have been rare. Nonetheless the last of these, in 1982, went as far as to force Lloyd's to appoint a Deputy Chairman and Chief Executive nominated by the Bank of England and endowed with significant powers, to work alongside an internally appointed Chairman.

The early days of Lloyd's, in the Edward Lloyd Coffee House, would not have led one to predict its worldwide expansion. It all began in 1668 as a sort of club for gentlemen and merchants who decided to organise a system of mutual security to protect each other from bankruptcy. As the risks incurred increased, it soon became necessary to rely on capital from outside the small mercantile community in the City. Today it is still a number of wealthy private individuals who provide that capital in the form of liquid assets (a minimum of £250,000) placed in the hands of underwriters. These non-professional members of the market are known as the 'Names'. There are about twenty-eight thousand of them, of which a sizeable proportion are foreigners. Though the profits they can make are huge, they also risk losing every penny of their personal wealth. In addition to the Names, Lloyd's includes five thousand active members, including the brokers, whose job it is to find the best possible deal for their clients among the different underwriting firms.

The City is still, primarily, made of and by men – a certain type of man. In spite of their diversity, a certain attitude – easy to recognise and hard to define – keeps these men subtly apart from the rest of the world. They cannot be distinguished by their way of dressing (contrary to what caricaturists would like us to believe) nor by their social origins or their accent (which can be the purest cockney), nor by their nationality. But whatever their origins, they have learnt to observe the rules of the club of clubs.

Americans are completely mystified by the courteous fog which envelopes dealings in the City. The French, energetic and forthright, are irritated by a nonchalance and lack of precision which they attribute either to laziness or bad faith. The Italians sigh at their lack of imagination. The Germans . . . Yet everyone envies them their style, which is their secret language; a language which seems so simple and yet is so difficult to learn.

Royal watchers would have searched the Court Circular in vain to find a mention of the intimate luncheon party, in 1975, at which James Capel – the City's most ancient stockbroking firm (now owned by Hong Kong & Shanghai Bank) – invited Her Majesty the Queen to join in the firm's discreet and dignified bicentenary celebration. This was a strictly private affair, and it was in her capacity as the firm's principal client that the Queen was being asked. According to the adage learnt by all those who aspire to succeed in the City, the important thing is not what one knows but whom one knows. Founded in 1894, the firm of Rowe & Pitman (R&P) also counts the Queen as a client, as well as an impressive array of multinational firms. Although the descendants of the original founders (presidents of the Oxford and Cambridge rowing clubs) are no longer involved, the grandest names in high finance still appear on the list of its associates. One of these, Lancelot Hugh Smith (Lancy to his friends) joined the firm before the First World War, and a few months before his death in 1941, wrote: 'I have always felt that if they keep their heads up and their overheads down, a firm containing three members of great City families must succeed.' The firm of Rowe & Pitman followed this prescription admirably. Among its associates could be found members of Lancelot's own family, the Smiths (bankers for the past two hundred years), a number of Flemings (including Ian Fleming, of James Bond fame), and a number of Barings. By associating with De Beers and Anglo-American – the two giants that dominate the world diamond market – R & P was able to increase its field of activities and its profits further still.

Stockbrokers, bankers, insurers, lawyers – the old boy network is still flourishing – but since the First World War, many newcomers have been infiltrating the ranks. For instance the founder of the important merchant bank, S.G. Warburg and Co., was a Jew of German origin, Siegmund Warburg. As early as 1933, Jewish financiers and entrepreneurs were driven to London by Nazi persecution, and integrated without difficulty into the City, where they prospered. The City welcomes anyone who has money, or knows how to make it – any man, but not any woman. The presence of women is tolerated rather than applauded, and although they sometimes hold positions of considerable responsibility, they are well advised to know their place. No doubt they will rebel one day, but they have not done so yet.

While admitting that the City has a special flair for discovering talent, Sir Christopher (Kit) McMahon, Chairman and Group Chief Executive of the Midland Bank and former Deputy Governor of the Bank of England, believes that its prosperity is largely attributable to a number of historical advantages. The first of these is longevity, with its corollary, confidence – a talisman which is a must for that superstitious sceptic, the financier. Since 1846, he explains, Great Britain has been importing more goods than it has exported – hence the vital importance of invisible returns, hence the need to turn the City into a pole of attraction, hence the City's success.

'Habit keeps money here, and once people are used to one place of business, they keep going there,' he adds.

The exceptional technical know-how acquired by the City over the centuries is another factor in its continued prosperity, enabling it to avoid political and economic decline, even when it affects the rest of the country. When President Carter decided to release Iranian assets frozen after the overthrow of the Shah in 1979, in exchange for the release of American hostages held in Teheran during the previous year, two English firms of solicitors (Stephenson Harwood for the Iranians and Coward Chance for the Americans) were given the task of defending the interests of the parties involved. Two English banks – Barclays and National Westminster – were also chosen to handle the considerable transfer of funds (more than four billion dollars) which this agreement involved. According to Erwin Brecher, a prominent financial entrepreneur during the sixties and seventies, 'only the City could have taken on so vast a transaction at such short notice. Wall Street would have had the greatest difficulty in doing so. In the City you can hand in a cheque for ten million dollars in the morning and collect the cash in the afternoon. In New York it takes at least twenty-four hours'. During the nineties Gulf crisis, this technical expertise was to stand the City in good stead once more, enabling it to handle the vast capital which exiled Kuwaiti financial institutions placed entirely in its hands.

In the eyes of the majority of financiers – especially those who operate beyond the shores of the United Kingdom – the City has another major asset: it operates under the jurisdiction of English law courts and enjoys the benefits of their rich jurisprudence, particularly in the labyrinth of maritime law, insurance policies, and more generally, in the arcane contractual complexities of commerce and of private international agreements.

The October Revolution

The City's real advantage, and the necessary – if not always sufficient – condition for survival, is its freedom. Even during times of strict exchange control, foreign capital (untaxable – for

Britain is also a kind of tax haven) has always been free to circulate without hindrance.

'We are characterised by light controls,' explains Sir Christopher McMahon. 'Our attitude is exemplified in the famous motto of the Baltic Exchange, "My word is my bond". We believe in self-regulation, and we discuss the rules with the interested parties.'

The Bank of England was nationalised in 1946. By the terms of its charter, it takes instructions from the Treasury, in the common interest, after consultation with the Government. Its external activities range from intervening in the money markets, to liaising with the central banks of countries still within the sterling zone, and collaborating with world monetary organisms, including most notably the International Monetary Fund (IMF). According to its former Deputy Governor, 'In the Bank of England the exercise of power is a matter of expertise more than it is a struggle for supremacy. The Treasury could formally direct us to do something, but in practice there is a dialogue between us.' The Governor makes public declarations, in which it is permissible for him to distance himself from official policies. 'It's a bit like the nuclear deterrent,' a City banker suggests, 'one has to know how not to use it.'

As far as the private banks are concerned, the Bank of England has the means to exert considerable pressure, but is reluctant to do so. There are many who are not satisfied with the results of this traditional equilibrium, not to say tightrope walking act, and others who believe that the government has a great deal more power over the Bank of England than either party is willing to admit. Now almost three hundred years old, the 'Old Lady' is a bit geriatric, they say; still with all her wits about her of course, but nowadays when she frowns, no one takes much notice.

Nigel Lawson himself, when he was Chancellor of the Exchequer, was quite blunt. 'I make the decisions,' he said in April 1987, 'and the Bank carries them out.' In 1988, he put a secret proposal before the Prime Minister, suggesting that the Bank of England should be put in charge of interest rate policy. Arguing in favour of the idea, Robin Leigh-Pemberton, Governor of the Bank of England, said: 'It would be easier for the politicians if monetary policy were taken out of day-to-day politics and were seen to be the responsibility of the Central Bank.' But Mrs Thatcher, who is not one to relinquish power quite so easily, rejected the proposal out of hand.

Clearing banks, with their fifteen thousand or so outlets, serve the public competently if unimaginatively, fulfilling their main role of collecting money and bills of exchange. The man in the street is the principal client of the British clearing banks, yet he is less familiar with them than the average Frenchman or Italian. For a long time, building societies wooed small savers by offering them interest rates on all kinds of accounts, and effectively kept them away from the banks, which on the whole they found intimidating. Over the past few years, this competition has become increasingly fierce. The building societies, which in 1986 were released from the last constraints on their freedom to compete with banks, have been multiplying the services they offer: cashpoint machines, credit cards, insurance. They have even been given the right to grant their clients non-mortgage loans. The banks, for their part, have launched numerous publicity campaigns, aiming particularly at small savers and the young – who are often the same people: they have made it simpler to apply for personal loans, and have enticed children with all kinds of small gifts, urging them to open a first piggy-bank account, in the hope of turning them into clients for life.

The jewels in the City's crown are the merchant banks. Though they may lack the power of their American counterparts, or the indomitable vitality of their Japanese ones, they have the pedigree, the *je ne sais quoi* of champions. It is the lightness of their structures, their freedom of movement and their speed which has often enabled them in the past to overtake their Wall Street rivals, weighed down as these are by heavy machinery of specialised committees, and slowed down by pedantic rules and regulations. Their representatives, who have abandoned bowler hat and rolled umbrella in some antipodean cloakroom, cross the skies to disembark in the Tropics or the deep North. They are not technicians, they are connoisseurs. Though they know about figures, their particular expertise is in people, and on their judgement of character hangs subsequent profit or loss. Public take-over bids, whether 'friendly' or 'hostile', private acquisitions and mergers all feature prominently on the City's menu, as they do in Wall Street where the recipe was first invented.

Gerald Ronson, 'Tiny' Rowland, Robert Maxwell – the names of these great business predators are as well known to the public at large as those of almost any boxing champion or film star. The popular press gives them front page headlines next to horror stories of sex and violence, while the serious press devotes breathless commentaries to their activities. Script writers of television soap operas have a hard time matching the intricate accounts of ruthless battles between the bad 'raider' and the good 'white knight' of these financial sagas. But whether flamboyant or discreet, all these tycoons have one point in common: behind each one of them – and behind every loser as well – can be found the name of a merchant bank.

The 27th of October 1986 will perhaps be remembered by historians as the date of the second October Revolution – not a socialist one this time, but on the contrary, an ultra-capitalist one. For this was the day of the Big Bang when years of Stock Exchange conventions were exploded; the day when the distinction between jobbers and brokers was wiped out, as was the fixed brokerage commission; the day, finally, when it became possible for banks and other financial institutions to take on the functions of a 'broker' (which had previously been restricted to specialists), thus opening up the market to all kinds of financial establishments at home and abroad. At the same time, the establishment of a powerful electronic network made it possible to register and transmit all transactions directly by computer, and to fix bid and offer prices automatically. Despite the ensuing invasion of their territory by foreign competition, British merchant and clearing banks could not fail to welcome a reform which enabled them to offer a whole new range of services to their clients; the Bank of England, too, was preparing to extend its interventions to these unexplored territories.

The press duly saluted the October revolution. In an effort to become more competitive, some brokerage firms were amalgamated, while others were either completely or partially taken over by major national and foreign banks. After a few minor and excusable technical hiccoughs, the computers were operating to everyone's satisfaction.

Yet barely a month after the Big Bang, a financial scandal shattered the public's faith in the soundness of a reform which seemed to be exposing the Stock Market to an uncontrollable surge of speculation and fraud. When on the 14th of November, the American financier, Ivan Boesky, was accused of insider dealing, the British press and public were interested in him only because of the fine of one hundred million US dollars which he agreed to pay in order to avoid civil damages. In addition he accepted to plead guilty to one of the many charges for which he could have been criminally prosecuted. Only a few days later the same scenario was to be repeated in London. Geoffrey Collier, head of brokerage at Morgan Grenfell – one of the most important merchant banks in the City – was forced to resign in a hurry after similar accusations of insider dealing.

Finally on the 1st of December, the City – which had successfully weathered the turbulence of the Big Bang – was shaken to its foundations by a major new scandal. Guinness, one of the most reputable and (thanks to its takeover of Distillers) one of the most profitable of British firms, was itself the subject of an enquiry by the Department of Trade and Industry and the Serious Fraud Office. Revelations and disasters kept piling up: blocks of shares bought and sold after secret agreements, to the detriment of the small investor; the Chairman of Guinness, Ernest Saunders, an American administrator and his French financial director, all forced to resign; one hundred million dollars entrusted to the infamous Boesky, and now irrecoverable; twenty-five million pounds paid out in questionable deals recovered with some difficulty, dozens of people charged . . .

In August 1990, after a six-month trial, Ernest Saunders and three others were finally convicted on twenty-eight counts of false accounting, conspiracy and theft. Saunders himself was sentenced to five years imprisonment for 'dishonesty on a massive scale'; Anthony Parnes, a city stockbroker, received eighteen months; Gerald Ronson, Chairman of the Heron Group, was fined five million pounds, and given a one year prison sentence; and Sir Jack Lyons, though fined three million pounds, was exempted from a term in prison on account of ill health.

All in all, the public – reacting against the euphoria of economic self-interest during the eighties – was well pleased with this crop of harsh sentences. The mightiest of the 'Me generation' were being laid low, and their fate would set an example to other City sharks, large or small. But there remain a few cynics who believe that the Guinness affair has merely served as the vehicle for a purging of the public conscience. In the upsurge of general moralising, numerous other shady activities are conveniently forgotten. Crime continues to flourish, and the criminal becomes ever more sophisticated.

Is the City, that esoteric temple of money, turning into a brigands' den? Its defenders are quick to point out that the regulatory system which was put into place at the time of the Big Bang reforms immediately came into operation, and that the procedural and judicial powers of enquiry and sanction are quite sufficient to rid the market of any black sheep. The only really effective weapon against abuse of the system is information. The day companies become entirely transparent in their transactions, insider dealing will become an impossibility. Secrecy is the main culprit and it should be ruthlessly tracked down and severely punished. Similarly, the most effective agent in policing the City is not the police, but money – money, the very thing that gives it its *raison-d'être*.

The abolition of the double monopoly of jobbers and brokers has attracted to the square mile a number of financial giants beside whom the most important of the old-style brokers look like pygmies. One hundred days after the Big Bang, the total number of Stock Exchange transactions had doubled, but the average rate of commissions had come down by half. Six months after having ventured into the Stock Market, the Midland Bank decided to pull out in a hurry in order to minimise losses. The massive increase in capital needed to compete in the post Big Bang financial services, the cutting of profit margins, and the exceptional qualifications required of personnel were eventually to lead to the disappearance of the majority of small and medium-sized firms. Though illegal speculation has been checked, as have the six-figure salaries of the Big Bang cowboys, the old City is gone forever. Gone are the crowds that once swarmed in the great hall of the Stock Exchange; gone are jobbers' top hats. The computer has replaced the bustle of the dealing room, and fortunes are made or lost in silence.

Just one year after the Big Bang, the Stock Exchange crash of

October 1987 was to vindicate the reformers. It is true that by December 1988, the accumulated losses incurred by City stock-brokers amounted to more than five hundred million pounds. True, also, that the financial establishments which had so hastily extended their activities to a stock market whose mechanisms they were unfamiliar with, now found themselves obliged to sack without notice the young prodigies of finance whom they had recruited for vast sums just a few months before. In 1988 some fifteen thousand jobs were lost in this sector. Yet by 1990, all but four thousand of those who had been unceremoniously sacked, had – like the *Independent*'s famous cartoon yuppie, Alex* – managed to find themselves another comfortable niche in the City. No doubt Wall Street and the Japanese Stock Market have the advantage of being based on national economies which jointly represent more than sixty per cent of the world's gross national product. Paris, which has followed the example of the British in liberalising its *Bourse*, now offers competitive services – particularly for the individual shareholder. And the current economic recession is contributing to a more sober assessment of the City's prospects. But for the time being it unquestionably retains its place as the foremost international financial market.

By the end of the century the market will be worldwide. Its activity (which is dictated largely by institutional investors, most notably the pension funds) will be concentrated in New York and Tokyo, because of the weight of their economies, and – more than ever – in London, thanks to its expertise. The majority of Stock Exchange transactions will be shared between the portfolios of three or four major American broking firms, two or three Japanese ones, and if they play their cards right, some four or five British firms. The only victim, perhaps, will be the finesse of which the City was so proud. The winds of the October Revolution are blowing it away.

* Now appearing in the *Daily Telegraph*.

3

Public Service or Civic Duty

The mercantile spirit is clearly deeply rooted in the individualism of the British, but the profusion of charities that flourish in the United Kingdom, with a combined annual income of some fifteen to sixteen billion pounds, are another less obvious expression of it. In 1989, a record 168,710 charities were registered in England and Wales – more than four thousand of these being founded during the previous year.

Well Organised Charity
No doubt the great medieval charitable foundations deserved the criticisms that were expressed, in similar terms, by the eighteenth-century Scotsman, Adam Smith, and his French contemporary, François Turgot. Both deplored their religious origins, their great wealth, and the fact that their permanent character shielded them from any kind of objective evaluation. In general, they were also less concerned with dispensing aid than with providing ecclesiastical livings. In France these criticisms foreshadowed the expropriation of the clergy's estates under the Revolution in order to 'return them to the Nation', that is to the all-powerful state. In Britain on the other hand, the usual kind of pragmatic compromises were reached, new foundations were set up to complement or replace the old ones, reforms were anticipated, and great social changes were gently introduced, thus avoiding the disruption of a grand plan.

The charity schools – also known as blue-coat schools because of the blue uniform worn by their pupils – were created at the beginning of the eighteenth century. They were not capable of providing genuine mass education themselves, but their initiative was at the root of compulsory education for all. Until 1947, for better or for worse, public health remained the major preoccupation of the charities. On the threshold of the Second World War, nine hundred of these charities collected and distributed some five million pounds, of which fifty per cent went to the thousands of private hospitals which provided one-third of the country's available beds. Half of the 115 nursing schools and one-quarter of the maternity units and childhood health centres in Great Britain were voluntary organisations. The second half of the nineteenth century also saw the emergence of a new kind of charity which offered global assistance to entire categories of the needy. Some of these, such as Dr Barnardo's and the Salvation Army, are still flourishing today, and have extended their activities throughout the world.

Faced with the most glaring examples of poverty in Victorian or Edwardian Britain, individual initiatives were little more than the crystallization of guilt felt by the privileged. They were also an antidote to it and as such received widespread support. But there were – and still are – more controversial causes. Yet these are no less strongly defended. On the contrary, they elicit the most ardent devotion and the most active proselytism. They are the jewels of British philanthropy.

For thousands of anonymous women in this country of men, voluntary work, collective action and political lobbying have long been an important outlet. A few of the most remarkable zealots stand out. The indomitable suffragette, Emmeline Pankhurst, flanked by her two daughters, Christabel and Sylvia, immediately springs to mind, as does the socialist Fabian, Annie Besant, who began with theosophy, and ended with the struggle for Indian independence. The women who chained themselves to the railings of public gardens and were arrested every weekend, in order to be released every Monday, were all sublime in their generosity, courage, and perseverance, all a little ridiculous but all ultimately successful in their struggle against masculine prejudice, indifference and egoism.

My favourite among these female militants is Marie Stopes. At the age of thirty-eight she was still a virgin, and by the end of a marriage that was never consummated, she was haunted by the desire to have a child. Yet during the First World War she embraced the unlikely gospel of contraception which she came to see as the salvation of the human race. From 1918 she began to preach the cause with missionary zeal, convinced that future generations would vindicate her. In the margin of a Catholic pamphlet condemning her, she scribbled that she would be canonised within two hundred years. She was beautiful and highly educated, as was natural for someone of her background: her mother, who came from a Scottish family that prided itself on its ancient lineage, was one of the first women in Britain to receive a university education and fight for equality of the sexes. From her mother who was intelligent but dour, Marie – deprived of encouragement and tenderness – inherited a feeling of guilt and inadequacy that was compensated for by overweening intellectual ambition. She and her father adored and admired each other, and from him she acquired a love of fossils that led to a doctorate in science and an international reputation as a paleo-botanist. But although the education she received from her parents – both of them resolute feminists – was much ahead of its time, it contained one major gap. 'I drew minutely the sex organs of earthworms and frogs, and discussed them simply and frankly with my father,' she wrote in 1935, in a book entitled *Marriage in My Time*, ' – but they did not come into marriage. In our home, human sex was never spoken of at all.'

After a platonic love affair with a Japanese academic, and a first marriage that was annulled because it was never consummated, Marie finally gave birth to a son by her second husband, but was not able to find physical fulfilment with him either. It was not until she was in her sixties that – in the arms of handsome young men who admired her – she was able to find what she called true 'erogamic love', combining the physical and the spiritual.

The book which was to bring international fame to Marie Stopes, *Married Love*, was part pamphlet, part revelation, part practical manual on contraception. Her thesis on eugenics had been familiar among readers of Darwin since the end of the nineteenth century; the audacity of her ideas about sex and marriage came from Edward Carpenter, the reformer, and from the South African Olive Albertine Schreiner (whose books had been equally successful in Britain and in the United States), while the most interesting things she had to say about sexuality were taken from Havelock Ellis. But although the work was not an original one, the overwhelming sense of conviction with which it was written gave it authority. Its publication coincided with a period of public lassitude and revulsion against the slaughter of the Great War, and its success throughout the world was extraordinary. A second book, *Wise Parenthood*, finally established the reputation of Marie Stopes as the invincible – if not the uncontested – champion of contraception. In 1921, she opened the first clinic in the British Empire to dispense free advice and help with contraception, and from then on the trend was set, with the number of voluntary groups devoting themselves to the same task increasing from year to year.

In 1934, the National Birth Control Association drew up a list of approved contraceptives recommended for use in clinics. And by 1938, some 650,000 women were receiving help from 935 Family Planning Association clinics (at the time there were only 524 such clinics in the whole of the United States), and more than eighty per cent of the female population in Britain were regularly using contraceptives. But Marie Stopes – solitary and incorruptible, with the egocentric altruism of many a great public benefactor – remained isolated from the movement whose principles and politics were rejected by her megalomania.

Europeans are forever astonished by the subjective, puritan and sometimes sectarian character of even the most respectable manifestations of liberalism, generosity and intellectual openness among the English, as well as among their spiritual heirs, the Americans. On the continent tolerance is easily intimidated. Born of cynicism and indifference, it is vulnerable to the turmoil of wars, revolutions or dictatorships. In Britain it is made of sterner stuff, and can be as aggressive as the fanatics of which it disapproves.

The most remarkable consequence of this vigorous English conscience is the absence of state jurisdiction in numerous areas of collective life. Individuals like Marie Stopes take individual initiatives, then form themselves into associations, train other individuals, and one day, the entire country is equipped with a network of highly professional information centres, clinics, animal hospitals, legal aid bureaux, and a doctrine for each of these questions. Government (and if need be, Parliament) will intervene only in the last stages to rubber stamp the accomplished work. Its role is a purely enabling and regulatory one.

Even at the height of Labour interventionism just after the Second World War, the party could not entirely ignore an attitude so deeply rooted in the national character, and Government in Britain remained more decentralised and less inquisitorial than it was in the supposedly liberal régimes of the other European countries. Yet in one of those contradictions of which nations are quite as capable as individuals, Britain relies more on the State than any other Western democracy for the organisation and running of its National Health Service.

When National Health is in Poor Shape

October 1980, Liverpool, the gynaecological unit of the Mill Road Maternity Hospital: Dr Robert Altay has just put nine names into a hat in order to choose the four patients who will spend the night in his ward before being operated on the next morning. The other five will be sent home in their dressing gowns. The degree of urgency is the same for all nine women, but there are not enough beds for all of them.

January 1982, London: Cyril Chantler, Professor of Paediatric Nephrology at Guy's Hospital in London, announces that in all likelihood, about one-third of all children afflicted with chronic kidney disease in the coming year will not be treated because of a shortage of necessary equipment. About two thousand adults suffer from severe kidney disease every year, but only about half this number are offered surgery or dialysis. For the rest, there is only one likely outcome: death.

January 1987, Sheffield: 4,286 patients have to wait more than one year for non-urgent surgical interventions. In Birmingham South, the figure is 3,536; in London's Bloomsbury, 2,886. In Hackney, one of London's poorest districts, 1,248 patients have to wait more than one month for an urgent operation; in Norwich, Newcastle and Southampton, more than seven urgent operations are also delayed by one month.

April to November 1990, during the run-up to the implementation of major National Health reforms in 1991, a record 4,500 hospital beds are closed, of which more than 1,000 are cut in

London alone. In October, the Department of Health announces that the number of patients in England waiting for operations has increased by a massive 31,000 during the past six months, bringing the total to a record 912,800. In November, twenty major London hospitals and seventeen of London's thirty-two district health authorities tell the Emergency Beds Service (which trawls the capital for beds in urgent cases) that they will accept emergencies only if ordered to. During this period, conditions in South London's King's College Hospital deteriorate to such an extent as a result of the closure of 120 beds, that some casualty patients are having to lie on trolleys for more than twenty-four hours before being admitted.

Is it possible that the true invalid is the National Health Service itself? According to the European Commission in Brussels, every social security system in Europe is suffering from similar chronic growth-related problems. The British themselves generally persist in believing that – despite some undeniable deficiencies – they still possess an exemplary medical system. They question only whether that system is safe in Conservative hands, or whether the series of reforms begun in April 1990 (particularly the provision – introduced in April 1991 – enabling NHS hospitals to apply for self-governing status) are in fact merely a preliminary to the privatisation of *their* National Health Service.

Every British resident today has the right to be treated, more or less without payment, from the moment of his birth until he dies. As in most other countries of the European Community, eyes and teeth are the only areas excluded from the general provision of free treatment. Patients are also required to pay a flat rate on any drugs prescribed to them, but in practice nearly sixty per cent of those treated – the oldest, the youngest, the poorest, pregnant women, women with children under one – are exempt from any payment. In all other respects, access to the NHS is not only free but remarkably unbureaucratic. All the patient need do is to register with a GP, and whether he is looked after at home or in hospital, no other administrative chore will be required of him. The only files kept on him will be medical ones. There will be no forms to fill in, no payments to be made, no refunds to be claimed. The NHS is a public service in the fullest sense of the word. The only restriction to this remarkable freedom was introduced in 1983, and applies only to foreign visitors, who are required to pay their hospital bill, unless their countries have a reciprocal arrangement with Britain. A great many hospitals, however, do not even bother with this requirement, which costs more to implement than it would raise in extra revenue.

In 1939 there were numerous analogies between health provision in France and in Great Britain. Both countries treated their medical corps – crowned by the prestigious élite of Harley Street practitioners in London, and the heads of the hospital services in Paris – with considerable respect. Doctors had an aura of scientific respectability; they were successful and disinterested, faithful to the Hippocratic oath. Praising the devotion and probity of the humble family physician, the affluent doctors of the affluent graciously gave of their precious time to work in the hospitals, and enhanced their reputations by effecting a number of free cures for the poor. But those who could, paid their doctor, and paid him well. They lived longer than manual labourers and the poor, and entrusted their teeth to the dentist's drill and not the tooth-puller's pincers. For them illness was a physical ordeal but not a financial disaster.

This twilight of Victorian harmony was to be entirely obscured by the advent of the Second World War. Rich and poor, humble and exalted alike found themselves in the operating theatres of remote country hospitals in the north of England, swept up in the advancing tide of the wounded from every front, or dodging the bombs which were pounding the major cities of the South and the Midlands. The victory of the Allied Forces, and their liberation of France, brought to power – both in London and in Paris – governments which were determined to put an end to the most glaring social injustices, beginning with privileged access to good health care. But from that point onwards, the policies of the two countries were to diverge. And this divergence is all the more surprising since it seems to have taken each nation down a path which would most naturally have accommodated the talents and temperament of the other. As if suddenly touched by the grace of Anglo-Saxon pragmatism, the French began to introduce a diversified system of social insurance – including health as its most important provision – which they gradually extended to increasingly numerous categories of the population. The British, on the other hand, abandoned caution and from one day to the next adopted an entirely unfamiliar system whose organisation was planned, French-style, down to the last detail. The new service, which was imposed from the top by legislative means, eliminated in one stroke the entire mosaic of independent institutions which had evolved to look after the nation's health. The medical corps, although regimented by four hard years of war and restrictions, nonetheless resisted being herded *en masse* into a civilian national service. Their objections forced the Labour government into major concessions to the senior corps of hospital specialists, thus splitting the profession and opening the way for the NHS.

Brian Jarman belongs to a practice of four doctors in Bloomsbury. They have eight thousand patients on their list – about the national average of patients per doctor, though the law allows a maximum of 3,500. The system of GP group practices, which is at the basis of the NHS, provides an extremely flexible service, allowing doctors to stand in for each other without upsetting their clients. It also gives them the opportunity of discussing difficult cases together informally, as well as enabling them to employ more staff and buy better equipment for their surgeries. In addition, the Medical Practices Committee is empowered to limit the number of doctors working in any given area, so that Britain now has a better geographical distribution of general practitioners than any other country in Europe.

Dr Jarman has a number of French patients on the register of his Bloomsbury surgery. 'When a mother comes to see me with her little boy who has a touch of the flu,' he explains, 'unless I give her a prescription for injections or suppositories and a list of five or six medicines, she has the impression that I'm not looking after her child, and she doesn't hesitate to tell me so.' Naturally, this would not happen with an English mother, for whom illness is not quite the done thing in so far as it obliges one to explain and complain. If the doctor makes light of the trouble, who is she to contradict him?

In her memoirs, *Pay, Pack and Follow*, Baroness Ewart-Biggs recalls how the teachers at her boarding-school, Downe House,

234

would allude to the hay fever and chronic asthma from which she suffered throughout her childhood only in order to complain of 'Jane's tiresome sniffle' and 'Jane's silly wheeze'. None of them, it seems, ever thought it necessary to take her to a doctor.

This asceticism which the English deprecate, with modest pride, as being one of their most admirable national faults, is not a purely Anglo-Saxon characteristic. In the last century, it was common to the ruling classes in all of Europe; it was a form of moral affectation aimed at justifying their privileged status both to themselves and to their social inferiors. Nonetheless, there is no doubt that the English today are less prone to feel sorry for themselves than their neighbours across the Channel. The consequences of this are clearly seen: while the frequency of medical consultations is roughly the same in France and in Britain, British doctors write only sixty per cent of the prescriptions lavished by their French counterparts. From Land's End to John O'Groats and Dover, patients are fully worthy of the name, as they meekly submit to the doctor, who knows best; in Calais, the doctor's client loses patience and turns consumer. But this difference in attitudes is not entirely sufficient to explain the respective behaviour of French and British doctors, especially when it comes to general practitioners. Ultimately their behaviour is dictated – or at least encouraged – by the institutions in which they work, and by the methods of their remuneration.

General practitioners have considerable power within the system, since patients can obtain access to a specialist or to hospital treatment only after referral from their doctor. There is nothing, in principle, to stop them changing GPs if they do not like their own, but such a move is frowned upon; doctors do not like having their competence called into question by a layman. By introducing a greater element of competition between GP practices, Mrs Thatcher's National Health reforms are meant to encourage patients to exercise their right to go to the doctor of their choice, and doctors to treat their patients more like clients than like supplicants. But in practice – with the proposed introduction of measures such as restricted drug budgets – the reforms are likely to increase even further the financial pressures under which GPs in Britain are forced to operate, making it likely that their impact in this sphere will not be very great. Critics claim that standards are bound to suffer, while partisans reply that increased competition will favour those who provide better services, and will therefore benefit the patients.

But though the reforms may reduce the stigma frequently attached to changing doctors, the basic structure of GP practices remains the same. In marked contrast to the French system, where doctors are paid according to the number of consultations they dispense, in Britain a GP receives a fixed salary, supplemented by additional sums dependent on the number of patients he has on his list, and – to a lesser extent – on his providing an effective service in certain areas of preventative medicine such as vaccinations and cervical smears. According to a family doctor working in a country practice in Oxfordshire, with a vocal and educated list of patients, the system enables him to withstand requests for unnecessary medication or hospital procedures.

'A British GP is not paid to treat illness,' he explains. 'He is responsible for looking after a defined population – for which he gets paid – and the healthier that population remains, the better off the doctor is, in the sense that he has less work to do. In countries like France, Australia and New Zealand, where doctors are payed for each consultation, it is in the direct financial interest of every GP and specialist to make sure that a patient returns to him for further consultations – even if that means dispensing unnecessary drugs. On the other hand, I am able to educate patients to avoid treatments which are useless and may be harmful to them, such as antibiotics for colds. But in some countries, a patient who comes presenting a headache immediately demands – and gets – a brain scan, in case he has a tumour.'

There are still, in Britain as in France, some decrepit hospitals whose inadequacy cannot be entirely disguised, despite the most conscientious efforts at modernisation; others, whose architectural splendours do not quite compensate for their design, are inappropriate to contemporary practice. In both countries, recently built hospitals usually satisfy the most demanding criteria. The only important difference between them is in the marked preference shown by the French for individual private rooms. But this greater comfort, like unrestricted access to specialists, and the growing appetite for drugs, all have their price: during the eighties, health expenditure per person was seventy per cent greater in France than it was in Britain, and was rising by about seven per cent a year in real terms for the French, as against only four per cent for the British. In France, as in Britain, the most serious cases and expensive treatments are ultimately paid for by the community.

This comparative underfunding in Britain goes some way towards explaining the growth of private medical insurance. Employers have been quick to spot the trend and now frequently offer their managers, and sometimes their entire staff, the perk of private medical cover. Individual premiums remain high and offer only limited protection. Visits to a general practitioner are automatically excluded, while hospital treatment and consultations with a specialist are subject to expenditure limits and all kinds of restrictive clauses. This compares with the French system of compulsory public insurance*, complemented by a network of self-financing private insurance funds, which together cover the refund of all medical costs, including not only prescribed drugs and treatment by GPs, specialists and state hospitals, but even private medical care in private clinics.

The writer and Conservative thinker, David Hart, would like to see the complete abolition of the NHS, and its replacement by a system of compulsory insurance, with a choice of insurance companies. The Government would limit its role to ensuring certain minimum standards and to paying the premiums of the least well-off. In this way, he believes, the resources of the nation would be redistributed according to the laws of the free market, and decisions about their use would be left in the hands of the consumer, who is always the best judge of how to spend his money.

This vision of a health service entirely guided by the market-place must have held considerable attractions for Mrs Thatcher. During her eleven years in power, she encouraged competition from independent private hospitals, and adopted a number of

---

* Compulsory health insurance covers from seventy per cent of medical costs for minor complaints, to a hundred per cent for chronic illnesses and major medical interventions.

measures (such as the appointment to the health service of managers trained in commerce, and the tendering out of hospital cleaning services) meant to introduce new dynamism to state-funded hospitals. But in the end, even she did not dare to attack that sacred cow of the British, the National Health Service. The reforms that were finally adopted by her Health Minister, Kenneth Clarke, amounted to a bold but curious compromise between the desire to adopt free market strategies, and the political imperative of preserving the NHS. While retaining a system of centralised Government funding for the Health Service, the reforms aim at separating 'purchasers' from 'providers' in an attempt to allow market forces to determine the most desirable distribution of finite resources. Under the reform, GP practices with at least nine thousand patients may apply for fund-holding status, making them responsible for their own NHS budget, and enabling them to choose – among other things – which hospitals to buy their services from. Hospitals, on the other hand, are encouraged to become financially autonomous self-governing bodies, offering competitive services designed to attract the maximum custom – and therefore an enhanced revenue.

It is probably too early to judge whether these changes will increase efficiency or reduce standards, as many people fear. There is no doubt that, both in Britain and in France, the pioneers of the two social security systems were entirely justified in their hope that, by providing generalised access to health care, there would be a corresponding improvement in the health of the nation. But their belief that the corollary to better public health was a decrease in health expenditure has proved to be entirely illusory. The principal reason for the world-wide inflation in the cost of health lies precisely in the success of medical research, and in the constant improvements which are being made to the available drugs, techniques and equipment. Britain has been more efficient than France in keeping down its health costs because the NHS is a monopoly supplier and therefore sole producer, while in France competition between the public and the private sectors tends to bid up the salaries of medical staff and the cost of equipment. But the rather passive reaction of the British public to this state of affairs has less to do with the respective merits of the two systems, than with the British standard of living, which has for so long remained lower than that of most other European countries.

Every European nation however, is faced with the question of the appropriate role of its doctors. Is their clinical autonomy compatible with an effective control of expenditure? The French tend to fight for the preservation of medical power and independence at almost any cost, whereas the British emphasise better coordination between the different social services, prevention services and paramedical auxiliaries, while diverting certain charges from the regional health authorities to centralised state bodies. What remains true for everyone is that, in spite of the promises and mutual accusations of conservative or progressive theoreticians and politicians, there is no solution, only a selection of options. Could we entirely forego those spectacular surgical interventions and miracle cures? Yet when the popular press enumerates the number of children who will die in Britain for lack of a kidney transplant, it should at least have the decency to specify how many schizophrenics and elderly cancer patients should be sacrificed to their recovery.

A Question of Trust

'Trust' – the monosyllabic English word rings clearer and stronger than its limp French equivalent, *'confiance'*. Its meaning is also stronger. In its secondary usage, it defines a specific charge based on confidence, and the trust which it expresses is an observation of fact, not merely a hope or an expectation. Legally, it establishes – with many variations – a subtle equilibrium between the interests of an individual and those of a family, a group, or even the entire nation. In that trust, British charities today find their most useful instrument.

A law adopted in 1887, in the cynical exuberance of a conquering era, set up a number of commercial and industrial trusts, legalising agreements between companies, and thus enabling dominant groups to impose themselves on the marketplace. A central administrative body of trustees owned the majority – sometimes all – of the shares in the companies which formed these trusts. It was their declared aim to fight against competition (and their unavowed aim to wipe it out) by reducing the costs of production and distribution to the common advantage of the trust members. Since then extremely strict legislation in Britain and in the United States has made it illegal for trusts to carve out a near-monopoly for themselves at the expense of consumers. In practice a trust – even when it is not set up with any commercial purpose – remains a legal concept calculated to outrage the doctrinaires, blurred in its outlines, a constantly evolving and precarious compromise between individual self-interest and some subjective altruism (embodied in the persons of the trustees) which the law does not determine, but which it ratifies, and guarantees. Trust and ideology are two contradictory concepts. A trust attempts to contain a fluid reality without constraining it; ideology defines or resurrects a utopian vision, describing it down to the last button of its outdated uniform, and establishing peremptory certainties which have been the misfortune of nations.

There is no such thing as a trust in French law. French legislators have always been wary of a formula which so completely escapes the control of the State. This hostility is the expression of one of the most profound differences in mentality between the British and the French. Perhaps its origins can be traced to the sale of the nation's property by the revolutionaries of 1789. What is certain is that the purchasers of that patrimony were long haunted by the fear that the vast domains which had been broken up to their advantage, would be reconstituted and returned to their original owners or to their heirs. 'In this ancient antipathy for what is known as mortmain*,' wrote Charles Gide in his *Traité d'économie politique*, 'there is both an economic and a political rationale. The first is the belief that property belonging to a collective body is likely to be maladministered, and will in any case be taken out of commercial circulation for an indefinite period. The second, more powerful reason, lies in the fear that these organisations could become over-powerful, challenge the State and take over from it in the provision of the major social services.'

The least that can be said is that the State, in Great Britain, does not share these fears. Trusts are flourishing under its benevolent

* The condition of lands or tenements held inalienably by ecclesiastical institutions or other kinds of corporation.

240

gaze, and whether their aims are highly creditable or somewhat dubious, they suffer from no intervention so long as they do not break the law. Throughout Great Britain, thousands of trusts manage thousands of properties on behalf of many different kinds of beneficiaries. For example, The Bournville Village Trust Group – founded by George Cadbury in 1900 to provide good quality houses for 'the labouring classes in and around Birmingham and elsewhere in Britain' – is a trust. Hospitals choosing to adopt self-governing status under the 1990 National Health Service reforms are also instituted as NHS trusts. Most important among them is the National Trust*, now – with 565,000 acres of land – the third biggest landowner in England and Wales (after the Crown and the Forestry Commission) and the largest conservation body in the world.

The National Trust began as a good idea dreamed up by three friends at the end of the last century. Miss Octavia Hill had fought all her life to improve housing conditions in Great Britain. Sir Robert Hunter, a lawyer, rightly believed that the Surrey grasslands were among the greatest glories of the English countryside. Canon Hardwicke Rawnsley liked nothing better than to relax after his literary labours by going for long walks in the Lake District, Cumbrian homeland of the poet Wordsworth. Together they raised some money and, in 1873, founded the National Trust with the aim of acquiring for the nation buildings of historical interest and natural sites of exceptional beauty. Their first purchase consisted of five acres and a cliff overlooking Cardigan Bay, in North Wales. Next they bought the half-timbered fourteenth-century Clergy House at Alfriston in Sussex. The idea took off and fourteen years later, in 1907, a law was enacted to give the National Trust legal status and confirm it in its mission. In legislating, Parliament was extremely careful not to define that mission in any way. It was not up to MPs to interfere with the trustees. But in order to ensure that no one could despoil the public – joint beneficiaries of the Trust – of its inheritance, they introduced a measure, unprecedented in English law, guaranteeing the absolute inalienability of the

* The National Trust for Scotland, founded in 1931, is run in the same way, with the same objectives, but is an entirely separate organisation.

Trust's acquisitions. The national patrimony could be indefinitely expanded, but nothing could ever be taken away from it. This statement of principle was given further substance in 1946, when Parliament enacted another law giving the Trust the right to refer any government proposal for expropriation of National Trust property in the 'public interest' to a joint committee of the Lords and Commons – even when such a proposal emanated from the Ministry of the Environment.

The State's trust in the maturity and objectivity of an organism over which it has no power; the National Trust's confidence in the State's determination to respect its independence: neither of these would count for anything if it were not for the trust which the general public places in both of them. Like many other essential British institutions, such as the BBC, Lloyd's or the Bank of England, the National Trust does not draw its strength from the statutes protecting it so much as from being closely in touch with public opinion.

The launch of 'Enterprise Neptune' in 1965, nearly a century after the purchase of the first two hectares in Bournemouth, was to introduce a new scale into the traditional activities of the National Trust. Whereas the early acquisitions of land had been the result of small scale individual effort, now the whole of British public opinion was being mobilised in an effort to save the nation's coastline. In eight years the public contributed two million pounds to the project, enabling the Trust to add another 175 miles of coastline to the 180 miles it had already accumulated over the previous century on the coast of Cornwall. Today it has acquired a total of 512 miles out of a target figure of nine hundred miles.

It was as the result of another personal initiative that the National Trust expanded its original brief, to include the preservation of the historic country houses of England and Wales. In 1934, Lord Lothian – then president of the Trust – matched words with deeds and bequeathed his home, as well as its entire contents and the surrounding land, to the organisation. Blickling Hall, a superb Jacobean house built between 1616 and 1624 in Norfolk, thus became the first of many outstanding country houses acquired for the nation. Once again, in 1937, the Trust's new vocation was ratified by law in one of those extraordinary English compromises an anthology of which might constitute the best possible handbook of political wisdom. Though the majority of the Trust's country houses are no longer lived in by their natural occupants, some of the most notable – Knole Park in Kent, Powys Castle, Near Welshpool, in the county of Powys, and Oxburgh Hall in Norfolk – are still inhabited by the descendants of their original owners. None of the National Trust's 1,860,000 members, nor its ten million or so annual visitors, are in the least resentful of a solution which appears to sustain a small number of families in a position of great privilege. On the contrary, most of them draw vicarious pleasure from the enchanted country-house life which they imagine these leisured families to be leading, as they sip their tea on immaculate lawns.

But the National Trust is not without its critics. In the puritanical view of those who defend the general interest, its board of directors contains rather too many Lords, too many of the powerful and the rich. More pertinently, it is also accused of having become an intimidating leviathan – too large, impersonal and arrogant. While its size enables it to tackle enterprises on a national scale, it has also increased its running costs to such an extent that the majority of country house owners cannot raise the amount of maintenance capital that is required as a precondition to accepting a donation from the Trust. A top-heavy administrative machine also tends to be insensitive to special cases and, in its restoration of family homes, to sacrifice the contribution of succeeding generations to a pedantic concern for historical accuracy. The *Sunday Telegraph* in 1988 gave a striking example of this, quoting an unnamed descendant of the distinguished Trevelyan family, whose family seat, Wallington in Northumberland, was taken over and redecorated by the Trust: 'In the family bathroom people used to lie in the bath and write witty poems, limericks and sayings (in Latin even) on the wall. There was a chip in the plaster where people had drawn mice running in. All this family history was simply wiped out and lost forever.'

But perhaps one should not be overly concerned about faults which have at least the merit of forcing independent-minded owners to constitute individual charitable trusts, enabling them and their successors to preserve the living character of their ancestral homes, maintaining and enjoying them with a more modest capital, without having to pay prohibitive death duties.

4
The Law

For years, Jimmy Downey, a young Trotskyite from the Militant Tendency, has been trying to penetrate the inner circles of the Labour Party hierarchy. 'What is certain,' he tells me with conviction, 'is that we would never break the law, whatever the provocations of the Right.'

It is hard to imagine an Italian, German or French left-winger swearing, hand on heart, that come what may he would submit to the bourgeois order he is proposing to abolish. But an English communist is an Englishman before he is anything else, and like every self-respecting Englishman, he has an even greater respect for the law.

Morals and the Law

For the man in the street the law is more than a guarantee of social order; it is his shield against the abuse of power and the arbitrariness of the State; it is his fetish, his lucky talisman.

The Jungle Book's monkey people, the Bandar-log – who, it is said, represented the French in the eyes of the fable's author, Rudyard Kipling – are a people without law. They become agitated for no reason, quarrel with no motive, make up without cause, and scream with no purpose other than to deafen each other with their noise. It is certainly true that for the average Frenchman, the law is primarily an imposition from above, the yoke which constrains his freedom – at best a necessary evil. It is his natural right to get round the law, to sidestep it, challenge it, and break it if necessary. Sometimes it is even his duty to do so, and his action is acclaimed as the splendid defiance of a man of principle. A number of

245

historical factors are generally advanced to explain the differences in popular attitudes on either side of the Channel: the early erosion of royal power (coupled with the Reformation and the growth of Parliamentarianism) in Great Britain, and in France, royal absolutism, Catholicism, and a tradition of centralism beginning with Colbert, continuing with the Revolutionaries, culminating in the *Code Napoléon*, and solemnly perpetuated by the Republic. On the whole it is true that, even when it was most crudely serving oligarchical interests, the law in England gradually evolved to the general benefit of the people.

During the 1984 miners' strike, the entire assets of the National Union of Mineworkers, consisting of more than eight million pounds, were sequestrated as a penalty for the leaders' refusal to comply with an earlier legal decision, and its President, Arthur Scargill, was forced to make a public apology in front of a tribunal before the funds were released, minus a hefty fine and legal costs. Labour leaders, for whom solidarity with the miners was a matter of principle, rightly judged that it was imperative to issue an unequivocal condemnation of any breach of the law. But the public, only half-convinced of their sincerity, demonstrated their disapproval of Labour by offering Mrs Thatcher – the undisputed champion of law and order – a third electoral victory in 1987.

Nothing seems to shake the popular confidence in English justice. It is often slow and costly. It is not infallible. It is still the bastion of the privileged classes, and remains suspicious of poverty and ignorance. It is too repressive towards petty delinquents, and (with the exception of a few cases like the Guinness trial, in which the crime is too flagrant, and the publicity too great) saves its indulgence for shady financiers and high-flying crooks. Yet it espouses, better than any other judicial system in the Western world, that confused feeling of equity which is shared, even if they are not conscious of it, by the innocent and the guilty, the victim and his executioner, the dupe and the conman. It has never been precisely defined or codified, but draws its authority from procedures that have been improved over the centuries. A number of practising barristers still remember a time when it was not necessary to have studied law in order to be admitted into one of the four Inns of Court that govern the profession.

Book learning was irrelevant at this stage. What mattered was hands-on experience in a good set of chambers. After three or four years of dining in the magnificent Hall of his chosen Inn, brushing shoulders daily with pupils and celebrated jurists alike, the aspiring young lawyer was thought to have received the best possible training. The study of learned manuals could be left till later to round off a largely completed education.

Lincoln's Inn and Gray's Inn, lying to the north of the Law Courts, in Holborn and Chancery Lane respectively, and the Inner and Middle Temples, set between Fleet Street and the Thames, flesh out with their chambers, their halls and their churches, the skeleton of the royal courts. Since their inception in the Middle Ages, the Inns of Court have been devoted to the technical study of English law, and from among the barristers who work there the High Court judges of England and Wales are chosen.

Barristers and solicitors together carve up the responsibilities of representing their clients at law. Like general practitioners in the health service, solicitors hold the key to the system. The barrister, aristocrat of the profession, legal specialist and sole permitted advocate in the higher courts, is chiefly dependent on the solicitor for his work although it is now possible for barristers to be briefed by other professionals such as surveyors or engineers. At present, though, barristers alone are permitted to represent clients directly in the higher courts. These two complementary and rival categories have long defended their respective prerogatives, while engaging in obscure internecine struggles that are both their torment and their delight. Their services do not come cheap, and it is becoming increasingly difficult to qualify for inadequately funded legal aid (though for the minority who do qualify, and who succeed in getting a solicitor to act for them, the funds are usually sufficient).

In January 1989, Mrs Thatcher's third Government brought out a series of three green papers that were to shake the Bar out of its historical complacency. Unaccustomed to outside interference, barristers were horrified to find that the reforming zeal which Mrs Thatcher had so successfully applied against the unions, was now being turned against them. Their historical monopoly was under threat, and the law of the marketplace, so dear to Mrs Thatcher, was apparently going to be extended to them.

Solicitors had been subjected to Mrs Thatcher's enthusiasms as early as 1985. Like chartered accountants (whose territory had been invaded by financial consultants) and opticians (who had seen the sale of glasses opened up to all sorts of unqualified newcomers), they too had seen the break-up of their monopoly over conveyancing. Today any individual or firm able to prove competence in the field has the right to draw up the relevant legal documents. Since more than half the business in the average solicitor's firm used to consist of conveyancing work, the profession greeted the reform with the most sombre predictions. But although a number of firms stepped in to take advantage of the new freedom, so far their intervention has not proved very successful. Conveyancing remains largely in the hands of traditional solicitors, and the most striking effect of the reform has been to reduce the costs of the service by about a third, with the most dynamic solicitors hastily forming new partnerships to offer old services at lower prices while seeking to scoop up some of the former clientèle of their less enterprising colleagues*.

With this audacious reform, another sacred cow had been slaughtered, a few more bowler hats thrown to the winds. Like so many venerable institutions, the Law Society, which represents the sixty thousand or so solicitors in England and Wales, had seen its authority called into question, and had been forced to change and adapt. No longer was its prestigious past sufficient justification for the present, nor its immutability thought to be synonymous with wisdom. In a profession which for centuries had been dominated by men, women had come to constitute about half the intake of new solicitors. In England, where the nation's law runs in such close harness with its customs, when Justice moves it means the country is galloping.

But from the perspective of the early nineties, the distance covered looks less spectacular – as do Mrs Thatcher's achievements in breaking down professional barriers and vested interests wherever she found them. Like numerous monarchs since the middle ages,

* The 1990 Courts and Legal Services Act has further opened up conveyancing to banks and building societies able to demonstrate competence in the field.

she was soon to discover that the legal profession does not take kindly to having its 'independence' threatened, and that its ability to fight back was far greater than that of the unions, weakened as they were by several years of unemployment and recession. While solicitors broadly welcomed proposals giving them rights of audience in the higher courts, barristers and judges immediately began a strident and systematic campaign against the Lord Chancellor's plans. The Lord Chief Justice, Lord Lane, attacked the principal green paper as being 'one of the most sinister documents ever to emanate from Government'. By threatening the independence of both lawyers and the judiciary, the proposals, he claimed, were effectively threatening 'the last bastion, the last protection between the citizen on the one hand and tyranny on the other'.

The Courts and Legal Services Act finally passed the statute book in November 1990 – a pale shadow of its earlier incarnation. In its 1990 Annual Report, the Bar Council congratulated itself on a campaign which – 'with the help of our friends in the Lords and the Commons' – had successfully defeated a number of proposals threatening to undermine 'the continued existence of an independent Bar'. These included direct lay access to barristers, partnerships between barristers and solicitors, and multi-disciplinary practices. As it now stands, the Act provides for the setting up of an 'advisory committee on legal education and conduct' charged with looking at the whole question of the training and education of lawyers, and drawing up a new set of proposals governing the conditions under which solicitors will be granted rights of audience in the higher courts. The Bar Council is now limbering up for the next stage of the campaign (which it envisages continuing over 'the next few years'), to ensure that barristers maintain privileged access to the higher courts, and that any extensions in the rights of audience 'are carefully monitored before a further stage is considered'. Crucially, the Council has successfully ensured that each of the country's four senior judges (including Lord Lane) retains an individual veto over the advisory committee's future proposals.

Clearly we are not about to see barristers and judges abandon their horsehair wigs and long robes in favour of track suits and trainers. Like everywhere else in the world, the principal actors in the judicial tragi-comedy are fallible and unsure of themselves; they need to surround themselves with trappings that distinguish them from common humanity. The robe has a timeless and universal character with a symbolic and liturgical value. But it is the wig that distinguishes the English lawyer. This anachronistic accessory, perched straight (or slightly askew) on the crown, preferably a little threadbare, and if possible matured on the skull of some venerable predecessor, brings to life the triple alliance of dignity, irony and whimsy without which Justice in England would not exist.

Barristers form one of the last major castes that the new middle class has not entirely succeeded in penetrating. Aspirants to membership should preferably be good lawyers, and preferably also white rather than black. Women used to have to be very clever – and know how to hide it – if they were to be accepted; but even at the Bar, their march forward is inexorable. Today nearly forty per cent of entrants into the profession are women.

In 1950, Sir John Senter, an eminent tax specialist, met a young woman who was sufficiently gifted for him to invite her to spend six months pupillage in his set of chambers. He went so far as to promise that at the end of the period, she could stay on as a tenant of the chambers – the key to entry into the profession, without which any number of brilliant qualifications are quite useless. But on the appointed day, influenced perhaps by the opinion of his young colleagues who thought that tax law was not a feminine enough occupation, he shut the door in her face. The people who knew her well during this period say that this stinging blow, the first rejection she had ever suffered, finally impelled Margaret Thatcher to throw herself more vigorously into political life, though she continued to practise off and on for about five years.

Once a man is an established barrister, his eccentricities are tolerated; he can express almost any opinion without fearing that indiscretion will put him beyond the pale. He is the prince of Contradiction, the king of Ambivalence, emperor of the For and Against. Truth, if the word has a meaning, is a matter of balance and degree. Ensconced in his chambers, he is protected from the outside world, a member of the seraglio. But, as always in the art of English living, there are undefined and indefinable limits beyond which he cannot go without breaking the ties of solidarity that bind him to his colleagues. His eccentricities and outrageously expressed opinions must be amusing, but never shocking.

Inside London's four Inns of Court, the Bar is a club – probably the most pleasant club in Britain. The chambers are contiguous; a few steps up or down, a corridor to follow, a courtyard to cross – colleagues, adversaries and judges cross paths, consult each other, and dine together like plotting schoolboys. The tastes, the obsessions, the mannerisms of one and all are familiar to everyone. The provincial Bars, which sometimes have fewer than a hundred members, are hardly less difficult to penetrate and get to know – though for obvious psychological reasons, they tend to adhere more closely to the trappings of legal fashion (striped trousers and watch-chains) than do their colleagues in London. Among more than six thousand practising barristers, there is the occasional black sheep. But in general, one is in well-bred company, among people whose integrity is tempered only by the art of bending the law, more or less skilfully, to advantage. There are the occasional tensions, naturally, between the bright beginners whose brilliant future does not quite reconcile them to their present drudgery, the drudges who vegetate without hope of better prospects, and the Queen's Counsels, prosperous aristocrats of the profession. The title, QC, is purely honorific, and does not signify that the Crown takes advice from those who hold it. But it is almost invariably from their number that High Court judges are recruited. The world of politics is within their reach, should they want to enter it, and their earnings reflect their status.

No democratic country, apart from England, would dare to select such an important category of people under so arbitrary a procedure. The Lord Chancellor, a man of the law, but also – and more importantly – a member of the government, receives the applications of those aspiring to this lucrative honour, who comprise some twenty to thirty per cent of the country's barristers. After having taken the advice of his civil servants and consulted with the judicial authorities and the most 'respected' QCs, he asks the Queen to confer the title on about a third to a half of these candidates. It is thought quite acceptable that anyone who has spoken openly against Queen or Government should see their chances of promotion singularly reduced.

A remarkable feature of English criminal justice, as compared with most other European systems, has been the continuing role of lay justices of the peace, who, like the jury in cases before the Crown Court, are supposed to reflect public opinion and bring ordinary common sense to bear on matters that are of concern to the whole of society. Magistrates' courts – normally consisting of three voluntary justices (JPs) advised by a professional lawyer, the clerk – try over ninety-seven per cent of all criminal cases, and have the power to pass a sentence of up to one year imprisonment or a fine of up to £2,000. Like barristers wishing to become QCs, aspiring JPs can apply to the Lord Chancellor's office, and after extensive screenings, about fifty per cent of candidates are selected for the magistrature. Any criminal record – even if it consists only of a minor driving offence – automatically eliminates any candidate. For the rest, impeccable references and a reputation for steadiness ensure that no firebrand is appointed, while a JP's comparatively onerous unpaid duties stack the cards against applicants from the ordinary working population.

Until 1971, following ancient tradition, judges could be chosen only from among the body of barristers. After lengthy protest, solicitors – who had recently been granted the right to represent their clients in person before the lower courts – were further given the opportunity of being selected as circuit judges. The High Courts, however, are still the exclusive terrain of the Bar (and are likely to remain so for a good many years despite any changes envisaged by the advisory committee under the 1990 Courts and Legal Services Act). Towards the age of fifty, at the height of his career, a barrister can expect to be offered a High Court judicial appointment. The prestige of the office is so great that most of them will not hesitate to accept the job despite a substantial cut in earnings. It is true that, apart from the honour, being a judge also gives them job security. They too are chosen in secret by the Lord Chancellor, in consultation with his permanent secretary (who is a barrister) and the more senior judges. Theoretically, such procedures could lead to shameless favouritism and to an intolerable politicisation of the judiciary.

In practice this clubbiness has been tempered over the centuries by the evolution of political morality, and to resurrect now some of the abuses of the past would provoke a political storm of such proportions that no government could survive it.

Common Law

English democracy is not so much an institution as a prevailing state of affairs. Its mainspring and its strength lies in the English system of justice, which is founded not on immovable principles, but on a diffuse popular will. Barristers, solicitors and judges co-opt each other. They are overwhelmingly from the middle classes, and often from a good public school and either Oxford or Cambridge. From such origins they derive sufficient qualities for their prejudices not to render them entirely hateful to the less fortunate. Even when they feel overwhelmed by the coalition between their prosecutors, defenders and judges, petty criminals – ever the submissive sons of paternalism – are more inclined to trust in the equity of their superiors, than they would in that of their equals.

In their overriding concern to legitimise the Norman succession to the Anglo-Saxon kings, the eleventh-century invaders were at pains to show respect for native customs, and abolished none of the existing jurisdictions. Gradually new ones were added to those already established, until at one time there were more than 150 overlapping jurisdictions in the kingdom. Some were local, others seigniorial, others ecclesiastical. Their competence was ill defined, and their jurisprudence varied from one area to another. Local jurisdictions, familiar and based on custom, were frequently just an instrument of oppression in the hands of the local petty tyrant. They were invoked, if necessary, for want of anything better – until the day when another, competing form of justice became available. This jurisdiction treated everyone equally, and emanated from the King himself, and with it came the development of common law, 'declared' by the royal judges, and overriding any custom that was deemed unreasonable or unproven. Here was a solid and reliable jurisdiction, 'common' to all the people and based on a single set of standards – a situation which contrasted strikingly with that in France, where a monarch ruled over a number of duchies and counties, each with its own customary law.

During the reign of Edward I in the late thirteenth century, the office of judge was transformed from a clerical position into a full-time career, and admission to the Bar was made conditional on the legal knowledge of the applicant. These developments saw the rise of the lawyer, Jack of all trades and indispensable intermediary. His training consisted of participating in simulated legal disputes (known as 'moots'), attending lectures or 'readings' given by senior lawyers, and – crucially – attending court, where he took detailed notes for future reference. From about 1290 student notes seem to have been copied and circulated, and in the sixteenth century they began to be printed and arranged by regnal year, coming to be referred to as the Year Books.

This early organisation of the legal profession in England ensured an effective resistance to attempted Royal innovations such as the import, during the sixteenth century, of experts in Roman law as advisors and administrators. Case law came to be the typical form of English common law, while practising lawyers became the principal interpreters of the law, as well as the agents of its development. Though bound by precedent in cases that were similar to each other, they had considerable latitude to innovate whenever novel circumstances arose. And in cases where the remedies afforded by common law (limited to the payment of damages and to the recovery of the possession of property) were inadequate or inappropriate, the lawyer could apply to the Chancellor, 'guardian of the King's conscience', to consider the client's case himself, according to the principles of 'equity' – thus avoiding all the restrictions of precedent incumbent upon common law. The Court of Chancery was free to develop its own procedures, unencumbered by formalities, and its criteria were moral rather than legal. From the mid-sixteenth century however, chancellors were increasingly chosen from among common lawyers, and began shaping equity into an established set of rules, so that by the middle of the seventeenth century, the equity administered by the Court of Chancery had become a recognised part of the law of the land. Today's Chancery Division is its heir, while the Queen's Bench Division proceeds from common law.

The same procedural skill that first enabled the lawyer to spare his client the arbitrariness and uncertainties of local jurisdictions is still his most important quality today. Although the vast expansion of statute law in the nineteenth and twentieth centuries has, to some extent, narrowed the differences in legal procedure between France and England, the English lawyer is not (like his French counterpart) bound by clearly defined principles enshrined in a written code of law, and he retains remarkable freedom to improvise in cases where there are no precedents to constrain him. Champions of the English system argue that this procedural freedom and the general respect for tradition enshrined in the principles of precedent have allowed the law to develop organically, in harmony with the evolution of society.

Yet this same respect for tradition is responsible for the multiplication of complex and sometimes absurd procedural rules and regulations. The preservation of Chancery Division and the Queen's Bench as two separate sections of the High Court has no particular justification apart from their different historical origins. And though the system has been rationalised to the extent that the two divisions now handle different areas of the law, there remains a certain overlap, leading to cases that could be referred indifferently to either division.

But there are also more worrying aspects to the problem of procedural complexity. It is procedure that led to the ruin of the unfortunate Richard Carstone, hero of Dickens' *Bleak House*, in the labyrinthine inheritance suit of 'Jarndyce versus Jarndyce'. And it is still procedural complexity that daily discourages people from availing themselves of long-winded and ruinous legal services. The long preservation of the dual and complementary monopolies of solicitors and barristers is just one of the most glaring ways in which the legal profession has defended the *status quo* to its own advantage, requiring clients to pay two sets of people for services that could sometimes be accomplished by just one.

Members of the legal profession agree with a touching unanimity on the need to remove or reduce the multitude of anomalies that survive only on account of their antiquity. They console themselves in the meantime, like the wealthy socialist heroine of Saki's 'Byzantine Omelette', who 'was conscious of a comfortable feeling that the system, with all its inequalities and iniquities, would

255

probably last her time'*. History has taught them that the slowness of the legal system is not necessarily a fault, and that the radical reforms so favoured by their neighbours across the Channel are not always to be preferred.

Although the primacy of common law, enriched by the jurisprudence of the Courts of Equity, was not finally enshrined in written texts until the Judicature Acts of 1873 and 1875, its supremacy had effectively been established long before that. No doubt the King of England had been forced to compromise with the landed aristocracy, and was willy-nilly under the financial tutelage of recalcitrant Members of Parliament. Yet he had seen his justice prevail over all the others and gradually eliminate by attrition local customs and jurisdictions.

In France by contrast, the highly centralised apparatus of the absolutist monarchy continued, until the 1789 Revolution, to come up against a multitude of customary jurisdictions, countless privileges in common law, and the obduracy of the *parlements*, all of which combined to whittle down its power. It was therefore with all the more enthusiasm that the revolutionary assemblies – which were largely composed of lawyers – set about their task. The French have retained ever since a passion for legislating, codifying and centralising. They not only instituted the *Code Napoléon* at home, but also imposed it on the rest of Europe, and it continues to flourish with endless additions and modifications dictated by subsequent political or constitutional evolutions and revolutions.

However convinced they were of the superiority of common law, the English carefully avoided imposing it on the far from docile Scots at the time of the Act of Union in 1707. The English distrust of Roman law was such that one of the charges in the prosecution case against Cardinal Wolsey, in 1529, was his intention of introducing it into England. Yet Scottish law is strongly influenced by Roman law. No matter – time, it was thought, would eventually harmonise the differing legislations of the two kingdoms. Until then, it was better to spare Scottish pride and

* From 'Beasts and Superbeasts', *The Complete Works of Saki*, The Bodley Head, 1980.

avoid unnecessary conflict. Scotland was to retain its own legal system, and its tribunals would not be subject to appeal in the English courts; the possibility of appeal to the House of Lords, where sixteen Scottish peers were given seats next to their 190 English brethren, was at first prudently left ambiguous, but was eventually confirmed as a right.

This cohabitation continues today. The distinctive nature of the Scottish system has never been put at risk: civil and criminal law, legal terminology, the names of tribunals, the titles of judges – all these are still different in contemporary England and Scotland. Yet the evolution of jurisprudence in the two countries has been similar. Westminster's legislation has been applied with increasing frequency concurrently with English and Scottish law. When, in the 1986 BBC Reith lectures, the highly respected Scottish lawyer, Lord McCluskey, argued the need for an improvement in the administration of justice, he did so without reference to a Scottish or an English tradition, but simply stated that justice had to become more efficient, faster, and less expensive. Ultimately, he argued, the important decisions determining the evolution of a society are the responsibility of that society itself. Perhaps this could be seen as a contemporary application of the dual principle of the 'reasonable and the equitable' which is at the basis of common law.

Law and Liberty

However reasonable and equitable, common law remains something of an enigma to the minds of those trained in the discipline of Roman law. The use of *Habeas Corpus* as a means of defending individual liberties illustrates the deep-seated distrust of the English for ideas, and their propensity to reduce a complex case to a number of clear and inescapable premises. *Habeas Corpus* requires that unless a detainee can be charged with a precise crime and presented in person before a court, he must be released. The writ permits of only two possibilities, and in all its simplicity, it is solemnly set out in *Magna Carta*. But in its execution the idea is complex enough for more than four centuries to have elapsed before it was given the full force of law in the 1628 Petition of Right, and particularly, in the Habeas Corpus Act of 1679.

From then on this piece of precision mechanism was to accomplish minor miracles: why bother to campaign for press freedom, since no law existed to curtail it? What need to enact the end of conscription into the army, or the abolition of slavery, since there were no laws to enforce them? *Habeas Corpus*, alone, could ensure that judges would be obliged to release prisoners who had broken no existing law, thus bringing an end to numerous repugnant customs. No doubt it was a long time before the poor could avail themselves of this expensive high-class justice, reserved for high-class people. Nor has it been enforced without a break. Between 1794 and 1804 fear of internal subversion and of the Revolution in France led the Government to suspend *Habeas Corpus* every year. The same was to happen during the Boer War. It was suspended in Ireland in 1866, during the height of the campaign by the Fenian movement, and again between 1971 and 1975, in an attempt to curb terrorism. The Prevention of Terrorism Act, which was first passed in 1974 and has been confirmed every year since then, replaced the notorious policy of indefinite internment with provisions for allowing the police to detain suspects for a full seven days before charging them. And on the mainland, during the Gulf War in 1991, special measures were introduced allowing for the indefinite detention for security reasons of individuals deemed to present a terrorist threat. Nonetheless common law, with its curious crab-like gait, has probably been more successful at protecting individual liberties than other legal systems which are more explicitly dedicated to the defence of the rights of man.

It is not at all clear that the same can be said of the English adversarial system. The French have long had mixed feelings about their own inquisitorial procedure and particularly about the enormous powers devolved on the *juge d'instruction* or examining judge, who is entirely responsible for deciding whether a case should be brought before a tribunal on the basis of his personal investigation and evaluation of the evidence supplied by defence and prosecution. But today, with the introduction of an appeal procedure allowing for his decision to be reversed, the anxieties of the French public have been largely allayed. On the other hand, they would be horrified if told that henceforth their police force was to be given extensive new English-style powers. In addition to maintaining public order and making investigations, they would now have the independent right to look for and arrest suspects, unrestrained by any outside authority such as that of the examining judge. Not only that, but they would also have to combine their role as investigators with that of the prosecution, and be required to take suspects to court themselves. Yet until the institution in 1986 of a national body of independent prosecutors – the Crown Prosecution Service – and with the exception of a limited number of cases which were referred straight to the Director of Public Prosecutions, this is precisely what used to happen in England and Wales – though not in Scotland.

Despite this innovation which has eliminated one of the worst anomalies of the English system, it remains surprising to anyone familiar with French procedure, that the Director of Public Prosecutions should be required to decide whether a case ought to be pursued entirely on the basis of the evidence put before him by the prosecution, and without any kind of consultation with the defence. This curious imbalance results in numerous cases coming to court which would have been dismissed immediately had the strength of the defence been known in the first place. Meanwhile delays accumulate, expenses mount, and the reputation of the accused inevitably suffers – even if the court's verdict subsequently vindicates his reputation.

The Power of the Police

The British police is not, one has to admit, a police force like any other. The soldiers at Buckingham Palace, in their red tunics and their bearskin hats; the Beefeaters at the Tower of London, in their ancient black and red uniform: these are just exotic images to stick into a holiday photograph album. But the unarmed bobby with his funny helmet, strolling peacefully down the street, greeting local shopkeepers or helping children and old ladies across the street, is more than a piece of colourful nostalgia. He symbolises a lifestyle and a level of civilisation unique in the world. Not only is this bobby still around, but over the past few years there has even been an increase in the number of beats that he covers at a steady pace, alone or accompanied by a colleague. The only sacrifice to modernity has been his walkie-talkie. Yet today he is just the visible tip of a huge iceberg. Faced with the insecurity of urban ghettos, with the threat of terrorism from Ireland and elsewhere, and with a galloping crime rate, the British police have responded with fast cars, computerised files, information networks, and specialised bodies of armed men used in high-risk operations and for the routine surveillance of airports. With every passing day, they look more like any other police force in the developed world.

Another cause for anxiety is the remarkable power which rests in the hands of the British police and which is inherent in the very structure of the force. It is not a visible power and many British people would be outraged at the very mention of its existence. The moderation and wisdom of prevailing custom gives the public a sense of security that is largely justified. But when, in 1984, there was an enquiry in Ireland concerning certain expedient practices in dealing with suspects, John Stalker, the officer in charge of the investigation discovered – on the day before handing in an embarrassing report – that he had been implicated in some shady affair and was suspended from duty. The accusations against him proved to be entirely unfounded and, in 1987, he was reinstated as Deputy Chief Constable. But the enquiry in Ireland was completed without him and he was left feeling that he had no alternative other than to take early retirement from the force.

And when James Anderton, Chief Constable of Greater Manchester Police, suddenly declared to the press that he had a mandate from the Almighty to condemn the loose morals of the times (to which the scourge of AIDS could be entirely attributed), and that he was responsible to God alone for his orders, the local Police Authority which theoretically controls him, was powerless to silence him, or to sanction him in any way. Meanwhile the Home Office could do little more than engage in a face-saving mediation exercise between the Authority and the Chief Constable, who continued to play the prophet with impunity.

It is frequently argued that the decentralisation of police powers (divided between a number of independent regions), the existence of independent elected bodies charged with monitoring the activities of their local force, and the relatively weak powers of the Home Secretary, combine to guarantee the democratic functioning of the police. Undoubtedly, the annual reports drafted by the country's Chief Constables could profitably be emulated by policemen throughout the world – many of whom would be astonished by their openness in discussing the weaknesses and excesses of their force and revealing the punishments meted out to corrupt or undisciplined policemen.

But this self-regulation has it limits. England's powerful police associations, headed by the Association of Chief Police Officers, constitute a sort of sub-legislature, endowed with a collective executive. It is not above the law of the land, but translates it into its own terms. The severity with which it comes down on its guilty members is that of a freemasonry anxious to maintain the purity of its faith and cult.

This freemasonry – like the other one, the real one – used to be respectable and easy-going. Its members were recruited largely from the middle classes or among blue collar workers, whose social status was enhanced by membership. It was correspondingly respectful of established values, and tolerant. But social pressures have changed the police force. Significantly, in recent years it has felt the necessity, for the first time, to denounce the dual allegiance of freemason policemen as being incompatible with the overriding duty they owe towards their colleagues and superiors.

The influx of racial minorities into the country has seen the police force turn in on itself, and despite official protestations, the number of coloured recruits is minimal. Faced with the petty delinquency of bored youngsters trapped in endemic unemployment, policemen have resorted to increasingly harsh repression in the inner cities and urban ghettos. The cancer of Northern Ireland, with its sequel of terrorism leading to the suspension of legal guarantees, and increasing urban violence (particularly in Greater London) have required new resources and methods. Police forces in predominantly urban areas have received more funds and personnel for their CIDs (Criminal Investigation Divisions), while the latter have been extending their networks of informers, and carrying out a growing number of secret operations.

The London Metropolitan Police is the only force not answerable to a police authority. But although it is directly responsible to the Home Office, it has developed a defiant autonomy: defiant towards government, which begrudges it men and materials; defiant towards Parliament and the press, who frequently question its methods and decry the results of its activities; and defiant towards a public who are less indulgent towards it than in the past, and whose indulgence it perhaps deserves less. In 1989, the Metropolitan Police paid out more than £500,000 in damages and compensation for wrongful arrests, malicious prosecutions and assaults. Meanwhile, the West Midlands Serious Crime Squad was being disbanded in disgrace, amid allegations of serious corruption, and the number of complaints against the police nationwide rose to more than two hundred a week.

For an important minority of British public opinion, there is another, yet more ominous danger looming. During the national miners' strike in 1985, the police forces of Great Britain were mobilised in an unprecedented nationwide collaborative effort to handle the situation, using common tactics and a common strategy. No doubt policemen were within their remit when they used strong-arm tactics to ensure that the law was not breached. But their huge and co-ordinated intervention created a pyschological gulf, not only between them and the striking miners, but also between the police and a significant section of the public at large. However respectful they might be of the law, this law-abiding minority could not but deplore the way the Queen's Peace was being violated in the name of the law.

This Queen's Peace is a common treasure. It exists only in so far as it is recognised as such. If tomorrow certain central values transcending all political divisions were no longer shared by the bulk of the population, the harmony that still survives between the police and the public – of which the British are justly proud – would be irreparably damaged. One of the most frequent criticisms levelled at Mrs Thatcher, not only by her opponents but also by some of her partisans, was that her taste for confrontation led her to ignore this danger, or even to accentuate it. But whatever her share of responsibility for the present situation may be, the core of the problem must be attributed to the natural evolution of a society that is becoming increasingly complex and fragmented.

It is partly because the police were finding it ever more difficult to reconcile their job of detecting crime and maintaining public order with their prosecuting role (as cases such as that of the Guildford Four and the Birmingham Six continue to demonstrate, years after the event) that, after much hesitation, the Government finally decided to create in England and Wales a national prosecution body comparable to the one already existing in Scotland under the authority of the Procurator Fiscal.

Several well-publicised scandals (notably in Northern Ireland) also played an important part in the Government's decision by highlighting the pressures facing policemen who were expected to act both as impartial investigators and as prosecutors. Naturally the temptation to tailor the evidence to the case sometimes proved irresistible. Indeed it could hardly have been otherwise in a system that is founded on confrontation – a system where the defence cloaks its own evidence and strategies in secret, the better to outwit the other side. At least now there exists an independent state prosecutor to cast a critical eye over the charges brought by the police before they are exposed to the onslaught of the counsel for the defence.

Law and Order

In spite of growing disillusionment, the British still admire their police – and their army – more than any other institution. Furthermore, they believe they have the best system of justice in the world, and are convinced that in Europe, and particularly in France – home of the arbitrary – a defendant in court is presumed guilty until proved innocent. Any suggestion that this is untrue and that the presumption of innocence is laid down quite as firmly in French as in English law, is usually greeted with an incredulous smile. This distrust of continental legal systems is even more marked among lawyers themselves, particularly when it comes to the criminal law.

To the equivocal French legal notion of a 'search for truth', which allows prejudice to creep into the judge's assessment of the evidence, they oppose the virtues of a system where every possible interpretation of the facts is explored by prosecution and defence, leaving it to the lay magistrates, or to the jury of twelve ordinary men and women, to come to an independent decision on the basis of the evidence. In marked contrast to the French system, in which the presiding judge (who comes from the same professional stable as the prosecutor and the examining magistrate, but not the defence lawyer) typically dominates the process of taking evidence and questioning the witnesses, English procedure in principle limits the role of the judge to that of legal interpreter. His function is to enforce the complicated common law rules governing evidence, and to ask supplementary questions if he feels the parties have failed to clarify the facts. In his final summing up, he is supposed to guide the jury as to the significance of the facts presented with regards to the law. In practice however, some judges play an important part in guiding the proceedings, and can make their own view of the substantive evidence quite plain.

English lawyers place great significance on the subordinate physical position assigned to the defence in French legal theatre (for while judge and prosecutor stand on a raised platform, the defence lawyer is apparently relegated to the level of the accused), and immediately assume this means the dice must be loaded against the defendant. They are also shocked by the way the accused is questioned in court about his previous history – a practice which violates the most sacred of all their precepts, that it is the circumstances of the crime that must be judged, not the man, and that any inference from the one to the other constitutes a gross violation of his rights. And they cannot entirely believe in the independence of lay assessors (equivalent to the jury in common law procedure) who deliberate in the presence of the presiding judge – even though he is supposed to restrict himself to enlightening them as to the legal aspects of the case they are considering. But these same English lawyers rarely stop to ask themselves whether in practice defendants in England receive a better deal than their counterparts on the continent. Yet the English Magistrates' Courts send nearly one person in a thousand to jail. In 1989, Britain had a higher proportion of its population in prison than any other Western European country except Luxembourg, with the prison construction programme set to continue growing (total prison capacity was due to expand by a massive sixty per cent between 1980 and 1996). Within the limits of their jurisdiction, English JPs belong to what is probably the most repressive judiciary in Europe.

Her Majesty's prisons are largely ancient and overcrowded. Conditions continue to deteriorate, and the number of suicides by prisoners has doubled in the last ten years. Between January and November 1990, fifty prison inmates committed suicide, of whom nine were aged twenty or under; five teenagers who committed suicide at the notorious Armley prison in Leeds between May 1988 and February 1989 were on remand, as well as another youngster who killed himself at Armley in September 1990. But while only the most vulnerable choose the ultimate solution, growing tensions among the prison population also lead to occasional violent protests. In April 1990, a riot erupted during the chapel service at Manchester's Strangeways prison, and inmates invaded the roof-tops, starting what was to become a five-week-long siege – the longest in modern British history. Speaking of the conditions at Strangeways, Her Majesty's Chief Inspector of Prisons, Judge Stephen Tumin, said, 'To place three men in a cell designed in the nineteenth century for one man, and to hold them there for some twenty hours daily with a chamber pot for company, creates a school for crime and corruption.'

Pickpockets and Saturday brawlers may spend anything between six to eighteen months in jail, and frequently emerge as hardened criminals. But the courts, who interpret and embody public opinion, are prone to deal more severely with an unemployed young black who has stolen a handbag, than they are with a well-educated crook whose fraudulent activities have led him to bankruptcy; and this because they are frightened by the former while they pity the latter, much as they might pity a distant cousin who has gone to the bad. Not content with imprisoning the guilty, in recent years magistrates and judges have been increasingly liberal in their use of prisons to lock up defendants pending trial. Yet, despite the intervention of the new public prosecutors, the case against many of those brought to court remains very weak. In 1988, sixty-six per cent of the women and fifty-three per cent of the men who had been remanded in custody were released after their trial.

One of the great principles of English justice gives any person accused of a serious offence the right to have his case heard before a jury. This right dates back to the thirteenth century and is often cited as one of the citizen's principal safeguards against arbitrary justice. Yet today it is not clear that it can compensate for major weaknesses in the English adversarial system, in which the parties and their attorneys are primarily responsible for finding and presenting the evidence. For while the police and the prosecution share similar interests, defence counsel cannot muster comparable resources on behalf of his client. And although prosecuting counsel is under the strict obligation to disclose all the evidence at his disposal, the only incentive to collect a full range of evidence in the first place, is the fear that counsel for the defence, working alone and with fewer resources, might ask awkward questions in court.

In the light of this imbalance between prosecution and defence, the practice of plea bargaining that has evolved in common law countries appears all the more dangerous. When the evidence against the defendant seems to be overwhelming, a barrister will sometimes advise his client to plead guilty to a lesser offence, such as 'malicious wounding', in order to avoid having to defend himself against a more serious charge, such as 'attempted murder'. In such a bargain, the prosecution agrees to drop the heavier charge in order to avoid the uncertainties of a full trial. According to French procedure by contrast, conviction on the basis of a plea of guilty is not permitted. When the accused is willing to admit his guilt, the court remains obliged to investigate the evidence fully – though the admission is considered as part of that evidence. This important difference between the two systems ensures that in France it is less likely that a defendant who may have been pressured into making a false confession will be convicted as a result.

There are also more subtle dangers to the confrontational English system of justice in which defence and prosecution use their considerable procedural and oratorical skills to trip each other up, while the jury is left to disentangle the complex strands of evidence presented. By contrast the inquisitorial system – with its examining judge and its possibilities of appeal before trial to assess the validity of the prosecution case – seems to offer the accused better safeguards than this merciless duel, even when the fight is presided over by the best system of justice in the world.

Overcoming the natural reluctance of the British courts to hand over one of their own nationals to a foreign tribunal, the Law Lords unanimously decided, on the 13th of July 1987, to quash a decision by the Court of Appeal refusing to grant Belgian courts the extradition of twenty-six young English football supporters implicated two years before in the Heysel football disaster, which had cost the lives of thirty-nine spectators – almost all of them Italian. This is perhaps one of the first signs of cooperation and – who knows? of fruitful cross-fertilisation between the kingdom of common law and the countries of Roman law. The cohabitation of English and Scottish law shows that such cooperation is not impossible. Britain's signing and ratification of the European Convention on Human Rights and its willingness to accept sentences pronounced by the court at Strasbourg – where judges appointed by all the members of the community preside together – are contributing to the creation of a genuinely European jurisdiction. That is how, after all, common law and the royal courts gradually replaced local jurisdictions in England.

The English contribution to this process could be decisive. Of all the cultural factors which – in spite of the gradual slackening in the 'special relationship' between Britain and the United States – have given the two peoples a certain feeling of solidarity, the most important is probably the legal heritage that England has bequeathed its former colony. It is possible that the adoption of a common legal language with generally accepted terms of reference and some of the flexibility of the common law could, in the same way, establish the most solid possible base for a European identity. But unlike their American spiritual heirs, the British have never accepted 'government by judges'. Despite strong pressure from a section of public opinion and a number of eminent lawyers, no government has consented to drawing up a formal Bill of Rights within the framework of a written constitution. Though Britain willingly subscribes to the European Convention, placing its citizens under the jurisdiction of the European tribunal, at home it is still reluctant to freeze general principles into binding legal texts.

The House of Lords is not the equivalent of the Supreme Court in the United States, and it is not the function of the Law Lords to interpret the Constitution. The justice of the people – the justice of the juries, chosen from among the people – can be entrusted to judges only if they remain under the control of the people, that is to say of the people's representative, Parliament – the only legitimate successor to the Norman Kings.

The law is good only if it is coherent, predictable, respectful of its principles, and if it produces socially acceptable results. Parliament reflects the evolution of public morality. It must not meddle in the administration of the law, but when a law no longer seems to reflect public consensus, it is best to change it, and it is up to judges to apply it in its modified form so that it becomes socially acceptable, while not flying in the face of the principles on which it is based.

There is, in this English-style compromise, a certain wisdom that is not easily compatible with the separation of the three powers so dear to Montesquieu; but in so far as it allows for the possibility of evolution, it may provide an example for an evolving Europe.

5

The Defence of the Realm

The December 1988 Soviet-American agreement on the gradual destruction of the medium-range atomic weapons stationed in Europe has put an end to one of those women's crusades that flourish in England. Over a period of some years, large numbers of women would gather at Greenham Common in Oxfordshire, camping in the vicinity of the air-base where the nuclear-headed American missiles were kept, singing and joining hands in 'human chains' of protest. Like many others involved in the peace movement, Mgr Bruce Kent – the Catholic prelate who used to preside over the destiny of the Campaign for Nuclear Disarmament (CND) – regularly visited the women, adding his gentle voice to their protest. Unilateral nuclear disarmament, he maintained, was the only reasonable option for Britain to adopt.

CND and the Greenham Common women achieved a high profile during this period. But make no mistake: though the great majority of the British love peace, they do not love pacifism. They were exasperated by these demonstrations which they judged to be demeaning, absurd, and perhaps even dangerous for the country. In 1983 and 1987, the Labour Party lost two successive elections, in large measure because it supported unilateral nuclear disarmament and the closure of American nuclear bases. And it was not until Neil Kinnock succeeded in reversing this policy in 1988, that the Party's hopes of forming the next government began to seem at all credible. In the aftermath of the Gulf War, it looks as though the defence policy of a future Labour Government would not be very different from that of the Tories. Like the Conservatives, Labour would find itself torn between the friends of the 'special relationship' with the United States on the one hand, and a pro-European faction on the other; between partisans of the national military-industrial establishment and those who advocate multi-national cooperation; and – as ever – between the Ministry of Defence and the Treasury.

Patriotism – their kind of patriotism – is a sentiment that the English find entirely natural but that is quite unintelligible to a foreigner. Frequently jingoistic, no other people love their servicemen as much as the English do; yet any manifestation of patriotism that is not their own strikes them as an expression of incomprehensible vanity, or of such childish aggressiveness as to deserve no more than an eyebrow cocked in disbelief. It is quite a different matter when their own pride is at stake: they are immediately on the warpath, ready to do battle for Queen and Country.

Queen and Country

'Queen', the queen, is common property, loved by the people and celebrated by the press – an ornament in any ceremony or inauguration. She no longer has an empire but remains the sovereign of a Commonwealth of races and creeds; the Queen, defender of the faith, guarantor of the unwritten constitution, protector of the rights and liberties of all her peoples, whatever their race, religion, politics or class; the Queen, living memorial of all those dates one has learnt at school.

And 'Country' – the United Kingdom of Great Britain and Northern Ireland, composed of four nations – of which three have been subdued by the fourth, England – and of a number of scattered islands whose history and common interests have, with the exception of Ireland, done more to tone down than to highlight the differences between them. Country – the familiar landscape seen through a delicate veil of rain that screens the sun, striating the fields in green and gold, or glistening in the clean light after a shower; the gentle contours that lead the eye across ancient frontiers, discovering new horizons along the meandering course of a river, beyond each swelling on the plain, or on the slope of every hill. Country – that distinctive civilisation carried across the oceans by merchants and soldiers for more than four centuries; the

Englishness that survives translation into any language and that, transplanted to the other end of the world, used to contemplate native custom from the safety of club windows or through the monocled eye of its officers, like some incongruous idol parked inopportunely on the impeccable lawns.

Clichés these may be, but whether faded or forgotten, they still feature in many a family photograph album next to pictures of the family soldier, sailor or airman in full uniform with gold braid, or dressed more soberly in the washed out colours of his combat uniform. This custodial trinity, whose features blend to give us the most recognisable of British archetypes, is not at the service of the State or the Government but of the Queen. We must not forget this, because Her Majesty's subjects in uniform never forget it themselves. And it is in so far as the Sovereign is without power and cannot therefore be identified with the power of the day – but only with the nation and her people – that the armed forces will not allow themselves to be highjacked by a factional interest, but are conscious of serving society as a whole.

The abolition of identity cards and conscription just after the Second World War is often cited by the British as proof of their attachment to civilian society (although conscription for one year followed by a longer two-year period was reintroduced in 1948 and lasted until the early sixties). It is true that thanks to its insular geography, it is always outside the national territory that Britain's generals have achieved glory. Britain's greatest naval victories have been won on distant seas, and the founding of the Empire has long kept the bulk of the nation's armies and ships at the other end of the world. Never has political life been influenced, either directly or indirectly – as in France or in Germany – by a dominant or frustrated army; and Wellington remains the only professional soldier ever to have been Prime Minister.

But the Falklands War revealed to an astonished world the passionate identification of the British with each young soldier of the shock troops sent out to reconquer those few tiny islands which most of them could not have found on a map. Their victory was as surely responsible for putting Mrs Thatcher back into 10 Downing Street a second time, as the promise to abandon the nuclear deterrent was responsible for closing its door first in the face of Michael Foot, and then of Neil Kinnock. There has been much talk in this connnection of nostalgia for past glories, of restored national pride, even of explosive jingoism – and no doubt there was something of all that in the popular reactions to this senseless conflict. But what really moved the British – uniting Argie-bashers and gentlemen in the same enthusiasm – was the reassuring discovery that the most precious resources of the national patrimony were not lost through negligence or weakness, as might have been feared, but were still there, ready to be tapped in times of need.

First of all there was the ability to be practical. Faced with the fact of invasion, recrimination was pointless. What was needed was action – and before action, organisation was required: rounding up enough Royal Navy units to join a Task Force on its way to the South Atlantic; transforming vessels of the Merchant Navy into troop carriers; sending engineers to Ascension Island – a necessary staging post between London and the Falklands; modifying the nose of the Vulcan bombers for ease of refuelling during the fifteen-hour non-stop flight to Port Stanley airfield, where they would be dropping ten thousand tonnes of explosives on the runway; feeding, equipping and training the troops during their long voyage to the shores of Goose Green.

Secondly there was courage – real courage, not vainglorious foolhardiness; the kind of courage that does everything possible to reduce danger before facing it squarely, and only resorts to heroism if it is absolutely necessary. But then, that kind of courage was the only commodity that the British were sure they would not lack.

Finally there was decency – a virtue the English are convinced they have invented. It was so very decent of Lord Carrington (then Foreign Secretary) to resign, whether or not he was responsible for mistakes in British diplomacy on the eve of the Argentine invasion. And, ignoring for a moment the usual demagoguery and xenophobic chauvinism of the tabloids, there was good old-fashioned English decency in the attitude of the quality press, the radio and television, all of which devoted plenty of space to explaining the Argentine point of view to the British. It was decent that a member of the Royal Family should be exposed to the same dangers as any other soldier of his age. It was decent that élite troop officers should expose themselves more, show greater endurance, and suffer with and as much as their own men. And it was decent that in the midst of victory, the Archbishop of Canterbury should have spoken in remembrance of the dead on both sides – even if ultra-Conservatives and *Sun* readers did not give a fig about this sort of decency.

The Iraqi invasion of Kuwait did not provoke in Britain quite the same spasm of patriotic indignation as was caused by the Argentine takeover of the Falklands Islands. Nonetheless it once again united the majority of the public, and politicians of every hue in a near-unanimous cry of condemnation.

And here again, the outspoken or implicit pride that the British feel for their armed forces became clearly manifest: the so-called 'desert rats' (a group of highly trained Marine commandos) were treated to enthusiastic descriptions in the press. And no sooner had they arrived in Saudi Arabia than they took up position next to the Americans, the better to underline the reality of those special ties between Great Britain and the United States. Meanwhile the French, displaying their own brand of independent chauvinism, and faithful to the Gaullist tradition, unilaterally sent their contingent to take its place alongside the Saudi troops.

On Land, on Sea and in the Air

The British Army does not command quite the appeal of the Navy, nor does it have the sentimental attraction of the Royal Air Force, which still bathes in the glory of the Battle of Britain. Nevertheless the splendid regiments of the Guard are indispensable actors in the famous Changing spectacle, which – behind the ceremonial minutiae – hides a well-oiled mechanism for the prosecution of war. And on top of it all, tourists pay good foreign currency to see the red tunics and bearskin hats, before their next ritual *rendez-vous* with the wax dolls at Madame Tussaud's.

It is no longer indispensable – though it helps – to be wealthy and to have been to a public school in order to belong to the corps of four hundred officers of one of the seven regiments of the Queen's Household Division. The Grenadiers, Coldstream, Scots, Irish and Welsh Guards, on foot, and the Blues and Royals and Life Guards on horseback, have been watching over their sovereign since the

reign of Charles II. Yet, despite the rumoured displeasure felt by
Prince Charles at such a deficiency, there have not been more than
a handful of black royal Guards. The regiments of the Household
Division take it in turns – when they are not on duty at Buckingham
Palace – to join the British Army on the Rhine (BAOR), and
with the exception of the Irish Guards, they have all served in
Northern Ireland. The Falklands War amply demonstrated that
for all their fastidious preoccupation with etiquette and clothing
and their predilection for young ladies of good family, when it
comes to training impeccable soldiers, their officers are the match
of any barking regimental sergeant-major.

While the Guards are somewhat distanced from ordinary mortals
by the mystique of royal majesty, the SAS (Special Air Service)
has captivated the popular imagination. Less well-known, the SBS
(Special Boat Service) selects a small élite from the already élite
Royal Marines in order to prepare them for high risk missions.
Both are specialised commandos trained in the fight against terrorism. They are skilled marksmen, acomplishing spectacular actions
(which is good), with discretion (which is even better). The decision by the Queen's youngest son, Prince Edward, to give up a
career in the Royal Marines was a great disappointment to the
general public, for whom it seemed strange that a royal Prince
should prefer the dramatic to the martial arts. While the liberal
Left is somewhat wary of these popular heroes who give off a
musky scent of war in the midst of peace, such doubts do not
affect the composure of men who wear their valiance with all the
inconspicuous elegance of a Savile Row suit.

The bulk of the Army is more or less invisible. The fifty-five
to fifty-six thousand men of the BAOR live in Germany like
privileged Indians in a luxurious reservation. In Britain, Infantry
and Cavalry remain inconspicuous in their quarters. Those officers
who chose to live outside the camps are easily integrated into
the middle classes from which they mostly come – though they
always retain a certain distinctiveness. Since this professional army
naturally remains small, the promotion pyramid quickly becomes
very narrow, and it is usually advisable to take early retirement
before it is too late to retrain for a second career in Civvy Street.
A former captain has no trouble finding a new place in personnel,

in the administration of an agricultural estate, managing a security firm, or – if he has acquired a particular competence in a specialised field – as some sort of expert. Fifty years ago he would have kept the title of his final rank for the rest of his days. But today the ghosts of Major Thompson and of the silent Colonel Bramble have joined those of stuttering aristocrats and impeccable butlers in the nostalgic mists of the past.

The Royal Navy is the prow, the shield, the pilot of the Kingdom, the guardian of its life-line. No schoolboy will ever be allowed to forget Drake or Nelson, and no Defence Minister can long ignore its admirals. Whether it makes itself heard or not, the Navy never loses an opportunity to repeat that what is good for the Royal Navy is good for the nation. Its natural reserve force is the merchant fleet, but the latter has seen its tonnage melt away dramatically, and the deep-sea trawlers which could be modified for use as minesweepers have virtually disappeared. Yet what is left of the Merchant Navy is still liable to be called in to assist the Royal Navy at the first necessity. The closeness, strength and suppleness of the ties that bind the civilian and military fleets is still one of the most remarkable traits of the British Navy.

In July 1987, the House of Commons Defence Committee (whose members are appointed in proportion to the numbers in the parliamentary parties) brought out a unanimous report paying unreserved tribute to 'the fortitude, bravery, ingenuity and professional skill' of those responsible for the 'achievement' of the Falklands campaign. Another Government paper, published six months after the Argentine surrender, had already examined the lessons to be learnt from the campaign. The paper's description of the 1982 expedition has the tone of an epic: 'In the space of seven weeks a task force of twenty-eight thousand men and over a hundred ships had been assembled, sailed eight thousand miles, effectively neutralised the Argentine navy, and fought off persistent and courageous attacks from combat aircraft which outnumbered its own by more than six to one. This in itself was no mean feat, but the task force then put ashore ten thousand men on a hostile coast while under threat of heavy air attack; fought several pitched battles against an entrenched and well supplied enemy who at all times outnumbered our forces; and brought them to surrender within three and a half weeks.'

But this heroic preamble is followed by a reminder of British losses – six ships sunk, twenty-two planes brought down by the Argentines, twelve further planes lost accidentally – and a plea to the Government to make good the deficiencies in equipment that the Falklands War had brought to light. Long neglected in favour of NATO's strategy and the submarines and rockets of nuclear deterrence, the surface fleet had been vindicated during a conflict that so clearly demonstrated the Navy's vital importance in an expedition of this kind. No doubt one could legitimately ask how long the Government would be able to continue deploying such considerable resources for the defence of the Falklands' 1,800 inhabitants, how long it would be in Great Britain's interest to forego good relations with a country of Argentina's importance, or indeed in the interest of the Falkland islanders themselves to be deprived of a friendly neighbour on the mainland, however much they claimed to be able to do without him. But in the meantime, the essential thing was to ensure that the Royal Navy had a secure future.

The Royal Air Force has a huge asset – its comparative youth. Though ridiculed by the other two forces when first created during the First World War, it soon became the object of envy – particularly by the Navy, from which it was stealing a good deal of credit. Its discipline rested on competence, rather than authority. Rank and social class were less important than the solidarity between pilots, navigators and mechanics. Today, the development of the British aeronautical industry into one of the world leaders in the field, coupled with the continual updating and astronomical cost of more recent aircraft, and the growth in civilian air traffic, have combined to put Royal Air Force pilots in an enviable position. Unless they become staff officers, their active career is short, but the high salaries of commercial airlines await the talented and the lucky, while engineers and technicians are also spoilt for a choice of new career when they go back into civilian life.

Over a period of less than fifty years, the role and strategy of the British armed forces have been radically changed by the loss of the Empire and the development of the nuclear deterrent. There are a few spots left on the globe where Britain is still entirely responsible for defence: Hong Kong – though not for much longer; the Pitcairn Islands, which were first settled by the mutineers from the Bounty and their Tahitian women, but which now have only some sixty inhabitants left; Belize, formerly British Honduras, which acquired independence from Britain in 1981 but could not now hope to maintain it in the face of Guatemalan ambitions, were it not for the British military presence; the Sultanate of Brunei on the north-west coast of Borneo, with its sovereign, Hassanal Bolkiah Muizzadin Waddanlah, its oil, and its newly acquired independence, none of which would have a fighting chance of survival without the garrisoned troops of its former protectors. The strategic bases in Cyprus, in the Ascension Islands and in Diego Garcia, and the presence of naval units in the Arabian Gulf and the Caribbean still lend a certain precarious credibility to official arguments about Britain's responsibilities in the world, and its capacity to face up to them.

The importance of the British military presence in the more exposed and unstable zones of the world should be measured in terms of influence as well as fighting units. There are multiple channels for this influence, not the least of which is snobbery. Anyone who has taken a meal in an officers' mess in India or Pakistan will recognise the unmistakable stamp of their common British filiation. Parades and marches – nothing of the imperial past seems to have been disowned, even where ideology and policy are firmly set against it. The Jordanian army – one of the best in the Middle East – still bears the imprint of its first commander in chief, Sir John Bagot, even though King Hussein showed little ceremony when thanking him, in 1956, shortly after he had taken Jordanian citizenship and changed his name to Glubb Pasha. Some thirty former colonies also continue to benefit from occasional training and advice by the British forces (not to mention countries where ex-members of the SAS have trained armies in counter-insurgency tactics).

It was with the help of the former colonial power for example, that the tiny African state of Gambia acquired a new land army after its democratic regime was nearly toppled in a military coup in 1981. The first officer training school in Bangladesh was set up by a British joint forces mission. The formation of a flotilla of coast-guards in Barbados, and the hydrographic survey undertaken in Fiji by the British military have not helped to slow down drug trafficking in the former, nor avoided a *coup d'état* in the latter. But there are several other examples where the British military presence has either extinguished, or at least moderated the convulsions that so frequently follow the accession to independence of third world countries.

In addition, the sale of armaments not only serves as an important source of profit, but also enables Britain to build up what is frequently a long-term relationship with its clients through the provision of technical training and assistance. Finally, there are seventy countries outside NATO that receive direct military training from the British – either on their own territory, or in institutions in the United Kingdom itself. The choice is vast, from the prestigious training courses at the Royal College of Defence Studies or at officer training schools, to courses in flying, engineering or electronics.

A Brave New World

Britain's membership of the Atlantic Alliance, its integration into the military organisation of the North Atlantic Treaty, nuclear deterrence, the continual updating of conventional armaments, and – even more importantly since it embraces everything else – the cost of defence: for many years these were at the heart of a highly technical debate, the vital importance of which was sensed by the general public, without their fully understanding its complexities. The rivalry between the three forces in defining a strategic policy was all the more acute since budgetary constraints meant that every government had to refuse them at least part of the funding they deemed to be indispensable. Many a complex theory of strategy might never have evolved had it not been for the Navy's desire to have more combat units, or the Air Force's wish to improve the performance of their high-tech aircraft. The infantry were usually the losers in these technical jousts, and for every anti-tank weapon or surface-to-air missile they acquired, they saw the Navy and RAF share out between them an entire arsenal of offensive and defensive weapons.

Today, the reunification of Germany, the break-up of the Warsaw Pact, the advent of more or less thoroughgoing forms of democracy in the former satellites of the USSR, and the disintegration of the Soviet Union itself, have all radically changed the world picture that determined the evolution of British military strategy after the Second World War. The end of the cold war, and with it, the end of those perhaps simplistic certainties that maintained a precarious balance of atomic terror between the two blocs, are forcing Great Britain (like every member of the Atlantic Alliance, and indeed, every nation in the world) to make a fundamental reassessment of its defence policy.

The world has not become less dangerous, but the dangers that exist are of a different nature: henceforth, instability rather than confrontation will determine the rules of the strategic game. The Gulf War was merely the first symptom of the resurgence of an ancient and endemic plague, temporarily forgotten during the vicious duel between communism and capitalism.

The unification of Western Europe and its possible or probable expansion towards the East of the continent, and the growing solidarity between national, regional and continental economies will enable Britain finally to bury the aged myth of her splendid isolation, which – truth to tell – has been on its last legs for a good many years.

In practical terms, Britain's defence strategies are intimately connected with those of its friends and allies. One of the few positive consequences of the invasion of Kuwait has been to demonstrate the suicidal madness of the escalating round of arms deals with Iraq into which Soviets and Westerners became enmeshed, each nation trying to outbid the other in the sacred name of individual 'national interest'. Not only was the strategy (or lack of it) manifestly dangerous, but in the light of Iraq's insolvency, quite nonsensical as well.

The only alternative to this kind of absurdity is the establishment – at least within Europe – of a truly integrated common armaments industry, accompanied by rigorous control over sales. Great Britain does not even have the means to guarantee her own national defence, let alone play the kind of international military role that she persists in claiming as her own. France is hardly in a better position; and should the two countries abandon the madness of competing on the world armaments market, while also refusing to be exclusively dependent on the United States for their defence, they have no choice but to cooperate with each other – in spite, or rather because of their independent nuclear deterrent.

6

The Unity of the Kingdom

The most common mistake made by the foreigner on crossing the Channel is to think that England and Britain are one and the same; the second is to believe the natives when they speak of insurmountable differences between England, Wales, Scotland and Northern Ireland, not to mention a number of islands scattered off their shores.

In a crucial Act in 1536, Henry VIII – pleading somewhat speciously that the principality had always been fully united with England 'as a very member and joint of the same' – finally extended the full operation of English laws and administration to Wales, thus effectively abolishing the last vestiges of the country's former independence. The 1707 Act of Union, which brought together the Parliaments of the two nations already united under one monarchy since 1603 (when James VI of Scotland becames James I of England), allowed Scotland a good deal of internal autonomy, but no longer permitted it to exercise its sovereign prerogatives, except through the intermediary of the King – who was above all the King of England and of the Westminster Parliament. Ireland effectively lost its sovereignty in March 1603, when the rebel army led by Hugh O'Neill, earl of Tyrone, surrendered to the English crown, though it was not until January 1801 that the Act of Union created The United Kingdom of Great Britain and Ireland, with one Parliament for all the nation. By December 1921 however, a new treaty with Britain had given Ireland – a part of it – Dominion Status, thus restoring it to its lost independence. Yet, in spite of vehement opposition from the Catholic minority, it was not coercion but a majority decision by the inhabitants of Ulster to remain part of the United Kingdom that deprived Independent Ireland of its Northern Provinces.

Wales

Is it possible today to speak of genuine nationalism in Cardiff or Carmarthen? The majority of Welsh people are the first to doubt it. Welsh, a Celtic language, is certainly still spoken widely in certain regions of the principality. There are some who go to great pains to learn and speak it in order to assert their identity in the face of the English usurper. Welsh also remains an official language, and is used, side by side with English, in government and in all civil documents. Furthermore, under the new National Curriculum for Wales, introduced in 1989, Welsh has become a compulsory subject. Road signs are also written in both languages. And after a long battle, supporters of Welsh language television programmes finally prevailed. But the programmes are expensive to make, and though the audiences are more numerous than had been predicted by its critics, they still constitute a tiny minority of the Welsh population.

Still, the game of rugby continues to arouse fierce nationalistic passions, and it is possible to hear Welsh politicians explain how the English have exploited their country for centuries, how after exhausting the coal mines they abandoned Welsh miners to unemployment, and how with their money they continue to drive the poor out of cottages which they turn into second homes for themselves. Welsh male choirs can be heard singing with grave melancholy about the beauty of their deserted valleys. In the Argentine region of Patagonia there even exists a living Welsh community which firmly refuses to speak either English or Spanish.

Wales, *Cymru* in Welsh, is a country of gorges and dark landscapes, leaving one in no doubt that this is no longer England. The Welsh too, are different: headstrong, drunk on their own rhetoric, quick to anger and ever ready to overturn the government of the day, whatever its colour – perhaps because it is based in London. During the First World War the Welsh were Liberal, firmly behind their compatriot, Lloyd George. In 1945 they switched allegiance, voting Labour into six seats which had been held by the Liberals since the beginning of the century. In 1979, a small majority joined the English to vote for Mrs Thatcher, and in the 1983 election, the Conservatives won a record thirteen out of thirty-six Welsh parliamentary seats. But this flirtation with power was short-lived, and by 1987 the Welsh were firmly on the side of Labour again, abandoning the English to their continued love affair with the Iron Lady. They were not alone in their defiance, for the Scottish are massively hostile to Thatcherite neo-liberal conservatism, while the true blue English regions of Yorkshire and Humberside also gave Labour a comfortable majority in the 1987 elections, placing their faith in the pure-blood Welshman, Neil Kinnock.

Wales and the north-east of England both vote Labour because both are hovering between the highly visible decline of the coal industry and the less prominent growth of new industries which – hungry though they may be for new technology – are not clamouring for manpower. Salvation, the Welsh are told, lies with the Americans, Germans, French and Japanese, all of whom have invested heavily in Wales. Since 1981, the Welsh have seen the establishment on their land of those strange Japanese factories which are clean, where workers and management wear identical overalls and eat the same food in the same canteen, and where the entire workforce is represented by a single union which, in complicated agreements, has signed away its right to strike.

While they are not exactly hostile to these new arrivals, neither are the Welsh entirely persuaded that they represent the key to the future. This uncertainty, this sentimental pessimism and an ill-defined dream for a different future are the sources from which *Plaid Cymru*, the Welsh Nationalist Party, draws its inspiration and its support. With 7.3 percent of the votes and three MPs in 1987, it survives from election to election, like the ghost of an independent Christmas yet to come. But though power seems to be forever out of reach, in the meantime the Party is not a negligible political force.

In 1966, forty years after the Party's creation, a *Plaid Cymru* candidate was finally elected to represent the Welsh National-ist cause at Westminster. But it was not until 1974 that the party was able (in conjunction with the Scottish nationalists, the Northern Irish deputies and two Independent Labour MPs) to disturb the cosy *tête à tête* enjoyed by the two major Parties without interruption since the end of the Second World War. Unable to raise a sufficient majority in Parliament to form a government without the support of this disparate coalition, the two major Parties were offering it the unique opportunity of arbitrating between them. But the paradox of this new-found power was that it emanated from the very London Parliament whose yoke these enemies-turned-accomplices were determined to throw off. Their implication in schemes and agreements far removed from their own original aims goes some way towards explaining the disaffection of which they were subsequently the victims. In exchange for their cooperation, they had extracted from the Labour Party the promise to hold a referendum on the devolution of a number of parliamentary powers to local assemblies and executive bodies. Called to vote on the issue in March 1979, the Welsh people inflicted a humiliating defeat on their representatives by overwhelmingly rejecting the opportunity offered to them. Henceforth the Party's momentum was lost, and all the indications are that devolution is now a dead issue.

Scotland

Despite their greater popularity, the Scottish Nationalists were no more successful than their Welsh counterparts in introducing devolution at home*. But by November 1988, the resounding victory of the Scottish Nationalist, Jim Sillars, in a parliamentary by-election for the Govan seat, gave a severe shock to the British political establishment. Would it have to relive the psychodrama that had preceded the 1979 Scottish devolution referendum?

After the 1987 election, the Labour Party – with its block of fifty Scottish MPs – seemed to have been institutionally invested with the role of guardian of the national identity, rather than that of champion of socialism. The Conservative Party, with only ten representatives from Scotland, was exposed to the uncomfortable

---

* Although thirty-three per cent of the electorate voted 'Yes' against 11.5 per cent who voted 'No' in the 1979 referendum, the law required a minimum majority vote of forty per cent before Scotland's autonomy could be strengthened at the expense of the unity of the kingdom.

feeling of having deserted and been deserted by the Scottish people. Yet within just a few months Labour's apparently inevitable identification with Scotland seemed to disintegrate. Jim Sillars' unexpected victory in Govan overturned a Labour majority of 19,500. At least a third of the Scottish electorate, no longer content to display their exasperation with that incarnation of English insensitivity – Mrs Thatcher – had come to feel an impartial resentment towards both sides.

Despite their election of a Nationalist MP, none of this meant that the Scottish electorate was necessarily ready for independence. In an opinion poll, only sixteen per cent of those who voted for Sillars at the by-election declared themselves in favour of such an extreme measure. What they wanted – in common with a good number of those who had not voted for the SNP – was the creation of a Scottish Assembly which would take over a large part of the powers at present exercised by the Westminster Parliament. But their enthusiasm was quickly tempered by the logical concomitants of such an assembly: increased taxation and fewer local MPs in Parliament.

The number of Scottish members of the House of Commons is, at present, greater than it would be if it had to conform to the rules of proportionality that are in force in England. This advantage is meant to make up for the constitutional imbalance from which Scotland would otherwise suffer in the Act of Union because of its smaller size and population, and its comparative poverty. But it is hard to see how it would be possible to give the Scots complete legislative independence while preserving their privileged position at Westminster, coupled with their right to vote on English affairs. Without sufficient authority, a Scottish assembly would be little more than another tier of government added to so many others. But if it were given real power, it would sound the knell of the Union. Both on the left and on the right, there are many who find the two alternatives unsatisfactory.

Scottish Nationalism is a good deal stronger, and rests on more recent memories than that of the Welsh, but its aspirations always founder on the economic and historical realities of a united Britain. Yet although it may not have found its constitutional expression, it has a political weight that is founded on social and cultural structures quite distinct from those in England, and as vigorous now as they have ever been.

How far back in history should one look to get a proper understanding of the Scots? The Picts were polygamists, and determined the royal succession matrilineally. Their art was highly sophisticated; their writing is still indecipherable. They were known by the Romans as the Caledonian tribes, and inspired them with extraordinary terror – so much so that the invading armies ended up by erecting a great physical barrier against them. Hadrian's Wall was of dubious defensive worth, but it was symbolically significant, marking the northern confines of the Roman Empire and of its Latin influence.

The nature and importance of the Pict inheritance in the genesis of Scotland remains a subject of erudite debate and conjecture, but there is a geographical factor whose significance is uncontested. The aberrant mildness of the Scottish climate is born of the ocean, carrier of the Gulf Stream with its gentle currents of warm air and rain wafted across the Western coast. The rain falls in sheets, softly, slowly, interminably; grey winter rain, penetrating and icy cold; furious spring rain, occasionally vanquished by a ray of sun which is all the more seductive for its infrequent appearance; summer rain, unvanquished, broken by wonderful explosions of summer heat; rain that whips the cheeks with stinging gusts in a melodramatic show of sombre clouds, painting the sky in shades of beige and brown, grey and black; frenzied showers between two moments of golden light against an emerald backdrop; October rain that frequently lingers in the sky, allowing stolen glimpses of autumnal reds before the next downpour. Take away the rain and there is no more Scotland – no grassland, no sheep, no Harris tweed, no torrents, no trout, no salmon, no glens, no whisky, no dreams, no escapes towards skies that are always blue, no transcontinental commerce, no soldiers of fortune, no colonies.

A passionate love for his tear-sodden land, and the desperate need to escape from its endless weeping has turned the Scotsman into a fine example of the proverbial split personality. From Dr Jekyll to Mr Hyde, the initial transition is easy – but to escape from that second self, born out of the curiosity of the first may be impossible. More significantly perhaps than the famous story's over-simplified representation of Good and Evil, this duality represents reality and the dream. Torn in different directions like his double hero, Robert Louis Balfour Stevenson was obsessed by ideas of adventures in distant lands so long as he remained at home. It was in his native Scotland that he conceived that masterpiece of adventure writing, *Treasure Island*, but it was while he was living in Western Samoa, Eden of the exotic, that he threw himself wholeheartedly into the boiling cauldron of Scottish history, writing *The Master of Ballantrae* – yet another parable of the eternal Scottish contradiction between the love of the familiar and the spirit of adventure, between common sense and romanticism, between the Jacobite and the entrepreneur.

Long before the Act of Union, London was swarming with Scots hoping to make their fortune. Without Scottish emigration, the East India Company would have gone bankrupt and the empire would have amounted to little more than a few trading posts scattered across the four corners of the globe. Though the Scots have had their share of internal struggles and conflicts with their English neighbour, they have not, like the Irish, been alienated by their history. Neither do they feel the need, like the Welsh, to seek refuge in a mythical past. Whether easy-going or bigoted, impetuous or industrious, the Scots look to the past for an image of vigorous and dynamic youth, as ready to learn, to work and to conquer, as it is quick to succumb to passion and to anger. The Scotland of hard work and restraint is inseparable from the Scotland of emotion and mad escapades. However different they may be from each other, they are so similar that the Scots themselves often confuse them. The support of the Jacobites for the Stuarts is the most revealing historical example of this similarity and of this divorce.

To be a Jacobite was to be the staunch supporter of a dynasty, most of whose sovereigns were unpopular so long as they reigned, in favour of a past and a future gleaming with all the jewels of which the present is shorn, in favour of yesterday's vanquished and tomorrow's impossible revenge. To be a Jacobite today is to honour the memory of Robert Bruce (medieval Scotland's unifying king), while conveniently forgetting his Anglo-Norman ancestry; it is to

287

glorify the immemorial clans, their tartans and their kilts, symbols of autonomy and family solidarity, while ignoring their bloody feuds and the collaboration of some of the most important clans – such as the Campbells – with the hated English; it is to celebrate the romance of Bonnie Prince Charlie's gallant defiance of the English, forgetting that his popularity among the Scots themselves was much greater after his death than it ever was during his lifetime. Above all, to be a Jacobite is to take refuge in timeless poetry which helps one to forget the prose of everyday life. Naturally, the real Scotland is different from the picture painted by this collection of colourful anachronisms, and the weavers of legend are blind to the subtle shades of their country's historical tapestry.

Scotland's Episcopal Church – which is a full member of the Anglican Communion – showed such loyalty to the Jacobite cause that the London Government, under George II, introduced a series of penal laws against it, almost eliminating it during the eighteenth century. Repeal of the laws in 1792 marked a turning point, and the Church began to revive – though it never again rivalled the Presbyterian Calvinist Kirk, which had been so favourably handled after the abortive Jacobite rebellions of 1715 and 1745.

Thanks to the initiative of its founder, the formidable John Knox, that same Kirk – supposedly sectarian and self-absorbed – was responsible for the establishment of an educational system that was open to the population at large. On the back of the printed catechism lesson distributed to young Presbyterians were printed all the multiplication tables. Prayer was a fine thing, no doubt, but in order to get anywhere in life one had to be able to count. And the clearest manifestation of divine grace was an entrepreneur's success.

Such healthy principles, combined with a first class education, were not slow to bear fruit. From as early as the seventeenth century, Scotland had been home to a great many outstanding scientists, from John Napier, who in 1614 originated the concept of logarithms, to the mathematical physicists James Clerk Maxwell and Lord Kelvin; to Sir William Ramsay, who discovered four of the noble gases (Neon, Argon, Crypton and Zenon), and Sir James Dewar, who discovered how to liquefy oxygen. But it was particularly in the area of applied science that Scottish talent and solid good sense came together with spectacular results: James Watt revolutionised the steam engine; William Symington built the first boat to be powered by this novel source of energy; Henry Bell, William Murdoch and several others successfully improved his original design. John Loudon McAdam gave his name to a new kind of road surface covering. Charles Macintosh was father to the famous waterproof coat. Kirkpatrick MacMillan invented the bicycle. John Logie Baird invented the television. And Alexander Graham Bell developed the Dunlop tyre before emigrating to the States with the secret of the telephone still in his head. To this day we continue to live off the heritage of these practical men. Finally, Europe's first industrial civilisation was to spawn two of the Scottish Enlightenment's greatest figures and two of the century's most important thinkers, David Hume and Adam Smith – fathers of critical empiricism and of the modern economy.

The rest was just a matter of energy and imagination. From Glasgow to Edinburgh factories mushroomed, with banks and insurance companies lending financial support. No doubt Mary, Queen of Scots and Bonnie Prince Charlie still had a place in some recess of the Scottish psyche, but in those days few people had the time to look for them.

Yet with the decline and fall of this first-generation industry after the First World War, there was a resurgence of nationalistic nostalgia. For a brief period during the seventies, the flow of oil from the North Sea was to give it a veneer of realism: the SNP were touching on a raw wound when they bewailed the pillaging of Scotland's natural resources by the eternal English profiteer. Their treasured independence, they argued, was not a costly utopia, but would on the contrary tap a vein of black gold. But however tantalising their arguments, at the crucial moment of choice Scottish realism ignored this mirage, and the nationalist movement was left to shrink back to insignificant proportions.

The reality of Scotland is less easily encapsulated than politicians – of whatever complexion – would like it to be. Dilapidated housing and failing industries can be found side by side with a standard of living that is higher only in the most prosperous zones of the south-east and east of England. At the same time as the closure of numerous large industrial plants was contributing to rising unemployment in the early eighties, new cities of steel and glass were accommodating a proliferation of sophisticated workshops specialising in the latest electronics. And, though the achievements of the service industries that mushroomed round the North Sea platforms were largely forgotten after the world fall in oil prices that followed the boom, their expertise is used in oil exploration and recovery the world over.

The growing popularity of Labour in Scotland can be attributed to a gut reaction against a certain English self-importance, of which Conservatism is perhaps the most irritating manifestation to anyone who neither is, nor wishes to become, English; against the cynicism of the wealthy that is as offensive to the generosity as it is to the parsimony of the Scots; and for a long time, against Mrs Thatcher herself, who appeared to have the gift of exposing every fibre of Scottish sensibility and pride. To add insult to injury, she seemed completely unperturbed by their ill-will, using the Scots as a sounding board for some of her most unpopular reforms, including the ill-fated poll tax, which she introduced in Scotland before anywhere else. For her part, Margaret Thatcher was relying on the popularity and long-term social implications of her 'right-to-buy' policy*. By putting up for sale the vast patrimony of council houses which had made Scotland into the champion of welfare housing, she hoped to break the rigid traditional mould of Scottish society, thus drawing together the two great nations of the union more effectively than any number of popularity-seeking concessions to a completely foreign culture. In the event she was to discover that increased home-ownership in Scotland did not automatically entail loyalty to the Conservative Party. John Major's less dogmatic tone and his apparently greater concern for problems of social and economic deprivation may prove less rebarbative to the proud Scottish nation than Mrs Thatcher's obstinate national and private individualism.

Anyone who has seen the peace of the Highlands invaded, in

---

* Two different Acts introduced in Scotland and in England and Wales in 1980 gave council house tenants the right to buy their homes from the local authority at preferential rates.

the name of progress, by dismal ranks of commercial conifers, will find it hard to suppress a shudder of apprehension at innovations which make light of custom, of cottage weaving industries and of those spectacular Scottish horizons where skies and mountains merge, in order to impose on this recalcitrant people an identity that is not its own.

Ireland

In Ireland, the myth, historical reference and ancestral totems that are to be found at the root of every nationalistic movement, are not an expression of mutual recognition and encouragement, they are a battle cry. To understand Irish history you need more than simple knowledge of the facts: you need to understand how every generation has relived and chewed over that history, nursing grievances ad infinitum; you need to monitor the nation's breathing, register its every shudder and palpitation, watch it seize up or shake with fever. Ireland's history is as obsessive as a passionate love and as hopeless as slavery. It is invoked or repudiated according to the occasion, in a litany of self-serving arguments. Catholic history text-books are full of tales of humiliation and defeat which fill the petty Protestant with pride, as if they were so many proofs of his natural superiority over the vanquished.

The six Protestant majority counties of Ulster that are still part of the United Kingdom and the three Catholic majority provinces of Munster, Leinster and Connaught, now under the authority of the Republic of Ireland, are forever lamenting their fates, eyeing each other suspiciously, exchanging insults and occasionally fraternising, living their friendships, their hatred and their inherited pain in the everyday banality of the present. What for others would be no more than a frontier, is for them an open gash – at best a scar so disfiguring that it can never be forgotten entirely.

Over the past few years efforts have been made to present school-children with opposing points of view and neutral interpretations of the events around which the two communities have woven their own political mythologies. Exchanges between Catholic and Protestant schools and interdenominational conferences of history teachers have made it possible to come up with a number of formulas to avoid mutual offence. Protestant schools used to stress the unequivocal nature of their ties to the United Kingdom by studying English history exclusively, without even touching its Irish dimension. Today their syllabus is more even-handed. But religion is now taking the place of history in the heavy artillery of the faithful. A tacit complicity between Catholic priests on the defensive and an Anglican hierarchy little disposed to offend its flock, strengthens the intolerance of the former and reduces the liberalism of the latter to mere words. Non-conformist Protestants, for their part, have ears only for the thundering tones of their leader, the Reverend Ian Paisley, who invokes the Lord in a frenzy of prophetic imprecations, calling on Him to strike down the idolatrous papists; and while they wait for the Almighty to bow before the injunctions of His pastor, they conscientiously continue to fan the flames.

The population of Ireland, which prides itself on its Celtic pedigree, is actually no more nor less Celtic than that of the British Isles. Invaded in turn by the Vikings, the Normans and the English, it was, until the seventeenth century, becoming increasingly integrated. Then a new wave of English and Scottish immigration put a stop to this process. The latest newcomers were fervent Protestants, and carefully kept their distance from the papist rabble. Every year their descendants commemorate the Battle of the Boyne in 1690, celebrating the victory of William of Orange over the Catholic James II, for all the world as if it were yesterday's battle. In the eyes of the original settlers, victory was a confirmation of the purity and supremacy of their faith – from which power and prosperity naturally flowed. It also brought in its wake a series of commendable laws, keeping the poor and idolatrous Catholics at a safe distance from the righteous Protestants. On the other hand, three centuries later, Catholics still treat their Protestant countrymen as hereditary invaders, condemned in perpetuity to the status of trespassers in the land of the only authentic Irish People – themselves, the Catholics.

Yet how many Catholics today remember the Society of United Irishmen (founded under the influence of the French Revolution) and its proposal to form an Irish Parliament composed of both Catholics and Protestants? Does anyone seize the banner of the abortive rebellion of 1798, organised by Presbyterians from Ulster exasperated by Anglican privileges? Sharing the same selective memory, Catholics and Protestants retain only the Act of Union, voted at Westminster three years later, in 1801, because it confirms and perpetuates the unequivocal division between its partisans, the Protestants, and its opponents – the Catholics. United by hatred and fear, they have no time to reflect on periods of uncertain loyalty. How can one fight without an enemy? For there is no doubt that the Irish are involved in a fight. But it is an internecine struggle; not – as the IRA* and the INLA (Irish National Liberation Army) would wish us to believe – a war of liberation against the English occupier. That war came to an end more than fifty years ago.

It is true that the Protestants benefit from the union with Great Britain, while the vote of the minority Catholics in favour of nationalist or republican candidates brings them no concrete advantage, and Dublin's moral support is but a poor consolation. The two communities, whether in the North or the South, can never quite forget this disparity, even though most of their members have only one desire: to live as if this absurd duel had nothing to do with them. But in spite of the allegations of the nationalists, the British Government has nothing to gain from this Protestant

---

* The Irish Volunteers, engaged in an armed struggle against British domination since 1913, were replaced in 1919 by the IRA (Irish Republican Army), a clandestine armed wing of *Sinn Fein*, the Irish nationalist party. Its guerilla campaign led to the creation, in 1921, of the free State of Ireland, under the dominion of the Empire. Only half of the IRA accepted this status, while the other half decided to continue the struggle. A two year civil war ended in 1923 with the surrender of the 'Irregulars', who did not, however, give up their arms, and continued to fight for a united and independent Ireland. It was declared illegal in 1931, and again in 1936, and after a series of terrorist attacks in England in 1939, the Irish Parliament, the *Dail*, adopted a procedure of internment without trial for any IRA suspects. Five IRA leaders convicted of murder were executed during the Second World War. Following Ireland's withdrawal from the Commonwealth in 1948, and the proclamation of the Republic the following year, Sinn Fein went through a period of hesitation, and the IRA split into two factions – the 'Officials', who accepted the legal line of the Party, and the 'Provisionals' who were determined to sustain the armed struggle for the reunification of the North and the South.

majority, which merely renders its task of arbitration the more difficult, while compromising its relations with the Republic of Ireland, and discrediting its Irish policy in the eyes of international public opinion. If tomorrow a majority in Ulster voted in favour of independence, the British would relinquish the Province with a sigh of relief, but in the meantime they have a constitutional obligation to uphold the Union, and their exasperation has to be held in check.

The IRA's need to cling to the fiction of Britain as a colonial power has already enabled it to forget how in 1969, British troops were called into Northern Ireland by the Catholics themselves, to protect them against the partisan brutalities of the local police, the RUC (Royal Ulster Constabulary), which was recruited exclusively from Protestant circles. Without the 'foreign' presence of British troops, the 'armed struggle' of the Republicans would be seen for what it is – a campaign of violence against civilians and law enforcement agencies. And their 'executions of traitors' would become plain murders of political opponents. Above all, their strategy of wringing surrender out of the Unionist majority by the use of force would be shown up in all its savage nihilism. For if the British were to withdraw from Ulster (a purely hypothetical suggestion), how could the revolutionary and Marxist 'Provisionals' hope to defeat the Protestants, who also have their extremists, organised, armed and ready to fight? Why should moderate Catholics in the North and the South suddenly start to support Sinn Fein – from which they have always withheld their votes – at the very moment when it abandoned its legal and democratic front in order to identify itself unashamedly with terrorism? How could the Irish Government – which has long outlawed the IRA – accept to compromise its privileged ties with the British Government for the sake of integrating into the Republic a territory whose population was overwhelmingly hostile to it, and whose leaders had sworn its destruction? Of all the myths on which Irish nationalism feeds, this is the most fanciful, but also the most perverse since it proves, by its very impossibility, that the true goal of the IRA's war is to bring down the bourgeois régimes in Dublin and London. Nor is the decision to play the democratic game by putting forward Sinn Fein candidates at local and general elections a sign that violence is being abandoned in favour of democracy. It merely constitutes yet another weapon in their arsenal of terror, destined to expose the contradictions of the rule of law. By challenging the prison authorities through devastatingly peaceful means, the 1981 hunger strikers – dying in the cause of Sinn Fein – gave the party an aura of martyrdom from which it subsequently gained significant electoral support. If Sinn Fein were now to be banned, that fading aura would be revived. Allowed to continue operating, it mocks the institutions that tolerate it, and tries to show, by its very existence, the weakness of a government tied down by the law.

The Protestant myth has two faces, one brassy and bold, the other reasonable, hesitant and self-deprecatory. Unionist Orangemen feed on certainties; their life is punctuated with commemorations and anniversaries (like that of the Battle of the Boyne), bedecked with sashes, medals, rosettes, and bowler hats, and accompanied by fanfares and religious rhetoric. They are devoted to the Queen, scandalised by the Pope, suspicious of the English. They are scornful of the Catholics (some of their best friends are Catholic, of course – and as for the rest, it's not their fault). They are shocked by the leniency with which the authorities treat terrorists (who should all be shot without trial, and since the authorities do not do the job properly, it is hardly surprising if a few angry Protestants take up arms to defend themselves against the assassins of the IRA); distressed that there should be greater unemployment among the minority community (but then Catholics are lazy), and that their housing should be less salubrious (but then Catholics are dirty); and conscious of their own superiority (they are Protestant, after all). That's how it is, and that's how it always will be: so long as politicians and the English don't meddle, they will always be British.

The second Protestant archetype is wholeheartedly British, and wears the earnest expression of the honest liberal. Its representatives speak the Queen's own English – with the hint of an Irish accent, polished by a good public school. They are liberal, not only in their tolerance and cosmopolitanism, but also in the professionalism of their calling, as bankers, lawyers, industrialists, doctors or civil servants. They know better than anyone the complexity of the Irish Question. They deplore extremism of every kind: that of the IRA, naturally, but that of the Loyalists too (and just as severely). They have learned the lessons of the colonial period. They are well disposed to the idea of an agreement between Ulster and the Republic of Ireland (where they often have relatives). And above all, whether they are Anglicans or Presbyterians, they realise the urgent need to do something for the Catholics. But that is where their difficulties begin.

They admit it frankly: helping the Catholics is a problem. They have tried, but for one reason or another, it never seems to have worked . . . An example: they would like to recruit some Catholics into their bank, their factory, their chambers, their doctor's surgery, or appoint one to head the administration of their company; but that's the problem – there are no good Catholic bank employees, no good Catholic engineers, no good Catholic lawyers, no good Catholic doctors; they simply don't have the makings of a high-ranking employee. What is to be done about it? It is true that the Catholics have had a hard life, but isn't it at least partly their fault? At heart, there is always a trace of fanaticism in the Catholic. That is why, when the chips are down, they see no alternative to voting for the Unionists – however reluctantly; that is why, with all the good will in the world, they find it difficult to imagine how Ulster could survive if it were no longer protected by British sovereignty.

The frustration of the Catholics is never far below the surface of everyday life. Unlike so many other demonstrations of feeling in Ireland, it is well justified. For the past three centuries the Catholics of the North have been kept in a state of underdevelopment by the alliance between the landed aristocracy, the civil service and the Protestant middle classes. Whether the government was based in London or Belfast, the situation for the Catholics has always remained the same. Even today, the only difference in their condition is due to a general improvement in the standard of living brought about by a generous public expenditure programme – about one-third greater in Ulster, per head of population, than it is elsewhere in Great Britain or in the Republic of Ireland. And though the rate of unemployment in Ulster is still much higher than the national average, unemployment benefit is also higher there than it is in Ireland. Yet the gulf between the Catholic and

Protestant communities remains, and any real improvement will not come from official declarations condemning discrimination and its historical victims. More important by far is better housing for the Catholics, and especially, easier, access to the liberal professions and better jobs in the public and private sectors.

Education would be the best vehicle for this improvement if it were not itself a fertile nursery for interdenominational rivalries, and if the Catholic clergy did not indulge in the national passion for double-talk, solemnly condemning the crimes of the IRA, while at the same time rejecting religious integration in schools (despite official encouragement and financial incentives) in the name of doctrinal purity. Thanks to this rejection, every year thousands of Catholic teenagers are sent out into the streets of Ulster, knowing nothing of the world outside their ghetto and their school, where the word 'Protestant' is at best ignored, and more frequently treated as anathema. For many of them, terrorism will then seem to be the best possible escape from such internal exile and unemployment, lending some meaning – however perverted – to their existence. Undoubtedly, this blind and brutal terrorism retains some kind of romantic attraction – and not only for Catholic youngsters in search of an ideal. More than a hundred thousand voters persist in placing their confidence in Sinn Fein and subscribe to the IRA's description of their campaign as a national liberation struggle against the British.

The ambiguity of the situation is certainly not helped by the composition and the role of the Army, the police, the RUC or the part-time reservists of the Ulster Defence Regiment. Servicemen are recruited all over the United Kingdom and do not belong to any particular denomination. In spite of that, the enemy, for them, is clearly Catholic since they are never subject to attack from Protestant armed groups. When stopped by a patrol, or questioned in front of an Army road-block, the Catholic is a natural suspect. Since London took over the administration of Ulster again, the RUC can no longer be labelled as the fighting arm of Protestant power. Nonetheless, its members are recruited almost exclusively among the Protestant community. The UDR does have a proportion of Catholic members, but they have become conspicuous targets of the IRA – which is hardly conducive to ease of recruitment.

The RUC is widely suspected of serious malpractice: of using strong-arm interrogation methods, sometimes bordering on torture; of shooting unarmed suspects on sight; of using paid informers as *agents provocateurs*. These suspicions and accusations have frequently created tensions between Dublin and London, and have been successfully exploited by IRA propaganda. In some cases the Government has responded by setting up inquiries; some policemen have been disciplined by the force itself, others taken to court and convicted. But in other cases the Director of Public Prosecutions has thrown in the sponge, giving the public the unfortunate impression that premeditated crimes committed by the police in difficult circumstances are – if not positively condoned – at any rate excused.

The conflicting demands of the protection of civil liberties and of the fight against subversion lead to endless tensions and compromises. In 1972, trial without jury was introduced into the Irish courts for terrorist crimes, and later other exceptional measures in the fight against terrorism were enshrined in law. In the early to mid-eighties, the uncorroborated evidence of so-called 'converted terrorists' (in legal parlance) or 'supergrasses' (in common parlance), against whom charges were dropped in return for their cooperation with the police, was admitted in court in a number of major and well-publicised cases. By 1987 however, the Government was having to admit that 'the recent rejection by the Court of Appeal of the evidence of converted terrorists, and the subsequent release of virtually all persons convicted solely on their evidence, have cast doubt on the future use of such evidence'*. Extradition and other anti-terrorist procedures are also a constant source of controversy between the Irish and British judicial authorities. It is recognised that without special measures the IRA would benefit from inordinate protection; witnesses could be influenced and juries intimidated. Yet it is these very measures that give the IRA a following. With every innocent person picked

* From a briefing paper compiled by the Foreign and Commonwealth Office in conjunction with the Northern Ireland office.

up in one of the wide combing operations that enable the police to break up terrorist cells, the IRA gains another propagandist.

Strict limits and supervision of special legislation, combined with discipline and a rigorous respect for the law in general, both by the police and the Army, and effective Anglo-Irish judicial cooperation (difficult as these are to implement) are the only way to reassure Catholic public opinion on the impartiality of the forces of law and order, demythologising the IRA and isolating it from a population that has had enough of violence, from whatever source. The RUC has proved that it is capable of pursuing Protestant para-military groups as well as the IRA, but the frailty of that commitment is manifest. In August 1989, a major political controversy developed in Westminster following the revelation that the Ulster Freedom Fighters (the cover name for the proscribed Ulster Defence Association) had killed a Roman Catholic man after obtaining security force documents naming him as an IRA suspect. Loyalist para-military leaders later confirmed that they frequently received approaches from frustrated members of the security forces offering information on known or suspected IRA or INLA members – though they admitted that this information was often unreliable, coming from low-level sources within the forces. According to a report in the *Independent* at the time, these revelations came 'as no surprise to the authorities' since security documents had 'often been found in searches of loyalist homes and offices', though such discoveries were 'given little publicity'.

In the face of this terrorism which nothing is able to quell completely, there subsists paradoxically in Ulster an order which no amount of violence seems to perturb. The Movement for Peace in Northern Ireland was founded in 1976 by two women, one of whom had lost three children, killed by a car full of terrorists fleeing from pursuit by the law. The Movement has not achieved its aims, but the dim hope raised by its creation persists. Small interdenominational groups try to go beyond reconciliation to the creation of a single community. Lagan College, founded in 1981 by a few Catholic and Protestant parents who wanted to give their twenty children an integrated education, now has four hundred pupils, has spawned a further three schools founded on the same principles, and is planning some more.

Those who believe in the inevitability of conflict between Catholics and Protestants should look at Liverpool, which has the highest proportion of Irish Catholics in the Kingdom outside Ireland, and where the two communities cohabit with exemplary tolerance. Scattered around the British Isles there are a million or so Irish men and women – most of them Catholics – who have settled down, work, vote and go to church, in complete harmony with their new surroundings. Did they shed all ethnic and national characteristics as soon as they crossed the Irish Channel in search of jobs? Or did they not leave their country to escape from the crushing burden of religious and murderous bigotry?

Ireland is not alone in being the prisoner of its own prejudices. Though widely disillusioned with the entire subject, the English press persists in giving a distorted picture of the conflict, highlighting IRA massacres of Protestants, and playing down loyalist killings. Few ordinary members of the public in England realise that Protestant loyalists have been responsible for a quarter of all political murders in Ireland since 1979, and that two-thirds of all victims are Catholics (of which a third have been killed by the Republicans themselves).

International public opinion has also frequently failed to distinguish between the situation in Northern Ireland and that in other trouble spots of the world, drawing conclusions prompted more by prejudice than by understanding. Irish-American immigrants, long humiliated by the haughtiness of the White Anglo-Saxon Protestants (the so-called WASPs), have almost all identified themselves with the 'resistance' of the unhappy Catholics, oppressed by the immoral coalition of their Protestant compatriots and the British colonial Army. Their feeling of solidarity with these victims of imperialism has been expressed by a flood of contributions – in cash and in arms – which have been the IRA's greatest war treasure. The American Government is finally beginning to recognise that the situation is not as clear as it wishes to believe – particularly when imminent election holds out the lure, for a future President, of securing the Irish vote.

Time, the improvement in Northern Ireland's standard of living, the secularisation of society, the determination in London and in Dublin – at last publicly declared – to cooperate in a joint effort to eradicate terrorism and to refrain from imposing any solution by force*: these things raise the hope of an eventual resolution. But it is the glimmer of a very faint and distant hope.

Forever England

An Englishman might be unhappy with his particular lot; the English are happy with theirs. Let the Scots and the Welsh claim their lost sovereignty and look to an identity they are afraid of losing; let the Irish shout themselves hoarse for or against a secession that leaves the rest of the United Kingdom indifferent: it is up to them. What Englishman would contemplate not being English? And if he decides to make tracks for the New World or escape to the antipodes, he will not fail to carry his corner of England with him to the green valley, the expanse of desert or the continent he plans to appropriate.

Even as the notorious Eurotunnel extends under the Channel, the English persist in the belief that they owe their singularity – and their tranquillity – to the arm of sea that separates their island from the continent. History has been the first to give the lie to this claim. In their quest for new territory to conquer, Romans, Saxons, Scandinavians and Normans were undeterred by the Channel, which they crossed without incident, like a river somewhat wider than the rest.

Well-entrenched on the two shores of their internal sea, the Anglo-Normans also thought nothing of recrossing that Channel. The struggles of the Angevin dynasty were those of a continental power of the first order, of which Great Britain was the northernmost province; and the Hundred Years War was just a dismal family quarrel between legatees whose claims were as well-founded or as dubious as each other's. For a long time, the finest jewels of the Angevin domain were inextricably embedded in the Franco-Burgundian feudal mosaic. And though confined to

* Under the 1985 Anglo-Irish Agreement, concluded between the Governments of Margaret Thatcher and Garret FitzGerald in the Republic of Ireland, an intergovernmental conference was established to deal on a regular basis with political, security and legal matters and with the promotion of cross-border cooperation.

their territory across the Channel, the heirs of the Plantagenets were to find a point of anchorage in continental Europe through their rivalry with the Capetians.

Then, for centuries to come, the defeat of the great Armada was to persuade the English that their principal stronghold was the ocean, rather than any territorial possession. Yet they were not the first to hear that famous call of the sea, which seemed to have broken the moorings tying the British Isles to the old continent. The whole of Europe had heard it long before them, and Spain and Portugal – for whom the Pope had divided the world in two, like an orange – had been the first to answer it.

But England alone was to see one of her colonies become not only independent, but immensely more powerful than herself. From that day, it was no longer the Empire (now transformed into an evanescent Commonwealth) that took her mind away from Europe, but the reversal of roles in the power struggle between the United States and the motherland. Like it or not, Britain's pole star now shone in Washington. Between the allied victory of 1918 and that of 1944, this phase reached its apogee, replacing the axiom of insularity with the fiction of the 'special relationship' between Great Britain and the United States. The expansion of Soviet power lent credence to this fantasy; the collapse of the Soviet bloc has done nothing to diminish its hold. It is high time the British came down to earth.

No more or less different from all the European nations than they are from one another; almost the twin of that insufferable France that blocks the view to the continent, England continues to believe in its singularity. Lumping all other European countries together, the English are convinced that the full meaning of the word 'democracy' is unintelligible outside their frontiers, that the States of written law are inevitably subject to the reign of the arbitrary, and that justice is codified only the better to suppress it. English civilisation is alone worthy of the name, since it alone allows for constant re-examination, while never doubting of itself. These fundamental truths emerge periodically from the collective unconscious and encourage a show of arrogance which too frequently masks the most precious English qualities: a sense of greatness – with its corollary, a horror of grandiloquence; a detachment bordering on coldness, but accompanied by the spontaneous acceptance of people's differences; the entire collection of paradoxes that feed the English art of *savoir vivre* – *a savoir vivre* that is not a question of class, as the English themselves believe, but a matter for every class. As well as the rules that are common to every stratum of society, each class has its own strict rules of observance, and its own equally arbitrary special dispensations; discussing these at length is a familiar pastime in every circle. From the top of the pile to the very bottom, all are convinced they can clearly distinguish a great lady from a social climber, a good boy from a lout.

From formal thank-you letters, to roll-calls of cryptic titles, toasts ceremonially barked, onomatopoeic acclamations, work clothes and party gear, epic variations on the theme of the weather and meteorological elegies: these are so many ways of sniffing the stranger, and require a sense of smell worthy of the pointer dogs in which British breeders justly take such pride. From birth to birthdays, house-warming parties, Saturday night outings or a prisoner's day out, from a triumph at the Derby or a win at the greyhound races to royal jubilees, illness and death: every circumstance has its own etiquette. Yet the strict application of this etiquette is not in itself a proof of quality, nor is the violation or apparent ignorance of it necessarily a fault; but its general adherence avoids the more embarrassing manifestations of good will or of pleasure, of aggression or of pain. In England as elsewhere, these forms of politeness are under attack from the tensions and the standardisation of the modern world, but they remain intelligible enough to most people for them to serve their purpose. Not only do they leave the way open for the dominant culture of the middle classes, but they can accommodate an evolving society with its clubs for single-parent families, its Thatcherite managers, its homosexual priests, its committees against sex and violence, its women-against-the-bomb and its women-against-male-chauvinism, its police support groups and its militants in support of racial equality, its law-abiding socialists and its old ladies on the war-path to restore capital punishment.

Other nations would do well to study the English art and science of everyday living. High principles are inaccessible to ordinary mortals, and too easily give way to cynicism to be reliable everyday guides. Instead of referring to them indiscriminately, the English believe that courage is above all a proof of common sense, and heroism the result of good training; that cowardice is sister to imagination, and that as it is right to condemn the former, it is essential to be wary of the latter. The dreams and madness that lie in wait for them (as they do for everyone), and occasionally seize them, have their own sphere, which is that of poetry, exploration and adventure. On the other hand, success and failure, which are our daily bread, are worthy neither of praise nor of recrimination. They are merely facts, and the English are rightly considered masters of the factual.

England is the home of the commonplace, which is sought after and cultivated like the rarest manifestation of good taste. It considers contradiction to be the least dubious manifestation of truth, and suspects logic of being no more than an elaborate attack on reality. Disorder and ambiguity have long intrigued its scholars and inspired its philosophers, for whom they are not anomalies, but the very stuff of life. And the English love this disorder, much as they love nature, without wishing to explain it, or claiming to dominate it, yet transforming it every time into an English garden.

7
Words and Images

Selling Paper

Fleet Street, the legendary newspaper street, no longer exists; or rather, it no longer is a street of newspapers. Before long it will have lost all the prestige it had gained as a centre of the world's press and become no more than a forgotten annexe of the City.

Like every other revolution, the one that is at present transforming the British press has its roll call of victims, heroes and traitors. It is all the more difficult to distinguish between them since their roles often seem to merge. Among them one could mention Rupert Murdoch, the insatiable Australian, bent on conquering a worldwide news and entertainment empire; the late Robert Maxwell, whose irrepressible personality earned him the nickname of 'the bouncing Czech'; Brenda Dean, heroine of a trade unionism destined for decapitation by technical progress, as surely as the Luddites were by the arrival of the spinning jenny; Eddie Shah, a small-time tycoon who distributed free local newspapers, the first who dared to confront the unions before whose power the magnates of the press had always cowered.

But there is another hero – or villain? – whose name was virtually unknown until the mid-eighties, and for whom I predict a glittering future: David Sullivan, owner of the *Sunday Sport* – a paper which, in the space of just a few months, with a derisory capital base and a team of eleven journalists, managed to capture a readership of five hundred thousand. Its success is due not, as one might think, to its coverage of football or of cricket, but to battalions of appetizing breasts and plump feminine posteriors, spread out each week, in colour, on broadsheet pages, with a sort of hygienic innocence which has won for the *Sunday Sport* a strategic position between pornography and culinary advertising. No need to get indigestion reading columns of text: the headlines are as appetizing and substantial as the photographs.

The growth of mass-circulation papers of entertainment at the expense of radical publications is a phenomenon, in England, that is as old as the freedom of the press, and is perhaps a natural and unavoidable consequence of that freedom. Censorship and restrictions are conducive to vigorous expression. Without the law on seditious and blasphemous libel (especially as amended by the 1792 Libel Act – steered through Parliament by Charles Fox – which required that libel cases should be submitted to trial by jury), the early nineteenth century would never have known such a flowering of radical writing. Stamp duty on newspapers, as well as taxes on paper and press advertising – 'taxes on knowledge', as they were known at the time – were designed to restrict the dissemination of information to respectable people, but in so doing they also provided radicalism with an unexpected source of protection. By preventing the growth of a vast undifferentiated popular market – which would have required enormous capital expenditure for the purchase of sophisticated printing technology – taxation provided the militant press with an effective safeguard against potentially savage competition, enabling it to survive on tiny print runs. With the failure of popular Chartism* in the mid-nineteenth century, a more sober, middle-class reformist movement called for and obtained the abolition of stamp duty and other newspaper taxes. But it was not in the name of freedom of expression that they fought, leaving such treacherous ground to the enemies of the established order. Their slogan was a much less threatening one: freedom of the marketplace.

And how right they were, these apostles of the marketplace, when

---

* The social and political movement of Chartism took its name from the Charter of the People, published on 8 May 1838, which called for universal suffrage by secret ballot, and for MPs to be salaried. It was the first expression of authentically popular aspirations, but became compromised – in the eyes of its own supporters – by its resort to violent protest and its internal disorganisation.

they accused their opponents of underestimating, in Palmerston's words, 'the loyalty and good conduct of the lower classes'. Within just a few years the radical publications were to disappear, smothered by the weight of a new generation of seductive mass-circulation papers. The development of rotary presses and Linotype printing at the end of the century further increased the circulation of established newspapers such as *The Times*, and contributed to the establishment of new titles, which successfully conquered the popular market despite a resolutely conservative political stance. The *Daily Mail* (founded in 1896) and the *Daily Express* (in 1900) still give daily testimony to the vigour of the idea which gave them birth.

Unlike the radical press, whose power was measured in terms of its capacity to provoke governments or shake institutions, the commercial press has tended to become a power in its own right, and to carve a place for itself among other major institutions. Its originality consists in its exceptional commercial success, not in any particular political ideology; and it is success that has both guaranteed its freedom and curtailed its expression.

Between the end of the nineteenth century and the beginning of the twentieth a series of newspaper mergers and acquisitions introduced the era of the great press barons. In 1884, the Scotsman Andrew Carnegie, founder of the American iron and steel industry, controlled a group of eight daily papers and six weeklies in Scotland. During the same period, Edward Lloyd, owner of two mass circulation papers, *Lloyd's Weekly* and the *Daily Chronicle*, was also building up an important group of newspapers. But this was just a beginning.

By 1921, three brothers were providing newspaper fodder for six million readers. The first, Lord Northcliffe, ruled over *The Times*, the *Daily Mail*, the *Weekly Dispatch*, and the *London Evening News*. The second, Lord Rothermere, controlled the *Daily Mirror*, the *Sunday Pictorial*, the *Daily Record*, the *Glasgow Evening News*, and the *Sunday Mail*. Together, the first two brothers also owned the Amalgamated Press, which specialised in the publication of magazines. The third, Sir Hildebrand Aubrey Harmsworth, had built up a chain of newspapers in the south-west of England. A further thirteen dailies, three Sunday papers and twenty-one provincial weeklies were shared out between two other newspaper groups.

After the death of Lord Northcliffe, the national press was never again to be concentrated in as few hands as it had been at the beginning of the century. Nonetheless, between the two wars a series of Homeric battles between competing newspapers culminated in the emergence of four figures dominating the national newspaper scene: again, two brothers, the Berrys (later respectively Lord Camrose and Lord Kemsley), Lord Rothermere, and the legendary Lord Beaverbrook, rumbustiously caricatured by Evelyn Waugh in his novel, *Scoop*. In many respects, Beaverbrook represented the epitome of brash and triumphant Conservatism – the colourful champion of individual enterprise and British imperial interests, thrusting his viewpoint on the editors of his papers for many years. Yet personally, he remained a much more complex and endearing man, inspiring fierce loyalty and admiration in the most unexpected quarters – as Michael Foot's moving essay on the man was to demonstrate even after his death*.

Socialists have always disputed the right of the formidable press barons to present themselves as champions of the freedom of information. Their collusion with political Conservatism, it is argued, has always been blatant. From the supposed objectivity of *The Times* to the strident partisanship of the *Daily Mail* or the *Daily Express*, the distortion of political reality is more or less obvious, but is just as real. In spite of their widespread distribution, former left-wing newspapers such as the *Reynolds News* and the *Daily Herald* received only a fraction of the advertising revenue enjoyed by Conservative dailies of comparable circulation. But it was not long before the market-place itself corrected this anomaly, with advertisers gradually abandoning their partisan discrimination against the socialist press. In 1933, for the relaunch of the *Daily Mirror* (which had been deserted by its middle-class readers and hurriedly sold off by Lord Rothermere), the advertising agency, J. Walter Thompson, advised the paper's new owner to address himself to the vast working-class public. It was irrelevant that such a measure implied a move to the left. The important point was

* From *Debts of Honour*, Reg Davis-Poynter, 1980.

that this was the best way of reaching a public of young workers whose purchasing power was growing rapidly. By 1939 the Mirror's distribution figures had risen back to a million and a half, and its advertising revenue was sufficient to ensure a healthy profit margin.

Throughout the Second World War, the *Daily Mirror* engaged in a battle of words with the Conservative majority over the question of government censorship, and their eventual victory was to extend the field of press freedom to proportions as yet unknown in Europe. In the summer of 1940, while Britain was anxiously expecting a German landing, the Government introduced 'Regulation 2D', which gave the Home Secretary, personally, the power to prohibit publication of any material 'calculated to foment opposition to the prosecution of a successful issue of any war in which His Majesty is engaged'. By the spring of 1942, the *Mirror*'s criticisms of the coalition Government headed by Winston Churchill had reached such a pitch that on 9 March, the Prime Minister called a cabinet meeting to obtain the enforcement of Regulation 2D against it. The only way of curbing the paper's invective seemed to be to ban it altogether. But as soon as Churchill's intentions were known, the opposition demanded that the question be debated in Parliament. The national press – setting aside all political affiliations – leapt to the defence of its threatened colleagues, and finally forced the government into an ignominious retreat. The *Daily Mirror* was safe, and Regulation 2D was never again invoked during the conflict. Henceforth, the freedom of the press itself was seen as one of the chief issues at stake in this war in which pluralist democracy was pitted against the evils of totalitarianism.

Nonetheless, had it not been for the need to ration paper during the war, the doctrine of press freedom would not – on its own – have been sufficient to allow for a significant expansion of the socialist press. Faced with a smaller field of action, advertisers were anxious to make use of every available opportunity to market their goods, irrespective of their own political leanings. And the publication of the Beveridge Report in 1942 would never have aroused such widespread enthusiasm had it not been endlessly reproduced, expanded on, discussed and saluted as a historical document by this vigorous left-wing press. The report, which formed the basis of the Welfare State, was later incorporated into the Labour Party's manifesto, and – thanks to its popularity – contributed greatly to the massive socialist vote in the 1945 elections. During this period, the combined circulation figure for all the dailies and Sunday papers with Labour leanings (the *Daily Herald*, the *Reynold News*, the *Daily Mirror* and the *Sunday Pictorial*) amounted to nearly nine million, not counting the four million or so readers of the illustrated weekly, *Picture Post*.

But with the end of paper rationing, advertisers once more began discriminating between papers according to the purchasing power of their respective readerships. At the same time, increasingly high salaries in the industry, as well as the imposition of restrictive practices by the press and printing unions, and their determined opposition to any kind of modernisation, all contributed to spiralling production costs. Between 1945 and 1979 (the first year of Mrs Thatcher's Government), these were to increase approximately thirty-fold for a London daily paper (compared to a six-fold increase in the general cost of living). In 1964, high production costs and chronically insufficient advertising revenue forced the *Daily Herald* to close down despite average daily sales of 4,744,000 copies.

The process which in the nineteenth century had led to the gradual elimination of the radical press in favour of the press of big business was once again set in motion in the twentieth. The unions, ignoring distinctions between right- and left-wing papers, continued to undermine them both during this crucial period of transition, unaware that they were ultimately playing into the hands of the capitalist press barons. It took some time before the owners of the more prosperous papers learned how to exploit the possibilities which an evolving marketplace offered them on a silver platter. Their lack of imagination provided one of the most spectacular examples of the kind of post-war management that was steadily leading a victorious Great Britain down the path to economic ruin.

Lord Hartwell, heir of one of the formidable Berry brothers, lost the *Daily Telegraph* (last of the high-circulation quality papers and unshakeable bastion of a stentorian conservatism), by yielding

– year after year – to the most unreasonable demands made by unions drunk on their own power. He only just avoided financial disaster by divesting himself of the paper that had been his entire life, and selling it for a song to a Canadian entrepreneur, Conrad Black. Hartwell did not long survive this incomprehensible *débacle*.

Incomprehensible because – despite their high quality and popularity – neither radio nor television have dented the popularity of newspapers among the reading public. Only in Japan is the press so favoured. Every day, from Dover to Inverness, more than eighty per cent of the adult British population reads at least one national or local daily. At the same time, the concentration of newspaper groups is increasing, as is their penetration of the audio-visual communications sector, and their internationalisation – principally in English language countries. The techniques of communication, storage and processing of information are also changing and improving at spectacular speed. Huge investment is sometimes needed to purchase this new technology, but thanks to radically changed working methods enabling a considerable reduction in the workforce, there is a proportional reduction in the costs of production.

A Worldwide Market

In 1979, seven multinationals – established in five continents, with interests in mining and banking, transport and oil, the food and construction industries, and in engineering and communications – between them owned nearly three hundred British dailies, and more than four hundred magazines, with a total circulation of about fifty million copies. At the same time, the five most important newspaper groups were together offering the public ninety-five per cent of the copies sold by the national dailies, ninety-six per cent of those sold by the Sunday papers, sixty-nine per cent of the copies sold by the provincial press in the mornings and fifty-eight per cent in the evenings, eighty-seven per cent of the print run of women's magazines, seventy-four per cent of paperback books, fifty-two per cent of cinema seats, seventy per cent of single records and sixty-one per cent of record albums and tapes. Since then increasing competition has led to a growing standardisation of writing styles, combined with greater differentiation in management techniques, and a growing internationalisation of the communications market.

Already deprived of most of its vehicles of expression, the Labour Party has seen its last support, the *Daily Mirror*, water down its message and cut down on the amount of space that it devotes to politics. This retreat in favour of human interest stories and entertainment journalism is in fact common to the press in general.

By introducing a more popular diet of news and features and launching an aggressive advertising campaign to promote sales, the owners of *The Times* (the Canadian group, Thompson Equitable Association) managed to increase the paper's circulation by sixty-nine per cent between 1965 and 1969. But the substantial increase in the paper's running costs which this entailed was not offset by a corresponding increase in revenue, since advertisers were already reaching this new category of low-income readers through the popular press, at much lower rates. From 1970, *The Times* began to shed its new readership with as much perseverance as it had put into acquiring it, and in 1971 the print run was voluntarily reduced to 340,000 copies, compared to peak sales of 432,000 in 1969.

Such measures were inadequate to revitalise an industry that was a prisoner of labyrinthine conventions built up over the years by the alliance of union obstructiveness and management pusillanimity. In the end, it fell to an unknown publisher of local free-sheets, Eddie Shah, to break the back of the unions' resistance. The Messenger group of free weeklies – distributed throughout the Manchester region – was financed entirely by advertising revenue, and employed the latest printing and publishing technology. When Shah (founder and owner of the group) engaged a number of non-union print workers on one of his papers in 1983, he was confronted by the wrath of the mighty National Graphical Association (NGA), and after a vain attempt at a negotiated settlement, was besieged by pickets of up to 6,500 participants. Armed with a series of laws recently enacted by the Conservative majority, and overwhelmingly encouraged by public opinion, he took the union to court – and won, thus obtaining what none of the press barons and multinationals had dared to fight for: the end of the closed shop.

Two and a half years later, the now famous Eddie Shah brought out a new, full-colour national paper, *Today*, using computer technology and the most modern printing techniques. His workforce was affiliated to the Electricians Union, rather than the NGA, and as such, was ready to accept flexible working hours and compulsory arbitration in case of conflict. In spite of high hopes, the adventure was not a financial success – but for the newspaper industry there was no turning back. Hard on the heels of Eddie Shah's light infantry, the News International group – led by Rupert Murdoch – was setting up the armoured divisions that were finally to break up the alliance of the National Graphical Association with the Society of Graphical and Allied Trades (SOGAT), which had dominated the production of newspapers in Great Britain.

As far back as 1980, Murdoch had purchased an abandoned site in Wapping (in the former East London docklands) and had invested one hundred million pounds to convert it into offices and printing workshops, as well as to build satellite printing works in Scotland. But despite two years of negotiation with the NGA and the London branch of SOGAT, he had been unable to come to a satisfactory agreement on the transfer to Wapping of the News International papers – the *Sun*, *The Times*, the *Sunday Times* and the *News of the World*. In 1985, working in the greatest secrecy, he created a new company for the exploitation of his Wapping premises, and set up a network of computers with software for the direct composition and typesetting of newspapers by journalists. He also hired an entirely new and autonomous team (belonging, like Eddie Shah's workforce, to the Electricians Union), and trained them to use the equipment. Meanwhile, without telling the unions about these preparations, he resumed negotiations with them to reduce production costs. During the last days of January 1986, the group's five thousand unionised workers went on strike to demonstrate, once again, their hostility to management proposals. Within forty-eight hours, Rupert Murdoch had moved his entire journalistic and administrative staff to the new offices, and began printing his papers with a salaried staff of a mere six hundred technical workers. Their publication had been interrupted by only one day. A one-year siege of the Wapping plant by NGA and SOGAT pickets did not succeed in halting the production of Murdoch's papers, and only briefly disrupted their distribution. It was becoming clear that the newspaper unions would have to negotiate if they wanted to avoid seeing all their members gradually sacked by employers following in the path of News International.

The rationalisation of production, coupled with the fruitful real estate deals carried out by newspapers as they abandoned Fleet Street to the developers, increased their profits beyond all the expectations of financial analysts. In the year to June 1987 alone, News International showed a tenfold rise in pre-tax profits, to eleven million pounds. Those of United Newspapers (publishers of the *Daily Express*, the *Sunday Express* and the *Star*) more than doubled between 1985 and 1987, as did those of the group controlled by Viscount Rothermere, publishers, amongst other things, of the *Daily Mail*. The Mirror group, which Robert Maxwell had purchased when it was in a state of advanced anaemia, tripled its profits between 1986 and 1987. The future of the *Daily Telegraph*, which had come within a hair's breadth of bankruptcy, was beginning to look more promising. But the *Financial Times* – despite a print run lower than that of its direct competitors – beat all records of profitability among newspapers, with an advertising revenue of one hundred million pounds. This feat demonstrated once more that while circulation figures are crucial in determining the advertising value of the popular papers, it is the precise targeting of a readership with high spending power that is the secret of success for the 'quality' press.

Rupert Murdoch's publications each have their own style, according to the public they want to capture, but – whether the content be popular or heavy – the tone remains distinctive. In theory, the objectivity of *The Times* is guaranteed by a group of independent directors who are required by law to sit on the paper's board. In theory the editor is master of the paper's editorial policy, which – in theory – Rupert Murdoch can in no way influence. In practice, with the exception of a few islands where the intellect still blows freely, the paper has been colonized by neo-liberal Thatcherite ideology, and has adopted – in a discreet register –

the strident ideological tones that are the imprint of its owner. It is a remarkable fact that all of these newspapers, dedicated – at either extreme of the market – to the most touchy brand of nationalism, should belong to an Australian company led by an American citizen, in which the principal share-holder is a family trust, managed entirely on behalf of its beneficiaries.

The *Sun's* recipes are applied, more or less – though with some nuances, and less obvious cynicism – by all the tabloid papers. Among the quality papers, the Conservative *Daily Telegraph* and the centre-left *Guardian* signpost their opinions with a clarity that makes their news coverage less suspect than that of the supposedly apolitical *Times*. The *Times'* former role as impartial arbiter of events has lapsed little by little, and been taken over by the *Financial Times*, which for some years has had a circulation extending beyond business circles to a broader public. The *Observer*, first published in 1791, is the oldest national Sunday newspaper in the world. During the protracted feud between Tiny Rowland (owner of the *Observer*) and the Al Fayed brothers over the purchase of Harrods, the paper's editorial integrity was put under severe strain by Rowland's exploitation of its columns to advance his case and discredit his rivals. But despite such threats to its objectivity, the *Observer* has maintained its reputation for a liberal and objective approach to reporting.

In 1986, a group of journalists, nostalgic for the past glories of *The Times*, launched a new paper to take up the torch. The significance of this event should not be underestimated. More than five years after its birth, the *Independent* has proved that there exists in Britain a readership determined not only by its prosperity but also by its genuine desire for impartial information, and that this readership is substantial enough to sustain a major modern daily. Spurred on by this success, 'Newspaper Publishing' launched the *Independent on Sunday* in January 1990. By June 1990 it had an average circulation of more than 362,000, and so far – despite renewed recession and a nationwide slump in advertising – it has not succumbed to the same fate as its rival, the *Sunday Correspondent*, which finally closed down in November 1990, one year after its first appearance, and just one month after being relaunched as the country's first 'quality' tabloid. Meanwhile, pressure of competition from the *Independent* has forced *The Times* itself to revert to less strident tones and a more dignified Conservatism.

The market for popular papers also remains vigorous and however much one is scandalised by this below-the-belt competition, however appalled at the drift into mindlessness, it should not be forgotten that without a *Sun* or a *Sunday Sport*, there might well not be a *Financial Times*, and the *Independent* might never have been born. The commercial dynamism of the press, its aggressiveness, the very abundance of its publications and the efficiency of their distribution combine to sustain the public's exceptionally voracious reading habits. And although at local level, the growing number of monopolies is restricting the reader's choice, nationally the choice is greater than ever.

To Be Different

Boredom with the conventions of the mainstream press has created a fertile ground for the growth of fringe publications, the most conspicuous of which is *Private Eye*. After more than a quarter century of publication, it still has the air of a loutish gate-crasher.

Founded in 1961 by a group of friends who had been to school together at Shrewsbury, and inspired most notably by the French satirical paper, *Le Canard enchaîné*, *Private Eye* specialises in scandalous revelations with political overtones. Few publications have ever provoked so much resentment, so many passionate denunciations – and so many libel actions. And even today when the magazine has lost much of its former bite, few issues can be read from cover to cover without leaving one – after one has finished laughing – with a slightly nauseous after-taste. It is not so much the periodical's objectives that produce this *malaise*, nor even its salacious indiscretions; rather, it is the use of masochism and contempt, of exhibitionism and scatology in the pursuit of the comic. This somewhat puerile approach to comedy is a much more typical product of an English public school education than is the famous 'English sense of humour', with all the wry subtlety that implies.

Between the mainstream press (tabloid and broadsheet), and the incendiary *Private Eye*, a multitude of periodicals, magazines and

316

free-sheets are born, survive, flourish or collapse. The essential role of the oldest among these – for instance, *Punch, Tatler, Country Life* and the *Illustrated London News* – is to preserve the flame (or the flickering light) of an ancient England more imagined than real. A faintly stilted smile, some polite small-talk (slightly tinged with commercialism), the fading beauty of an increasingly polluted countryside, a bit of news (slightly out of date) – of such things are these magazines made. Fishing, hunting, gardening, society gossip and celebrity pages: their subjects have hardly changed. Reality escapes them, but that hardly matters when mythology has taken its place. They still have many successful years ahead of them.

The tradition of political journalism survives as best it can. On the left, *Tribune* has sobered up and thrown itself into the arms of Neil Kinnock's moderate Labour left while the socialist *New Statesman* has merged with its former rival, *New Society*, and modernised its presentation. Today its tone is careful and judicious – too well-informed to swallow the socialist line uncritically, it remains sentimentally attached to it. It criticizes Labour, but rather as one might castigate a child, to improve its behaviour. The Communist publication, *Marxism Today*, seems to discover in itself a vitality that is inversely proportional to the strength of the Party. It offers an iconoclastic but fascinating interpretation of Marxist dogma, in which the old faith is substantially secularised. The anti-racist, anti-sexist, right-on *News on Sunday* was launched in the spring of 1987 with a twelve point editorial programme, to carry the torch of an unreconstructed socialist creed. It survived for just a few months – and even that was only thanks to injections of capital from the millionaire Owen Oyston, who claimed to be sympathetic to the paper's objectives. Malicious gossip has it that the working class – like everyone else – prefers reading articles on football, sex and beer than on nuclear disarmament and the civil rights of animals.

On the right, behind the ranks of the mainstream daily and Sunday papers, the *Economist* takes itself so very seriously that its readers are beginning to ask themselves whether it really is. Alas, it remains one of the best weeklies in the world. Under the new editorship of Dominic Lawson on the other hand, the *Spectator* has fun tripping up prominent public figures who are too confident about the layout and comfort of the club furniture. During a now notorious interview with the *Spectator* in July 1990, Nicholas Ridley, then Secretary of State for Trade and Industry, clearly felt completely at ease. Speaking frankly about the future of Europe, and in particular Germany's role in it, he said, 'This is a German racket designed to take over the whole of Europe . . . I'm not against giving up sovereignty in principle, but not to this lot. You might as well give it to Adolf Hitler, frankly.' Within days of the article's publication Mrs Thatcher found herself regretfully having to accept the resignation of one of her staunchest allies in the cabinet.

The major women's magazines – *Woman's Own, Woman, Woman's Weekly*, and *Woman's Realm* (all owned by IPC Magazines) – have seen their territory invaded by numerous competitors, starting with feminist and post-feminist publications such as *Spare Rib* and *Cosmopolitan*. More recently they have witnessed the arrival of the English edition of *Elle* – fresh and charming in her Parisian dress – and of her cousin, *Marie-Claire*, swarming with ideas for herself and for her house. Contrary to the pessimistic predictions of the eighties, these magazines do not seem condemned to extinction.

Since its birth in the cellars of Liverpool, pop music has become more middle class. Pop music lovers have outgrown adolescence and their purchasing power has increased. Their magazines – *Arena, Q, Smash Hits* – speak to them of fashion (male as well as female), of perfumes and of after-shave lotion; it is here that advertisers begin their campaign of indoctrination, hoping to turn the products they sell into the habits of a lifetime.

The fate of the printed word in Britain has confounded the prophets of doom. Far from succumbing to the assault of radio, television and cinema – and to the greater prosperity of the international conglomerates which have invested in it – its future looks healthier than ever.

The Last Church

Faced with a written press that has not always treated objectivity as a sacred duty, it fell first to radio, and later to television, to set out the dogma of impartiality – the contemporary equivalent of divine revelation. Its commitment to this cause was to found the reputation for integrity and the worldwide prestige of the British Broadcasting Corporation, the mother of information services, as Westminster is the mother of parliaments. But the truth of this article of faith is far from universally accepted. On the occasion of its fiftieth anniversary, in 1986, the BBC was subjected to more criticism than praise. The political Left accused it of obscuring its struggle (and the irreconcilable social contradictions that are at the root of it) by appealing to a supposed patrimony of common values and assumptions that never really existed. The right reproached it with having a monopoly that disrupted the operation of the marketplace, and also claimed left-wing bias.

The BBC can justifiably congratulate itself – and does so frequently – on being the object of contradictory charges, which cancel each other out. It remains no less true that its freedom to inform derives more from a tacit agreement with the Government (the subtlety and complexity of which does not in any way diminish its constraints) than from a clearly defined institutional principle.

Contrary to elated and alarmist predictions alike, the launch in 1954 of Independent Television (a group of privately owned stations, better known under the collective logo of ITV) was not to change the rules of the game. Like the BBC's Board of Governors, members of the Independent Broadcasting Authority (IBA – commercial radio and television's regulatory body) were all nominated by the Queen on the advice of the Government; they had identical profiles, and were easily interchangeable. No less than the BBC, the private companies were charged with maintaining strict impartiality on matters of controversy. The restricted number and regional allocation of licences distributed by the IBA, as well as their limited duration of ten years, placed the private sector in a position of dependence on the Government that was even greater than that of the BBC.

The supposed competition between commercial television (which, for its part, has a monopoly on advertising) and the two BBC channels, has for a long time been more apparent than real. No doubt the battle for the best rating figures is not entirely irrelevant, but the most popular programmes are carefully timed so that the

public can imbibe them all. The two rival cultural channels –
BBC2 and Channel 4 (which shares out its advertising revenue
between all the independent stations collectively financing it) –
also conduct themselves in a most gentlemanly manner. In spite
of a thirty-three-year cohabitation with commercial stations, in
spite of the development of new techniques (videos, transmission
satellites, cable), in spite of the incursions of the great sharks of
the printed media such as Robert Maxwell and Rupert Murdoch,
the shadow of the BBC's first Director General – John Reith –
still hovers (though increasingly faintly) over British radio and
television, conceived and fashioned by him more than half a
century before.

Over the years, innumerable experts, government missions,
researchers and specialist journalists have come from all over the
world to study the BBC – thought to be an unrivalled model –
and have left, considerably disconcerted by the extreme theoretical
dependence of an institution which is, in practice, so jealous of its
independence. The BBC started life as the British Broadcasting
Company, an ephemeral association of private interests with no
clear objectives. When the company was wound up, the Corporation was granted the monopoly of radio broadcasting by
Royal Charter, which also stipulated that it should operate as a
public service, independent of the State. But though the newly
constituted BBC did not owe its existence to an Act of Parliament,
the Government was responsible for nominating the chairman and
members of the Corporation's Board of Governors (who were in
turn responsible for appointing the Director General). If it had
got into the habit of exercising control over the airwaves by this
means – as happened in the majority of other European countries
– there would have been little that anyone could do about it.

John Reith – Managing Director of the defunct British Broadcasting Company before taking over as Director General of the
new Corporation – was alone in appreciating the BBC's potential.
He gave politicians no time to get the measure of these small
wireless electric boxes that delivered music into the heart of
people's homes. Unlike them, he immediately understood that the
revolutionary aspect of radio was not technical: the main principles
of broadcasting had been understood since the beginning of the

century, and had in fact been used during the First World War in the form of wireless telegraphy. The true novelty of radio lay in its social potential; in the fact that it was – in Reith's own words – 'a reversal of the natural law that the more one takes, the less there is left for others'.

Reith was a man with a mission, obstinate, irascible, religious and something of a megalomaniac. With some justification, he believed himself to be alone in having a clear perception of what the BBC's destiny should be. Neither financiers, with their obsession for sums, nor politicians, with their short-term perspective, could be trusted to jeopardise their investments or their popularity in the interest of a public good transcending their own narrow preoccupations.

Terrified at the thought of having to debate the Arts in front of their colleagues in Parliament, MPs were only too happy to leave the mysteries of culture to an appropriate organism, rather as one leaves illness to be dealt with by the hospitals. They were doing quite enough, they felt, by ensuring that the BBC was kept unpolluted by commerce through the institution of a licence fee on every radio set.

During the Parliamentary debate at which these matters were discussed, the talk was entirely of 'education', never 'news' or 'information'. It was Reith, once again, who had successfully substituted this word for one that had previously been more common: 'entertainment'. As far as the Members of Parliament were concerned, this substitution had the virtue of lending more gravity to their deliberations. For Reith, the concept of education was pivotal to his vision of the BBC's mission. Education, as he conceived it, did not consist in the transmission of knowledge. It was a kind of religious initiation aimed at preparing an ever-increasing public to receive a cultural eucharist, blessed and consecrated by the nation's élite.

Light entertainment, such as comedy and vaudeville, was included in the programming as a concession to popular taste. But it was also exploited as a vehicle of transition, capturing an audience that could then be led to nobler pastimes: to a classical music concert played by one of the BBC's eleven orchestras; to the plays performed by the BBC's own troupe of actors; to the hymns written especially for the BBC; and finally to unashamedly educational programmes such as Julian Huxley's investigation into the Origin of Species, or Keynes' lectures on economics. This association of the greatest names in science, philosophy, literature, art and music with the BBC, was to confirm the Corporation in its role as arbiter and guardian of the nation's values. If Bernard Shaw, H.G. Wells and the Bloomsbury literati did not scorn to be heard on the radio, it clearly deserved respect. And if its cultural programmes were praiseworthy, then its journalists and presenters must be so as well. It is true that the public at large frequently ignored the most ambitious of these programmes, while the intelligentsia mocked the fake starchiness of the BBC voice. But when all was said and done, one inevitably ended up praising the Corporation's merits, and – especially – saluting its independence.

Yet this independence remained a relative matter. As well as nominating the Corporation's governors, the State retained the right to issue (or withdraw) the broadcasting licence, and to determine the amount of the licence fee paid by the public. It was also empowered to veto any BBC programme it disapproved of, as well as to impose the transmission of official messages. During the General Strike of 1926, the BBC unashamedly drew its stance of hostility to the strikers from that of the Conservative cabinet, led by Stanley Baldwin. Reith himself never denied that the Government had full legal authority to give him orders. Nonetheless, his deep-seated loathing of politics prevented him from falling under the sway of government. Inter-party quarrels held so little interest for him that he felt able to ignore them with an entirely clear conscience. With the exception of a few Foreign Office interventions (which his patriotism easily accepted), and the occasional example of political censorship (such as the Government's banning of any interviews with the Conservative Party's black sheep, Winston Churchill – which did not trouble Reith in the least since he was equally hostile to all politicians), his general lack of interest and involvement in political controversy made it easy for him to avoid substantial interference from on high.

Most importantly, the BBC enjoyed the protection afforded to it by the political mores of the parliamentary system, and most notably by the institutional role of the opposition in the House of Commons. In gradually taking the place of the Liberals as the party in opposition, the Labour Party did not reject the rules of conviviality evolved over the centuries between Tories and Whigs. It would have been inadmissible for a national body like the BBC not to conform, at the very least, to the requirements of parliamentary civility. Though it would be an exaggeration to talk of objectivity with regard to the BBC's coverage at the time, there was at any rate a measure of bipartisanship – which is more than could be said for broadcasting in many other countries.

In Italy, Germany and in Spain, emergent totalitarian régimes were the first to discover the suggestive power of the radio waves, and soon put their discovery to use with the invention of propaganda. Compared to them, the British Government's intervention seemed positively benign, and the BBC's bipartisanship all the more to be valued. By reflecting the plurality of British society (even if under the same banner as the party in power, and sharing its prejudices), the BBC established its reputation as champion of democracy.

Reith – yet again – was obsessed with the unexploited possiblities of short waves for intercontinental broadcasting. And yet again, the technician in him was entirely at the service of the apostle with a gospel to spread throughout the world. In 1927, he was granted permission to use the relay station at Chelmsford to broadcast the BBC's internal programmes beyond the nation's frontiers. In December 1932, he inaugurated the first transmission of an English language service aimed at the Empire. It was understood that this service would be governed by the same Royal Charter as the BBC. Its mandate was to tell the truth. The BBC World Service still exists. It broadcasts in some forty languages to more than one hundred million listeners, and its reputation is such that a number of its programmes are actually sold to foreign radio stations, and are not merely transmitted free.

With the Second World War, the BBC's halo acquired a new brilliance thanks to the Corporation's identification with British democracy and its contribution to the war effort during the sombre hours of the Blitz. The formation of a Cabinet of national unity, the entry into the war of the United States, the presence in London of numerous European governments exiled from their countries by German occupation: all the circumstances conspired to turn it into a symbol, not only of national unity, but of the unity of the entire Allied camp; a symbol of the freedom for which they were all fighting. Towards the end of the war, it also became the echo of those – every day more numerous – who were beginning to draw an idealised picture of the Peace to come. The Beveridge report outlining the Welfare State of the future seemed largely consonant with the principles of benevolent regulation (not to say despotism) governing the Corporation. Naturally, the BBC became the enthusiastic herald of Beveridge's plan. After the war however, Beveridge himself expressed severe reservations about the 'secretiveness and self-satisfaction' of the BBC, though he finally recommended that the Corporation's licence be renewed because the alternative – American style commercial broadcasting – seemed far worse.

Auntie

The regular transmission of television programmes started on 2 November, 1936. By 1937 there were already twenty thousand operational receivers, and thus some fifty thousand viewers within a radius of about sixty miles from London were able to watch the coronation of George VI. But at £100, a television set cost almost as much as a small car, and only a tiny minority could afford to buy one. With the war, the experiment came to an end. In 1946, as if to wipe out the very memory of the war, the first programme to be shown on television offered viewers the same Mickey Mouse cartoon as had been shown at the end of the final pre-war programme in 1939. And it was another coronation, that of Elizabeth II in June 1953, that finally established television in the nation's mores. With twenty million viewers, eyes glued on their young Queen, television's audience exceeded that of the radio for the first time. Anticipating the advent of commercial television in 1954, the prophet of public service broadcasting compared it with smallpox and the bubonic plague. But far from doing the BBC any harm, it imposed on the Corporation a number of much needed reforms, without forcing it to alter a single one of its articles of faith.

Having seen more than seventy per cent of its audience desert to the independent channels, the BBC mounted a brilliant counter-offensive, and regained substantial lost ground. It was in its news coverage and presentation that the BBC had received the most severe battering. Its unchanging style, inherited from the radio, and its anonymous presenters and freeze frames compared badly with the dynamic young journalists who appeared on the screens of Independent Television to comment on the news, giving way whenever possible to filmed sequences from danger spots all over the globe. The BBC responded by replacing its distinguished speakers with journalists in the studios and roving reporters on the field.

After a few skirmishes which were to define its internal equilibrium, the new duopoly rapidly reached a *modus vivendi* that suited both parties. The public was more than happy to alternate between the two channels – since nothing essential differentiated them – while rejoicing in the resulting increase in programme choice. The only real change in the system was introduced in the name of the free market, but was actually its very negation: the Independent Television Authority (ITA), and later its successor, the Independent Broadcasting Authority (BA), were given the exclusive licence to determine their advertising tariffs, thus effectively delivering the advertisers into their hands.

In 1964, BBC2 was introduced to take over the role of purveyor of culture (which had been somewhat sacrificed in the interests of audience ratings), and was to carve a place for itself in the affections of the public with programmes such as the historical documentary series, *The World at War*, the literary serial, *The Forsyte Saga*, and the famous art historical series, *Civilisation*, presented by Kenneth Clark. The introduction of colour to BBC2 in 1967, two years before BBC1 or Independent Television, was further to extend and establish its audience.

The allocation in 1982 of a new, mainly cultural channel – Channel 4 – to Independent Television, followed by the birth a year later of two breakfast television programmes (one devolving to a new commercial company, TV AM, and the other being offered by BBC1) maintained the parity between the two sectors, while spurring them on to bring novel ideas and programmes to the screen. The success of Channel 4 has been remarkable, both in the history of British television and worldwide. It has vindicated the improbable, yet effective strategy of combining an educational vocation in the best BBC tradition with the ambition to please, capturing significant (if somewhat fragmented) audiences, gradually leading them to untrodden pastures and finally reassembling them around a number of general interest programmes. Masterminding this *tour de force*, we find once again, a single person, Jeremy Isaacs, Channel 4's first chairman*, and the eighties interpreter of the gospel according to Reith. Music played against the backdrop of an urban ghetto, or sung by Jamaicans or Pakistanis; an exploration of Japan or Germany in the 1930s; Polish experimental theatre; a Brazilian soap, or a French, or Italian one; forgotten treasures of early cinema; American football; humorous sketches; an investigation into homosexuality or the War of Secession: this assiduously applied alternative programme has exasperated more than one editorial writer, provoked a fair few contemptuous remarks from television critics, and sent a good number of dismayed viewers back to more familiar channels. Yet the Channel 4 viewing figures are often greater than those of its direct competitor, BBC2; in 1987, its advertising revenue was sufficient to cover the finance it had received from other private companies; it had acquired a loyal audience, and was becoming the object – as once the BBC had been – of worldwide curiosity and admiration. Little by little, both BBC and ITV expanded their programming to occupy the last open spaces in the television landscape, imposing their presence on almost every moment of the day and night.

A nation's mores are never simple and coherent. There have been times when radio or television have jostled or run ahead of general public opinion, and compromises have been needed. At other times, the reverse has been true. Between 1937 and 1986, the administration of the BBC had tolerated, as a matter of course, the unofficial enquiries that M15 made about all its journalists and any candidate for management position. It was not until outraged press commentary revealed the full extent of this collusion on the occasion of the BBC's fiftieth anniversary, that the practice

* Replaced by Michael Grade in January 1988.

was ended. At this time it was also revealed that the BBC had sometimes authorised the police to make use of its footage in order to identify participants in political demonstrations. On the other hand this same BBC had resolutely held out against the pressures placed on it by the Conservative leader, Anthony Eden, at the time of the disastrous Franco-British Suez landings in November 1956, and, a few years later, had defended its colleagues against the anger of the Labour Prime Minister, Harold Wilson. On the burning question of Northern Ireland, it had also defied official displeasure several times and shown programmes that were disapproved of by the Government, agreeing only to make a few token changes and to delay their transmission.

British television was (and still is) neither as virtuous as it is claimed to be, nor as shameless as some people would have it; it remains a good deal more pleasant, decent and better behaved than many others. It knows how to provoke laughter and how to educate, can face up to its responsibilities and is not afraid to resort to sarcasm when the circumstances call for it. Its hypocrisy – to which it is the first to admit – protects its virtue more than it masks its vices. In an imperfect world, perfection is frequently found to be more scandalous than crime, and to do justice to British television, it has more often caused a stir thanks to its probity than because of its compromises.

The competition between the BBC and ITV has led to the evolution of the British television product *par excellence*: the warts-and-all soap opera. Like every other country, the United Kingdom has a high consumption of American and Australian soaps such as *Dallas, Dynasty, Falcon Crest, Twin Peaks, Neighbours or Home and Away*; and even a French melodrama such as *Châteauvallon* finds an audience. British television, both state and commercial, produces high quality serials inspired by famous novels. Dickens, Thackeray, Trollope and Galsworthy have all been exploited and no doubt will be again. These productions, as well as numerous admirable documentaries, are exported throughout the world and often receive prizes at international festivals. But the distinctive feature of programmes such as *Coronation Street* – interminable chronicles of everyday life, dispensed year after year – is that they are a projection of the lives of humble people, or at any rate of the lives of a middle class that is similar enough to them to remain accessible. Their enduring success cannot be attributed to a thin veneer of fiction, nor even to the very relative suspense of succeeding episodes. What has truly caught the public imagination is the identification of the actors with the central characters they play. Blending the imaginary dramas of the television plot with the genuine accidents of life, the popular press has contributed to this identification, making the two both inseparable and irreplaceable: the actor who dies drags his fictional double into the grave, and the death of a soap opera character sometimes puts an end to the career of the actor who incarnated him.

And finally there came *Eastenders* – saga of the humdrum, narrative of picaresque platitudes, ravelling and unravelling the intrigues and adventures of its anti-heroes, twice a week, before some seventeen million avid viewers. Much water has flown under the bridge since the first truly successful television serial, *Coronation Street*, introduced viewers to a nostalgic working-class world in the imaginary town of Weatherfield, near Manchester. In the seventies, London Weekend Television brought out the immensely successful *Upstairs Downstairs*, a symmetrical description of the golden age of Victorian opulence in which, week after week and year after year, masters and servants lived, loved and suffered in the shared respect of social hierarchies. But in spite of their contrasting settings, the differences between the two serials were less stark than it first appeared: the simplified vision of a world of laughter and tears in which the good were very good, and the bad were horrid had merely been complemented by a nostalgia for luxury and family secrets.

Eastenders belongs to another genre: a liberating psychodrama dispensing a little pop sociology, while providing a manual on the nation's evolving mores – though carefully packaged in a wrapping of melodrama that makes it quite unusable as documentary. The Eastenders are to be found in Albert Square; in a permanent, life-size outdoor set, specially built for them. We bump into them in their pub, the Queen Vic, whose lovably villainous landlord 'Dirty Den' was finally killed by his enemies on a canal bank. We drink to their health. We take part in their quarrels and reconciliations and in the minutiae of a life punctuated by expeditions to the corner shop run by that West Indian family, whose son – poor lad – has sickle cell anaemia; expeditions to the fruit and vegetable market stall, to the launderette (the last of the big gossip factories); visits to the caff and the local doctor's surgery – such a decent man. We know them, we recognize them all: the blacks, the whites, the abandoned wives, the unfaithful girlfriends, the homosexual couples, the dear old granny who drank a little too much, then died, her chronically unemployed son-in-law, and her grandson, who has found out he is HIV positive. We will not find out any more about their sex lives than what they tell us themselves, and what the neighbours know. However promiscuous they may be, we are not allowed into their beds: *Eastenders* is shown at a time when the children are still awake. Nonetheless, the picture is clear, the euphemisms less blatant than in other similar soaps. *Eastenders* is not only an exceptionally realistic description of everyday life in the impoverished heart of London; it is also an outlet offered to all those who can recognize themselves in a character or transpose a moment of their lives into an episode.

With *Eastenders*, BBCI – 'Auntie', as she is known by her millions of nephews – beat all previous ratings records; another battle won. But her enemies (they are numerous and powerful) swear that she has lost the war. Mrs Thatcher's third coming in 1987 did not quite spell the death of the old aunt, but it did brutally expose her to national and international competition. Nonetheless, the BBC is likely to survive relatively unscathed into the next millennium thanks to one of the contradictions inherent in the neo-liberal philosophy espoused by the Conservatives. For while they swear, as usual, by the sovereignty of the consumer and his inalienable right to choose, they are also partisans of the sternest moral vigilance over television output, including careful control over that eternal couple, sex and violence, whom they bracket together for equal opprobrium.

The 1990 Broadcasting Act has drastically changed the network profile (both public and private) of radio and television in Britain*. Independent television licences are being auctioned to the highest bidder, subject to certain quality controls and diversity requirements,

* From January 1993, ITV will be replaced by Channel 3, which is to

and an elaborate new impartiality code is placing further restrictions on the way news and a wide range of other issues are being covered. But although the Act has been widely criticized for threatening the standards of public service broadcasting, and inevitably leading to bland and timid programme-making ultimately technology is likely to make much more of a difference than all the institutions and reforms set up by Mrs Thatcher. The reign of video-cassettes and *à la carte* television by cable or satellite makes a mockery of attempted censorship, and despite early teething problems, the industry continues to expand rapidly, with the number of homes receiving cable or satellite television increasing month by month. In February 1989, 650,000 homes received television by satellite dish or cable transmission. By November 1990, the figure had risen to 1.7 million homes, and by January 1991 it had risen again to 2.25 million homes – an increase of 505,000 in just two months.

Auntie, the Beeb, has always been a kept woman, unconcerned by money matters – a fact that used to scandalise Mrs Thatcher. But the BBC's supporters believe she could never survive unaided in the marketplace. The public at large is behind the Beeb, even when they betray her for a less lofty programme on another channel. The battle-field is circumscribed, the stakes are known. If the market wins, the general public will be the loser. If public service broadcasting survives, even in another form, it will survive to tell another tale and cast another spell. Rivals in the marketplace will occasionally succumb to the temptation of trying to do as well as the Beeb. And beyond the shores of the United Kingdom, a dissatisfied public will continue to wonder how on earth those confounded Brits manage to have the best radio and television in the world.

be serviced mainly by regionally based companies. A new Channel 5 will provide a nationally based service. Licences to both the channels will be sold by the new Independent Television Commission (ITC), and programme makers will be subject to a code of practice to be drawn up by the Broadcasting Standards Council, which the 1990 Broadcasting Act has placed on a statutory footing. A new commercial Radio Authority will be empowered to allocate up to three new national licences by competitive tender, subject to diversity requirements, and in the course of the 1990s, it is estimated that a further two to three hundred local and minority interest stations could come on air.

8

The Practice of Democracy

The British are not political animals. Around a quarter of the electorate does not bother to vote. They let themselves be guided by an easy-going sociability, combined with a sense of personal independence and an innate respect for established hierarchies. In making up their minds on any subject, they are more likely to trust to common sense than to take any notice of speechifying, and since their minds are usually made up, they resent it as an unnecessary imposition when some declaration of political principle replaces their favourite radio or television programme in the evening. But every year, for a few days in early autumn, this indifference tinged with boredom gives way to a certain animation as the conference season gets under way and the trade unions and party faithful gather before their leaders.

The Politics of the Unions

Although the Trade Union Congress (TUC) is not a political party but a federation of unions, its annual conference is nonetheless primarily a political event. And with their millions of block votes, the unions are still, in practice, the true masters of the Labour Party conference.

Since Mrs Thatcher came to power in 1979, this ritual has become charged with emotion. In the days before she became Prime Minister, about half of all employed workers belonged to a union. By the beginning of 1987 this proportion had fallen to thirty-four per cent, a drop of about three and a half million, bringing the total figure down to nine and a half million – that is to say, less than the total number of shareholders in the country. Of the twenty most important unions, fourteen had seen their membership drop during this period, while the six that had prospered were all white collar unions such as the Banking, Insurance and Finance Union, which had acquired forty thousand new members during the previous eight years. This general exodus from the unions was in large measure attributable to unemployment, but was also the symptom of a more general feeling of disillusionment which the Conservatives played on with great virtuosity, introducing new legislation that considerably reduced the power of the unions.

The most remarkable thing about this legislation – characterised by Mrs Thatcher as a liberating charter for workers tyrannised by a dictatorial union leadership – is that it really was perceived as such by large numbers of union members. The ban on secondary picketing, and the requirement that the union leadership submit itself for regular re-election and consult its members by secret ballot before embarking on strike action were all measures violently opposed by the TUC and the Labour Party. Yet despite the official union rhetoric, a mere forty-two per cent of trade unionists voted Labour in the 1987 General Election. The only measure which did not command the undivided support of the rank and file was the provision enabling individual union members to carry on working, without being subject to union discipline, despite a majority vote in favour of strike action. Nonetheless, only six out of ten union members still consider the principle of strike solidarity to be an article of faith.

Faced with this erosion of traditional union values, the leadership is in a state of disarray and increasingly divided. Since 1980 the formal jousts between unions of the Right and Left that used to take place regularly at the Trade Union Congress have been disrupted by the intrusion of a 'modernist' contestant unconcerned by the established rules of the tournament.

The moderate and reforming tendency within the movement is as old as British trade unionism itself. Though successive General Secretaries of the TUC have differed in many respects, they have on the whole reflected this tendency, with variable results. Today the moderates find themselves engaged mainly in trying to avoid a split within the TUC between the left-wing unions (implacably opposed to the iniquitous Conservative laws that have broken union power), and the modernists who not only accept these laws, but use them in an effort to establish sustainable cooperation between their members and employers.

Another major worry for TUC leaders has been that of finding a strategy to revive the Labour Party without depriving the unions of their dominant role in its organisation or in the definition and implementation of its policies. In addition, they have finally had to face up to the problem of declining trade union membership, but despite the creation in 1987 of a TUC Special Review Body to examine the issue, results have been mixed, with the lapse of another 240,000 membership subscriptions between the end of 1988 and the end of 1989. And this further drop has itself created financial problems in expanding a programme of co-ordinated recruitment drives started in Manchester and London in 1990. For the time being, suspicion between competing unions, afraid of losing members to their rivals, has proved stronger than the common will to strengthen the trade union movement as a whole.

Phantoms and Militants

In terms of entertainment value, the Labour conference beats the others hands down every time. The staging – though untidy – is better, and the plot less predictable. Even when the twists and turns of the action are carefully planned and the outcome known in advance, there is always a certain suspense – an unexpected development in the drama, or the unscripted improvisation of some secondary character.

From the very beginning of the October 1987 Labour conference, for example, speaker after speaker was forced to admit – either with fatalism and regret, or occasionally, with a note of admiration – that Mrs Thatcher had to be credited with the immense popular success of her council house sale and privatisation policies (nothing, at this stage, could have led one to predict the great Stock Exchange crash that was to take place just a few days later).

On the other hand, 1990 was the year of the image makers. Neil Kinnock and his henchmen and women were carefully groomed, American-style, to appeal to the public viewing the proceedings on their television screens. Delegates were dressed to impress, women in suits, men looking like business executives. In the background, a red rose was set against reassuring grey, and as the conference ended, Kinnock threw red roses from the platform at the adoring crowds. Even the opposition speeches could have been scripted (though they were not). In the words of a commentator: 'As Arthur Scargill roared from the conference rostrum against Labour's new union law policies, Mr Blair* could only just suppress his famous grin. How lucky he was: he had got his policy through – and had been opposed by Arthur Scargill into the bargain.'

Some of the participants at Labour Party conferences act for no one but themselves. Others have been mandated by their constituency party and represent tens, hundreds or sometimes thousands of members. The votes of the trade union delegates represent tens of thousands, hundreds of thousands or even millions of men and women who have not opted out of paying the 'voluntary' political contribution in favour of the Labour Party at the same time as their union dues. The number of votes cast by each delegate is determined by the size of the mandate written on the cards that they whip out of their pockets at every opportunity, ensuring that the unions have a crushing majority. The disproportion in power between the army of phantoms summoned by three or four grim-faced union bosses and the squad of militants represented by a noisy crowd of activists can throw the innocent spectator into an abyss of perplexity. It ensures that, behind the noisy front of public controversy, the Labour Party's organisation is strictly controlled by a small group of trade union leaders. Not only are they masters of the Party's political orientation, they are also its main source of finance. Only their own internal divisions and the need to maintain the prestige of the Party in the eyes of public opinion oblige them to tolerate a degree of independence among Labour MPs and to accept, reluctantly, the authority of the Labour leader.

When, in 1987, Neil Kinnock tried to extend the responsibility for the selection of parliamentary candidates to all the members of the local Labour Party, removing it from the exclusive domain of the Labour constituency committees (which were increasingly

---

* Tony Blair, Labour Party employment spokesman.

infiltrated and dominated by left-wing militants), the unions could not resist taking advantage of the opportunity to extend their influence even further: they imposed an electoral college on him, in which they would be guaranteed forty per cent of the vote, next to the Constituency Party members. During the 1988 Labour conference, Neil Kinnock was given an overwhelming vote of confidence in his role as leader of the Party. Yet during that same conference, he was to see the union block votes support – once more, and against his will – a motion confirming the Party's adherence to the policy of unilateral nuclear disarmament.

By 1990 the unions seemed more docile, agreeing in principle to a number of measures that would curtail their power somewhat in the constituencies, and cutting their own block vote from ninety to seventy per cent in conference decisions. Yet cynics would argue that these changes are largely cosmetic, introduced with an eye to public opinion, yet allowing the unions to retain overwhelming financial and structural power over the Labour Party. The real reason for their present docility has little to do with Party organisation and everything to do with their public standing – or lack of it. Ultimately, the unions need the Labour Party as much – if not more – as the Party needs them, and their very real power cannot hide a fact that is as disagreeable to them as it is to Labour: the fact that the first voters to slip through the Party's fingers were the unionised voters.

It is not the first time that union members have deserted the cause. During the 1987 conference there were plenty of veterans who could remember another conference, in 1959, at which delegates were similarly trying to draw lessons from another trio of General Elections won by the Conservatives over Labour. The explanations put forward then for the decline of the Labour Party could all be deployed once more: the Party was archaic and its identification with the toiling and exploited masses was old-fashioned. Class solidarity had been shattered by an avalanche of television sets, washing machines, cars and holidays abroad. Increasing numbers of working-class families, then as now, were buying their own homes. Hugh Gaitskell, who had been elected as leader of the Labour opposition in 1955, had already declared himself hostile to the left wing of the Party and in favour of the abolition of a clause in the Labour manifesto advocating the nationalisation of the means of production. He had also refused to bow before the then slender majority of those who wanted unilateral nuclear disarmament. But his death in 1963 made way for Harold Wilson whose remedy for the ailing Party was a little less unpalatable to the traditional Left. After the Conservative Government of Sir Alec Douglas-Home – a charming but dated escapee from Mme Tussaud's wax museum – the new brand of Wilsonian socialism, with its trendy style and love of technology, combined to give the Labour Party a new look, without inflicting on the faithful the full revisionist agony envisaged by Gaitskell.

Nonetheless, in October 1974, Labour only just avoided losing the elections again. Five months later, they had fewer seats in the Commons than the Conservatives. And in 1976, Labour's minority Government under James Callaghan survived only because of an agreement with the Liberal Party, the so-called 'Lib-Lab pact'. But it was the Conservatives themselves who contributed most to the survival of their rivals. Despite Edward Heath's success in negotiating Britain's accession to the European Economic Community, the Tories seemed incapable of offering the people what they really wanted: an alternative to the meagre but consistent security offered by the Welfare State.

In 1979, the Thatcher tornado swept away everything in its path. The Conservative Party abandoned the prudent paternalism that had prevented it from challenging the unions or touching any of the welfare structures inherited from previous Labour governments. In the event, Labour discovered that no one – or hardly anyone – cared much about this devalued inheritance, and that the power of the unions was being called into question by almost everyone, beginning with trade unionists themselves. In 1959, sixty-two per cent of all employed workers voted Labour. By 1987 this figure had fallen to forty-two per cent. Conversely, while forty per cent of employees owned their own homes in 1959 (a figure which already implied a perceptible improvement in the general standard of living), by 1987, this proportion had risen to sixty-six per cent. I like to think that historians will remember the phrase used by Ron Todd, General Secretary of the Transport and General Worker's Union, and later taken up by Neil Kinnock in his address to the delegates at the 1987 Labour conference: 'What do you say to a docker who earns four hundred pounds a week, owns his own house, a new car, microwave and video, as well as a small place near Marbella? You do not say – let me take you out of your misery, brother.'

By making contact with reality once more, Labour has been attempting to find the path that leads to power. But although the rhetoric of the annual conference is bracing in times of victory, its effects are less predictable in times of defeat. It lances the boil without revealing the cause of the infection. It anaesthetises instead of healing. The patient is examined by numerous specialists, none of whom agree about the diagnosis or the treatment, and finally great-auntie's famous cure is applied – the one that worked so well until the patient died.

In Blackpool, Brighton, Scarborough or Bournemouth, every evening, in some deserted street, down a badly lit *cul-de-sac*, or in the cold light of an empty square, a door opens slightly, a gate creaks: a meeting is about to start in the backroom of a pub, in a community theatre or in some disused church. It has been advertised at the conference with notices and posters, sometimes slickly printed, sometimes untidily scrawled with a felt tip pen. Groups of activists foregather, with or without an audience; there are discussions and arguments, sometimes fluent, sometimes woolly, and the range of subjects covered is as broad as the meetings are monotonous.

Tonight, after leaving the huge hall of the Labour Party conference, there is just time for a quick pint of ale or bitter before going to that fringe meeting where the Party's official ideologists are bound to get their come-uppance. In the event the meeting is something of a disappointment. It was not for nothing that, at the time of its inauguration in 1883, the Fabian Society placed itself under the patronage of Quintus Fabius Maximus Verrucosus Cunctator, master of tactical temporisation. Ranging from speculation to discussion, the Fabians – today and yesterday – continually put forward ideas or prudently retreat, and leave it to others to do the work.

The Tribune group, before a full hall, abandons the white robe of its left-wing virginity in order to don the latest collection of socialist styles presented by Neil Kinnock. Nearby, Militant – the Trotskyite Trojan horse, expelled from the heart of the Labour citadel before it could exterminate the garrison – escapes through one breach, sneaks in through another and begins again: the treachery of the Labour leadership is bound to be unmasked one day.

Even though the deals that really matter are struck behind the scenes, the Labour Party conference remains an open contest whose outcome can turn on unexpected manoeuvres right up to the last moment. The climax of the conference (as with the Conservatives) is the leader's speech, but though this speech sums up the Party's official line, it does not entirely cover up discordant minority voices. None of this prevents the final session of the conference from presenting a fine display of democratic fervour and unity. Manoeuvres, machinations, feints and stratagems are all submerged in a wave of unanimity. On the platform, Party leaders cross arms and hold hands in a chain, singing the farewell song, 'The Red Flag', enthusiastically taken up by the rest of the hall.

The Apotheosis of the Leader

The Conservative Party conference is positive and dynamic, like its young participants. It has the ruddy complexion and directness of the gentlemen farmers who attend it. It is as neat and well-tended as those militant Tory ladies of a certain age whose presence is inevitable at any Conservative meeting. The speeches are timed to the last second by a conference president who is as serious, and almost as sure of himself as the impeccable, excellent and irreplaceable Mrs T. used to be before the inevitable day when she was finally replaced.

With every conference there is a slogan, rousing but vague enough to justify any policy. There are motions from the floor that are in fact official, and motions of opposition officially aired for the sake of appearances, though everyone knows that ultimately they will not be carried – so many democratic gestures that give the appearance of argument without challenging the faith. When it comes to voting, the issue is too serious to be left to chance. Each vote adds up to a unanimity that is expressed, in a final apotheosis, by the intervention of the leader.

When ministers take the floor, their speeches are applauded as a matter of course, but from the intensity and length of that applause observers can gauge the speaker's popularity with the rank and file. Traditionally, the Home Secretary alone has the privilege of being heckled by the Conservative assembly, particularly if he is personally opposed to the restoration of the death penalty. Of all the subjects discussed in conference, law and order alone can arouse passions strong enough to disrupt the smooth and predictable progress of the day.

The ordered agenda of conference days is complemented by a crop of evening meetings – some political, some social – where it is possible to be a little more spontaneous. Important minority groups, such as the 'wets' under Mrs Thatcher, are at liberty to vent their bile, deploring the Government's lack of compassion and accusing it of widening the gulf between the proverbial 'two nations' of rich and poor, which Disraeli – who first coined the expression – had tried so hard to bridge.

Back at the conference, one of the Party's policy groups, such as the Bow Group, or perhaps some member of the European Parliament tries to attract attention with a particularly elegant dive into the sea of majority opinion. Elsewhere, a Conservative trade unionist manages to obtain a perfunctory handshake from Mrs Thatcher by placing himself strategically in her path during a reception for foreign delegates. His colleague will no doubt receive an equally abstracted pat on the shoulder from the classless Mr Major. Another activist, celebrating fifty years of electoral canvassing, is given a commemorative medal by the Secretary of State for the Environment. Sometimes it takes a real effort of concentration to remember that this is the Conservative Party conference, not the Labour one, or vice-versa.

But from the beginning of Mrs Thatcher's tenure, the leader's closing speech could never have been mistaken for any other. It was a general's exhortation to the troops before an assault. Her tactic was to galvanise rather than persuade. The troops for their part, remained standing throughout their leader's oration, and finally, still standing, renewed their oath of allegiance to her with an ovation that became longer and more enthusiastic with every passing year, until in 1987 it was lasting a full thirteen minutes.

By 1990 however, it had shrunk to a mere ten minutes – an omen of impending doom.

With this gesture the troops were committing themselves to pursuing – under Mrs Thatcher's leadership – the task of re-conquering society from socialism and crime, and of defending it from the cowardice of those lost Conservatives who refused to hear the call of their leader. The tone was no longer that of the old Tory Party, which disliked political platforms and much preferred the general mumblings – whether pleasant or grumpy – of leaders who were hostile to ideas but were destined by birth, and trained by the public schools, to govern the lower classes.

The election of John Major to the leadership of the Conservative Party may see a return to a less charismatic tone, but is unlikely to allow the true blue Tory to go back to his old ways. As colourless as the grocer's daughter was dynamic, Major, the acrobat's son, remains committed to the same kind of meritocratic, anti-establishment society as his predecessor. The best that the old-style Conservatives can hope for is that Major will be a 'good chap', ready, at least, to give his elders a hearing. But though they may secretly smile at the gaucheness of this 'self-made-his-own-man', so keen to emphasise his independence from the formidable Mrs T., the chances are that they will be as mistaken about him as they once were about 'poor Maggie', with her cultured voice, carefully nurtured at elocution school.

Ultimately, Conservatives of every shade are pragmatists. In 1947, Churchill's Party adopted an 'industrial charter' which, in R.A. Butler's words, insured that 'in the interests of efficiency, full employment and social security, modern Conservatism would maintain strong central guidance over the operation of the economy'. This unreserved endorsement of an interventionist State policy should have been anathema to the Tories, but they were realistic enough to realise that the electorate would never accept the loss of the advantages it had gained under a Socialist government – whatever complaints it may have had about Labour in general. The Welfare State was no longer a vague utopia in the heads of a few left-wing dreamers. It was a political reality. The 'industrial charter' was effectively a non-aggression treaty between the two parties. For more than thirty years the Tories were to accept its terms without wasting time on idle questioning, running a sporting political contest in place of social war. For the rest, nothing had changed: real politics, the politics that determined the position of Great Britain and the Empire (and subsequently the Commonwealth) in the world, remained the affair of a self-perpetuating élite which sat alternately at the head of the Government, or on the benches of Her Majesty's loyal opposition.

In 1955, Anthony Eden had smoothly taken over the reins of government from Churchill, at whose side he had served with distinction as Foreign Secretary. When the failure of the unfortunate Franco-British expedition to the shores of the Suez Canal, coupled with a very real deterioration in his health, forced Eden abruptly to hand in his resignation in January 1957, Harold Macmillan quite naturally stepped into his shoes. Once Macmillan had decided to retire, the choice of his successor seemed obvious – but to the great surprise of everyone but those whose business it was to know, the choice fell on Alec Douglas-Home. It was the most unexpected – and the last – manifestation of those peculiar processes of gestation within the body of the Party from which, in the fullness of time, a new premier would be brought forth for the country.

The unwritten law regulating this process excluded anything resembling an election. Officially, Parliament – even when reduced to the Conservative Parliamentary Group – had no voice in the decision; the party even less so. At most, a few Tory dignitaries would sound out the feelings of their fellow MPs so that the leader could take them into account if he wished. During the first days of October 1963, Macmillan had to undergo an operation of the prostate and, on the eve of the annual party conference at Blackpool, resigned from all his party duties. This meant that a candidate had to be found to take over from him as Prime Minister at the earliest opportunity. To the consternation of the Party king-makers, groups of MPs immediately began to form around possible successors, who – for their part – were canvassing more or less openly.

Lord Hailsham – one of the most popular contenders with the rank and file – completely ruined his chances of being chosen by seriously underestimating the repugnance felt by the Tory notables at the sight of the mass of the Party interfering with what was none of their business. Rab Butler was by far the most experienced contender, having been Chancellor of the Exchequer under Churchill and Deputy Prime Minister under Macmillan. He was also much admired in the country for his unassuming style of statesmanship, but among his constituency workers he was thought to be competent and uninspiring – a view that was shared by Macmillan. He was easily eliminated. Reginald Maudling lacked sparkle as a minister, and had not enough enemies to provoke an opposing groundswell in his favour.

Alexander Frederick Douglas-Home, fourteenth Earl of Home and Peer of the Realm, was Foreign Secretary at the time. For every candidate whose name was rejected, his name was thrown up. But there was a problem: he had been a member of the House of Lords since 1951, and for the past thirteen years he had not been elected. Furthermore, he was relatively unknown to the general public, and was of a retiring disposition, modest and discreet – not a man to impose his authority. But these very shortcomings would make it easier for Butler, Hailsham and Maudling – the three prima-donnas, deprived of the star part – to serve in a cabinet headed by him. On 18 October, the Queen paid a visit to Macmillan in hospital, from where he gave her the recommendation to call Lord Home to the Palace. This nomination was the result of the most successful – but also the last – manipulation undertaken by the charmed circle of wealthy or titled amateurs who had ruled over the historical force of Conservatism since its beginnings.

The choice, in July 1965, of Edward Heath as Leader of the Opposition, marked a turning point in the history of the Conservative Party. On this occasion there was no discreet exchange of views between the leading lights of Toryism. For the first time it was an open fight between three contenders, each conducting a proper electoral campaign before placing his name for a vote before the entire Parliamentary Party. Heath had been to Balliol College, Oxford, true enough, but it was only thanks to a scholarship that he had been able to afford his three years of study. His accent was a little too polished, and it was difficult to forget entirely that his father had been a builder, and his mother a lady's maid. Maybe these plebeian origins could explain his indifference to the past glories of the Empire, and his determination to integrate Great Britain into the European Community.

Edward Heath's major political achievement was to moor the United Kingdom to the continent through the admission of Great Britain to the EEC. But triumph was soon to be followed by defeat at the hands of the National Union of Mineworkers, which had engaged in a strike that was paralysing the nation. Uncommunicative, artistic and intelligent (too much of an intellectual to be a true Tory), even at the best of times Heath had been tolerated rather than loved. In Opposition, at the head of a demoralised Party, it was not long before he was removed from office. But though the man had been rejected, the popular Conservatism he represented was to survive and flourish. In another open leadership contest, the carpenter's son was replaced by the Methodist grocer's daughter, Margaret Thatcher, and the old boy network was also gradually replaced in Parliament by a new style Conservative hierarchy.

Nonetheless, the swift and ruthless dismissal of Margaret Thatcher after her third electoral victory, with an unshakable majority in Parliament, but obviously heading towards a major elector defeat, proved that the Party king-makers (the 'men in grey suits') had not entirely lost their influence. Though the choice of a new leader was conducted entirely according to the book, with every Conservative MP casting his vote in a secret ballot, it soon became clear that such a small-scale election (entirely excluding the Party rank and file) was still vulnerable to behind-the-scenes manipulation and lobbying. Once again, the Party displayed a remarkable sixth sense of survival, pitilessly abandoning their leader as soon as she threatened to become a liability, while shedding tears over her demise, and burying her under the flowers of their respect and admiration.

The Legacy of the Whigs

Tories and Whigs have between them shared power for so long that most British people – whether interested in politics or not – have some idea about the choices and attitudes that these two words imply. Yet from the moment they first entered the English language, they were charged with all kinds of contradictions. *Whig* comes from the Gaelic word *whiggamore*, which means expedition, and referred specifically to a raid against Edinburgh by Scottish insurgents in 1648. Another seventeenth-century term, *Tory* was taken from the Irish word, *toraighe*, which had come to refer to those dispossessed Irish who became outlaws, subsisting on plundering and killing English settlers and soldiers. Later the term was applied to any Irish Papist or Royalist in arms, and by the end of the century, *Tory* – with a capital T – was being inflicted as a term of abuse on the legitimists who wanted to ensure that James – the Catholic Duke of York – would succeed his brother, King Charles II, on the throne. The term *Whig*, on the other hand, was first applied to Presbyterian Scots, and was later transferred to those strict Protestants for whom the Catholicism of the Duke of York was sufficient cause to invalidate his succession to the throne.

Whigs, defenders of Parliament's prerogatives and of the non-conformist churches, against the royalist Tories, champions of the Anglican faith; liberal and reformist Whigs against conservative and authoritarian Tories: these convenient characterisations gave only a superficial approximation of reality. The wealthy landed Whig aristocracy could find no consensus when it came to the introduction of really major change, whereas Tories such as George Canning, Robert Peel or Lord Liverpool were genuine reformers. In 1809 tensions between Canning and Viscount Castlereagh, Secretary of State for War, were running so high that the two men fought each other in a duel.

Until the beginning of the twentieth century, the public was generally satisfied with the regular alternation in power between these two *coteries* which ensured regular progress without notice-ably altering the structure of society. The First World War, and the split in the Liberal Party behind the irreconcilable rivalry of Asquith and Lloyd George, did not put an end to this duality. But whereas the Conservatives responded to the growth of Socialism by closing ranks, the Liberals retreated in disorder, giving way to the emerging Labour Party. Thereafter it became an open question as to whether the traditions of Whigs and Tories could be said to be still alive. For the Socialists, coming into power for the first time in 1945, these traditions were an irrelevance masking the real struggle of the people against capitalism. But the Conservatives continued to set great store by their Tory credentials. Today, after many twists in the tale of British Liberalism and Social Democracy, it is still unclear who, if anyone, has inherited the legacy of the Whig tradition.

In 1981, the Social Democratic Party was created in an attempt to offer the electorate a centrist option that would break the now entrenched duopoly of the Labour and Conservative parties. The SDP soon joined in partnership with the established Liberal Party and by October 1985 a public opinion poll showed that thirty-five per cent of British voters supported the Alliance, against only thirty-three per cent who backed Labour, and thirty per cent who were in favour of the Conservatives. The SDP's leader, Dr David Owen, who until then had declared that there would be no clear majority at the next elections, now predicted an easy victory for the new coalition. His optimism turned out to be misplaced – yet, in this June 1987 election, there were some seven million three hundred thousand votes cast in favour of the Alliance. It was the brutality of the first-past-the-post electoral system which cheated him of an honourable showing in the House of Commons. This success (in terms of votes), and failure (in terms of seats), prompted the Liberal leader, David Steel, to suggest an immediate fusion of the two parties, with the hope of finally bursting the dam of Labour and Conservative power. He was supported in this by Roy Jenkins, Shirley Williams and William Rodgers, co-founders of the SDP with David Owen, and – like him – Labour Party apostates. Surrounded by a small group of true believers, David Owen refused to drown the identity of the SDP in that of a Party which he believed to be without principles, born of an opportunism without perspective and a political ambition shorn of policies. But by June 1990, nine years after the creation of the Party, Dr Owen was forced to admit defeat, and the rump of the SDP was finally disbanded.

The huge building that houses the Liberal Club and served as the party's headquarters is just a stone's throw from the Prime Minister's residence, and is a good deal more imposing. Looking at it today, one is overcome by a feeling of unreality. Even though it possesses some fine remains, contemporary Liberalism has little to offer the future apart from the dubious guarantee of past glory.

Like ruined aristocrats, the Liberals for a long time accepted without difficulty the need to cut down on essentials – as long as they were not deprived of superfluous luxuries. They could manage without power, so long as they had ideas: militant ecology, pacifism, the prickly defence of every kind of social, racial and sexual minority. There was less to distinguish them from the left wing of the Labour Party, than there was between the left wing and the Labour Party majority. Former Labour Party members and the numerous voters and activists – neither Labour nor Liberal – who came to the Alliance convinced they were joining a new political force, believed they would be able to knock some sense into the Liberal idealists. Dr Owen's Social Democrats thought it was an impossible task. Paddy Ashdown has stepped into the shoes of the retired Liberal leader, David Steel, to take over the merged party, and has indeed imposed a more measured – and uninspiring – tone on former Liberal enthusiasms. But in any case the question is now irrelevant since bickering over the merger has destroyed the electoral credibility of both parties. The SDP has disappeared, and in December 1990, the Social and Liberal Democrats could command barely nine per cent of support in the national opinion polls.

The real loser in these internecine squabbles has been the public at large. For some time the British people believed that the situation was clear: between a disappointing Left and an arrogant Right, a great new centre party was taking shape. Today, in the aftermath of disillusionment at the kind of pettiness that prompted the Liberals – or was it the Democrats? – to keep changing their official titles and acronyms, few people even know the correct name of the merged party. And today, hardly anyone mourns the SDP – though political analysts still occasionally regret the wasted talents of a man of David Owen's stature. Yet none of this means that the SDP has ceased to be a powerful political force. On the contrary, it is very much alive: it is led by Neil Kinnock and it now calls itself the Labour Party. It remains to be seen whether Kinnock will be successful in his bid to rally the more dynamic elements of the middle classes, without which no party can hope to govern.

9

The Exercise of Power

The Parliament of Westminster has so successfully kept up the appearance of its past greatness, that it still believes in its reality. It has even managed to impart the belief to the rest of the world. This is one of the myths on which British society is founded; but one can legitimately ask whether it is a source of inspiration, or merely a delusion. The role of Parliament is both vast and derisory. Most of the time, the general public does not concern itself unduly with examining its functions. Yet whenever there is a crisis, it is around Parliament that the country's passions are mobilised.

The Queen's Speech
Every autumn, the parliamentary year is solemnly inaugurated by the monarch. Dressed in her royal finery, she delivers the Queen's Speech, which has been written – down to the last comma – by the Prime Minister. Her Majesty is there only to dignify the will of the people, expressed by the parliamentary majority of the day.

In the House of Lords, before her vassals, the peers of the realm, attired in their robes, a bespectacled Queen Elizabeth II reads the Government's legislative programme. Before she does this, the Gentleman Usher of the Black Rod (her personal representative at the Lords) is sent to the other side of the Palace of Westminster to summon members of the Lower House before their Queen, in the House of Lords, so that they may all hear her speech together. At the sight of Black Rod, as he is known for short, the Commons Serjeant at Arms slams the double doors of the chamber in his face. This defiant gesture commemorates the rebuff inflicted on Charles I, in 1642, on the occasion of his abortive attempt to arrest five members of Parliament. Lifting up his ebony cane surmounted by a golden lion, Black Rod then strikes on the doors three times, and they are finally opened. He relays his Sovereign's orders to the honourable members of the Commons, and they promptly comply. Preceded, in pairs, by the Speaker and by the Serjeant at Arms, bearer of the Mace, escorted by Black Rod and the bewigged Clerk of the House, led by the Prime Minister and the Leader of the Opposition, followed by the ministers and their shadows, the nation's elected representatives humbly join in a procession to hear the Royal mouthpiece express their will.

No symbol of the supremacy of Parliament could be more eloquent: the more grandiose the homage paid to the monarch, the more dazzling the consecration of the sovereign people. Numerous other symbols of this supremacy – some grand and others insignificant – are meticulously preserved by custom, giving British democracy the esoteric charm that so fascinates foreigners. The Mace is not the least evocative of these symbols: originally a bludgeon, this ceremonial weapon recalls the former right of arrest vested in the Commons. Until the reign of James I, the Serjeant at Arms, carrying his protective club, did not need a warrant to perform an arrest. It is from this ancient privilege that Parliament – like all English courts of law – has inherited the right to punish for contempt*.

The Speaker's state robe of black satin damask trimmed with gold, his full-bottomed wig and black silk three-cornered hat and white gloves, the bob wig worn by the Clerk of the House, his court suit of black cloth with knee breeches and knee and shoe buckles of cut steel, his lace cuffs and jabot, the chaplain's silk cassock (not too long to cover his black silk stockings and court shoes with silver buckles): such archaic modes of dress no longer

* Contempt is defined as 'any act which offends the dignity of the House or which obstructs or impedes any member or officer of the House in the discharge of his duty . . .', and includes behaviour such as disorderly conduct in the House or abuse of the Speaker. The House retains the right to punish offenders by imprisonment, fine, reprimand, admonition or – in the case of a member – suspension or expulsion. Imprisonment may be for a specified time, or until the end of the session when the committal automatically lapses.

have any function other than that of recalling the great age of Parliament, and the respect that it should inspire. But these adornments have the additional incidental property of infusing each member of Parliament with a sense of his own importance.

Between the pomp of great circumstances and the banality of everyday life, there are other, more workaday customs and conventions that also contribute to this climate of familiar strangeness in which the nation's elected representatives and their acolytes move: the colour of the carpets – red at the Lords and green at the Commons – distinguishing their respective territories; the different bars and tea rooms, each with their own particular rules of admission and tacit codes of conduct; the House of Lords restaurant with its distinctive decorum and its bad cooking, and the one in the Commons (somewhat better), with its unofficial segregation between the Conservatives, wearing jacket and tie, and the socialists, at ease in their shirt-sleeves – unless they happen to subscribe to the new brand of well-groomed, executive socialism. In order to understand the workings of the Commons, it is pointless to look for a rule-book (there isn't one), to consult an absent written constitution, or even to look for some doctrine of power. Better to observe the exact topography of the scene, and to try and pierce the exact meaning of certain words and phrases that punctuate parliamentary life: whip, taking the whip away, pairing, backbencher, frontbencher, catching the speaker's eye, question time, standing committee, select committee, the press gallery, the lobby.

The debating chambers in the Commons and Lords are both rectangular. Opinions and Parties cannot fan out in the rainbow of their nuances and factions, from the extreme Left to the extreme Right, with the ease afforded by the semicircular continental assemblies. The opposing benches, Government majority on one side and opposition on the other, give out a clear message at the beginning of every debate: 'Whoever is not with us is against us'. The House of Lords reserves a few transverse benches for those 'cross-benchers' who refuse to accept any political affiliation and vote entirely according to the merits of the occasion, for or against the Government. The Commons has no such provision. The reductive effect of this uncompromising opposition, added to the brutality of the first-past-the-post electoral system, clearly encourages a radicalisation of extremes and accentuates the country's division in two. On the other hand, its advocates rightly point out that the system is responsible for ensuring large parliamentary majorities and hence a remarkable continuity in government.

There is another aspect to this stark parliamentary division that is less often mentioned: it is the ritual, almost playful quality of the proceedings. It has more in common with the rivalry between opposing football teams (with their supporters sometimes behaving like cacophonous hooligans), than it does with the hatred dividing two armies about to tear each other apart. The solidarity that unites the adversaries when faced with an outsider foolhardy enough to poke his nose into their family quarrel is even stronger than their antagonism. The Liberals and their Social-Democratic successors have had long experience in measuring the collusion between the two opposing forces which has so successfully made light of millions of votes, too evenly distributed across the electoral map to threaten secure local Labour and Conservative fiefs.

In the language of Westminster, the 'whip' refers both to the head of a parliamentary group and his assistants, and to the written notice, which is an expression of his authority, and which summons the members of his group – with more or less force – to the House to cast their votes as instructed. A 'one line whip', in which the written text is literally underlined once, amounts to a request to vote. A 'two line whip' is a more pressing invitation that cannot be declined without good reason. A 'three-line-whip' is an order: to defy it, except in case of *force majeure*, is equivalent to a desertion.

Pairing could simply be regarded as an ingenious device enabling MPs to retain a certain freedom of movement. It ties one member from the majority party to another from the opposition, allowing them both to be away from the Chamber – even when they have received a two line whip – without their absence having any effect on the result of the vote. But it is also a device that helps to crush every semblance of a third voice between that of the majority ruling party and a monolithic minority, waiting in the wings to take over. When there are just two of you, it is always possible to reach some *modus vivendi*, and a regular alternation in power encourages a discreet exchange of favours, which would become difficult or embarrassing in the complex negotiations and personal conflicts that accompany any coalition.

In this bi-partisan climate, the two Chief Whips – helped by their staff of promising young party hopefuls – are given better offices and are generally better treated than those of the skeletal marginal parties. They are like fathers to their parliamentary parties, and their families are often turbulent, causing them frequent anxieties. Despite the eminently personal character of pairing, they exercise a discreet supervision over it. It is also the Government Chief Whip – under the direction of the Prime Minister and the Leaders of the two Houses, and in consultation with the Opposition Chief Whip – who settles the detailed arrangements of Government business. Before any important debate, the ground is carefully prepared. Talented Whips know how to smooth over disagreements of principle in the interests of order and harmony in debate. Fights and skirmishes are generally staged to avoid unnecessary violence; insults are decently clothed in courteous formulas. 'Taking the whip away' is more painful than it sounds. It excludes the Member of Parliament from his parliamentary group; deprives him of his life-blood. The sanction is rare, and though it does not spell the political death of the patient, it is likely to send him into a profound coma.

The Speaker of the Commons is akin to a chairman. He is elected by a majority which has previously checked his popularity with the minority, but not necessarily with the Prime Minister. His is a subtle and discreet art, requiring a careful balance between severity and tolerance. 'Catching the Speaker's eye', or in layman's language, obtaining the right to speak, is one of the parliamentary exercises where his mastery is revealed. With the frontbenchers (ministers and members of the Shadow Cabinet, seated – as the expression implies – on the front benches of the chamber), the question does not arise: a comment or speech from one side calls for an answer from the other. But the backbenchers, the parliamentary rank and file, are entirely at the mercy of the Speaker. It is up to him to see or to turn a blind eye to the unspoken solicitation of the aspiring orator; up to him to show prudence and judgement in his choice. Once again, the arbitrariness of the institution is justified by an observance as restrictive as the most meticulous rules.

The Waning of Sovereignty

Four times a week members of the government come before the House to answer MPs' questions. On two of those days, the Prime Minister is also required to take the floor. It is the best opportunity to see him and his colleagues in action, and the Chamber is rarely as full as it is at Question Time.

Today the time for questions has come round again. One of the Government's faithful backbenchers has been instructed to ask the Minister a well-phrased question that will give him the opportunity to preen his feathers, unruffled by this call to lay modesty aside. The next question is more awkward; though the questioner is also a member of the Party in government, he is trying to dissociate himself from a measure he knows to be unpopular with his constituents, without risking his career by defying the whip. The questions from the Opposition benches are heavy with innuendo, and – potentially – explosive. To a practised minister, they are rarely dangerous. But, with a little presence of mind, the questioner can still have the last word in this lightning dialogue which is frequently more dramatic and more revealing than a real debate. Indeed the press is quite aware of this, and much prefers these jousts to the interminable debates in which the orators themselves seem to fall asleep at the sound of their own voices.

Parliamentary standing committees are neither as important as the imposing American Congressional committees, nor do they have the prestige of committees in other European parliaments. Select committees, set up to take evidence on particular problems, have the power to summon witnesses such as civil servants and scientific experts, and to order the production of certain documents. The institution is respectable, and perhaps unduly respected. Its reports, like the silver cutlery and bone china reserved for special occasions, are too grand for everyday use.

The British Parliament, which has been so frequently and excessively praised, has also inevitably attracted extreme criticism: though constitutionally it is the most powerful in the world, its sharpest critics claim that in reality it offers no more than a pitiful caricature of elective democracy. One should not believe them. Whatever its weaknesses, the House of Commons has the power to make or unmake governments, and its members are quite aware of the fact. More subtly, a promising politician has few chances of being picked out for a ministerial post if he has not first demonstrated in his parliamentary career that he has the ear of the House. This primacy of Parliament is reflected even in small details: on the envelopes of correspondence addressed to the Prime Minister (or any other minister), his name, unaccompanied by any title, is simply followed by the two letters, MP, Member of Parliament. The practice is in marked contrast with the custom in France, which requires that a parliamentarian who has held ministerial office – even if only for 48 hours – should be called 'Monsieur Le Ministre' to the end of his days. Nonetheless, in Great Britain as in all modern democracies, the authority of the executive is increasing at the expense of the legislature, and the strong majorities produced by the first-past-the-post electoral system have accentuated this tendency by sheltering governments, not only from the opposition, but also from disaffection within their own party.

The increasing complexity of administrative mechanisms (even in today's post-Thatcherite society), combined with greater centralisation at the expense of local authorities, have developed the role and expanded the responsibilities of central government, while the privatisation of major industries has, year by year, reduced Parliament's field of intervention without weakening the State, which retains the usual means of applying pressure politically, financially and economically.

Every elected assembly has its swamp; Westminster is just such a swamp, and the Mother of Parliaments is slowly sinking. But her decline cannot be attributed to an oppressive constitution, nor to the abuse of power by the State. Hers, uniquely, is an old woman's voluntary abdication of power. Members of the House of Commons do not think of it as a centre of action. According to their inclinations, they see it as the channel of the popular will, the antechamber of the Government, or merely as a debating society. These subjective interpretations are variants of an opinion that is shared, not only by the Commons backbenchers, but also – to varying degrees – by the Lords, the whips and their staff, the Civil Service, the Government (which dominates the House with its overwhelming authority, but which remains a part of it, and is therefore never entirely felt to be a foreign body), and finally by the press gallery, particulary the lobby.

Seen in this light, politics is not a profession but a sort of public-spirited activity. Without being unpaid (since men and women of independent means are a breed in danger of extinction), it should at least remain disinterested. Remuneration is not a right but a regrettable necessity, and should therefore be as modest as possible. Parliamentarians are expected to be enlightened amateurs; specialisation or technical competence ill becomes them. They are badly paid and crammed into narrow offices, with woefully inadequate secretarial help. When they are not being called on to deliver their votes for the party, they are left entirely to their own devices. The consequence is fierce resistance to any proposals to advance the start of business from the quaint hour of 2.30 p.m.* (since so many MPs need the morning hours to make a living), and horror at the suggestion that the receipt of remuneration from interested parties might conceivably compromise the integrity of an MP in pursuit of the public good. Divided between their constituency and the capital (where they frequently camp in somewhat precarious conditions), MPs can pay dearly in discomfort and hard work for the privilege of representing the People. The great majority are driven by a real – if strangely passive – aspiration towards the public good.

But for the ambitious (not necessarily the most gifted), a parliamentary career is nothing if it is not crowned by a job in the shadow cabinet and by ministerial office. The only form of power which backbenchers, on both sides of the House, have agreed to reject is that which is expressly conferred on them by the Constitution: effective control over the State budget and over the activities of the government. For although they can scrutinise the accounts, the reality of government expenditure escapes them;

* Except on Fridays when business starts at 9.30 a.m. and finishes at 3 p.m., allowing MPs time to return to their constituencies at the weekend.

though they examine the legislation, they are not parties to the choice and implementation of policy. Kings of the *fait accompli*, they are called to give their verdict only on cases that have already been heard. In theory, they have the power to approve or reject legislation. In practice, they will rarely sacrifice the possibility of ministerial office for the sake of parliamentary privilege. And even their powers of amendment and criticism – powers lying halfway between approval and rejection – depend entirely on what latitude the government of the day, which is theoretically subject to their judgement, chooses to accord to them.

Proposals for the reform of the system include an extension of the Standing and Select Committees' right to summon witnesses (including the most senior civil servants), strengthened with a procedure for the disciplining of contempt; a systematic right of access to independent national and international experts on both sides of a question; and a broader and more precise definition of the prerogatives of committee presidents and their staff in relation to government ministers (particularly in the case of the Treasury, Foreign Affairs, Home Office and Environment committees). But there is little chance that these expensive American-inspired amendments will ever be implemented, though the growing 'presidentialisation' of the executive makes them increasingly necessary.

The complacent puritanism of official posturing on the question justifies its own parsimony in terms of the traditional austerity of the public service. The electorate, for its part, is convinced that its representatives already have too many privileges, and is naturally hostile to any suggestion that they might be increased. A fastidious respect for tradition; a pantomime dialogue between the rumbustious approval of a majority and the barracking of an institutionalised minority: everything conspires to reduce Parliament's role by imperceptible degrees to that of a constitutional rubber stamp.

Much Loved Anachronisms

Deprived of its dearest anachronisms, Britain would survive, no doubt, but the nation would languish. The survival of the House of Lords, with its majority of hereditary peers, is regularly denounced as being an unacceptable challenge to democracy. But each time the abolitionists reflect on the practicalities of getting rid of it, they retreat in horror at the implications of the sacrilegious gesture. Over the years, from one constitutional revision to the next, they have contented themselves with limiting its powers. But reformism has mysterious properties, and several vigorous new shoots are growing on the stumps of the aristocratic tree where the democratic axe has struck.

The House of Lords rightly prides itself on being the oldest parliamentary institution in Europe. Its origins can be traced to the *Witan*, a council of nobles advising the Anglo-Saxon kings, and later constituted by the Norman dynasty into a *Commune Concilium* or great council of leading feudal lords. Today it is difficult to suppress a smile at the sight of grown men and women, laden with honours and responsibilities and dressed in a comic opera outfit, doffing their three-cornered hats three times in salutation before an assembly of peers who are solemnly welcoming them, for the first time, into the medieval setting of the Upper House, gilded by a Victorian architect. It is difficult not to pity them their arthritis as they kneel, like characters in some swashbuckling movie, to swear a feudal oath of loyalty to their sovereign; difficult also not to be amused by their tunics, decorated with heraldic symbols, and their numerous strange titles, including the very *franglais* title of *Rouge Dragon Poursuivant*.

It remains no less true that, in the eighth century of its existence, the House of Lords still exercises a direct influence on politics, and actively participates in the elaboration of the nation's legislation. Furthermore, the immutability of its ceremonial should not blind us to the remarkable powers of adaptability demonstrated by the Upper House throughout the ages. During the seventeenth-century interregnum, its members wisely kept their heads down when Cromwell conveniently forgot his formal promise to respect their rights. But after the Restoration, they paid him back in the same coin and gathered in the House for the next parliamentary session, at the usual time and the usual date, without even mentioning their long enforced holiday. They showed the same tact in 1911, when the Lower House passed an Act withdrawing their right to veto Commons legislation. Their docile acceptance of this measure made it possible quietly to forget the preamble to the Act, which had recommended that the House of Lords be replaced by an elected second chamber.

In 1958, they remained equally unmoved by the Conservative Government's creation of a non-hereditary peerage*, and absorbed the newcomers with remarkable ease. If transformation there has been, it has not been that of the institution. As if marked by a kind of predestination, from the moment they take part in the ancient ceremony of allegiance, newly elevated peers of the Realm – retired politicians or trade-unionists, leading lights of the academic world, industrialists or financiers – find themselves on an equal footing with the nineteen Law Lords and twenty-six bishops and archbishops, as well as the three royal dukes, the twenty-five dukes, the twenty-nine marquesses, the 157 earls, and all those other Lords who owe their titles not to merit – like themselves – but to their lineage. With the elevation of some and the death of others (a not infrequent event in an ageing household), the number of members hovers at around 1,150. The cordial understanding that exists between life peers and their eight hundred or so hereditary colleagues is not surprising when one knows that sixty-three per cent of the letters patent of nobility of these dyed-in-the-wool aristocrats go back only to the beginning of the century, that only fifty-five peers can claim an ancestry dating from before the sixteenth century, and that there are only seven families left whose title has been transmitted, without interruption, since the thirteenth century.

The Queen ennobles, decorates and otherwise rewards her subjects. But though it is the Royal hand that disposes, it is the Prime Minister who proposes. With a few rare exceptions where Her Majesty has free rein (such as with titles conferred on her own family, the Order of the Garter, the Order of Merit, the Order of the Thistle and the Royal Victorian Order), the twice-yearly Honours List is entirely drawn up by the Government. Whereas in France such decorations are colourfully displayed on the lapel, in England they take on the manifestation of mysterious suffixes such as MBE, GCMG, CH, which – following other punctuated acronyms

---

* Under the Life Peerages Act, 1958.

designating some degree, diploma, or position – enrich certain visiting cards with large sections of the alphabet. In addition, knights and baronets prefix their names with the title *Sir*.

The 'Honours List' is a shining example of the way in which the system so perfectly reconciles arbitrariness with moderation – if not with equity. Though it was the Conservatives who introduced life peerages, the new institution has had the effect of substantially increasing the number of Labour Peers, who – nonetheless – remain much less numerous than their Conservative colleagues. In addition to the honours conferred entirely on the basis of merit, without reference to ideology or political considerations, custom allows the Prime Minister to approach the Sovereign on behalf of a number of personalities who are politically close to him. But that same custom also requires him to include in the list he puts forward for Royal approval a proportion of names chosen by the Leader of the Opposition and other party leaders. There is no rule to determine the precise number of honours allocated to each grouping, but it is assumed that it should be more or less proportional to their strength in Parliament. Nothing obliges the occupant of No 10 Downing Street to accept all the suggestions put forward by the opposition, but a refusal to take account of them could shatter this constitution in which constraint is all the more imperative for being implicit.

Yet scandal has not entirely spared this noble institution. Just after the First World War, Lloyd George did not hesitate to put peerages up for sale, hoping perhaps to undermine a body for which the Liberals had little respect, eventually replacing it with a truly democratic second chamber. In 1976, the 'exceptional Honours List' drawn up by Harold Wilson on the occasion of his retirement as Prime Minister (an entirely customary procedure), included peerages for a number of personal friends of dubious credentials – provoking widespread acid comment. One of these – Lord Kagan – was to receive a prison sentence for tax evasion a few years later. The Tories, who had cried foul at the time, were not to be outdone; and after 1979, it became hard to ignore the coincidence between the largess bestowed on the Conservative Party by certain companies, and the elevation to the peerage of those company presidents.

But the blazons of the noble Lords still shine, despite these hints of tarnish and Labour's persistent threat to abolish the Upper House. Indeed, the Upper House enjoys health that is at least as good as that of the Labour Party itself, and a good deal better than that of the Social and Liberal Democrats, who have also felt it necessary to come up with a reform-cure for the Lords. Mrs Thatcher more than once expressed her exasperation at the petulant independence of these Lords. Yet it was also Mrs Thatcher who revived the custom – which had fallen into abeyance since 1958 – of asking the Queen to create new hereditary peerages. William Whitelaw, her most faithful ally in the Party, was honoured with the hereditary title of viscount in 1983; but in 1984, she also selected the former Prime Minister Harold Macmillan – whom she did not particularly like – for the title of earl. Thus today, at least a third of the peers of the realm can be relied on to respond to a three-line-whip from the Government, voting for or against a crucial amendment as directed.

A long-standing joke has it that the one way of ensuring a full Upper House is to initiate a debate on poaching, or on a modern English version of the Book of Common Prayer. By now the pleasantry has lost its sting. The Lords make useful contributions in all sorts of areas, from housing to health, education, the rights of old-age pensioners, and the jurisdiction of local authorities.

Faced with a massive majority of 438 Conservatives, of which a good many are hereditary peers, the 112 Labour Lords try to make up for their small number by a more assiduous attendance record. Their fifty-three Liberal Democrat and seventeen Social Democratic colleagues* sometimes join forces with them, but it is the support of the 243 cross-benchers that can tip the balance. Many of them are high-flying experts. Their eminence in a particular field is what has led them to the Lords, and they expect to bring their expertise to bear on relevant subjects in debate, remaining on the look-out for any *faux pas* by the Government or any error of judgement on the part of the majority. Their personal authority

---

* A minority of Social Democratic peers chose not to join the merged Social and Liberal Democratic Party despite the demise of the SDP in June 1990.

is usually more significant than the weight of their numbers. Conscious of the doubtful character of their legitimacy, the Lords are often more sensitive to public opinion than their elected colleagues in the Lower House, whose position is sanctioned by the people's vote. They were the first, in the nineteenth century, to admit the press to their public debates, and the first again, in 1985, to accept television cameras, followed by the Commons in 1989. The Lower House is the battle field in which the political armies confront each other, but it is in the Upper House that their strategies are refined.

The Fourth Estate

The expression 'the Fourth Estate of the realm' was used in writing for the first time, by Macaulay in 1828, to refer to the press gallery. Today, Parliament's relations with the press are still those of one power with another.

In their protracted constitutional struggles with the monarchy in the seventeenth century, members of the House of Commons felt they needed to preserve the secrecy of their deliberations. To protect themselves from the power of the King, it was essential that nothing be revealed to him that he might use against the House. Major conflict first arose under Charles I, when – in a famous speech – Speaker Lenthall threw his lot in unambiguously with the Commons, saying 'I have neither eyes to see nor tongue to speak in this place, but as the House doth direct me whose servant I am.' By the time the King was no longer to be feared, the habit of secrecy was well entrenched. Though censorship before publication was abandoned in England as early as 1695, it was not until nearly a century later, in 1771, that the right to publish proceedings in Parliament was granted. The final breakthrough came in 1803, when a speech by William Pitt about the war against France was ignored by the press because no reporter had managed to find a place in the crowded public gallery. Henceforth, on the speaker's orders, the last bench in the gallery was set aside for the exclusive use of the press.

Today the Palace of Westminster press gallery not only has its own benches, separate from the public, but also its own press offices, a library, a newsroom, a television room, a restaurant and a bar. For a long time the gallery was the lucrative monopoly of London journalists, who would sell their copy to the provincial press. In 1881 it opened its doors to newspapers from all over the kingdom, and eventually even accepted a hundred or so correspondents from overseas. These restrictive practices, which are now dictated only by lack of space, make it appear that the covering of parliamentary news is a privilege rather than a right. Yet for the ambitious journalist, the press gallery is merely an antechamber. The hacks who frequent it are the rank and file; their task is limited to the straight reporting of parliamentary debates. Their generals do not mingle with the troops, but meet in the privacy of the Lobby – staff headquarters for tactical analysis and strategic reflection. Before 1914, it would have been inconceivable to see them entering the Commons without a top hat, and it is only recently that light suits have been tolerated.

It was in 1884 that an outsider was first authorised to penetrate the Lobby, which had hitherto been reserved exclusively for members of the Commons. History does not record the name of this privileged individual. A small number of others were gradually allowed to mingle with MPs, in the sanctum of the House. Together they came to form the 'Lobby', in its other meaning: that informal club of initiates who are both interpreters to the public and watchdogs of Parliament and Government. At present, about one-third of the members of the press gallery are also members of the Lobby. They gravitate mainly towards Annie's Bar, which is open only to them and to Members of Parliament. The conversation consists mostly of gossip, rather than secrets of state; but friendships are struck, more or less disinterestedly, and old hands can sometimes detect, in the bar's either dull or animated atmosphere, the foretokens of an impending crisis or some dramatic turn of events.

The daily briefings of the Lobby by the Prime Minister's press secretary provoke envy and hostility. They are frequently denounced as the inadmissible privilege of a freemasonry, in the secrecy of which information is improperly manipulated. In practice, they have lost much of their importance, and political journalists with no other source of information would be sadly failing their public. The real advantages of the Lobby are the same as those of any good club: it creates special ties between its members and the members of that other great club, the Commons; it places them on an equal footing with each other and gives them a vantage point from which to look down on those who belong to neither club.

But there are also critics of the system within the Lobby itself. They object to the rules of anonymity that bind the members of the club, and would like to put names to the information they receive from Government spokesmen, and in particular from the Prime Minister's press secretary, who under Mrs Thatcher was the powerful Bernard Ingham. The *Guardian* and the *Independent* have started a rebellion against these rules, which they believe to be prejudicial to the clarity and objectivity of news reporting, and are refusing to attend Lobby briefings altogether. The opposition is committed to abolishing the system, but experienced journalists are all the more sceptical about these promises, having seen the skill with which these recent converts played the system when they were in power.

The backbenches contain the odd eccentric whose pronouncements often make good copy, and the views of a former minister might also be thought worth listening to by a member of the press gallery. But on the whole, political journalists are unlikely to take much notice of the eager backbencher, trying to get his opinions aired in the papers or on television. Only Hansard, which is obliged to, will print his every word, page after page. The neutralisation of the average MP has created a void in political life which leaves the press hungry for more substantial fare. Government is only too happy to step in and fill the void, though it hardly chooses to do so through the unsubtle medium of the daily Lobby briefings; a rumour, a half-revelation will be carefully spread, or – even better – a secret document is leaked, exclusively, to a newspaper which makes all the more of it for being able to boast of a scoop.

Some British journalists, however, are beginning to ask themselves with increasing anxiety whether the scandal hounds and their discoveries are not ultimately detrimental to the truth. Caught up between governmental secrecy, which favours every kind of manipulation, and the routine of Parliament, which rumbles on away from the public eye, it is easier for the press to offer its public a few good melodramas, complete with hero and villain, or some elegant and witty commentary which gives the author an opportunity to shine, than it is to chip slowly away at the mask of official truth.

10, 11, 12 Downing Street

His name is Murdo MacLean. His title is Private Secretary to the Chief Whip, and he has two offices: one in the Palace of Westminster, and the other in an elegant eighteenth-century house at No. 12, Downing Street. No. 12, No. 11, residence of the Chancellor of the Exchequer, and No. 10, the Prime Minister's official residence, are three separate but intercommunicating houses. All that separates the offices of the head of the Government from the offices of the head of the Civil Service, is a padded door.

This architectural trinity of modest yet elegant exterior, reveals the symbiosis that exists between matters political and economic, between the executive and the legislature, between the Government and the Civil Service. As for MacLean, he is the perfect guide to this mysterious world of British politics – a world still protected by the secrecy that remains an obsession with every British government. This secrecy casts a shroud on trivial and important matters alike, making no distinction between the national interest and the passion for political manipulation. At the end of the labyrinth, there is an enigma: authority does not open its heart to the first-comer who – through perseverance or good luck – has succeeded in penetrating its lair. To subdue the monster one must know the solution to the riddle. In Great Britain, it is the Private Secretaries who are the keepers of the magic word, and their model – the most accomplished example of that permanent contradiction of which they are the incarnation, but which their professional duty requires them to transcend – is probably the Private Secretary to the Government Chief Whip.

Like every other Private Secretary, MacLean is a civil servant, and therefore apolitical by definition; which in no way stops him from collaborating directly with the Whip, whose function is not only political, but partisan. In his capacity as the Whip's right hand man, he is party to the strategy and plans of the majority, quite as if he were the most devoted member of the Conservative

Party. And if the Conservatives were to be defeated tomorrow, that same Murdo MacLean would become the Private Secretary to the Labour Chief Whip, or the SLD Whip, or the Devil himself, were the Devil to become the next majority's Whip. Remaining in this most political of jobs, he would serve his new master (yesterday's opposition) with zeal and probity, without however jeopardising his relations with today's opposition, nor betraying his old master in favour of the new one. From the leader of the Party to the most junior minister, every new member of Government has his own Murdo MacLean, who will work as faithfully for him as he did for his predecessor. The Minister may or may not like his new Principal Private Secretary*; he may wonder about his personality, his efficiency, his faults – but never for a moment will he question his loyalty. To do so would be an attack on the constitutional requirement that the nation's administrative service should remain impartial. Worse still, it would be an impropriety.

The Principal Private Secretary is an honest broker; his fellow team members in the Private Office are, like him, intermediaries between the Minister and the Civil Service of which they are a part, and where most of them are likely to remain for the rest of their careers. In fact, the Private Secretary has a dual loyalty to the Minister, and to the Civil Service. In his book on the Private Office†, Sir Nicholas Henderson – former Ambassador to Bonn, Paris and Washington, and Private Secretary to five different Foreign Secretaries, Labour as well as Conservative – elaborates: 'it is this duality that gives him his exceptional influence; he represents to the Minister the opinions of the Office, and to the latter the will of the Minister. Neither commission would carry the same weight if it were not balanced by the other'. 'Impresario' and 'hinge' are two other words used by Sir Nicholas to describe the irreplaceable function of the Private Secretary.

The memorable BBC satirical series, *Yes Minister*, has staged for posterity the archetypal dialogue between the civil servant and the politician. Though the principal role undoubtedly belongs to

---

* A Minister has one Principal Private Secretary and several Assistant Private Secretaries working for him in his private office.
† *The Private Office*, Weidenfeld and Nicolson, London, 1984.

the Minister, that of Permanent Secretary to the ministry runs a close second. There are forty-one Permanent Secretaries, each in charge of the administration of his own ministry. They are masters in the art of conversation and of silence: conversation, as it was understood in more polite centuries – courteous, and neither sententious nor too revealing, but amusing and sometimes instructive, always avoiding rhetorical effects and cynical observations; silence, their principal defensive and offensive weapon, a silence made of omission and numerous well-placed pauses, which the most skilful practitioners subtly embellish with the rhetoric of modesty. For the friend and ally, what is not said goes without saying, but when words are spoken in an open conflict, they can break the adversary or ruin the chatterbox himself. Like war, the art of evasion is all in the execution.

These forty-one Permanent Secretaries belong to the smartest trade union in the Kingdom, the First Division Association, which covers the eight thousand or so civil servants in the highest streams of the British administrative service. It is often objected that a vastly disproportionate majority of them have had a public school and Oxbridge education; but though it is true that these shared origins cut them off from the common run of mortals and give them a sense of solidarity that is stronger than their rivalries, they have also endowed them with a moral and intellectual training uniquely well adapted to their function.

The Art of Quiet Confidence

On the 1st of January 1988, Robin Butler, Second Permanent Secretary, Public Expenditure at the Treasury, was promoted to the top job in the Civil Service, that of Secretary to the Cabinet. As such, he became the Prime Minister's right hand man, coordinating the Government's action, and serving as principal intermediary between Government and Civil Service. The Honours List, published the day before, had announced his elevation to the rank of Knight Commander of the Bath, which gave him the right to the initials KCB after his name, as well as the title of Sir. On the same day, his predecessor, Sir Robert Armstrong, had received a life peerage with the title of Baron.

For the student of British politics, it is an illuminating exercise to play the biographer for a while, and explore the parallel lives of these two Civil Service luminaries. For despite eleven years of Thatcher government, despite the rise of the entrepreneur and the promise of a classless society under John Major, the old school tie still dominates the higher reaches of the Civil Service.

Robert Armstrong received his early education at the Dragon School in Oxford, a preparatory school for the children of an intellectual élite. The Dragon School quite naturally led on to Eton, from where it was but a step to be offered a place at Christ Church, one of the smartest of Oxford colleges. Robin Butler went to Harrow, where he already displayed enough wisdom to divert attention from his clear intellectual gifts through the excellence of his performances in the best rugby and cricket teams. At University College, Oxford, he will perhaps be better remembered for having been a rugby Blue, than he will be for his meteoric career in the Civil Service. He is also the founder of an exclusive cricket club, 'The Mandarins', which only Whitehall civil servants can join.

Robert Armstrong and Robin Butler were both recruited by the Treasury, which carries the same prestige in the higher spheres of the State in Britain, as the *Inspection des Finances* does in France (it is by virtue of being Lord of the Treasury, not Prime Minister, that the head of the Government is entitled to reside in 10 Downing Street). Even more significantly, they were both put through the indispensable training provided by the private secretariat.

Robert Armstrong was Private Secretary to the most remarkable Conservative minister of the post-war era, Richard 'Rab' Butler (whose outstanding qualities probably cost him the Prime Ministership). Between 1970 and 1975 he was an equally successful Principal Private Secretary first to the Conservative Prime Minister, Edward Heath, and then to the Labour Prime Minister, Harold Wilson, before finally becoming Secretary to the Cabinet in 1979 and head of the Home Civil Service in 1983. Robin Butler was Private Secretary to the Financial Secretary at the Treasury in 1964, and followed closely in Armstrong's footsteps, working with him in the Prime Minister's private office as an Assistant Private Secretary to Heath and Wilson between 1972 and 1975, and eventually returning to 10 Downing Street as Principal Private Secretary to Mrs Thatcher between 1982 and 1985. In 1988, he, in his turn, became Secretary to the Cabinet and head of the Home Civil Service.

In spite of such brilliant beginnings, none of these achievements would have been sufficient to guarantee these men the ultimate prize had they not both possessed that mysterious gift, that indescribable ease, that *je ne sais quoi*, without which an Englishman in the Civil Service – whatever his merits – will forever be condemned to playing secondary roles. Robert Armstrong's father was director of the Royal Academy of Music, and the young Robert – an accomplished pianist and a pretty good tenor – sang in one of the most famous of English choirs, the Bach Choir. Later he was elected to the board of trustees of the Royal Opera House, Covent Garden, and continued to be an active member even after he was made Secretary to the Cabinet and took up his functions as head of the Civil Service (when he became the honorary secretary). A man of taste, and of passions, Robert Armstrong was not prisoner to a single ambition. It is perhaps because he had within him the potential for another destiny that he was accorded an undisputed primacy among his peers.

Robin Butler frequently used to bicycle to work. It was not an affectation, but a practical way of staying fit. In the slightly starchy atmosphere of scepticism prevalent in Whitehall, his natural enthusiasm and open delight in action and decision-making must have compelled recognition. True superiority is sometimes revealed in such nuances. At any rate, in a country where self-importance is self-defeating, these fine distinctions can be decisive for the prospects of anyone who aspires to greatness.

Behind the higher echelons of the Civil Service where such subtle strategies take place, there is an indistinct mass of public servants who do not enjoy particular prestige in the outside world. Though their honesty is not generally questioned, they are certainly not credited with great efficiency. The compartmentalisation of the different ministries and the absence of any national bureaucracy at a regional level – such as the *préfectures* in France – far from reducing the power of central government, effectively increase it and considerably slow down any decision requiring the approval of several ministries. Local authority employees are even less popular. They are credited with more prejudice than sense or efficiency, and are either accused of pandering to the lunatic Left or of falling in with the heartless Right. Whether for reasons of administrative efficiency or political expediency, Labour and Conservative governments have been continuously gnawing at the power of the local authorities since the end of the Second World War – to the great indifference of the general public.

Thatcherite pragmatism was never more appreciated by the public than when it translated this diffuse sense of irritation into action. During her second term in office, Mrs Thatcher engaged Lord Rayner – Managing Director of the immensely successful and efficient Marks & Spencer – to infuse the Civil Service with something of that fighting spirit that enables dynamic companies to get the better of their competitors. By the end of 1985, 206 separate suggestions for improvements by the barbarically named Efficiency Unit and Financial Management Initiative had resulted in savings. Certain proposals for reform were drafted and well received; but they were soon to be lost in the sea of studious negligence that is common to all bureaucracies. Nonetheless, between 1979 and 1989, the number of public servants was reduced (largely by reclassifying their jobs) from 732,300 to 567,200 in line with the Government's policy of controlling administrative costs and efficiency.

Doctrinaire as ever – but for the last time – Mrs Thatcher was persuaded by her advisers that the best strategy for forcing the local authorities to be less profligate was a fiscal one. The introduction of the poll tax (officially called the community charge) to replace the old property rates was designed to make local government more 'accountable to the people' by obliging everyone – including the least well off – to pay the same amount for the local services they were getting. Only the least well-off would be entitled to pay a smaller portion, set at twenty per cent. Not only were the old rates inequitable, she believed, placing excessive burdens on industrial and commercial establishments as well as the propertied elderly; they also shielded a significant proportion of the electorate from the financial implications of the policies for which they were voting. When forced to pay exorbitant local charges, so the argument ran, the local tax-payer would know whom to blame, and extravagant local authorities would be forced to curtail their spending through the power of the vote.

But what Mrs Thatcher – normally so sensitive to the vagaries of public opinion – had completely failed to anticipate, was the deep-seated anger that the new tax provoked, not only among its victims, but also among a significant proportion of those who benefited by it. The new tax was immediately opposed for its regressive character both by Labour and by moderate Conservatives, until Mrs Thatcher was forced to concede defeat to the extent of introducing a package of rebates for the less well-off. Despite these changes, the tax remained deeply unpopular, and many people believe that it proved to be the first nail in the Thatcherite coffin. When in November 1990, Michael Heseltine challenged Mrs Thatcher for the leadership of the Party, he picked out the community charge as being one of the issues most likely to bring down the Conservatives at the next election. And when finally, John Major was chosen as the Party's new leader, he effectively endorsed this judgement by appointing Heseltine to the job of Secretary of State for the Environment, with responsibility for reforming the poll tax.

But although the first woman Prime Minister could not last forever, her legacy cannot be ignored. When she won the June 1987 election, she became the first party leader in Britain this century to carry off three successive electoral victories. On the 1st of January, 1988, with a reign of eight years, 244 days, she exceeded this century's record of political longevity for a Prime Minister, previously held by Herbert Henry Asquith, Liberal Prime Minister from 1908 to 1916. It would be impossible to discover in Thatcherism a coherent strategy founded on logical reflection, but the style is eminently recognisable. Over the years it has led to a considerable strengthening of the executive's power, and with it the equilibrium of every institution has been modified.

Nonetheless, one should not credit Mrs Thatcher with virtues or with faults that were not hers. She, too, inherited certain practices which she had to accept and which she transmitted to her successor unchanged. She had always deemed herself lucky to have been elected leader while her Party was in opposition, for the salaried head of Her Majesty's loyal Opposition, *ex officio* member of the Queen's Privy Council, is kept abreast of events and decisions related to the nation's security and vital interest by the very person whom he intends to supplant. He receives twice-weekly parliamentary practice in leading the attack against the policies of the moment, and is indeed a Shadow Prime Minister, each day better prepared for the moment when a new majority will give him the mandate to govern in the flesh. John Major, the youngest man to have been elected to the British Premiership this century, had not benefited from any of these advantages when he was plunged head first into the nation's biggest crisis since Suez – the 1991 Gulf War. By taking over from Mrs Thatcher while the Conservatives were still in power, he was being elevated to the job of Prime Minister with only three years' experience in the Cabinet, and no experience whatsoever in the Shadow Cabinet. Such a situation, some people believe, must never be allowed to arise again.

The Tyrant, the Mandarin and the Entrepreneur

From the moment a new leader is installed in his official home, he disposes of more discretionary powers than many a potentate. He is not even tied by traditions of loyalty to the Shadow Cabinet that was formed around him and is dissolved as soon as the Queen calls him to the Palace, and his authority over the members of his actual Cabinet is also immense. A Secretary of State needs to be a strong personality not to be intimidated by the impartial authority of his Principal Private Secretary and the longevity of the ministry's Permanent Secretary; as if that were not enough, he is not even given responsibility for choosing the Junior Ministers who are to help him run his own department. Almost everyone is nominated by the Prime Minister. The only concession to the Secretary of State is that he may choose two political advisers, whose joint influence, however, weighs little in the balance against a Civil Service that is disinclined to welcome intruders. Only two posts generally escape this Prime Ministerial expansionism: that of Chancellor of the Exchequer, the most important and prestigious, and that of Foreign Secretary.

When the leader of the Government chooses the members of his Cabinet, he takes account of different internal party factions and of the balance of power between them, as well as the popularity or docility of those he appoints. But when it comes to choosing a Chancellor of the Exchequer, the Prime Minister gambles on his own future. The Chancellor's skills are too technical for the Prime Minister to fear being overshadowed by him, and he does not usually provoke any passion on the part of the public. But an ill-judged increase in the level of income tax or of the taxes on beer or tobacco, and the whole Government becomes unpopular. He is the sole architect of the Budget which, every year, is elaborated in the most impenetrable secrecy (one of the many veils of secrecy behind which the executive in Britain shrouds itself), and – as the purveyor of the public purse – he dominates all his colleagues, who have no recourse against him other than appeal to a Star Chamber hearing, presided over by one of the PM's faithful, or by the Prime Minister himself. An intimate and permanent dialogue between the occupants of No. 10 and No. 11 Downing Street is a crucial condition of success or failure – a success for which they share the praise (with a premium for the Prime Minister), or a failure for which the entire party will have to pay the price. With hindsight, it is obvious that the resignation in October 1989 of Margaret Thatcher's Chancellor, Nigel Lawson, and his unusually frank condemnation of the Prime Minister's policies, along with Sir Geoffrey Howe's resignation speech, sounded the knell of Maggie's downfall. It was left to her pack of backbenchers to do the rest.

What happens outside Great Britain does not greatly interest the public at large, except on occasions when the Government is given an opportunity to silence those foreigners who have the presumption to place their own interests before those of the British. The attitudes of the political élite are not substantially different, but they believe themselves to be uniquely equipped to understand and guide the foreigner. Undoubtedly, few bureaucracies in the world are as well adapted to their task as The Foreign and Commonwealth Office. Humility is not its strong point, but neither is vanity a major weakness. It fosters conformity, in the guise of humour, and contains a good deal of sensitivity, sometimes enhanced and sometimes smothered by intransigent patriotism. Within it, one finds the unconscious romanticism of old families that have been forced to sell their silver but have kept their manners, and the scepticism of witnesses who have seen lies and truthfulness result in similar massacres, with victims and executioners impartially forgotten by posterity. In a word, one finds professionalism.

There have been many good Foreign Secretaries, and a few great ones. Their duet with the Prime Minister is more difficult to handle than that between the PM and the Chancellor of the Exchequer. Foreign Secretaries feature too frequently in the headlines not to be seen as rivals or possible successors to their leader; and tradition has frequently opened the doors of No. 10 to them. A high-profile leader is always sure of reaping the credit for a successful economic policy, but he does not necessarily lose face by admitting to a lack of expertise in technical matters which he leaves in the hands of a financier. Foreign policy on the other hand, is above all a matter of politics; the Prime Minister must be seen to be its author, and his Foreign Secretary merely the interpreter. Neither the Prime Minister, nor *a fortiori*, the Foreign Secretary will ever admit to the reality of these tensions. The Government doctrine of collective responsibility has it that all important questions should be debated in cabinet, before a decision is collectively reached, and thereafter collectively defended. In these deliberations, the Prime Minister is merely *primus inter pares*. As is so frequently the case however, practice belies the theory.

In November 1987, Lord Hailsham – in his first address to the Upper House since retiring from the Government, where he had held the post of Lord Chancellor – spoke in praise of the Cabinet as 'one of the permanent gifts conferred by British political genius on the science and art of civilised government'; but he immediately went on to deplore the increasingly frequent use of secret Cabinet Committees (which he numbered at far more than a hundred) to replace its collegiate meetings.

When Mrs Thatcher first came to power, her aim had not been to increase State intervention, but on the contrary, to restrain it. In 1982 she got rid of the Central Policy Review Staff (more generally known as the Think Tank) – which was supposed to provide the Government with non-partisan analysis – preferring instead a French-style cabinet of advisers who shared her neo-liberal views on the limited role of the State, and whose role was strictly limited to giving her personal advice. Her sincerity was not in doubt: she shared the parliamentarian's hostility to bureaucracy, and she had a grocer's daughter's faith in the sanctity of profit; but after twelve years of uninterrupted power, it became possible to distinguish between changes that she had brought about herself, and the ambitions that she had sacrificed – by choice or necessity – to the *éminences grises* of Whitehall.

After the Liberal, Herbert Asquith, son of a small businessman in the wool trade, whose record tenure at the head of the country she surpassed; after Edward Heath, son of a builder and a domestic servant, whom she supplanted as leader of the Conservative Party to become Prime Minister; not to mention her Labour predecessors on the other side of the barricade – it was the turn of Margaret Thatcher, born Roberts, to demonstrate that, without repudiating any of its prejudices, the establishment could be made to bow before talent and energy, however lowly their origins.

Nonetheless, it would have been difficult to imagine Margaret Thatcher, with her immaculately groomed hair and her affable official smile, repeating the easy gesture of Harold Macmillan on the day of his admission into 10 Downing Street, in 1957. Scribbling casually on a piece of scrap paper, he had written the following 'motto for the Private Office and Cabinet Room', taken from Gilbert and Sullivan's operetta, *The Gondoliers*: 'Quiet, calm deliberation disentangles every knot'. This amateurism, bred of experience, wisdom and humour, belongs to an age which she buried without regret.

But she was even more unlike her predecessor Edward Heath, whose biography is in many ways so similar. Both received scholarships to go to grammar school and Oxford, and both started out in power with similar principles. Heath was haunted by the post-war spectres of inflation and spiralling wage demands, and was elected on the promise of reducing the hold of the unions and of the State over the economy. But he very quickly realigned himself with the Keynesian model employed by all his predecessors, Labour and Conservative, and following their example, resorted to the exorcism of dialogue. As a music lover and amateur musician, he diverged from the philistinism of traditional Tories, and had a passion for sailing. They could not quite accept him, but they admired him.

Margaret Thatcher's programme did not differ substantially from the one drawn up by Edward Heath, but the style was all her own. Instead of dialogue, which she considered synonymous with capitulation, she chose confrontation. Three million unemployed, record levels of interest rates, a fight on an unprecedented scale with the unions, the collapse of obsolescent industries – none of these made her give an inch of ground. And once she had established a reputation for sticking consistently to her policies, she profited from a combination of good luck and judicious – and discreet – amendments to these very policies. In particular, the subsequent abandonment of the strict tenets of monetarism in favour of a financial liberalization that allowed easier access to mortgage finance and a consequent rise in the value of the houses owned by mortgage-holders; a halving of unemployment due to a rise in demand as great as those she had accused previous governments of irresponsibly seeking to engineer; a fortunate reduction in the world price of commodities; a sustained reduction in union militancy; Labour's disastrous defence policy; and a dramatic and genuine improvement in the performance of public sector industries: these developments, partly serendipitous and partly deserved, earned her a third term of office against an Opposition that had failed to convince of its competence in government.

The notables of the Conservative aristocracy allowed themselves to be seduced by the conquering euphoria of Thatcherism, and she continued to handle them with tact. But she was finding it increasingly difficult to hide her irritation with the traditionalist 'Wets' within the party. She responded to the belligerence and scorn that united artists and intellectuals against her by treating them with the hostility and disdain of a plain-speaking housewife. On the other hand, top civil servants – who had not been spared by her while she was leader of the Opposition – were surprised to find favour with her in her new incarnation as Prime Minister, and thereafter treated her with a protectiveness born of gratitude. This she exploited with all the skill and charm of a femininity which her enemies were quite wrong to deny her.

Making full use of her constitutional authority during her first premiership, she was able to pick as many as nine Permanent Secretaries to fill the posts of their retiring colleagues. According to the judgment of one civil servant who owed her nothing, 'she had the intelligence to choose "can do men" rather than "yes men"'. Nonetheless, the great crusade that she had launched to revive the public services, enfeebled – in her view – by years of Socialist interventionism, was not successful. In 1979, she had placed Sir John Hoskyns – one of the businessmen whom she had mobilised to lead the offensive – at the head of a group of personal advisers. Three years later, returning to the private sector, he admitted to having failed all along the line: not a single one of his proposals for reform had been implemented, nor even properly examined. He attributed this defeat not only to the passivity of the Civil Service, but also to the indifference of the press. Mrs Thatcher did not appear to be unduly upset by this defeat of the entrepreneurs by the mandarins. No doubt she was beginning to see the advantages of a closed circuit between the executive and the top echelons of the Civil Service – especially when the executive tended to mean the person of the Prime Minister.

Churchill's War Cabinet (or even the Government that he constituted just after the defeat of Labour in 1951) and the Governments of Eden and Macmillan all contained a number of outstanding personalities around the Prime Minister, however formidable his presence. The crucial role played by the Cabinet could be attributed as much – if not more – to their presence within it, as to the nature of the institution, or to God-knows-what doctrine of collective responsibility. Its meetings were like gatherings of old friends, with all their rivalries and petty quarrels, but accompanied by a good dose of conviviality and cheerfulness. Labour Cabinets did not have quite the clubby atmosphere of their Tory analogues, but whatever the authority – not to say the authoritarianism – of the Prime Minister, he remained a friend among companions. Struggles for influence and underhand tricks were commonplace within it, and personal enmities flourished behind closed doors. However, a Bevin, a Bevan, a Gaitskell, a Michael Foot or a Tony Benn had personalities that were too flamboyant to be hidden under a bushel.

In spite of the secrecy that surrounded them, everyone knew that Mrs Thatcher's Cabinet meetings were not conducive to laughter. 'A brilliant tyrant surrounded by mediocrities': with this quip that did the rounds of Parliament, Harold Macmillan (whom the tyrant had just elevated to the hereditary title of Earl of Stockton), gave – shortly before his death – the best explanation of the phenomenon. Margaret Thatcher was alone. She did not seek out this isolation, but power – the prolonged exercise of power – progressively created a vacuum around her. The first to leave her were the wets, followed by her first Foreign Secretary, Lord Carrington, and some of her most faithful followers – her mentor, Keith Joseph, Norman Tebbit, and William Whitelaw, the wisest, the most useful, the last member of the old guard in her cabinet. The corollary to this solitude was the increasing weight of her *entourage* – her Private Secretary, her Press Secretary – who exercised greater influence over her than any of her cabinet members. A few top civil servants even began to express fears for the famous independence of the bureaucracy that had always been left unmoved by the winds and tides of political change. Governmental longevity meant that numerous civil servants were now spending the crucial years of their career entirely serving the leader of one party, quite as if they were that leader's exclusive servants. But – unknown to her – the dangers attendant upon such longevity were also threatening Margaret Thatcher herself. Her increasing isolation had shielded her too long from growing public and party disaffection – until the day, in November 1990, when the resignation of her Deputy Prime Minister and Leader of the House, Geoffrey Howe, proved to be one resignation too many, and set in motion the chain of events that were to lead to her downfall.

Secrecy

There would be no threat to the integrity of the Civil Service nor to the autonomy of ministers and the authority of Parliament over the executive, and the press would immediately shine its spotlight on Whitehall's active hive, were it not for one massive obstacle – secrecy, or the unwritten but stringent law of silence that confounds misplaced curiosity with obstruction and chicanery. This secrecy behind which the executive hides (in Great Britain more than in any other Western democracy) probably owes more to tradition and education than it does to reasons of State.

The people of Britain have never really had to fight for power. Over the centuries the establishment has adopted the path of prudent reform, gradually conceding power to the majority. But this piecemeal approach to change enabled it to preserve certain corners of privilege, and the people have always been excluded from ceremonial halls too small to admit the crowd, or from clubs with restrictive membership. Important matters are not for discussion in public; it is officers who are responsible for strategy, not the other ranks; the great and the good may have their foibles, but it is not for the public to know about them, or they may lose confidence in their leaders. Like Venice with her doge, Great Britain – a nation of landowners, merchants and seamen – was, under her monarch, a patrician republic; and her patricians did not scorn to use the tool of democracy to gain support for their enterprises. At the same time, they never intended to relinquish control. By cloaking their activities in secrecy, they had just one goal: to rid themselves of interference.

One only has to read the diaries of Samuel Pepys to see another kind of secrecy fully displayed. This secrecy is not always official; it hovers around the periphery of power, engendered probably in public schools and religious congregations. It disguises faltering steps or a wrong turning, a lustful glance or a hand grasping at the forbidden fruit. It is the unofficial secrecy that cloaks itself in the mantle of discipline, delivering sermons and *communiqués*. It derives from the ancient conflict between public morality and private transgressions. Because it has concealed or minimised the predictable risks of any action, it is subsequently forced to disguise or dissimulate any unexpected failures.

In 1987, after years of procrastination, it was finally decided to revise that Bible of secrecy, the 1911 Official Secrets Act. Before such a momentous decision was arrived at, numerous civil servants had been charged, some condemned, others acquitted; journalists had repeatedly been ordered to reveal their sources and countless reputedly secret documents had been embargoed – despite the fact that their contents were widely known. The definition of secrecy contained in the Act was so broad as to deny the very existence of the Secret Services. Its revision, begun in 1988, has eliminated some of the most absurd provisions, but such changes can make little difference while the scope of the Act remains as broad and imprecise. And real change can be achieved only when Parliament and the press demand and obtain greater control over its application, and when there has been a sea-change in the mentality of governments, the Civil Service and the judiciary.

In Western democracies, the secret services tend to conflate revolution, conspiracy and the political Left, enveloping them all in the same distrust. MI5 and MI6 are no exception to this rule. From 1909 to 1939, the heads of the British special services were all men of the Right, and only clear and unequivocal right-wing opinions could reassure them entirely. So they did not hesitate to employ Kim Philby, a member of an Anglo-German association with Nazi sympathies. His Soviet masters knew just what they were doing when they chose that particular cover for his activities.

With the advent of Fascism in Italy and National-Socialism in Germany, General Franco's victory over the Spanish Republicans, followed by the Second World War and the strong movement of public opinion against totalitarian ideologies, the Left was finally rehabilitated. But this rehabilitation was not without ambiguity. Following the example of Philby and his accomplices Burgess and Maclean, Anthony Blunt had allowed himself to be recruited by the Soviets, and justified this action to himself by arguing that they were Britain's allies; but in 1964, after the defection of Kim Philby, he was confronted by the authorities and secretly confessed his Soviet connections. The greatest damage done by his treachery was to plunge the secret services into an exhausting and demoralising struggle against those real or mythical agents infiltrated into their own midst, as well as into the Labour movement, the unions, and even – why not? – the Government itself. Since then, those in charge of the special services have been haunted by two obsessions: unearthing the moles buried in their midst, and restoring security to the services by the imposition of even greater secrecy over their activities.

Mrs Thatcher did not show herself more flexible than her predecessors on the question of the executive's right to secrecy. In early 1988, her troops – tiring of official prevarication – threatened to preempt the Government's promised action by voting in favour of a private Bill, put forward by a Conservative colleague, to reform the Official Secrets Act. She was forced to brandish a three line whip, but succeeded in containing the rebellion and forcing the Party to wait for the Bill that was being prepared by the Home Secretary.

Proving once again (if proof were needed) that the Thatcher Government remained faithful to a doctrine of State secrecy, another law was passed in 1988, to forbid the media from publishing or broadcasting interviews with Irish terrorists or with members of Sinn Fein – which supports terrorist action but is itself a legal organisation. In the name of a security whose frontiers move like shifting sands, the public's right to information is effectively made to depend on the Government's discretion. In practice, the reform of the Official Secrets Act (finally passed in December of the same year and presented by the Government as an updating and liberalisation of the 1911 Act) had the effect of emphasizing the State's commitment to a broad definition of secrecy, encompassing not merely matters relating to national security, but equally a whole area that one might describe as the domain of high politics, a domain reserved to the Cabinet and a few top mandarins, convinced – as they always have been – that mistakes are more easily forgiven if they are never discovered in the first place.

Quite independently of official restrictions, the press is beginning to question the reality of its freedom, which is already limited by the concentration of newspaper titles in the hands of a small number of multinational financial groups. An increasing number of journalists are also calling for the Lobby, with its selective revelations, to be replaced by official representatives who can be quoted, by name, as authorised spokesmen for their minister. In spite of the indifference of a public grown accustomed to the timidity of the quality press and the excesses of the tabloids, what is at stake is far from trivial: from Downing Street and its secrets to Westminster and its debates, there is all the distance between 'elective dictatorship' and true parliamentary democracy.

The Sovereign

Everyone knows the Queen of England; but no one knows exactly who the sovereign of the United Kingdom and Northern Ireland is. In America, in Germany, in Italy, in France and in other republican states, it is written in black and white: the people are sovereign. In most of Europe's constitutional monarchies, the rights and prerogatives of the monarch are clearly established. Great Britain is an ancient and well-established democracy, yet it remains attached not only to the pomp and ceremony of its monarchy, but also to its indefinable nature, which expresses so well the gut refusal of the British to use the artifice of logic in a futile attempt at defining and understanding an incomprehensible world.

More than a century ago, Walter Bagehot – the Darwin of constitutional law – stressed the evolutionary nature of the English constitution. For the most part, his definition of the powers of the monarch still holds true today. The monarch has 'the right to be consulted, the right to encourage, the right to warn'*. At present, the Queen's most visible and most important action is her appointment of the Prime Minister. For as long as there are two major parties alternating in power with substantial majorities, she has no choice. But if a third rogue party were to upset the balance of power, creating a hung Parliament, it would be up to the Queen and the Queen alone to decide who was to be made responsible for resolving the crisis. A few of the rare politicians who are hostile to the monarchy believe that – since true legitimacy derives from universal suffrage alone – this royal prerogative should devolve to the Speaker of the House of Commons. But their demands have met with little enthusiasm from their colleagues.

The Monarch has other, more significant constitutional rights which no one has thought of abolishing because, to this day, they have never been improperly used. Let us refer, once more, to Bagehot's splendid catalogue: 'The Queen could disband the army . . . she could dismiss all the officers, from the General Commander-in-Chief downwards; she could dismiss all the sailors too; she could sell off all our ships of war, and all our naval stores; she could make peace by the sacrifice of Cornwall, and begin a war for the conquest of Brittany. She could make every citizen in the United Kingdom, male or female, a peer; she could make every parish a University; she could dismiss most of the Civil Servants; she could pardon all offenders.'†

* From *The English Constitution*, Walter Bagehot, 1867.
† ibid.

The part of sovereignty that has been retained by the Crown does not emanate from the majority, nor is it merely the shield of the minority; it is the guarantee of those traditions and rights that neither encroach on the rights of the individual, nor on those of the community in general. In a speech in Parliament in January 1988, Margaret Thatcher stated that the Crown had the right – on the advice of the Prime Minister – to waive prosecution in special cases, as for example when a secret agent had broken the law in the course of a mission. The Master of the Rolls, Sir John Donaldson, confirmed the constitutional validity of the Prime Minister's interpretation: the law of the kingdom is the same for everyone, including the Queen, but she transcends it, and in her name its application can be suspended.

In practice these powers – though vested in the monarch – can be seen as strengthening the executive, to whom they ultimately devolve. But they have an important additional constitutional function. For so long as the monarch remains alive and free, neither a foreign invasion, nor the impossibility of calling Parliament or holding elections, nor even the disappearance of the Government itself would be enough to create a constitutional void. The Queen's powers would be extensive enough to enable her, quite legitimately, to ensure the survival of the nation until such time as normality could be restored – with the additional asset that the sworn allegiance of the armed forces is due to the monarch and not to the Government. In France, Article 16 of the Constitution of the Fifth Republic (introduced by General de Gaulle) provides for national emergencies by placing every power in the hands of the President of the French Republic. But the French have felt obliged to hedge these powers with all kinds of precautions and provisos – which many of its critics still find insufficient – whereas the majestic silence of the British constitution can accommodate itself to the most unforeseen circumstances without in the least disturbing delicate consciences.

By maintaining the monarchy – with its pomp, its privileges and its still immense implicit power – Parliament seems concerned less with preserving royal authority as a resort in case of national emergency, than it is with staging the spectacle of its own supremacy. But in this respect, the British people are not at one with their representatives. They do not want a submissive monarchy shorn of all power. According to an opinion poll carried out by International Communications and Marketing (ICM) for the *Today* newspaper in February 1991, fifty-eight per cent of them do not think the power of the monarch should be reduced entirely to ceremonial work. When Princess Elizabeth was crowned in Westminster Abbey, she was not encroaching on the democratic powers devolved to Parliament in its palace across the road, but on the contrary, was confirming them through the sacred character of the coronation; thanks to her, and through her, sharing in her sovereignty, the British can enjoy the Divine Right of the People.

By offering Queen Victoria the title of Empress of India in 1876, Disraeli was creating one of those legal monsters that terrify our countries of written law, but which British tradition takes in its stride. The day the Empire (born of conquest), turned itself into the Commonwealth (of freely associating and equal independent States), several of those States decided to keep the sovereign that Great Britain had given them as their King;* others opted for republican regimes with more or less respect for universal suffrage; but all of them, today, recognise Elizabeth II as the Head of the Commonwealth. Whether this recognition is personal or hereditary will become clear when her successor inherits the throne. What is certain is that, in her role as leader of the Commonwealth, the Queen has no constitutional obligation to ask for advice from Downing Street. Her adviser, in this field, is the Secretary General of the Commonwealth, who has the same rights of direct access to her as does the Prime Minister. Similarly, in each of the States of which she remains Queen, it is the Governor General, her representative, who advises her – though personally he has no political latitude beyond following the directives of government.

---

* The modern Commonwealth, comprising republics and national monarchies as well as monarchies under King George VI, became possible when it was agreed in 1949 that India, on becoming a republic, could continue to be a member. Since then, almost all of Britain's former dependent territories have attained their independence and have voluntarily joined the Commonwealth. (Fiji's membership lapsed in 1987.)

The Queen attaches great importance to her role as head of the Commonwealth. She is convinced that, in a dangerous world, the ties that bind its members together – however tenuous – help to reduce international tensions, contribute towards understanding between developing countries and the First World, and preserve a precious common cultural heritage. The fact remains that an open conflict between one of the States of which she is the sovereign and the United Kingdom would place her before an insoluble constitutional dilemma. But the participants all know the rules of the game; it is up to them to avoid an impasse. For as long as they keep prudently to the open road, she will continue to reign serenely over each of her kingdoms and will remain the leader of this community of nations which a breath could disperse, but which no storm has yet succeeded in breaking down.

Titles and Honours

Twice a year, in January and June, peerages, knighthoods and medals are spread like dew over recipients for the most part chosen by the Government, but honoured by the Queen. This distribution of prizes, known as the 'Honours List', is notable for the antiquity of some of the titles dispensed, and for the ceremonial which surrounds them; but the most prestigious amongst them are in the gift of the Queen, not the Prime Minister.

On the 15th of June 1987, the former Prime Minister, James Callaghan (the Queen's favourite Head of Government, it is rumoured), was installed as Knight Companion of the Most Noble Order of the Garter. Appointments to this Order, the most senior of all the British Orders of Chivalry, are usually announced on St George's Day (23 April), but the ceremonies are held on the Monday of Ascot Week. Sir James Callaghan (now Lord Callaghan of Cardiff) was invested with the insignia of the Order that morning at Windsor Castle, and after lunching with the Queen and the other Companions in the Waterloo Chamber, he was formally installed in St George's Chapel. At his investiture he received from the Sovereign the following items:

– the Garter, made of midnight-blue velvet, with the motto *'Honi soit qui mal y pense'* embroidered on it in gold thread, and

383

worn – as is customary for men – beneath the left knee (women, for decency's sake, wear it around the left arm);

– the Mantle, also in midnight blue, with the badge of the Order embroidered on the left shoulder;

– the Hood, of crimson velvet;

– the Hat, of black velvet, adorned with a plume of white feathers;

– the Collar, weighing thirty ounces and made of gold knots alternating with enamelled red roses, each encircled by the Garter;

– the Badge, known as the 'great' George, worn suspended from the Collar, and made of gold with an enamelled image of Saint George on horseback thrusting his lance down the dragon's throat;

– another Badge, known as the 'lesser' George, oval, made of gold, and again showing Saint George and the dragon, but this time within the Garter (it is worn on the right hip, suspended on a broad blue sash which passes over the left shoulder);

– the Star, with its eight silver rays, decorated in the centre with a red enamel cross of Saint George, surrounded by a blue Garter with the Order's motto and worn on the left breast.

The story goes that King Edward III picked up a garter dropped by the Countess of Salisbury during a ball, and putting it round his left leg, cried out to his mocking courtiers, '*Honi soit qui mal y pense*'*. It little matters whether the anecdote is true or false. What counts is the antiquity of the Order, which was probably founded in 1348; its exclusivity (membership is restricted to twenty-six including the Sovereign and the Prince of Wales†); the associated etiquette and legendary aura; the invocation of the Holy Trinity, the Virgin Mary, and especially Saint George and Saint Edward the Confessor, England's two accredited protectors.

Every state dispenses such inexpensive knick-knacks; none other possesses so complete a panoply of dignities, uniforms, coats of arms, banners and parchments. The assiduous heirs of King Arthur

* 'Shame on him who thinks this shameful.'
† There are also a number of supernumeraries known as 'Extra' Knights and Ladies, including members of the Royal family and foreign sovereigns.

invite their honoured guests to a Round Table in the heart of an Enchanted Land, from which they rise – in the footsteps of so many heroes, saints, bankers, cricket players and pop singers – charmed and transformed into the mascots of crowned Democracy. One should not laugh at these theatricals nor at the actors; a monarchy stripped of ornament and deprived of dedicated servants would lose the power of transmuting clichés into moral principles, of maintaining a social hierarchy without freezing it, and of offering the poorest members of society the vicarious pleasures of luxury.

10

Thatcherism and the Pride of Nations

After their emergence from the epic of the Second World War
with renewed self-confidence, it had begun by the seventies to
look as if the British people were allowing themselves to sink into
a complacent torpor. Thirty years later, waking suddenly to the
imminent danger of drowning, they decided to throw their excess
baggage overboard, dispensed with glorious memories of the past
and the deadly certainties of the present, and rediscovered a taste
for adventure and a new hopefulness for the future.

War and the Welfare State

But in the seventies, Britain was still imbued with philosophical,
aesthetic and social ideas and references reflecting the extraordinary intellectual and moral flowering of the thirties, which was
itself a product of the First World War and its geo-political legacy.

The roaring twenties had been an attempt to bury the appalling
memories of war butchery in nights of frivolous revelry inhabited
by Nöel Coward's bright young things and the contemporaries
of Bertie Wooster – sworn enemy of all things serious. But the
arrogant complacency of the Right and the timorous inactivity of
the Left were unable to ward off the crisis affecting the traditional
sectors of national prosperity: coal, textiles and shipbuilding.
Neither the expansion of agriculture nor the development of new
industries in the south of England to the detriment of the north
were sufficient to contain the depression, aggravated in 1929 by
the great Stock Market crash.

With the Labour Party's political advance during the inter-war
years, the working classes – who feared being cheated of the fruits

of a victory to which they had contributed so significantly – were able, for the first time, to express their heartfelt aspirations towards social justice. Over these two decades, Labour was gradually to replace the Liberal Party entirely in the predictable alternation of power with the Conservatives.

This transformation of Labour into a party of government was effected to the detriment of its radicalism and revolutionary faith. Nonetheless, although Communism was firmly rejected by the Party, it did not disappear entirely from the political scene and was to maintain a durable influence within the trade union movement. But it was among intellectuals that the ideas of Communism were most influential. The Civil War in Spain and the rise, in Italy and in Germany, of totalitarian doctrines founded on anti-Communism, were to lend to those ideas the romance of martyrdom as well as a kind of democratic and moral legitimacy.

When in 1979, Sir Anthony Blunt, former Surveyor of the Queen's pictures and an art historian of world repute, was publicly unmasked as a Soviet spy, public opinion was dismayed to discover that the gangrene of treachery had spread so far within the body politic. Blunt justified himself by declaring – with a candour that it would perhaps be too easy to tax with cynicism – that by spying for the USSR, he had never felt himself to be passing secrets to the enemy. After all, had not Russia been Britain's ally against Nazism? The rise of Nazism had driven the first victims of totalitarianism to Britain – and those victims had long haunted Blunt and his Cambridge friends. There is little doubt about their thirst for social justice.

This ideological fervour was to see a brief renaissance in 1968 for a new generation of exasperated or confused young people. The debate, which was given a new lease of life by the re-emergence of an arrogant conservatism in the face of the ideals of socialism, is only now coming to an end with the collapse of world Communism before our eyes. But the extraordinary resilience of these ideas (by now well over a century old), would be incomprehensible without the war, the terrible forge that moulded a new order out of the lazy cohesion of British society and its Empire in 1939.

It is due to the war, and to its length, that the plan for a global reform of British society – a hundred times still-born and a hundred times redrafted – did not end up, like so many others before it, in the dusty files of some well-meaning visionary. The conjunction of two factors was to lead to the publication, in 1942, of a report which charged the British leadership with the task of ensuring 'freedom from want' for all of its people. The first of these was a latent determination not to repeat the mistakes of the past by depriving the poor of the fruits of their great victory; the second was the personality of one man, William Beveridge, a liberal reformer in the great English tradition. The Beveridge report was no sooner published than it became a bestseller, outstripping all others that year.

The electoral defeat of Winston Churchill in 1945 was not so much a rejection of the Conservative Party as a change of emphasis. Churchill had been a fine war leader; his lieutenant, Clement Attlee, was thought to be a better peace-time technician. Those voters who brought Labour into power (some forty-eight per cent) hoped to continue a project that was very much in the spirit of their wartime alliance. The Tory opposition was in fact well aware of this. Until the late seventies, whether in government or out of it, the Conservatives never seriously questioned the principles of state interventionism underlying the Welfare State.

Consensus Politics

Emerging after 1940 from his role as general critic, Maynard Keynes was charged by the British leadership with offering alternative perspectives and solutions, and was soon hailed as the prophet of a new alliance between *laissez-faire* capitalism and socialist interventionism. For according to Keynes, increased government intervention in the financial markets was not only compatible with political freedom, it could actually encourage economic activity.

The impact of Keynes' theories on full employment (which was effectively achieved in Britain until the seventies) is still a subject of controversy among economists. But the fact remains that for more than a quarter of a century his emphasis on the role of government in sustaining economic activity was accepted as an article of faith by successive British governments, Labour and Conservative.

In the sphere of foreign policy, there was an even greater measure of agreement between the two major Parties. Whether on nuclear deterrence, membership of NATO or decolonisation, the continuity of Government policy was remarkable. Within ten years of India and Pakistan gaining independence in 1947, a further thirty former colonies did the same. Only the 1956 Suez expedition, rashly undertaken by the Conservative Prime Minister, Anthony Eden, had been condemned by Labour – but in so doing Labour was merely echoing the criticisms of the American Government.

Edward Heath's premiership foreshadowed the imminent demise of interventionist socialism, but it was his fate to be the precursor – Saint John the Baptist to Mrs Thatcher's Christ. The assault by the unions, crowned by the electricians' and miners' strike during the winter of 1973 to 1974 (against the background of a world oil crisis) helped to undermine Heath, his Government, and his reforming ambitions. He called a snap election, hoping to profit from his handling of the crisis. Inflation, however, remained the number one issue in the poll and he lost his majority.

Heath's failure was due not to an excess of zeal, but rather to the timidity of his reforms, which left the Welfare State limping on unsatisfactorily as before. Taking over from him, the Labour Party was inevitably brought up against its shortcomings, but could not bring itself to admit this publicly nor take appropriate action. Paradoxically, it was the very weakness of Labour's Government, headed by James Callaghan, that constituted its strength. Even the unions – which were asserting their role as guardians of the Party with increasing insistence – were too frightened of seeing power slip by them not to bow before the moderating arguments of the new Prime Minister; yet this new-found moderation was in fact the first symptom of the unions' loss of influence and finally quashed any hope of a return to the consensual euphoria of the immediate post-war period. Prompted by persistent inflation, the continuing fall of pound sterling, and the need to borrow heavily from the International Monetary Fund (IMF), the Labour Government introduced a programme of austerity unprecedented since 1945.

So it was that in 1977 – one year before the monetarist prophet, Milton Friedman, was awarded the Nobel Prize for economics – the Labour Chancellor, Denis Healey, set himself a number of strictly monetarist goals that were entirely in step with the American economist's thinking (something which Mrs Thatcher never achieved despite her declared intentions). But the union rank and file were unwilling to accept compromise agreements negotiated by their leaders, and engaged in a prolonged series of official and unofficial strikes. By the spring of 1979 the notorious 'winter of discontent' had taken its toll on the nation, leaving an indelible mark on the collective memory, and prompting the Liberal Party to withdraw its support from Labour (which depended on it for a majority in Parliament), thus precipitating the fall of the Government.

Though the financial policies advocated by Healey were Thatcherite before Thatcherism (indeed, more Thatcherite than Thatcher), the Labour Party was operating under constraints that were too heavy to be shaken off. Edward Heath too, had been a prisoner of the unspoken pact that bound Tories and Socialists in a partnership for the preservation of the post-war social heritage they had fought for together. Margaret Thatcher, on the other hand, did not hesitate to turn her back on that heritage, firmly rejecting policies of State interventionism in economic affairs.

Thatcher and Thatcherism

On becoming Prime Minister in 1979 Mrs Thatcher put her exceptional energy at the service of her convictions, displaying the ease she had acquired while criticising her predecessor as Leader of the Opposition. Thatcherism was about to step into history, leaving historians with the difficult task of describing this apparently plain phenomenon. But although Mrs Thatcher's personality can be clearly outlined, the sum of her ideas and the line of her conduct are less straightforward than either her supporters or her detractors have claimed, or than she believed herself.

Neither Churchill nor Pitt ever enjoyed the honour bestowed spontaneously by the public on the nation's first woman Prime Minister – the honour of having their name enshrined in a new English word. What lies behind this key word, Thatcherism, which did duty as an ideology, a set of moral principles, a philosophy even, to an important minority of the British population, not to mention a majority in Parliament – a philosophy which, for more than eleven years, was the guiding force behind Government? Thatcherism: a secular religion that fired the imagination of a populace yearning for tangible miracles and scandalised the piety of those who – in the midst of galloping prosperity – persisted in painting a picture of misery as desolate as the poorest of the nation's poor. The nation's intellectuals, who thought they were well armed against false or simplistic ideas, found themselves strangely disorientated by the dynamism of the High Priestess of efficiency, whose message seemed so clear, yet proved to be so hard to pin down doctrinally.

More concretely, and perhaps most importantly, Thatcherism is the sum of eleven years of continuity in government – of reforms (or, for those who reject them, of counter-reforms), of victories and setbacks, and above all, of action. Thatcherism is a crusade against improper State intervention. It is systematic privatisation of nationalised enterprises and by the same token, the (not altogether successful) encouragement of popular capitalism; it is a charter for the individual, for tenants wanting to buy their homes from the council, and for parents wanting to exercise a choice over their children's education. At the same time, Thatcherism is a victory for the State and for management (Tories would say a victory for law and order) over the unions. It also involves rigorous control over the State budget (much helped, it must be said, by the sale of the nationalised industries); it implies a reduction in income tax, particularly for high earners; it means intransigence in the face of Irish terrorism and conciliation with the Republic of Ireland; it is the masterly negotiation for the independence of Zimbabwe; it is victory in the Falklands; it is the endlessly repeated affirmation of a 'special relationship' with the United States – without special advantage for Britain – yet loudly proclaimed once more in the face of the annexation of Kuwait by the Iraqi dictator, Saddam Hussein; it is a prickly cohabitation with Britain's European partners who are irritated, yet secretly in admiration of an obstinacy they are incapable of denting.

For most people, Thatcherism is the expression of a character which combined common sense with courage, and self-confidence with a taste for confrontation in the face of facile optimism and complacency; it is an unyielding pursuit of ideals that were well-defined and understood by the majority and a refusal to compromise principles in an impossible attempt to reconcile contradictory policies.

And contradictory many of them indeed were. Mrs Thatcher could assert the virtues of free competitive markets while privatizing large monopolies and increasing the sternness of controls on standards in broadcasting. She could proclaim faith in monetarist theory while abandoning monetarism in practice, and in thrift and good housekeeping while presiding over the largest credit boom and consumer spending spree in the country's history. Only a conviction politician could embrace inconsistent convictions with so little unease. And only an effortless command of political theatre could have dared to persuade the population that the assertion of successive deeply held convictions was all the consistency that mattered. Mrs Thatcher's genius lay not in a refusal to make U-turns but in the speed with which she could ensure they were forgotten – not least by her.

For Thatcherism, finally, is a consummate piece of stage management designed to enhance the prestige of the show's heroine. Let us examine a few of the scenes that highlighted her personality most effectively. The first has the tragic overtones of a warning by fate: March 1979, on the eve of the General Election that was to open the doors of 10 Downing Street to the Tory leader, Airey Neave, spokesman on Northern Ireland in Margaret Thatcher's Shadow Cabinet, is killed by an INLA* bomb placed inside his car. He is not only a weighty ally (one of the principal architects of Maggie's election to the Party leadership), but also a personal friend. His death causes her genuine grief, but also serves as a keen reminder of her vulnerability – a vulnerability that will only be increased by her subsequent accession to power.

Two years later, a minor IRA fighter, Bobby Sands, dies after a sixty-six-day hunger strike undertaken to obtain political prisoner status for IRA detainees. His death is followed by that of nine other prisoners belonging to the IRA. Questioned in the House of Commons about her intentions with regard to the death of Bobby Sands, she replies that Mr Sands was 'a convicted criminal who chose to take his own life. It was a choice that his organisation did not allow to any of their victims'.

* Irish National Liberation Army.

On the 11th of October 1984, during the Party's annual conference, Mrs Thatcher narrowly escapes a bomb placed by Irish terrorists in the Grand Hotel, Brighton, where the Prime Minister and her colleagues are staying. Just a few minutes after the explosion, which has killed five people and injured many more (including two of her own ministers), millions of people see her on television, speaking with the most calm assurance. At Chequers a week later however, a few witnesses will see her crying as she recalls the horrors of that evening. It falls to her to sign a unique agreement with the Irish Prime Minister, Garret Fitzgerald, giving the Republic of Ireland a say in the affairs of Ulster for the first time since partition.

Violence distresses Margaret Thatcher; it does not intimidate her. The Argentinians made this painful discovery in the Falklands. Iraq's invasion of Kuwait might have left the British as indifferent as the eight-year blood bath of the Iran-Iraq war, the interminable fighting between Ethiopia and Eritrea, or the tribal massacres in Liberia; but from the moment the aggression allowed Britain to cast herself in the role of guardian of the rule of law, a large majority of the population, forgetting all political or social indifference, appeared to rally round Mrs Thatcher once more. When it came down to essentials, there seemed to be a continuing understanding between herself and the British people.

Ultimately, Thatcherism – in so far as such a thing existed – was not a political doctrine, still less a philosophy; but it did embody a rejection of the establishment, be it patrician or working class. Ignoring the nice distinctions between 'us' and 'them', it swept away all superfluous nostalgia in an effort to restore national ambition. It did not herald the reform of the ruling class, so much as its submission; it did not promise an improvement in the condition of the working class, so much as its abolition.

The middle class had been appointed by Margaret Thatcher to sovereign power. The new British citizens of her creation would all be home-owners, all share-holders, all entrepreneurs, and together they would resurrect the splendour and adventure of the past. This utopia was based on something of a reality. Though Mrs Thatcher did not transform society, she recognised that people' attitudes were changing, and set about moulding the country's institutions to meet the challenges of change.

The palace coup that drove Mrs Thatcher from power can in fact be seen as a sort of apotheosis. Thatcherism, stripped of its partisan stridency, was reasserting itself in the election of her successor, whose lowly origins finally confirmed an irreversible social mutation. Indeed, her elimination from the Premiership was in some way the inevitable result of that mutation. When in November 1990, her leadership was seriously challenged for the first time in eleven years, she was, in some respects, the victim of her own past victories. For by inflicting three ignominious defeats on Labour, Mrs Thatcher had effectively forced reform on the party. Cautiously returning to a policy of multilateral nuclear disarmament, forgetting about nationalisation and recognising the virtues of the market economy, this new Labour Party – one of Thatcherism's most successful secondary products – was rising steadily in popularity from one opinion poll to the next.

With inflation taking off once more towards the end of Mrs Thatcher's reign, the trade unions – long demoralised by her successful assaults against them – were rediscovering their old fighting spirit and refusing to accept sermons on the virtues of the market as adequate consolation for the decline in their purchasing power. In spite of the Government's repeated entreaties, they were asking for – and getting – substantial increases in salary, as untroubled as ever by the inflationary implications of their success. Despite their natural tendency to vote Conservative, industrialists were becoming increasingly worried about the Government's apparent economic mismanagement, and public opinion – which had been all in favour of the early privatisations – was beginning to worry about the sale of lucrative monopolies (such as the water and electricity boards) to businesses whose primary motive was profit rather than the public interest.

The inadequacy of health funding during this period and the attempt to introduce market forces into the health service also provoked a general outcry among the medical profession and from the general public. Cuts in the education budget, attacks on the cherished status of the BBC and on the rules governing the output of commercial television and radio, lack of sympathy with the Scottish, a dubious treaty with China over Hong Kong – Mrs Thatcher was definitely losing her touch.

While the large Conservative parliamentary majority had long enabled her to ignore criticism from the opposition benches, the introduction of the poll tax, her handling of the economy and the increasingly acrimonious tone of her disagreement with the other members of the European Community were, for the first time, provoking considerable anxiety among her own supporters. Even the powerful unifying effect of the Gulf crisis and the threat of another war were not sufficient to rally public opinion around her as spontaneously and unanimously as the Falklands campaign had done. Everyone knew, of course, that political leaders of every hue were in agreement with her over the need to meet Iraqi aggression. Yet even as the crisis was gathering force, people were plotting against her, openly and in secret. The time-bomb threatening her Government was already in place, ticking and visible to everyone – the hated poll tax that was so offensive to the British sense of natural justice.

It fell to Geoffrey Howe, the number two in the Government, to introduce a European detonator into the bomb. Contrary to the profound conviction of Mrs Thatcher, upheld by a vocal minority of traditionalist chauvinists, public opinion – which had long been largely indifferent to the European question, not to say suspicious of it – was beginning to be persuaded that there could be no viable future for Great Britain outside the European movement. Naturally, neither the poll tax nor the European question could, on their own, account for the Parliamentary Party's sudden disaffection with their leader; more prosaically, they were worried about their prospects at the next General Election. By openly charging Mrs Thatcher with authoritarianism and insensitivity in a devastating resignation speech, Geoffrey Howe paved the way for the charismatic Michael Heseltine (who had resigned from Government several years earlier, making similar accusations) to make his bid for the leadership.

So it was that on November 14, 1990, having repeatedly denied that he had any intention of taking over from Mrs Thatcher, Heseltine announced his candidature in the forthcoming routine annual leadership election. Margaret Thatcher's unconvincing majority after the first ballot was to activate one of those mysterious processes beneath the surface of British democracy. While the two stars of the show were engaged in a public confrontation on stage, the real battle was being conducted in whispers, behind the scenes. Heseltine's major problem was his very strength – he was too popular at large to be effectively controlled by the Party's dominant right-wing faction, and seemed to present all the disadvantages of Thatcherite authoritarianism, while causing considerable anxiety about the soundness of his policies.

Mrs Thatcher however, had definitively alienated the Party's king-makers, who no longer believed in her ability to lead the Tories to a fourth electoral victory. Giving way before the threatening predictions of her opponents and the entreaties of friends anxious to avoid her humiliation at the second ballot, she withdrew from the leadership contest, knowing at least that her fall would inevitably bring Heseltine down with it, making way for the election of her right-hand-man and Chancellor of the Exchequer, John Major.

From Downing Street to Dulwich

In recognition of eleven years of discretion behind the scenes, Denis Thatcher – model husband and satirists' harmless whipping boy – was awarded a baronetcy – a modest title, like its recipient, but a hereditary one at least, giving him the right to be addressed as Sir Denis. Mrs Thatcher, on whom the Queen (who, it is said, does not much like the former PM) nonetheless conferred the high dignity of membership of the Order of Merit, is also entitled to be called 'Lady' in her capacity as the wife of a baronet. But she has rejected the title, preferring to retain the name that made her famous. As she put it in an interview shortly after her husband's elevation to the peerage, 'I have done pretty well out of being Mrs Thatcher'.

On leaving their long-standing home in 10 Downing Street, the Thatchers were restored to the status of ordinary private citizens – or almost. Their planned retirement home, a neo-Georgian house in Dulwich, South London, built to withstand explosives, was in fact put up for sale and they moved to an exclusive central London square. The press has not lost interest in them either, speculating avidly on the millions the Iron Lady could make by writing the memoirs she disdained to think about in the days when she was still confident of a fourth electoral victory. Meanwhile Mrs Thatcher continues to sit on the backbenches of Parliament, and has accepted the presidency of the 'Bruges Group', composed of Tories opposed to a federal Europe. Though she no longer holds the reins of power and announced her departure from the Commons at the 1992 election, we have not heard the last of her.

Historians and political commentators will long continue to speculate about the evolutionary and the revolutionary aspects of the Thatcher years, and no doubt she will add her own contribution to the debate. But whatever their respective conclusions, it seems to me that the British people now feel that her mission – like Churchill's after the war – is over. They expect new things from her successor – a new perspective that she could probably never have opened up for them. Like Moses – deprived by his God of the right to enter the land of Canaan – she was forced to bow out by her inability to see beyond national horizons, and it has fallen to the new Joshua, John Major, to lead the British people into that promised Europe that she did not love enough.

From l'Entente Cordiale to l'Alliance Vitale

The dismantling of the Socialist State and the rehabilitation of the market economy will no doubt be seen by posterity as the two major monuments of the Thatcher era, to which perhaps, should be added a third – the restoration of national pride. On the other hand, few historians today would stake anything on the guess that Mrs Thatcher will prove to have been a crucial player in the final integration of Great Britain into the European continent. Yet history has more than once proved historians wrong. Long after the Iron Lady's flamboyant rhetoric has been forgotten, the fact will remain that it was she who signed the Single European Act in 1986 (the single most important European document after the Treaty of Rome), creating for the first time a market that is truly open to all members of the European Community. And – with the exception of the Germans – it was also Mrs Thatcher who was the first to abolish exchange controls.

In the Thatcher moral code, the sacrosanct right of the individual to look to his own interest merges with the nation's sacrosanct right to defend the best interests of its citizens. But these rights are balanced by an obligation to accept all the risks that accompany opportunity – the risks of the entrepreneur in the face of competition, and the risks of a nation in the face of its rivals. Ultimately, there is only one justification for the pursuit of self-interest (be it individual or collective), and that is excellence.

Europe, she kept asserting, yes, she believed in Europe, but a Europe founded on realism and not on the hollow socialist dreams of the Brussels bureaucrats. In a *Financial Times* interview on the eve of her resignation she was still insisting: 'I do not like monopolies of any sort. And like most people in this country I am suspicious of blueprints, especially where institutions are concerned. My own vision of Europe can be summed up in two words. It should be *free*, politically and economically. It should be *open*.' She had not liberated her country from the suffocating constraints of socialism in order to see them smuggled in through the back door. She was not going to abandon the sovereign prerogatives of Britain's democratically elected Parliament to a bunch of irresponsible bureaucrats.

These suspicions and parochial quarrels were to be swept away with the last winter leaves by the wind of liberty that had so suddenly arisen in the East at the close of 1989. The new dawn that had been promised to the twelve member states of the EEC in 1992 suddenly took on the aspect of a faint flicker on the horizon, while the reunification of Germany dominated the foreground.

As honoured guests at the wedding feast, the chorus of enraptured democrats could hardly change tune in mid-festivities, complaining that the bride was too beautiful and the groom too wealthy. It fell to Mrs Thatcher once again to sound a discordant note in the concert of good wishes – after all, this was a second marriage, and first time round the couple had behaved so badly that they had had to be separated by force. They had changed, no one was denying it; and they were made for each other, undoubtedly. But there was no need to rush, and they had to guarantee that they would never again break down their neighbour's door claiming there was not enough room for them at home.

No doubt, it was not the done thing to sulk at the very time when the Berlin wall was collapsing amid universal cheers. But freedom is more than just a symbol. It is a property that must be defended, and the survivors of the Battle of Britain are the last to forget it. At a time when the Soviet-American duumvirate born of the Yalta agreements was becoming little more than a memory and the Soviet empire was crumbling, Europe found itself back at square one, and Britain – returning instinctively to its historical role as European arbiter – did not hesitate to pose the blunt question already set out by a British columnist just after the 1918 armistice: 'And now, are we going to europeanise the Balkans, or balkanise Europe?'

Reflecting on the problems thrown up by the reunification of Germany, the British Foreign Secretary, Douglas Hurd, was at pains to emphasise that he felt the French and British had almost exactly the same interests in the matter, and that by working together as closely as possible, they should be able to reach a consensus on appropriate action. This identity of interests is in fact authentic and far-reaching, and has always existed despite the longstanding (and equally authentic) rivalries between the two nations.

Collective civilisations have always been more than just the sum of all the different cultures they have crossed or dominated; they are a tangled web of borrowed or stolen influences. If today's Europe remains an abstract notion, the fault lies with the cautious or imprudent claims and counter-claims of nationalism. The world-wide avatars of English or Spanish, the defence of French and its Francophone echoes, the greatness of Germany and the proliferation of Slav nationalisms, the protection of minority languages and cultures – these will long continue to flatter, affront or mortify different national and sub-national susceptibilities, and to fuel interminable controversies and the occasional bloody ethnic feud. And it is not from their resolution that a European identity will be created, nor from some more or less laborious compromise, but only from a surge of irresistible vitality. To discover the nature and power of this vitality we should turn to the United Kingdom where English, Scots, Irish, Welsh and immigrants of every colour have learnt to live together – even if the experience is sometimes painful and difficult to make sense of.

As the French are well placed to know, vitality finds its first expression in language. The English language has amplified the voice of Celtic bards, Welsh singers and Scottish philosophers, and has continued to spread steadily outwards through the world. There is vitality also in England's Common Law, inherited from the Normans with a faint lingering smell of France. Taking over from native customs only when these were moribund, the King's common law was able to accommodate local differences without sacrificing justice; it became the flexible arbiter between the collectivity and the individual, whose rights it successfully protected without ever having to carve them in stone. And there is vitality finally in a constitution which – being unwritten – has never become frozen in the past from which it draws its authority, and continues to foreshadow a future that it does not need to know. This United Kingdom, whose two principal nations – England and Scotland – have maintained their own specific laws and are tied by virtue of a treaty, is by its very structure more European than it knows, and than we are prepared to believe. The only decision left for it to take – and that France must incessantly urge it to take – is that of extending a pragmatism that has served it so well in its islands to its neighbours on the continent.

For the third time in a century, the French and the British have been invited by the Germans to pronounce themselves – in spite of themselves, and, as it happens, in spite of Germany too – on a new European order which they do not fully understand. To brandish the spectre of Prussian militarism or of the Final Solution is as stupid as it is dangerous and unjust to the people of Germany today. On the other hand, it is not only legitimate, but imperative to ask what counterweight might be found to the demographic size, the industrial dynamism and the financial strength of a united Germany. In this light, it is all the more important that all the European associates – reflecting on the contributions that each of their different cultures could make – should harmonise their vision and political action, and stand together in the face of the rest of the world.

The reconciliation of France and Germany in the aftermath of the Second World War was the gesture of reparation without which Europe would forever have remained paralysed. But when Edward VII came to Paris in 1903 to inaugurate the *Entente Cordiale*, his visit (the first of its kind by a member of the dynasty) marked a truce in a war that had lasted some thousand years. The King, then, was astonished to discover the extraordinary love that the French bore the British Royal Family. The same is true today; yet, although the truce has now lasted nearly a century, and despite repeated alliances between the two countries, it remains no more than a lengthy armistice.

Let us forget for a moment the academic quarrel between partisans of a federal Europe, and those who would prefer to see a community of independent nations. The smaller nations of Northern Europe and the countries of the Mediterranean tend to favour a federation, while the British Isles (because of their famous insularity, once again), and the French (sole heirs of de Gaulle's unique legacy) dislike the idea of a supra-national body which would, in the former case, ride roughshod over the sovereignty of Parliament, and, in the latter case, sacrifice the nation's precious identity.

Barely a year after the end of the cold war, the invasion of Kuwait on the 2nd of August 1990, its annexation by Iraq and the armed conflict that ensued plunged the world into a profound crisis. It is illuminating in this context to examine the behaviour of both Britain and France after the Iraqi aggression, not forgetting the reaction of Europe as a whole, dominated and obscured by Germany's giant shadow.

Responding to the crisis in a characteristically forthright manner, unconcerned by the sensitivities of other European Community Members, and unaware of the Party coup that was brewing to deprive her of the power she was still exercising with so much vigour, Mrs Thatcher immediately declared that Great Britain and the United States stood as one on the matter. At the hour of danger, the place of the British was not among muddleheaded and timorous European bureaucrats, but – armed from head to foot – at the side of the only ally that counted: the United States of America.

This unreserved support, this immediate alignment of Downing Street with the White House was not just a political statement: it was a symbol. By identifying itself with the greatest power in the world – as during the terrible and glorious days of the Second

World War – Britain had found the best possible approximation to its past greatness. Better to be second in Washington than first in Brussels. The role of thirty thousand troops, placed directly under American command, as well as numerous squadrons of the Royal Air Force (including several Tornado aircraft which were to be among the first casualties of the war), was not limited to the liberation of Kuwait. It was to remind the world that in London, as in Washington, *Liberty* is an English word.

Stepping into Mrs Thatcher's shoes, John Major squarely pursued her policy, basking modestly in the praise which America did not begrudge its most reliable ally. And here too was the perfect opportunity to emphasize that – in his view – the European Community was ready neither for political union, nor even for a common foreign policy. Neil Kinnock, faithful to the neo-Thatcherite line of the Labour party, did not demur. Only Paddy Ashdown – leader of the surviving fraction of the old Liberal and Social Democratic alliance – was to express a platonic attachment to a nebulous Europe in the name of an insubstantial Party.

In contrast to Britain's martial stampede under the starred American banner, France preferred a hesitant waltz. As convinced as Mrs Thatcher and Mr Major that President Bush was determined to act, and believing, like them, that France was duty bound to take its place in the allied camp, Mr Mitterrand nonetheless showed the world a spectacle more reminiscent of Italian *Commedia del Arte* than of the great political and military drama which the President of the Republic had hoped to offer the public both at home and abroad. Expressing his astonishment at France's 'novel posture', Claude Imbert, one of the most subtle French political commentators, described it as 'puffing up one's chest while dragging one's feet'.

Although fully decided (whatever he said in public) to maintain a close alliance with the Americans, Mitterrand felt obliged to propitiate the French public – which was reluctant to go to war – by donning the old Gaullist uniform, unaware that it was threadbare, and in any case, too large for him. The President's first aim was to underline that the French position in relation to the Arab-Islamic countries was quite different from that of its allies. A bevy of unofficial emissaries, their smiles laden with innuendo, persistently denied that they were mediating, exploring or proposing solutions for peace in the President's name. As guardians of the Lebanon by divine right, impartial purveyors of arms and advice to the Middle East, neighbours separated by just a stretch of water from the Arab countries of Northern Africa, and hosts – whether they liked it or not – to some four million Moslems, the French displayed all the more self-importance when comparing their experience with what they considered to be the blunders of British diplomacy (whose duplicity was deeply hurtful to the Arab Soul), and the clumsy manoeuvres of the Americans which succeeded in antagonising both friend and foe.

Carried away by the logic of this strange display, President Mitterrand achieved the *tour de force* of presenting an ambitious six-point peace plan (which was to be ignored as categorically by the Iraqis as by the allied coalition), on the very eve of his unconditional promise to cooperate in the armed struggle to force Saddam Hussein out of Kuwait. The dispatch to the theatre of operations of an aircraft carrier without its aircraft (to underline its purely defensive mission), and the protracted failure to get rid of a Defence Minister who had not waited to resign before expressing his hostility to French military involvement in the war – these laborious and useless manoeuvres were to lead finally to the straightforward acceptance of an unavoidable conflict. Ultimately, neither Britain's reflex enthusiasm for America's position, nor France's touchy insistence on its own singularity were to make any difference. They both played their part in the military operations with some panache, and were both able to claim some credit in the victory – but their joint action did nothing to advance the cause of European unity. It is clear that the slowness and clumsiness of the European Community's institutions, and the priority its members place on the mysterious dictates of the national interest, is primarily due to the vanity and reciprocal suspicion of the French and the British, whose leaders persist in preferring prestige to the reality of power.

Nonetheless, there are a few signs allowing one to hope that a number of politicians, both in Paris and in London, are beginning to look beyond the swagger, at the real possibilities of coopera-tion between European countries for their common defence. The

Atlantic Alliance has won the cold war, and it can now no longer continue in its present form. The dissolution of the Warsaw pact and the departure of Soviet troops from the countries that used to form its protective shield should at the very least lead to a reduction in the number of American troops stationed in Europe, if not to their complete withdrawal. Similarly, the presence of French and British soldiers on unified German territory is no longer justified. But as the conflict in Kuwait clearly demonstrated, and as we are constantly reminded by regional conflicts from Kashmir to Eritrea, from Cambodia to the Lebanon – not to mention national and ethnic tensions within the former Soviet Union – despite the extension of democracy, the world has not become a safer place. In spite, or perhaps because of its conquering economic dynamism, Japan does not, on its own, seem to have the capacity to contribute positively to the balance of world power.

With America the last remaining power still able to intervene on every point of the globe, Europe seems to be the only possible partner in a position to cooperate actively with the United States for the maintenance of an acceptable international order. But although Europe is no longer split in two, it remains confused by events that have in one sense united it in shared aspirations for pluralist democracy, yet have left it more divided than ever over the definition and application of that democracy, and as divided as before by culture, language, historical traditions and ancestral rivalries.

In spite of the theoretical differences between those who favour a united Europe and those who remain attached to the notion of national sovereignty, the EEC is a viable entity, as has been clearly demonstrated by the economic progress and political stability it has enjoyed since its creation. Nonetheless it would be extremely dangerous to ignore the significance for the Community of Germany's new-found unity. It is clear that, despite any crises that might be encountered on the way, the collapse of Communism in Eastern Europe will eventually lead to the opening up of those markets whose primary focus has always been Germany in the past, and the German economy – which is already more vigorous than that of its European partners – can only become even more dominant as a result.

It is no secret that the British have misgivings about the implications of German unification. In July 1990, Nicholas Ridley,
then Secretary of State for Trade and Industry, was forced to
resign after saying aloud what many of his colleagues thought
in secret: that although an overpowerful Germany might well
be acceptable to those 'French poodles', it was not something to
be stomached by the English bulldog. But in the meantime, the
Foreign Secretary, Douglas Hurd, has not missed an opportunity
(both before and after Mrs Thatcher's resignation) to propose a
revision of European defence policy, including most notably, a
strengthening of the Western European Union* 'to become truly
the European pillar within the NATO alliance'.

In spite of numerous failures in the past, the French and the
British are once again talking of cooperating in the field of arms
production. In particular, they are planning a joint project to build
a multi-purpose frigate for the year 2000. It has been difficult to
reach a compromise on the requirements specified by each of the
partners; fortunately the extra volume required by the French to
stock their wine will come in very handy when the British sailors
want to store their beer. More and more frequently too, there
has been talk – in London and in Paris – of the advantages
that accrued in the past from closer cooperation in the areas
of nuclear research and the manufacture of weaponry. In the
diplomatic and political arena, collaboration is more prevalent
than dissension. The French President and the British Prime
Minister meet every year at a political summit; there is also
an annual conference bringing together the administrative élite
of the two nations to discuss problems of common interest, and
the Franco-British Council – created by Edward Heath to promote better mutual understanding – valiantly pursues its task by
organising regular encounters between influential people on both
sides of the Channel.

Neither these occasional efforts, however, nor the Channel
Tunnel, are sufficient to bridge the chasm that still separates
the two countries. Yet unless we can find a way of bridging that

---

* Comprising France, Germany, Italy, Britain, Spain, Portugal and
Benelux.

chasm, there is a danger that the whole of Europe may founder in it. If submitted to the pressure of overwhelming German economic superiority, the Franco-German reconciliation that has been so frequently celebrated by Kohl and Mitterrand, in the footsteps of Adenauer and de Gaulle, Schmidt and Giscard d'Estaing, could shatter like glass.

Germany's great culture, which for so long seemed to have been smothered by defeat and the reductive standardisation of Communism, will now find new direction, looking once more towards Central Europe, the Balkans and Ukraine and Russia – and this is all to the good. But were this great nation to become weighed down by too many riches, it would be imperative for the countries of the Western Atlantic and the Mediterranean – strengthened by such curious love affairs as the one that has survived between Britain and Portugal for the past three hundred years, and invigorated by Italy's repeated economic miracles and the democratic renaissance of Spain – to place themselves, in all their diversity, side by side with the peoples of the Rhine and the North Sea, not forgetting those of the Baltic, the Poles and the Finns, all of whom are more or less closely tied to the West through trade, memories of war and shared convictions.

Warm greetings exchanged between Paris and Bonn – or Berlin – are not sufficient proof of this European unity that must transcend so much diversity. That patent and irrefutable sign can come only from France and England – those two former powers, now widowed of their empires, abandoned by the heirs of their cultural supremacy, and incapable of meeting alone the ransom that the future demands of them. Separately neither France (which lags behind Germany both financially and economically), nor Great Britain (whose industrial might has done nothing but shrink in the face of German dynamism) have sufficient weight to guarantee a political equilibrium in Europe. But the conjunction of British financial power and the expertise of the City, of a solid democratic tradition and of France's growing capacity for industrial innovation and for producing better and cheaper goods, as well as her knack of creating fruitful alliances between public investment and private initiative could provide that essential counterweight to German power. Only when France and Britain have achieved much closer economic integration and a profound and lasting consensus over foreign policy, as well as a common approach to many domestic problems, will the future unity of Europe be assured. And for that to be achieved, all that is required is for the French and the British to accept a few home truths that cannot ultimately be avoided; to accept that although they have not chosen each other, although they will perhaps never love each other, they belong to the same family and are condemned either to the fratricidal struggles of centuries past, or to a peaceful – even advantageous – cohabitation.

In fact, it is more often poor reasoning than bigotry or chauvinism that divides and opposes the two nations. Each country imagines that it is alone in having to face problems that the other would never understand. It is true that France and Britain do not share the same colonial past, that Britain does not have the Arab nations of North Africa at her doorstep, nor their Muslim workers under her roof. But Cyprus and Gibraltar have long provided Britain with a link to the Mediterranean, while – for better or for worse – the face of the Middle East today owes more to the geo-political mysticism of T. E. Lawrence, or to the prophetic implications of the Balfour declaration, than it does to an entire century of French diplomacy. The Rushdie affair broke out in Britain, not France, while the British – with their significant minorities of Indians, Pakistanis, Africans, West Indians or Chinese – are faced with problems of social integration that are quite as complex as those of the French, with their immigrant populations of Algerians or Vietnamese.

There are many other areas where apparent differences between the two nations turn out – upon closer inspection – to be similarities which might benefit from common reflection and a common approach. Instead of falling back on habits of antagonism inherited from the past, the Foreign Office, in liaison with other European nations, could work with the French to defuse the over-emotional tenor of Franco-Arab dialogue in North Africa, and restore more balanced relations between the French (rightly or wrongly accused of pro-Christian bias) and all the different Lebanese communities.

France and Britain are the only countries, apart from the United

States, China (and the Soviet Union before its collapse), to have a permanent seat at the United Nations Security Council and an independent nuclear deterrent. To date, both nations have seen in this situation a decisive reason for maintaining their autonomous positions. The 'subservience' to the US of which Paris accuses London is yet another factor dividing the two semi-greats, and at the present rate of progress, it will not be long before they get relegated – behind Germany and Japan – to the status of insignificant small powers.

The integration of Europe must be preceded by Franco-British solidarity in the Security Council (a solidarity that is already frequent, but is unplanned and almost grudging), by a common approach with regard to the United States and other regional blocks, and finally by an integrated defence policy (even if the British remain within NATO while the French opt out of the Organisation itself, though remaining firmly inside the Alliance). In their tireless search for European unity, France and Britain should be working with Germany, rather than against her; and rather than trying to dominate the lesser European nations, they should be helping them to look for clearer political and economic options and a common defence strategy. Unless they give top priority to these tasks, both French and British will discover one day that their most precious asset – the national sovereignty that they both defend so jealously – will imperceptibly have become emptied of content. For how can one talk of sovereignty without economic or military power, and without political clout? Diehard patriots will argue that anything is possible, and they are not wrong of course: the Republic of San Marino is a sovereign state.

On the 16th of June 1940, General de Gaulle, Jean Monnet, Chairman of the Franco-British Economic Coordination Committee, and Robert Vansittart, Chief Diplomatic Adviser to the British Government, hastily met to discuss the content of a message that Winston Churchill intended to send to the French Government, bluntly requesting that its fleet – then stationed in Tunisia and vulnerable to German attack – should immediately be ordered to sail for Britain. The three men were convinced that a conciliatory approach would be more helpful and fruitful than this humiliating request, and drafted an alternative text for Churchill to deliver. In spite of his scepticism, the British Prime Minister agreed, and on the same day, addressing the two nations on the radio, he made the historic offer of Anglo-French political union – including a single government, common citizenship and associated parliaments.

It is not surprising that this offer should have met with so little response. Yet the personality of its authors and their agreement over its terms gives it great symbolical force: Vansittart represented what was most fiercely hostile in Britain's reaction to Nazism; Churchill and de Gaulle stood for English and French patriotism at its most exacting; and no one can deny Monnet the title of Father of Europe. It can only be hoped – though the hope remains a faint one – that the symbol will one day be seen as foreshadowing the future, and that the selfishness of individuals and of nations, so dear to Mrs Thatcher, will give way to something more than the ephemeral *Entente Cordiale* – the *Alliance Vitale* which could cement the future of Europe.

Acknowledgements

In October 1980 I took on the task of studying with a little method this Great Britain which I was sad to see so little known and so badly understood beyond its shores. Sir Michael Paliser, then Permanent Under-Secretary of State at the Foreign and Commonwealth Office and Head of the Diplomatic Service, was the first to encourage me in my enterprise and to undertake to help me. Lord Nicholas Gordon-Lennox, his assistant (before being named British Ambassador to Spain), provided that help in the form of tireless interventions on my behalf with the most eminent personalities in the most varied private and official circles. I am all the more grateful to him since the slowness of my progress must have made him increasingly doubtful that my book would ever see the light of day.

The Central Office of Information (COI) organised a series of trips and interviews with all the efficiency and impartiality that an author – jealous of his independence – had the right to expect, as well as the good will imparted to it by its two representatives, Stella Mummery and Susan Curtis-Bennet, for whose help I am profoundly grateful.

It is with some emotion that I call to mind the two meetings I had with the then Archbishop of Canterbury, Dr Runcie, two years later. For the two people he asked to help me in my attempts at understanding the mysteries of the Anglican Communion were his chaplain, the Reverend Richard Chartres, and his personal assistant, Terry Waite, who, thankfully, has now been liberated.

Countless old friends and new acquaintances have also contributed invaluable ideas, observations and anecdotes. Christopher Soames (who sadly has died since then), and his wife Mary, daughter of Winston Churchill, did not think they were wasting their time by telling me about their childhood memories. Ben and Janet Whitaker gave me their – sometimes divergent – vision of that public school education which I had just begun to study on the ground. Among the dozens of schools that I visited over the years, I would like in particular to mention the bilingual school at Llanharry, in Wales, where Welsh and English coexist in perfect harmony; Lagan College, in Belfast, which – in the face of tides of hatred – has bravely erected the frail barrage of a common education dispensed to Catholic and Protestant children alike; and finally, the Scottish Community School at Wester Hailes, whose headmaster convinced me that the idea of truly popular education was not utopian.

What better guides could I have hoped for to explore the gardens and secret corners of Cambridge than Bernard Williams, then Provost of Kings College, and his wife Patricia? At Oxford Polytechnic I was to meet the sociologist Peter Marsh, who has devoted numerous years of study to the problem of violence among the young, particularly on football stadia. I am also grateful to Arthur Marwick for explaining to me the nature and role of the Open University.

My background reading for this work has not been systematic, and that is by design. The book is not meant to be a comprehensive account; it is a portrait. Its only justification lies in the author's prejudices and impressions. For this reason, I have not thought it useful to draw up a bibliography, the choice of which would have been quite arbitrary. Nonetheless, there are a few works from which I have borrowed extensively, and without which I would never have been able to see beneath the surface of life in Britain. Among the most important of these are the articles and books by Mark Girouard about the country house in Britain.

The details of everyday life revealed themselves of their own accord, while the regular examination of six morning papers and as many weeklies, in addition to numerous trips from north to south and east to west, all helped to expand my horizons. Sir Edward

Pickering, whose entire career has been in journalism, gave me
the basis for a more in-depth study of the written press. Concerts,
exhibitions, plays and novels played the same part in my life as
they would have done had this book never seen the light of day.
On the other hand, I could not so easily have entered the closed
world of Glyndebourne without the help of Helen O'Neill.

The list of industrialists, businessmen, employees and trades-
unionists who gave me interviews is too long to detail. They were
of enormous help to me, as, thanks to them, I was able to examine
the true economic and social face of Thatcherite society. I thank
them all for their contribution.

High flying financiers welcomed me into their banks, as well as
into Lloyd's and the Stock Exchange – they are also too numerous
to list and do the justice they deserve. I will limit myself to an
expression of enormous gratitude to my dear friend Raymond
Bonham-Carter, whose letters of introduction opened all doors
and seemed to carry the force of law, endowing me with a prestige
which my work or personality alone could not have claimed. His
experience and critical eye were far greater than the use I made
of them. I thank him for inspiring the best parts of my text, and
hope he will forgive any inadequacies, for which I take entire
responsibility.

The Honourable Sir John Donaldson, Master of the Rolls, who
presides over the highest court in the land, apart from the Lords,
takes the first place, as befits him, amongst the judges, lawyers
and clerks who welcomed me into their Inns. I would also like
to remember myself gratefully to Sir Jack Jacob, Q. C., Senior
Master of the Supreme Court, Queen's Bench Division, and
thank him for his kindness and good humour as well as for his
erudition. His son, Robin, a lawyer like his father, supplied me
with valuable information about his beginnings in the profession.
Another friend gave me a view from the inside without which any
circle must remain inpenetrable: Andrew Geddes, a lawyer and
occasional judge, decoded for me the usages and customs of one
of the oldest professions in the country.

I must also thank Mr Hayden Phillips, Assistant Under Secretary
at the Home Office; Sir Kenneth Newman, then Commissioner of
the Metropolitan Police; the staff and inmates of Lewes Prison,

who agreed to talk to me; Dr C. Bertram, Director of the International Institute for Strategic Studies; Vice Admiral Sir Roderick Macdonald, who not only introduced me to his friends in the Royal Navy, but was also my guarantor to Admiral Lord Terence Lewin, at that time Defence Chief of Staff; and to the Admiral of the Fleet Sir Richard Clayton, Air Vice Marshall D. G. Bailey, Air Vice Marshall B. Brownlow, and the staff of the R.A.F. Training College at Cranwell, who looked after me for two days.

It is with great sadness that I mention a friend who is now dead, Wynford Vaughan Thomas, to me an incarnation of the poetry and warmth of the Welsh nation. I can still see him on his terrace feeding a pet seagull. I thank all my Welsh friends for their help. The Scots, too, were not ungenerous with their friendship: I have fond memories of the superb, eccentric, erudite and high-spirited Sir Ian Moncrieffe of that Ilk, who died a few years ago. I can only name a few of those who gave me so much of their time and attention: Lord Polwarth, who gave so much more than he had promised; unionists such as M. J. Milne, then General Secretary of the Scottish T.U.C.; David Coulter and the team in charge of the renovation of Glasgow in the eighties; His Grace the Duke of Hamilton; Mr Ian Fyffe, the distinguished distiller; M. E. Moffat, who organised the Edinburgh Festival Fringe; Mr Stewart Bart, who worked on the development of the new town at Glenrothes; Stewart Murray, at the time captain of the Thistle Alpha oil platform off Shetland. In Ireland, where I met leaders of all parties, Catholics and Protestants, fanatic Orangemen and Sinn Fein supporters, and probably, without realising it, IRA terrorists, I will not mention anybody for fear of offending everybody. My numerous Irish friends will understand this discretion as being only further proof of my affection for Ulster and the rest of Ireland.

From Mrs Thatcher to the other Party leaders, politicians of all hues, extreme Right to the most radical Left, all saw it as their duty to help a French writer attempting to interpret the English in his own way. Again I thank them all without naming them: they, like writers, regard it as their purpose to enlighten and serve the public. I must however, name a few of those Members of Parliament from both sides of the House, who did more than simply grant an interview or give advice: Sir Anthony Meyer, a friend of all things French; John Roper who, on the many occasions when I lost my bearings, piloted me safely between the sandbanks of parliamentary life; John Cope, who gave me a job as secretary, enabling me to wander at will through the corridors of Westminster; Joan Maynard, the grandmother of the Labour Left, thanks to whom I met militants for whom political activism is a way of life; Paul Boateng, the black M.P. whose anti-racism sets out to rescue whites from their prejudices.

My warm gratitude to Robert Armstrong, a peer since 1988, for his frank and energetic explanations, extends also to the officials under him who facilitated my task. Sir Nicholas Henderson, who was Ambassador in Bonn, Paris and Washington, and whom I am honoured to count as a friend, was also the most reliable mentor from the upper echelons of the administration, thanks both to our conversations and to an invaluable little book, *The Private Office*, which describes an institution almost incomprehensible to a Frenchman.

Finally, I must acknowledge three books, and thank their authors for always guiding me back to the right path when I thought I was lost: *The Changing Anatomy of Britain* remains a classic of its type – its author Anthony Sampson was always ready to advise and encourage even when he knew I disagreed with him. *La Société Anglaise* (1851–1972) by François Bédarida provided me with a solid base for my vision of present-day England. François Crouzet, whose most recent work *La Supériorité de l'Angleterre à la France* is a delight of erudition and talent, was kind enough to read a draft, pencil in hand, and to assure me that a book would emerge. Michel Mohrt did me the great favour of forcing me to put in order a text in which he appeared to find some merit.

I would like to remind those who want to obtain a precise and fair picture of Great Britain, without wasting time, of the excellent *L'Angleterre, cette inconnue* by Monica Charlot. To complete the picture I hope we will soon see a revised and up-to-date version of the *Encyclopédie de la civilisation britannique*, which she edited and which was published in 1976.

I am also indebted to the Franco-British Council, its members and guests, who for years continued to increase my knowledge of

British life, and to enlighten me as to the complex nature of the relationship between the two peoples.

I owe Jane Morton far more than a passing thank you; she may be assured that my friendship for her, now twenty-five years old, is truly undying. She has been my dictionary, my *chef de protocol*, my address book and go-between through all the years of research; a word from her was worth any number of introductions when it came to gaining access to inaccessible people.

I must now confess to a fraud so advantageous to myself that it will be easily understood why it has taken me so long to reveal it: all my English correspondence was written by my secretary, Angela Morpeth. Her style, her tact, her subtlety, gained me a reputation for courtesy and talent amongst my correspondents; it is time she was recognised by her compatriots.

I must pay particular tribute to my son-in-law, Paul Seabright, who, having felt obliged to read my book in French, found himself suffering for a whole year from the doubts and scruples of the translator, his wife and the author, his father-in-law, and tirelessly applied himself to solving their problems. The formidable linguist Barbarina Digby-Jones neglected her latest acquisition, Turkish, in order to guide Isabelle firmly through the most difficult passages of her translation. Jim McWhirter's advice led the reader through the labyrinthine reforms in the National Health Service. David Hart, a barrister, and Mark Ormerod from the Lord Chancellor's office chased up errors that betrayed all too clearly to the public the author's legal incompetence. Henrietta Miers contributed her academic experience and her generosity, which seems unlimited, to bringing the present edition to light, researching the corrections which in a book like this one can seem never-ending. Euan Cameron was brave enough to publish the work and make me believe that I did not owe this luck to our friendship alone. Emily Read eliminated the last mistakes in the manuscript, leaving behind only those due to the ignorance or the obstinacy of its author.

Finally, I am grateful to Dr Anthony Barker of the University of Essex for his help in revising the paperback edition.

Index

INDEX

Hart, David 237
Hartwell, Lord 310–11
Hazlitt, William 162
Healey, Denis 390
Heath, Edward *xiv*, 90, 336, 342–3, 366, 373, 390–91, 406
Heim, Mgr Bruno 61
Henderson, Ian 200–201
Henderson, Sir Nicholas 364
Henry VI, King 88
Henry VII, King 63
Henry VIII, King 32, 54, 157, 281
Heseltine, Michael 369, 397
Hill, Octavia 241
Hobbes, Thomas 162–3
Hogarth, William 159
Holbein, Hans 157
Home, Sir Alec Douglas (*later* Lord Home) 336, 341, 342
Hoskyns, Sir John 375
Howard, Sir Ebenezer 13
Howe, Sir Geoffrey 376, 396
Howson, Peter 157
Hughes, Richard *xi*, 171
Hume, David 163, 289
Humfrey, Pelham 153
Hunter, Sir Robert 241
Hurd, Douglas 400, 406
Huxley, Aldous *xi*, 171
Huxley, Julian 322

Ingham, Bernard 362
Ireland 60, 258, 281, 291–301, 400; see also Northern Ireland; Republic of Ireland; Ulster
Isaacs, Jeremy 326
Ishiguro, Kazuo 174

Jackowski, Andrzej 157
Jackson, Tom 194–95
Jacobs, Eric 137
James I, King 281, 348
James II, King 164
Jarman, Dr Brian 234

Jenkins, Roy 345
John, Augustus 156
John, Elton 134
John, Gwen 156
John Paul II, Pope 56, 61
Johnson, Ray 185
Joseph, Sir Keith 81–82, 376
Joyce, James *xi*, 172, 175

Kagan, Lord 358
Keble, John 56
Keeler, Christine 137–8
Kelman, James 175
Kelmsley, Lord 308
Kelvin, Lord 288
Kennedy, Margaret *xi*, 171
Kent, Mgr Bruce 269
Keynes, John Maynard, Baron 322, 389
Kinnock, Neil 93, 196, 269, 283, 317, 333–5, 338, 346, 403
Kipling, Rudyard *xi*, 171, 245
Kneller, Sir Godfrey 157
Knox, John 288
Koestler, Arthur 160
Korda, Alexander 148

Lane, Lord 249
Laughton, Charles 148
Lawrence, D.H. *xi*, 171
Lawrence, T.E. 171, 408
Lawrence, Thomas 158
Lawson, Dominic 317
Lawson, Nigel 202, 220, 371
Le Brun, Christopher 156
Lehmann, Rosamond *xi*, 171
Leigh-Pemberton, Robin 220–21
Leighton, Frederick 158
Lely, Peter 157
Lenthal, Speaker 360
Lessing, Doris 175
Lewis, C.S. 72–3
Lewis, Matthew Gregory 169
Lipton, Thomas 28

More Autobiographical Non-Fiction from Headline:

WILLIAM WHITELAW
THE WHITELAW MEMOIRS

THE NUMBER ONE BESTSELLING AUTOBIOGRAPHY

'A delightful volume. Anyone reading it will quickly realise
what a shrewd, good and lovable man the author is'
Sunday Telegraph

Member of Parliament for Penrith from 1955 until his
elevation to a viscountcy in 1983, Lord Whitelaw has served in
Government and in Opposition under Macmillan and
Douglas-Home and as a Cabinet minister under Heath and
Thatcher. His popularity among members of his own party is
legendary; the respect he commands among his political
opponents is both rare and remarkable.

The Whitelaw Memoirs are no dry, self-serving re-enactment
of a life in politics. They are, instead, a thoughtful and concise
recollection of the events and moods of the day in a political
career which has spanned the posts of Leader of the House of
Commons, Secretary of State for Northern Ireland,
Chairman of the Conservative Party, Home Secretary and
Leader of the House of Lords. For, while never courting
controversy, Lord Whitelaw presided over such politically
sensitive issues and events as the Iranian Embassy siege and
the knife-edge complexities of the Northern Ireland situation
of the 1970s.

The Whitelaw Memoirs tell the engaging lifestory of an
outstanding family man who has come to embody for many
such old-fashioned virtues as loyalty, fairness and political and
personal decency. Most tellingly, they reveal – for the first
time – the inner thoughts of a politician of consummate skill
at the various crisis points of twenty-five years at the centre of
British public life.

'The characteristically graceful memoir of a delightful,
instinctively decent and – genuinely – popular public figure'
Guardian

'An eminently enjoyable, sometimes deceptively informal,
personal story' *Evening Standard*

'Eagerly awaited . . . engagingly written' *Sunday Express*

'This excellent book' *The Times*

BIOGRAPHY/POLITICS   0 7472 3348 9

More Political Non-Fiction from Headline:

THE
CHINESE
SECRET SERVICE

ROGER FALIGOT & RÉMI KAUFFER
TRANSLATED FROM THE FRENCH BY CHRISTINE DONOUGHER

'A racy story of naked ambition . . . The final message
is that China is still a poor country seething with suppressed
violence, where a minority political movement is using its
secret police and massive army to maintain power by
repression' *Sunday Times*

For the first time ever, the veil is truly lifted on the Chinese
secret service, the *Tewu*, and its shadowy founder, Kang
Sheng, who died – mourned publicly by millions, privately
by few – in 1975. The culmination of years of painstaking
research all over the Far East and Europe, *The Chinese
Secret Service* probes into the life of Kang Sheng and the
crucial role he and his secret services played in the
shaping of modern China.

Exploring every aspect of the Chinese secret service, from its
inception in Shanghai in the 1920s to its current role at
home and abroad, the authors lay bare a world of violence,
mystery and ruthless ambition: the merciless struggle
between Mao and Chiang Kai-shek, the incredible story of
the Chinese atom bomb, the turmoil of the Cultural
Revolution and beyond. By casting a cold and piercing light
on China's secret past, *The Chinese Secret Service* offers
vital historical illumination on the country's troubled
and confused existence today.

'An interesting new book' *Sunday Express*

'The book in its popular and vivid style serves to highlight
the treacherous, secretive, violent and factional nature
of the Chinese Communist Party and government'
The Times Educational Supplement

NON-FICTION/CURRENT AFFAIRS   0 7472 3368 3

MY
MOUNTBATTEN
YEARS

IN THE SERVICE OF LORD LOUIS

WILLIAM EVANS

A six-year-old 'city urchin' evacuated during Hitler's war to the
Yorkshire Wolds in 1939, William Evans joined the Royal
Navy, due to conscription, in 1950. Rising to the rank of Chief
Petty Officer, he achieved his life's ambition when he was
appointed to the Royal Yacht *Britannia* in October 1959.
But he only managed one brief cruise of the Caribbean before
being whisked off by Lord Mountbatten, then Chief of the
UK Defence Staff, to head his Naval Retinue after
the death of Lady Louis in Burma.

There followed ten of the most hectic and exciting years of
William Evans' life. His duties took him to the four corners of
the world and gave him opportunities only dreamt of to rub
shoulders with kings and prime ministers, members of the lost
tribes, and eminent and distinguished people from the worlds
of business and entertainment. At the centre of it all, though,
was Lord Louis himself, one of this century's most charismatic
and intriguing statesmen. Evans served him selflessly and
devotedly, never taking a holiday, attending to his every
requirement, whether for a State visit, a military tour or a jolly
weekend with fellow Royals. Eventually, stress took its toll and
Evans left the service of Lord Louis, only to be reunited with
him, tragically, four days before he was killed by an IRA bomb
in his boat off Classiebawn Castle in August 1979.

Honest, simple and endearing, *My Mountbatten Years* is a book
to be read and treasured by all Lord Mountbatten's
many admirers.

NON-FICTION/AUTOBIOGRAPHY   0 7472 3417 5

More Non-Fiction from Headline:

FIRST CONTACT

THE SEARCH FOR EXTRATERRESTRIAL INTELLIGENCE

EDITED BY

BEN BOVA AND BYRON PREISS

'REALLY EXCELLENT' PATRICK MOORE

'I read the book with great interest. It is, I think, really excellent, and presents some viewpoints not found elsewhere . . . It is a book I will certainly add to my library' – Patrick Moore

Some of the world's leading scientists and scientific writers have come together in this timely, mind-stretching and highly readable book to confront their greatest challenge for the 1990s: the search for extraterrestrial intelligence.

An intriguing combination of observation and speculation, FIRST CONTACT presents the state-of-the-art answers from people at the forefront of space research to the ultimate questions: What is the nature of intelligence? *Is* there intelligent life beyond this planet? Where and how should we look for it? What will it be like? How will we recognise it? What should we do once we make contact?

Not only does this book show us a possible path into the future, it also provides practical advice to anyone interested in joining humanity's quest for its neighbours in the stars. With original essays from such distinguished writers as Isaac Asimov, Arthur C. Clarke, Ben Bova, Frank Drake and many, many more, FIRST CONTACT provides a tantalisingly imaginative glimpse from the pool of our collective knowledge into the outer limits of man's understanding of his place in the Universe.

'A comprehensive overview that inspires as well as informs' *Kirkus Reviews*

NON-FICTION/POPULAR SCIENCE   0 7472 3508 2

More Biography from Headline:

ROD STEWART

THE BESTSELLING BIOGRAPHY

TIM EWBANK AND STAFFORD HILDRED

**The definitive biography of one of the world's
most enduring sex symbols.**

In this searching yet affectionate account of the
man, his music and his life so far, Tim Ewbank
and Stafford Hildred follow Rod's inexorable rise
from the backstreets of Highgate via a short-lived
soccer career and busking in Paris, through times
spent with Steampacket, The Jeff Beck Group
and The Faces until he finally achieved the
pinnacle of international stardom that he enjoys
today. And then there are, of course, the
blondes...

Based on first-hand interviews with those close to
Rod at every stage of his life – including ex-
girlfriends – this biography highlights the many
contradictions and ambiguities that make up Rod
Stewart. Stripping away the hype and the hysteria,
it reveals at last the man.

NON-FICTION/BIOGRAPHY   0 7472 3585 6

A selection of bestsellers from Headline

FICTION

DANCING ON THE RAINBOW	Frances Brown	£4.99 □
NEVER PICK UP HITCH-HIKERS!	Ellis Peters	£4.50 □
THE WOMEN'S CLUB	Margaret Bard	£5.99 □
A WOMAN SCORNED	M. R. O'Donnell	£4.99 □
THE FALL OF HYPERION	Dan Simmons	£5.99 □
SIRO	David Ignatius	£4.99 □
DARKNESS, TELL US	Richard Laymon	£4.99 □
THE BOTTOM LINE	John Harman	£5.99 □

NON-FICTION

ROD STEWART	Tim Ewbank & Stafford Hildred	£4.99 □
JOHN MAJOR	Bruce Anderson	£6.99 □
WHITE HEAT	Marco Pierre White	£5.99 □

SCIENCE FICTION AND FANTASY

LENS OF THE WORLD	R. A. MacAvoy	£4.50 □
DREAM FINDER	Roger Taylor	£5.99 □
VENGEANCE FOR A LONELY MAN	Simon R. Green	£4.50 □

All Headline books are available at your local bookshop or newsagent, or can be ordered direct from the publisher. Just tick the titles you want and fill in the form below. Prices and availability subject to change without notice.

Headline Book Publishing PLC, Cash Sales Department, PO Box 11, Falmouth, Cornwall, TR10 9EN, England.

Please enclose a cheque or postal order to the value of the cover price and allow the following for postage and packing:
UK & BFPO: £1.00 for the first book, 50p for the second book and 30p for each additional book ordered up to a maximum charge of £3.00.
OVERSEAS & EIRE: £2.00 for the first book, £1.00 for the second book and 50p for each additional book.

Name ....

Address ....

....

....